SHARED VALUES
SHARED RESULTS

Positive Organizational Health as a Win-Win Philosophy

Dee W. Edington, PhD
Jennifer S. Pitts, PhD

Printed in the United States of America

Library of Congress Cataloging-in-Publication Data

ISBN: 978-0-692-56153-9 (paperback)

Shared Values—Shared Results: Positive Organizational Health as a Win-Win Philosophy. Foreword by Ken Blanchard.

Book design, cover design, and cover illustration by Jennifer S. Pitts

LCCN Imprint Name:

1. Health, Wellness, and Well-being. 2. Organization Effectiveness—Wellness.

First Edition

To those early, current, and future visionaries
who seek to bring wellness and high performance
to individuals, families, organizations, and
communities.

To two, of many, influences on our work:
Lewis Robbins, MD (1913-1984)
John Holland, PhD (1929-2015)

Acknowledgments

We acknowledge our families and friends, who stood by us over these years to pursue the dream that has now come to fruition in the form of this book. We are pleased to share our everlasting gratitude for their understanding and extreme patience and encouragement.

DWE—I acknowledge the patience and encouragement of Marilyn who shared her vast and relevant workplace health, creative writing, learning experiences and her feedback related to content and style. To David and Stacie, I am grateful for always reminding me of the value of family and relationships. As always, I am thankful for the life lessons passed on to me by my parents. Thanks to our many friends in Ann Arbor and throughout the country, especially Ken and Margie Blanchard who are always ready and willing to share their experiences and vast knowledge of the work they have done during our friendship of 45 years. My friends in workplace health management are a major source of my 37-years of continuous energy and dedication to this field. During those years (1978-2012) the knowledge generated by the University of Michigan Health Management Research Center made it among the top research centers in the world for documenting the sustainable business case for workplace health management. Finally, and most directly related to this book, I acknowledge the talents of Jennifer Pitts, who generated much of the content and writing of this book. Her experience, knowledge, and creativity exceeded my original expectations.

JSP—I am grateful for the patience and support I received from my family and friends while researching and writing this book. Especially to Dave, my mother and father, my sister Shannon, my good friends, including Nancy and Angela, and the many others who helped keep me sane while I wrote this book with Dee. I am also appreciative of the many life experiences; personal, professional, educational, and even a little bit of kismet, that converged to prepare me for my contribution to the framework, content, and design of this book. Finally, I am eternally grateful to Dee for allowing me to partner with him in this great adventure.

We both gratefully acknowledge the many individuals who made valuable contributions to each of us during the long process of writing this book. We especially recognize individuals who made thoughtful comments on early drafts of the book: Nancy Barnes, Joel Bender, Ken and Margie Blanchard, Wayne Burton, Gary Earl, Angela Camilleri, Marilyn Edington, Jennifer Flynn, Jessica Grossmeier, Pat Materka, Sharon Milberger, Michael Parkinson, Brian Passon, George Pfeiffer, Jackie Richardson, and Nancy Spangler. We also acknowledge those contributors whose quotes we embedded throughout the book.

We want to give special recognition to Angela Camilleri for her creative input during our work together at Edington Associates and for her writing of special sections in this book. The book is better for her input and our lives are better for her friendship.

Since the publication of Zero Trends in 2009, we have visited many worksites and have heard firsthand the unique stories of hundreds of professionals in the field. We will forever be grateful to each and all of these individuals who unselfishly gave their time and energy to speak with us and to share their diverse experiences which helped us see the unique value of each organization and each person.

Every day we read, see, or hear of organizations and individuals who report the benefits of wellness to individuals and organizations in terms of a higher quality of life and performance and less pain and suffering. We honor and acknowledge the extraordinary professionalism and enthusiasm of individuals directly engaged in the wellness and well-being field. We also acknowledge those positive organizations and employees who find value in living healthy and high-performing lives. We are dedicated to the premise that there is no one-way to arrive at positive organizational health and the health of individuals, families, organizations, and communities.

Foreword

Shared Values—Shared Results™ brings a refreshing new vision for organizational success. The book combines the economic business case and sustainable culture of health concepts from Dee Edington's 2009 book *Zero Trends: Health as a Serious Economic Strategy* with new thoughts developed for a win-win organizational philosophy. Dee Edington and Jennifer Pitts carefully explore how shared values and results take organizational and individual health to a higher level of organizational success. As Margie (Blanchard) of The Ken Blanchard Companies says, "We believe that everything that happens in the organization impacts the health of the people." Dee and Jennifer add that "…the health of the people impacts everything that happens in the organization." I could not agree more.

Results from measuring what matters are key to the win-win philosophy. The authors promote this philosophy through positive organizational health that added to my understanding of caring for the well-being of us all.

This book builds on the *Zero Trends* focus on cost avoidance and the construction of a sustainable, five-pillar culture of health. *Shared Values—Shared Results* adds a positive organizational health initiative that recognizes the contributions of all levels of employees as leaders and stakeholders in the outcome.

The authors challenge organizations to take more responsibility and accountability in creating positive organizational health in partnership with employees. They absolutely make their case that organizations win when employees win, and employees win when organizations win.

I'm alert to what is new and cutting edge. Dee and Jennifer promote "next" practices in support of the vision while they acknowledge "best" practices as starting points. They emphasize that "people matter" through every step of the journey they present.

Thanks, Dee and Jennifer, for bringing your complementary talents to the table and for continuing to push the boundaries of positive disruptive innovation.

Ken Blanchard, PhD
Co-Founder of The Ken Blanchard Companies
Co-Author of *The New One Minute Manager*
October 2015

Contents

PREFACE

Organizations throughout the world face an unprecedented opportunity to optimize the health, creativity, and engagement of their employees while achieving sustainable benefits to their financial performance and bottom line. The need for new approaches is urgent and timely as both organizations and individuals pay heavily for poor health and well-being in terms of high healthcare costs, poor performance, personal pain and suffering, and poor quality of life. The price is intensified by individual and organizational disengagement, lost productivity, and high rates of employee turnover.

We have been aware of the need for a different level of thinking for decades. One of the most often used quotes we see is from Albert Einstein.

We cannot solve our problems
with the same level of thinking that created them.

— Albert Einstein

As a society, we pay homage to this wisdom, yet we continue to look to the past for tomorrow's "solutions." We make tweaks to, put more energy into, and push harder and harder on yesterday's solutions. We must open up our creative thinking and innovations to emerging future possibilities. This will take setting our egos aside, opening ourselves up and seeing with fresh eyes—use a beginner's mind and observe, observe, observe. It will take being willing to be wrong, and incorporating ideas and emerging practices from disciplines and sources we have not looked to in the past. It will take having greater empathy for ourselves and others around us, locally and globally. It will also take being collaborative and creative in the process of co-creating, and experimenting with new and innovative solutions—collaboration is key—engage, engage, engage!

Thinking differently also takes a broader sense of what it means to be healthy as individuals and organizations. Although man has examined the nature of individual health for centuries, and the concept of organizational health only relatively recently, the learning process continues for both. Regarding individual health, western medicine has relied heavily on treating the physical body with pharmaceutical solutions, medical procedures, and surgery. Meanwhile, organizational consultants have concentrated on implementing cost-cutting strategies, including wellness programs, which also focus on the individual employees. Efforts to improve organizational health have focused primarily on financial metrics, reorganization, and leadership effectiveness, while largely leaving the health and well-being of employees out of the strategy equation.

With this book, we describe a win-win philosophy that embraces the synergy between organizational health and individual health. We are excited to present a collaborative vision for Shared Values—Shared Results™ and outline a flexible process for developing positive organizational and positive individual health. There is growing evidence that this new level of organizational and individual performance, health, and well-being can create sustainable value for both employers and employees, and can lead to flourishing organizations.

None of us is as smart as all of us.

—Ken Blanchard

To capture the power and energy of this integrated strategy will take committed and collaborative efforts involving executive leadership, management, and employees. Our goal is to help organizations leverage real collaboration between leaders and employees to co-create comprehensive strategic approaches that evolve healthy and high-performing workplaces and workforces.

We invite leaders of organizations to join with your employees to evolve healthy and flourishing workplaces and workforces that support the values, vision, and purpose of both employees and the organization.

Dee W. Edington, PhD
Jennifer S. Pitts, PhD
December 2015

The definition of insanity is doing the same thing over and over again but expecting different results.

—Albert Einstein

Introduction

Knowing is not enough; we must apply.
Willing is not enough; we must do.

—Goethe

Why This Book?

It's time to create realistic solutions to maintain high levels of health, performance, and thriving in organizations, individuals, families, and communities.

Being fully healthy is about much more than our physical attributes. Societies across the globe are reexamining what it means to be healthy and exploring more effective ways to support high levels of health and sustainable high performance. There is a growing awareness of the inseparable connection between mind, body, and spirit. The impact of our attitudes, work environment, climate, and culture, and the influence of our families, friends, and communities is also becoming clearer.

Well-implemented wellness and well-being programs can help the motivated employees who actively participate and work to lower risks and improve their health. However, we have seen only marginal reductions in risks and disease in the total population. The earliest wellness initiatives emphasized a multidimensional, whole-person approach to improving health. However, most corporate wellness programs over the past three decades have focused on helping individual employees reduce health risks to reduce healthcare costs. Until recently, very little attention has been given to the ways that organizational systems influence employee health or, more important, how improving organizational environments and cultures can better support healthy and thriving employees.

You can't put a recently changed person back into the environment from which he or she came and expect to maintain the change.

To better understand how wellness initiatives can more positively impact employee health and performance, we have examined the health-related effects of the complex organizational systems where people work and live. We knew that to support healthy employees, we needed an approach that would encourage organizations to modify their health-related environments, cultures, and climates. At the end of the day, no matter how good an organization's wellness program, employees cannot realize their fullest potential health in an unhealthy workplace or in unhealthy families and communities.

> *When I became CEO of Steelcase, I had a strong inkling that what was true for me personally was also true in a larger context: that the well-being of individuals and the well-being of the organization they work for are inseparable. The better off employees are in terms of their personal well-being, the better off the company can be in terms of fiscal fitness, agility, and capabilities for innovation and growth.*
>
> *By personal well-being, I mean the "whole" person at work—mind, body and soul—and I realized that the physical workplace could be a powerful agent in providing an environment in which people can thrive, which would in turn allow us to build the kind of resilient and agile organization we wanted to be.*
>
> *Jim Hackett*
> *Former CEO, Steelcase, Inc.*

This realization led to the 2009 book *Zero Trends: Health as a Serious Economic Strategy. Zero Trends* outlines five fundamental pillars that provide the foundation for evolving more positive environments, cultures, and climates for employee health and well-being, and strengthening workplace wellness initiatives. In this book, we have built upon those pillars in the following ways:

Zero Trends	Win-Win Philosophy
Pillar 1: Senior Leadership	Pillar 1: Engaged and Committed Leadership
Pillar 2: Operations Leadership	Pillar 2: Positive Environment, Culture, and Climate
Pillar 3: Self-Leadership	Pillar 3: Self-Leadership and Positive Individual Health
Pillar 4: Rewards and Recognition	Pillar 4: Positive Personal Motivation
Pillar 5: Quality Assurance	Pillar 5: Measure and Communicate What Matters

As in *Zero Trends*, the pillars still emphasize the importance of strong leadership support for employee and organizational health initiatives (pillar 1). Thriving workplace environments and cultures are also imperative (pillar 2), as are resources, opportunities, and practices that support and develop employee self-leaders (pillars 3 and 4), and meaningful measures and feedback about progress (pillar 5).

In this book, we describe advances in research findings, in our thinking, and in our practices for each of these pillars. We also highlight their place in a larger strategic process for evolving thriving workplaces and workforces. With *Zero Trends*, we focused primarily on the "why" and "what" of the pillar concepts. Here we include many ideas for "how" you can strengthen the pillars in your organization.

> *There is no singular solution or product that solves our problems. What we are trying to change and/or solve is much too complex for any one solution. We must be open to working from ground zero to build a better organization with a common vision that drives all organizational policies, projects, and programs toward a common objective of improved health and productivity.*
>
> *Brian Passon, MS*
> *President, ARCH Health and Productivity, ArchHP.com*

Who Is This Book For?

At its core, this book is about leadership. It is about committed, engaged, and visionary leadership. Most important, we believe that everyone is a leader and can play a significant role in his or her organization.

Because of the fundamentally complex and social nature of health, our solutions must be social, collaborative and creative. Therefore, we have written this book for multiple audiences that represent all parts of the organization. Senior executives, leaders in management, and labor union leadership are all core to the kind of evolution it will take to make a sustainable difference in the health and well-being of your workplace and employee populations.

We also believe that all members of organizations are leaders in their own right and are all valuable contributors to high levels of health and thriving of employees and organizations. Therefore, this book is also about engaging employees at all levels throughout the organization to create a win-win philosophy.

Everyone is a self-leader, from the chairman and CEO to middle managers, to all employees

We provide a highly customizable approach along with practical tools and resources that will help everyone throughout the organization understand how they can engage in the evolution of a win-win strategy. Close collaboration among all stakeholders is imperative. Every-one in the organization is a "stakeholder" so involve everyone in the process:

- **Senior Leaders.** The evolution of a healthy and thriving environment, culture and climate will be most successful when all leaders (executives, union leaders, managers, and supervisors) embrace a win-win philosophy.

- **Wellness and Well-Being Leaders.** Wellness coordinators, occupational health professionals, third-party wellness program providers, and training and development personnel are all critical to creative, comprehensive, and effective approaches to support positive organizational and individual health.

- **Operations Leaders.** Individuals with backgrounds in organizational development, human resources, human capital development, wellness, safety, quality, and benefits management will be core to evolving healthy policies, processes, benefits and the built environment, or physical plant of the organization.

- **All Employees.** It is crucial that we include the voices of the employees throughout the planning and implementation process. It is also critical that approaches and conditions foster intrinsic motivation for everyone in the organization. As with safety and quality, wellness and well-being are the responsibility of all stakeholders throughout the organization.

It takes a village.

It is important to remember that this approach will only be successful if everyone has a voice and a stake in each part of the collaborative process of developing healthier and more thriving workplaces and workforces.

How to Read This Book

If you are looking for a quick fix, a blueprint for success, or low-hanging fruit, this might not be the book for you. If you are looking for a new level of thinking and operating, you will find value here.

This book is simultaneously a business justification for a win-win philosophy and a how-to guide to help you play a role in developing a win-win strategy. Wherever you sit in your organization—in the C-suite, or on the shop floor—this book can help you. We hope you will take the time to read carefully through this book and fully digest and reflect on the concepts and practices we outline throughout. We believe this will provide the best chance for success in your efforts to create conditions for healthy and thriving employees and a healthy and thriving organization. However, we acknowledge that there is a lot in this book to digest, and recognize that many of you are busy with full-time responsibilities. For this reason, we have included the following design elements throughout the book to highlight the core narrative in each section. Some of you may just want to skim the book at a high level and dive deeper into areas where you have the most need or interest. Others may want to read every word.

We have included bolded text throughout the book to emphasize the key aspects of the story line throughout.

We emphasize our own key statements.

We include quotes from prominent individuals both living and from history to emphasize the broader intellectual context of the ideas and practices presented.

Real-world stories and case studies provide practical examples of approaches in use in more forward-thinking organizations.

We have also included many tables and figures throughout the book that include distilled information from each chapter.

How Is the Book Organized?

Throughout this book, we underscore the value of a win-win philosophy and strategy for organizations and the people who work in them. It might be helpful to think of the **win-win philosophy** as the guiding beliefs and principles of the approach (the "why and "what"), and the **win-win strategy** as the overall comprehensive plan created to evolve the environment and culture (the "how"). We base our approach on the awareness of the complex and multifaceted nature of human and organizational health. The framework of the book begins with a call to AWAKEN to a bigger way of thinking about the health and well-being of employees. It then follows the three main themes in the win-win strategy (see figure 1):

1) *Create Shared Values—Shared Results:* The ideal work culture and environment is one where employees and the organization share core values (shared values), and what is good for employees is good for the organization and vice versa (shared results).

2) *Evolve Positive Organizational Health:* Positive organizational health encompasses having a positive environment, culture, and climate, as well as employees with strong positive individual health and positive personal motivation. Organizations with strong positive organizational health provide caring and positive environments, cultures, and

climates. Individuals and employee work teams engage in healthy choices. The organizations and employees make shared decisions that contribute to flourishing workplaces and workforces. We describe each of these concepts in more detail later, but for now it is most important to understand that they go hand in hand; you can't have one without the others.

Figure 1. Three primary themes of the win-win strategy

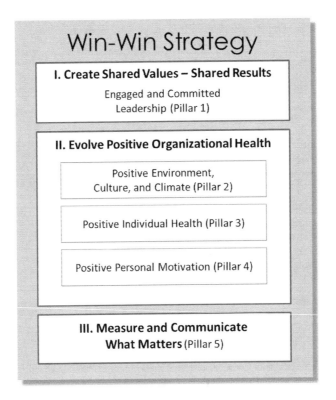

3) ***Measure and Communicate What Matters:*** Measuring and communicating what matters demands that we respect what is important to both the organizations and employees. The organization will continue to value productivity, performance, being an employer of choice, social recognition within the community or industry, and financial objectives among others. Employees are likely to value trust, happiness, autonomy, recognition, respect, quality of life, meaningful work, and fair wages.

The major sections of the book outline the value and fundamental principles of a win-win philosophy. We address not only the "why" and "what" for each of our major themes, but also provide ideas for "how" you can create your version of a win-win philosophy.

Our employees are the single most critical factor in our corporate success and in providing outstanding service to our customers. We understand the value each employee brings to the organization, and we want to help them feel and live their best because we understand that a healthy employee is a happy and productive employee. Wellness is a collaborative effort. The company must do its part to provide the tools, resources, and environment to help employees manage their health—and employees must cultivate their intrinsic motivation to change behavior and achieve personal health goals. Ultimately, it is up to each individual employee to change their behavior to become healthier, but it is the company's responsibility to help facilitate that change through our culture, environment, and financial incentives.

Rick Chiricosts
Chairman, CEO, President, Medical Mutual of Ohio

To read the full case study go to appendix B

Awakening

We begin with a challenge to leaders to think and act in a bigger way when it comes to the health and well-being of both employees and the organization.

In chapter 1, we outline the value of the win-win philosophy for all organizational stakeholders. It is important to note that we believe that "stakeholders" include the organization, its shareholders, senior leaders, employees, and their families. We also believe that communities and the larger society have a stake in the success of employees and employer organizations. We describe the senior leaders' agenda and role in awakening stakeholders throughout organizations to the power of a win-win organizational philosophy.

Over the past decade, we have seen employers expand their view of the total costs of health care to a more inclusive view of the broader economic impact of health. This broader view includes in the cost equation the impact of absence, disability, health-related performance, and lost productivity. Health-care reform has played a key role in this transition but so has the influence of CFOs asking a new set of questions about why to invest in workforce health. The next phase is for more employers to understand better how health influences employee contribution to the business—bringing health to the top line.

Thomas Parry, PhD
President, Integrated Benefits Institute

We believe "stakeholders" include the organization, its shareholders, senior leaders, employees, and their families.

We next challenge the reader to adopt a (1) broader view of health that represents a higher level of thriving for employees, and (2) more comprehensive awareness of the factors that influence whether employees and organizations flourish (chapter 2). We use the terms "thriving," and "flourishing" throughout the book to represent strong positive levels of health and well-being across a broad set of dimensions. These include, but are certainly not limited to mental, emotional, spiritual, intellectual, physical, social, occupational, environmental, cultural, and financial health.

We discuss the breadth and depth of the many known dimensions of health, and the potential for thriving and flourishing. We also describe the concept of *positive individual health* and present a graphic depiction of health that can be used to represent the unique constellation of health's many known and unknown dimensions for any individual.

Next, we introduce the *model for positive organizational health* (chapter 3). The model provides a framework for understanding the impact of the five fundamental pillars on the environment, culture and climate in organizations, families and communities. It also highlights the influence of all of the factors listed above on the health and thriving of employees. We discuss the importance of using systems thinking and human-centered design (HCD) as we develop meaningful, engaging, and compelling innovations that support and enhance health and well-being to allow employees and organizations to flourish.

Finally, we introduce a framework for the win-win journey process (chapter 4), a comprehensive set of flexible and customizable practices that you can draw from to create a win-win strategy in your organization.

The next three sections of the book follow our three primary themes. We provide practical tools and resources for strengthening the five pillars and moving organizations, employees, their families, and surrounding communities to a higher level of performance by

- promoting shared values and an inspired vision for all stakeholders

- assessing the current status of organizations and developing a plan for a strategic, systematic, systemic, and sustainable approach

- implementing concrete positive organizational health strategies

- implementing concrete positive individual health strategies

- introducing key life skills for continuous learning and growth

- enhancing conditions for positive personal motivation

- defining measures and measurement that matter to all stakeholders; and

- creating communications that motivate

Each organization is unique, so you will need creativity and flexibility to create your organization's distinctive approach to developing positive organizational health.

There is no one-size fits all formula and no step-by-step blueprint for creating positive and thriving workplaces and workforces. There are as many paths along the journey as companies on the voyage.

Theme 1. Creating Shared Values—Shared Results

Organizations win when employees win,
and employees win when organizations win.

In the ideal work culture and environment, the employees and the organization share complementary core values (shared values), where everyone understands what is good for the health and well-being of employees is good for the company and vice versa (shared results). When it is clear to everyone involved how employee and company health and thriving can benefit each in ways that matter to them (shared results), we have the ultimate win-win situation. Organizations that practice Shared Values—Shared Results and help employees live according to their personal and professional values and purpose will have a significant competitive advantage.

We begin this section by discussing what it means to lead the effort to evolve a win-win philosophy. Most understand that leadership is critical, but not everyone appreciates what it looks like to embody the type of leadership needed. We briefly outline what are currently considered "best practices" for leadership related to wellness and well-being programs. We then present emerging "next practices" for leaders that can help them start a movement to permeate wellness and well-being into the culture and fabric of the organization. We challenge leaders to think beyond the status quo and explore a new generation of approaches to help both individuals and organizations flourish.

To create a true culture of well-being that is sustainable, the leadership must view well-being as part of their overall business strategy with a clear set of strategic objectives, a defined process, and meaningful measurement. These types of programs can have a far greater chance to be seen as an essential element of the human capital management strategy, thus resulting in more effective and higher employee engagement.

Colleen M. Reilly, MBA/MSM
President, Total Well-Being

Theme 2. Evolve Positive Organizational Health

We imagine thriving organizations whose criteria for success are about more than power and wealth.

We see a world where resilient, thriving individuals are engaged in high-quality and meaningful work, collaborating with creative and inspired colleagues in organizations where they feel supported, challenged, and valued.

This section is intended to provide concepts, practical guidance, techniques, and methods that will help you develop flexible and creative strategies and put them into practice. We encourage keeping an open mind to integrating a broad range of ideas from a variety of disciplines that will help make the initiative more appealing to all stakeholders.

Whereas moral courage is the righting of wrongs, creative courage, in contrast, is the discovering of new forms, new symbols, new patterns on which a new society can be built.

—Rollo May, The Courage to Create (1975)

Evolving a win-win philosophy and strategy in your organization requires environmental and cultural practices that help both employees and organizations operate at their highest potential. This approach also involves creating policies, benefits, development opportunities, and environmental and cultural practices that align with and promote positive individual and organizational health. In organizations with strong positive organizational health, organization and union leaders and all employees are committed to respecting and trusting each other, and structuring workplace environments and cultures that produce the best possible results.

Employers didn't fix safety by ignoring culture—they purposefully created cultures of safety. Similarly, organizations need to see choices about health and medical care as reflecting the absence of a culture that truly values health as human capital. Healthy companies grow healthy employees and families through projecting every day that contributing to the best of one's ability is an expectation—and shared responsibility.

Michael Parkinson, MD, MPH, FACPM
Past President, American College of Preventive Medicine

Theme 3. Measure and Communicate What Matters

For many years, evaluators of wellness programs and initiatives have focused on a relatively narrow set of measures, methods, and questions. In this section, we outline our recommendations for taking measurement and communication to a higher level by:

- Using a broader lens on the types of information that we collect to evaluate progress and gathering information that matters to all stakeholders throughout the organization.

- Evolving our questions to get better answers.

- Collaborating with all stakeholders during evaluation planning and implementation.

- Expanding our methods for collecting and synthesizing the information that we collect —methods that encourage collaboration and engagement of all stakeholders.

Measuring and communicating what matters is about evaluation and feedback for decision-making, momentum, and sustainability. It is about generating and distributing meaningful information that demonstrates to all stakeholders how the organization is progressing toward the vision. It is also about using measurement to achieve what you seek.

Like all companies, we've seen a steady rise in healthcare costs for many years. The hospital employee population is not immune to the cultural changes that have contributed so hugely to the health epidemic in our nation. I believe we in the healthcare profession have a special obligation to "walk the talk" if we are to impact the downward spiral of health in America. As it turns out, initiating health-focused steps for our workforce is helping our bottom line as well. Healthy, thriving employees have a direct and positive impact on a healthy, thriving, and high-performing organization.

Margaret Sabin
President and CEO, Penrose-St. Francis Health Services
President, Centura Health South State Operating Group

Final Words

In our "Final Words," we provide a call to action to organizations and stakeholders worldwide to embrace a new way of operating, and engage in disruptive innovation that will take the health and well-being of individuals and organizations to a higher level. We challenge our readers to embrace and undertake a more strategic, systematic, systemic, and sustainable approach to achieving positive individual and organizational health.

What Does It Take to Evolve Positive Health in Your Organization?

A win-win strategy is core to the long-term success of your organization

It will take collaborative, creative leadership to develop a healthy and thriving culture and climate and thriving employees. So it is not coincidence that three of the five pillars are about leadership. It will take committed senior leaders, motivated and aligned operations leaders, plus the engagement of self-leaders throughout the organization. A clear and inspiring shared vision based on shared values and shared results is imperative.

> _As time goes on, high-performing, talented workers are going to be in short supply and high demand by thriving companies. And one of the things that these workers are going to look for in a company is not only a place where they can grow professionally, but where they can reap the personal benefits of health and well-being. Research shows that organizations can make changes that will improve the well-being and performance of their workers. The company that can provide both professional and personal growth will attract and retain better talent and reap higher productivity and loyalty from their workers._
>
> _Michael Friedman, PhD_
> _Clinical Psychologist, Medical Advisory Board, EHE International_

All stakeholders need to see how their health and thriving contributes to the organization's vision and understand the value they bring to the success of the enterprise. They also need to recognize the value they receive from the organization's success. As all stakeholders come to understand their respective key roles, their sense of engagement, retention, and performance will grow, as will their loyalty to the organization and their sense of ownership in the vision.

Involve all levels of leadership—embrace everyone as a leader!

> _Coming together is a beginning, staying together is progress, and working together is success...[a] company will not be successful unless employees are successful, and employees will not be successful without the company being successful._
>
> —Henry Ford

AWAKENING

It is time to **AWAKEN** *to the power and competitive advantage of positive individual and organizational health as a win-win strategy.*

CHAPTER 1:
The Win-Win Imperative—
Taking Wellness and Well-Being to the Next Level

The cost of health is much less than
the cost of sickness and disease.

It is time for employers to **AWAKEN** and to expand their thinking about the link between employee health and thriving and the financial success of the organization. There are some fundamental truths that can help us better understand this link:

- *The Win-Win imperative.* Organizations must better understand the full value of healthy and thriving employees and organizations to be successful and thrive in the emerging future. Without thriving employees, organizations will not thrive. Employees will not be fully healthy or flourish in unsupportive, unhealthy organizations.

- *Health has many dimensions and can have extraordinarily positive end points.* Medicine, pharmaceuticals, public health, and many of our wellness and well-being initiatives do not currently address the most positive potential for health. Our purpose is to awaken the hearts and souls of individuals and organizations to the highest levels of organizational and human capacity.

- *Many factors influence health.* Man has studied the domains of health for thousands of years, but we built the Western medical model on waiting for risk or disease to occur and then treating it. There is now a compelling body of research on how factors like attitude, resilience, creativity, and meaningful work enhance health in all its dimensions. The evidence is also mounting about the health effects of the workplace environment, culture, and climate, support from family and friends, and connections with the community. We need a collaborative and comprehensive strategy that can address all of these factors.

*When employers believe employees
are their most valuable resource, and employees
believe their employer is the best possible,
we have a win-win situation.*

The solutions in this book respect each of these complex and fundamental truths. We offer a framework for creating healthy workplace environments, cultures, and climates for health, wellness and well-being in employer organizations. We also provide a set of organizing principles that can shape any effort to create a thriving workforce. We have expanded on the importance of each of the five pillars introduced in *Zero Trends: Health as a Serious Economic Strategy* based on both new and previous evidence from a broad range of traditional and nontraditional areas of study. We also embed the pillars within the broader context of the systems surrounding the organization (families, communities, and society) and present a framework for evolving a win-win organizational philosophy. We recommend comprehensive, systems-level thinking to develop effective solutions that address systemwide influences on the health of individuals and organizations. The key is to tap into the power of a healthy, thriving, high-performing, and sustainable workplace and workforce.

We are at a critical point where the problems we are facing are far more severe than in any other modern era. Our solutions must rise to the occasion. While this may sound formidable, the alternative of continuing with "business as usual" in many areas, including effectively addressing poor employee health, is far more daunting. Organizations with strong shared values and shared results can anticipate high levels of employee health and thriving, and can ultimately produce the highest possible quality products and services. They will also bring far more value to their surrounding communities and the larger society.

We have included a brief pillar assessment on the next page to help you use this book in a manner that best serves your need.

We strongly encourage you to read through all the sections and chapters of the book, but we hope this assessment will prime you to be looking for areas that represent your greatest strengths and your best opportunities for making a positive difference in your organization.

Indicate the degree to which your organization currently engages in each of the practices in the assessment on page 5 using the following scale:

0=Not at all true, 1=A little true, 2=Somewhat true, 3=Very true, 4=Completely true. If you don't know the answer, enter "0."

Quick Assessment

Pillar 1: Engaged and Committed Leadership	Score	Location
1. Our senior leaders are deeply committed to employee health and well-being	_____	Ch. 5
2. Our vision and values reflect the importance of healthy and flourishing employees	_____	Ch. 9
3. The vision and values were created with input from employees at all levels............	_____	Ch. 9
4. We have a strategic plan to align the vision for health with the business strategy....	_____	Ch. 10
5. Leaders and managers are authentic role models for health and flourishing	_____	Ch. 11
Subtotal for pillar 1 (sum of the 5 item scores above)...	[____]	

Pillar 2: Positive Environment, Culture, and Climate		
1. We have aligned our policies and procedures (including benefit design and job design) to support health and well-being...	_____	Ch. 10
2. We have sufficient resources dedicated to support employee health and well-being......	_____	Ch. 10
3. We have designed the environment of the workplace to support healthy choices	_____	Ch. 11
4. All leaders and managers are trained to support employee health and well-being	_____	Ch. 11
5. We engage employees in designing our health and well-being approaches.....................	_____	Ch. 11
Subtotal for pillar 2 (sum of the 5 item scores above)...	[____]	

Pillar 3: Self-leadership and Positive Individual Health		
1. We provide resources that help employees across the health continuum live healthy and thriving lives (beyond the absence of risk and illness).................................	_____	Ch. 12
2. Our initiatives* promote self-leadership, mindfulness, and positive outlook...................	_____	Ch. 12
3. Our initiatives* are designed to support health at the family and community level........	_____	Ch. 12
4. Our culture encourages building connections and fosters strong collaboration	_____	Ch. 12
5. We help employees understand their purpose and find meaning in their work and lives	_____	Ch. 12
Subtotal for pillar 3 (sum of the 5 item scores above)...	[____]	

Pillar 4: Positive Personal Motivation		
1. Our leaders and managers understand the basic principles of human motivation	_____	Ch. 13
2. Our work culture and initiatives* are designed to support intrinsic motivation...............	_____	Ch. 13
3. We help employees understand the relationship between their motivation for living a healthy lifestyle and their ability to fulfill their life purpose....................................	_____	Ch. 13
4. Our initiatives* provide choice over whether and how to engage	_____	Ch. 13
5. We recognize employees in a way that best supports their fundamental need for competence, relatedness, and autonomy	_____	Ch. 13
Subtotal for pillar 4 (sum of the 5 item scores above)...	[____]	

Pillar 5: Measure and Communicate What Matters		
1. We track outcomes that matter to both employees and the organization	_____	Ch. 7
2. We evaluate the full value of our investment in the health and well-being of our employees (i.e., value of investment and value of caring)	_____	Ch. 14
3. We use quantitative and qualitative methods to capture the richness of the culture	_____	Ch. 15
4. We have a comprehensive evaluation strategy based on a guiding framework...............	_____	Ch. 16
5. We frequently communicate with leaders and employees at all levels of the organization about progress toward our vision	_____	Ch. 17
Subtotal for pillar 5 (sum of the 5 item scores above)...	[____]	

TOTAL (add the five subtotal scores from above)... [____]

Initiatives may include any programs or initiatives to support wellness and well-being, or manage health risks or conditions.

There are 100 points possible on this assessment. In addition to calculating your overall score, you may want to you review your answers to the individual questions and note those where you responded "Very true" or "Completely true." These likely represent areas of strengths of your organization in terms of health management. You may want to find ways to celebrate and build on these areas of strengths. Also, you may have several questions with "Not at all true," "A little true," or "Somewhat true" or even "Don't know" responses. These likely represent opportunities for development in your organization. You may want to pay special attention to the chapters listed for those items to learn about ways to build strength in those areas.

The Win-Win Challenge

*In essence, we believe everything that happens in the
organization influences wellness and well-being of employees and
the positive health and thriving of the organization.*

In the six years since the publication of *Zero Trends,* there has been increasing recognition that the environment, climate and culture of organizations have a substantial impact on employee health and thriving. Organizations and their leaders are being challenged—even expected—to demonstrate value not only to their shareholders, but to their employees, and to the communities and larger societies they serve.[1] The challenge and expectation works both ways. Employers expect employees to demonstrate value to organizations by pursuing positive health, wellness, and optimal performance.

> *Hope is not a health strategy. Just as we cannot hope the national obesity epidemic will go away because of a few public service announcements, we cannot expect that there will be any real and sustainable reduction in healthcare costs for an employer because they implemented a basic wellness program. We have to be more sincere in our efforts. On a national level, our strategies have to address the toxic food environment we live in, where supersized foods have supersized our bodies. At an employer level this means strategies must address the culture, where wellness is not a box to be checked, but values around which the entire organization is built.*
>
> *Sami Beg, MD, MPA, MPH*
> *Founder and CEO, Proactive Living*

The win-win philosophy is designed to create workforces and workplaces where excellent health, meaningful work, high-performance, loyalty, happiness, and quality of life are the norm. In such organizations, performance and shareholder value are at their highest possible levels. Each organization must find a balance of philosophy, strategy and tactics within its setting. These efforts will help maximize the total value of the win-win philosophy by:

- evolving a positive organizational environment, culture, and climate to optimize positive organizational and individual health and performance;

- increasing revenues by developing and supporting a high-performing workforce and workplace; and

- minimizing costs associated with lost work time and avoidable healthcare utilization.

With this approach, everyone wins. Organizations win by increasing revenue and decreasing costs, and all employees win by improving their health, quality of life, and the meaning they find in their work and other areas of their life.

The Win-Win Strategy for the Success of Employees and Employers

Organizations are in a unique position to positively impact their employees' health and well-being. However, employers have been attempting to manage the costs associated with disability, poor work performance, and excess healthcare utilization the same way for over thirty years. While many individuals have improved their health through the wellness and well-being programs employers have implemented, the impact on the overall population has been minimal. Senior leaders in organizations and unions must choose whether to continue to pay excessive costs for poor health or to invest in developing positive individual and organizational health outcomes. Our bias is toward the latter approach. It is imperative that we find a new way of thinking and behaving for success.

Investing in good health is less expensive than paying for poor health.

Employee and employer results take many forms. Currently, most of the perceived value of wellness and well-being programs is focused on financial savings for the *employer*:

- increased productivity
- reduced time away from work
- reduced disability cost
- decreased healthcare costs through cost avoidance
- high financial return on investment

Employees will be skeptical unless efforts to create strong positive organizational health are based on the genuine desire to improve the quality of health and thriving for employees, as well as to create value for the organization. When people see that the efforts are genuine, they understand the connection. This kind of honest intent is especially needed in organizations that have eliminated jobs, shifted costs to employees, and lowered employee compensation while the company grows increasingly profitable.

The win-win philosophy for *employees* includes the following benefits:

- stronger health and well-being for themselves, their families, and their communities
- higher levels of energy, resilience, optimism, creativity, and fun during work and leisure
- a sense that the employer cares about them, respects them, and values their opinions
- an overall greater satisfaction and meaning from work and life

Communities also benefit when local employers and employees thrive. Financially healthy companies are a source of revenue for local merchants. They pay taxes to local governments, which are then used to provide community services. Successful organizations are also more likely to support the arts and other community resources. Conversely, employers depend on local communities for basic infrastructure services and a source of qualified job applicants. A high level of employment has a positive economic impact, and successful employees often participate in the communities in which they work and live. This is another example of the win-win relationship.

Thriving employees and thriving organizations
contribute to thriving communities!

Dee Edington not only helped build the foundation of our industry, but he continues to help shape its evolution. Zero Trends helped us recognize that we need to move away from a find it and fix it one solution approach towards a systems approach that addressed the organizational side of wellness in creating a champion company that had been neglected for too long.

Brian Passon, MS
President, ARCH Health and Productivity, ArchHP.com

We challenge senior leaders to ensure their organizations create value for employees, family members, communities, and the larger economy and ecology of societies. We also challenge the leaders of organizations that operate internationally to demonstrate value on a global scale.

People look to the top to see what's important. When leaders include health and well-being as a major strategic initiative and are serious about it, good things happen.

—Margie Blanchard, PhD
Co-Founder, Former President and CEO, The Ken Blanchard Companies

CHAPTER 2:
What Is Health?

The first wealth is health.

– Ralph Waldo Emerson

While dictionaries define health as "the state of being free from illness or injury," a more comprehensive definition of health goes further to include factors beyond physical health. In 1946, the World Health Organization (WHO) defined health as "a complete state of physical, mental and social well-being, and not merely the absence of disease or infirmity."[2] In 1986, WHO said that health is "a resource for everyday life, not the objective of living. Health is a positive concept emphasizing social and personal resources, as well as physical capacities."

Some have taken issue with the word "complete" in WHO definition. However, most people would agree that the concept of health, as outlined by WHO, is a more advanced and desirable view than the dictionary definition. Even so, it has been nearly six decades since WHO published its definition, and we do not use mental and social health concepts as much we could in our wellness approaches. There are several likely reasons for this.

The earliest wellness programs grew out of the human potential movement of the seventies and eighties and addressed many important health dimensions.[3-9] Corporate wellness programs began to grow in popularity in the mid-eighties when rising healthcare costs for employees were a growing problem for organizations. At that time, there was a growing body of evidence about the relationship between healthcare costs and health risks, and reducing risks would result in lower costs.[10-14] Wellness programs began to focus on reducing health risks and costs. Given this focus, the primary metrics of success for these programs were often reduced risk or disease and lower costs associated with medical care and time away from work. The implied health continuum represented by these practices and measures ranges from high risk and cost to lower or no risk and cost (see figure 2).

Figure 2. Health dimension represented by many current wellness programs

There is increasing evidence that underscores the importance of social and personal resources for health and thriving.[15-18] Only relatively recently have providers of wellness services begun to embrace these concepts in their approaches. One reason for this may be that the workplace wellness industry has largely followed the medical model of identifying individuals with risks and disease and then intervening with that subset of individuals.

For years, many commercial wellness programs have informed or coached people about reducing risks such as smoking, poor nutrition, and inactivity to improve blood pressure levels, cholesterol numbers, and body weight. Understandably, many wellness coaches have backgrounds in fields like nursing, exercise physiology, and nutrition counseling. Fewer have had training in areas like mental health, social work, and other psychosocial health fields that focus on support for mental and social well-being. For many wellness and medical providers, WHO's broader type of health prompts a major rethinking in the way they bring products and services to the workplace.

Past and Current Questions:
How can we reduce risks and chronic disease?
How can we reduce costs?

We must fundamentally enhance the way we view and support health to reverse the negative patterns we see in the health and performance trends in America. We must embrace the reality that health is far more than the absence of physical illness and, more important, that health plays a huge part in the overall economic and productive outcomes of organizations.

Elevating health as an organizational value will involve expanding beyond the questions of "How can we reduce risks and chronic disease?" and "How can we reduce costs?" Clearly we're not saying we should ignore these questions; the answers to these questions are necessary but not sufficient to help create thriving populations. From the employer's perspective, a broader notion of health can have an important impact on the workplace, given that thriving employees translate into thriving businesses and organizations.

"Health Is in the Clouds"

To fully appreciate our current understanding of health and thriving, it might help to use the metaphor of a cloud. Imagine within this cloud are the dimensions of health we have mapped today (2015), given the tools and instruments available to us and the mindset of our times. The cloud of health also contains aspects of health we cannot yet measure or comprehend with our current tools and mindset.

Over the years, many have contemplated this "cloud" of health and have attempted to measure its nature using their current level of understanding and the measurement instruments of the time. Researchers have synthesized the data they collected into useful dimensions based on the relationships of individual data elements to one another and their ability to predict various outcomes of importance to us. Depending on the purpose of the exploration and the methods used, different representations of health have emerged. Some say health has three, four, five or six dimensions, some say seven or eight, and some say twelve or more. Some represent the dimensions of health as a wheel. Some use a pyramid with foundational layers and an apex that represent health's different dimensions.

Each of these explorations has helped us better understand the true nature of health, but none has truly captured health's full character. Each is merely a map of health colored by the individual and various lenses through which we have viewed it.

We may never fully understand human health, let alone the health of the dynamic social and ecological systems of which we are a part, but we can become better explorers of health.

Becoming Better Health Explorers

As we stated earlier, the medical model has been a narrow lens for exploring the full terrain of health and thriving. Until relatively recently, we had been operating with a narrow view of health and have heavily weighted our approaches to reducing physical health risks and treating illness. We can draw an analogy to the time in our history when we believed the world was flat—a belief reflected in the maps of the time and in the way we contemplated the universe. Explorers of the day took great risks and demonstrated courage when setting out to find new trade routes and expand territories. Their journeys helped us better map and understand the true character and boundaries of our world terrain. We now know much more about our planet, including the basic truth that the world is not flat. We have now re-charted most of the world's regions, and we are continuously increasing our understanding of Earth's place in the larger solar system and galaxies. Today we wouldn't dream of behaving as though the world were flat.

Like the world explorers of the past and present, we must expand the way we view and support health for individuals at the workplace, in families, and in communities worldwide. We will need to embrace a new level of thinking about health and thriving and use a much more holistic and expansive mindset. Our knowledge of health continues to evolve as we make new discoveries about its various dimensions, evolve our measurement tools, and expand our willingness to view health through new lenses. As modern day "health explorers" we can use the emerging knowledge, tools, and technology to evolve our view of humanity and rechart the breadth and depth of human health.

Modern-day space exploration continues our search for deep mysteries of space with the July 2015 accomplishment of a Pluto "flyby." We feel this example helps us to see that there are still many unknowns out there, and continual exploration will uncover today's unknowns and at the same time clarify that tomorrow's knowns lead to tomorrow's unknowns. In this book, we adopt this same attitude to allow room for today's definitions but hold onto tomorrow's additional knowledge about our view of health and its many dimensions.

NASA to Pluto: We did it!

In addition to gathering incredible science, one of my hopes for the flyby was that we'd excite people about the power of exploration, the sheer audacity of our species, and the great things we can achieve. And it's working—from an unprecedented response on social media to global news coverage, the exciting and historic nature of New Horizons has really caught on! It took us more than nine years to cross the 3 billion miles of space to get to Pluto—and you have followed our journey, supported us, and believed in our mission. We can't thank you enough for that, or for your support of NASA that made New Horizons possible.

Alan Stern
Principal Investigator, NASA New Horizons Mission

A Broader Perspective on Health

While we continue to pioneer better methods for detecting and treating illness, we have been myopic about how to help people truly thrive. It may never be possible to chart the full and definitive landscape of the human condition, but there is a confluence of relevant findings from nearly every area of scientific study that underscores the need for an expanded view of health for the twenty-first century. We are learning a lot about the dynamic relationship between the mind and body from the social sciences, including positive psychology, positive leadership, positive organizational scholarship, social neuroscience, sociology, anthro-pology, and philosophy. "Harder" sciences like physics and epigenetics are also yielding new break-through insights into the fundamentally interrelated nature of all aspects of our universe and their influence on our health. We now understand far more about how the mind and body interact and how the brain and body shape the mind. These disciplines and others can help us gain a fuller understanding of health's true character.

Figure 3 outlines the very simple yet powerful driving idea behind many of the new "positive" disciplines—pushing the old boundaries of scientific study to help humans truly thrive. The most positive outliers in this revised health continuum represent a level of thriving far beyond neutral or the absence of risk.

Figure 3. A broader perspective on the overall health continuum

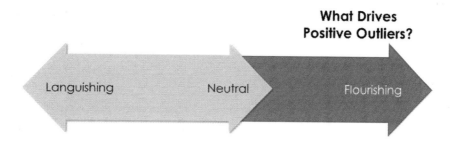

Recognizing this level of thriving helps us ask new questions such as "How can we help healthy people stay healthy?" "How can we create conditions that support positive outliers?" and "How can we help people flourish?" Ultimately we would like to answer the question "How can we make today's positive outliers tomorrow's norm?" We believe this new positive emphasis will have a profound impact on the health and energy of individuals and the performance and sustainability of organizations.

Challenges Are Sometimes the Drivers of Innovation

The current and emerging questions shown in table 1 illustrate new directions to take us to a higher strategic level for the workplace and workforce. We want to be clear—we are not proposing a new definition of health. Instead, we are urging a new level of openness about the way we view the health and well-being of individuals and organizations. We are encouraging broader thinking, taking more risks, and demonstrating greater courage as we become better explorers of health. We also urge a greater level of creativity and open-mindedness in our approaches to supporting and impacting health. We must expand our thinking about the domains that we consider to be part of health and extend our awareness of the positive end of the continuum for each of those domains. We must also expand our thinking about the relationships among the many domains of health and ask new questions. To what degree do the domains overlap? Are some domains more important than others?

...we are not proposing a new definition of health. We are urging a new level of openness about how we view the health and well-being of individuals and organizations.

Table 1. Current and emerging questions, solutions, and metrics for health and well-being

Current Questions:	Emerging Questions:
How can we reduce health risks and poor behaviors in employees and healthcare costs for companies?	How can we help people thrive?
	How do we help healthy people stay healthy?
	How can we help create conditions for positive health outliers?
Current Solution:	**Emerging Solutions:**
Worksite wellness programs focused on individuals with risk and disease	Support thriving, health, and quality of life in the total population
	Create healthy and thriving workplace cultures and environments
	Embed our wellness programs within the organization's overall business model
	Create positive organizational health
Current Metrics:	**Emerging Metrics:**
Change in health risks	Metrics of positive individual health and thriving
Change in healthcare costs	Metrics of positive organizational health
Return on investment (ROI) of wellness programs (primarily financial calculations)	Value of investment (VOI), including indirect financial results such as recruitment and retention, morale, loyalty, etc.
	Value of caring (VOC), including the tangible and intangible impact of strong positive relationships at work, at home, and in the community on the organization and its employees

To create thriving organizations that provide the conditions for employees to flourish, we must begin by pushing the historical boundaries of the health continuum. We must also apply a broader lens as we explore what we mean by "health."

It is misleading to think of separate dimensions for health and view them singly without considering the full tapestry of the territory—the entire expanse of the terrain.

Positive Individual Health

Keeping in mind that the true nature of health and all its influences are currently unknown, we are using the term "positive individual health" to represent the state of an individual's functioning across many dimensions of health. Each dimension has outer boundaries that represent the poorest levels of languishing and the most optimal levels of thriving.

Figure 4 is a graphic depiction of positive individual health. Because the dimensions are related to one another, we represent health as more of a flower with overlapping petals, rather than as a pie chart or a wheel, like many other depictions of health's dimensions. The upper half of the figure outlines dimensions that represent internal, personal characteristics. The lower half of the figure depicts domains with an external component—that enable the health and flourishing of individuals. The personal characteristics and enabling factors are strongly related to one another and overlap to varying degrees with one another. Just as every flower is unique, every person's ability to fully flourish is unique to his or her personal and enabling characteristics.

Note that figure 4 includes placeholders for "other" currently uncharted dimensions. We are in a relatively early stage of understanding the full realm of human health and the potential for influencing health in a positive way. We know far more now about health than we did fifty years ago, and we will know far more in fifty years than we know now. So it is important to acknowledge that our understanding has room to grow.

These dimensions also interact with other factors that influence an individual's overall level of health. Individual preferences for what energizes people, such as introversion and extroversion may also play a part in social connection. For example, an individual's values and belief system may highly inform his or her spiritual dimension. These interrelationships are complex and fascinating, and all contribute to what constitutes a thriving and fulfilled human being. While it is not possible to fully map all aspects of and influences on health, we encourage a broader, multidimensional view of health as we embark on creating more meaningful and impactful approaches.

Emerging questions:
How can we help healthy people stay healthy?
How can we help people thrive?
How can we create conditions that support healthy
outliers?

How can we help today's positive outliers
become tomorrow's norm?

Figure 4. Interrelated dimensions of positive individual health

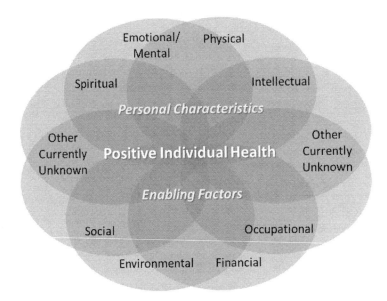

As health explorers, let us continually remind ourselves that our conceptualizations of health are just maps of the real underlying territory that is true health. Let us keep our minds open as we traverse the terrain of health and build upon our collective knowledge as we make new discoveries.

But most of all, let us not confuse the map for the territory.

In table 2, we outline some example characteristics of individuals who exemplify the most positive and negative ends of the continuum for each of eight core dimensions. We recognize it is impossible always to embody the most positive characteristics of every health dimension, and it wouldn't be "healthy" overall in the long run to do so. However, we do believe the "healthiest" individuals in this broad sense, strive to be at their personal best in all or many of the dimensions of health while still acknowledging the growth that can be associated with experiences on the more negative ends of these dimensions.

> The goal of our efforts should not only be to reduce risks and disease but also to increase our capacity for energy, flow, vitality, creativity, and happiness.

We believe individuals can flourish even if they are not at the most positive end of the continuum for all of these dimensions.

Table 2. Negative and positive characteristics of eight health dimensions

Health Dimension	Most Negative	Most Positive
Personal Characteristics		
Mental/Emotional (Focus)	Debilitating stress, anxiety, depression, negative emotions	Contentment, joy, self-esteem, self-efficacy, optimism, resilience, positive emotions
Spiritual (Meaning in Life)	Doubt, despair, fear, disappointment, dislocation	Live by a clear set of values, sense of purpose, meaning in life
Intellectual (Engagement)	Disengaged, bored, "burned-out," stagnant learner	Strong engagement in lifelong learning
Physical (Vitality)	Chronic, debilitating physical condition	High energy, vitality, and capacity for high performance
Enabling Factors		
Social (Relationships)	Destructive social relationships, detached, isolated	Thriving, positive relationships with family, friends, workplace colleagues, supervisor, connected to others
Occupational/ Professional (Meaningful Work)	Job insecurity, mismatch of skills/interests and vocation	Contributing to work in a meaningful way, connection to qualifications and interests
Environmental (Environment)	Live and work in unsafe toxic environment (workplace, home, and community)	Live and work in environment, climate, and culture that strongly supports health
Financial (Security)	Unable to support self or family, no health insurance or underinsured; debt, living outside of means	Sufficient income and savings for the future; financial security and consistency

Other currently uncharted dimensions yet to be discovered

We each have our positive personal end point on our overall health continuum. The approaches outlined in this book are designed to help individuals and organizations create conditions (both internal and external) that allow each of us to achieve optimal personal health to the degree possible. In the remainder of this chapter, we briefly discuss each of the areas represented in our current depiction of positive individual health.

Personal Characteristics

Mental and Emotional Health

One of the earliest and most prominent disciplines to formally expand the boundaries of its parent field of study is positive psychology. Positive psychology evolved in the late nineties as a response to the predominant focus on healing mental disorders in the practice of clinical psychology. Helping a person overcome a negative psychological state was previously considered a success in clinical psychology. As part of his tenure as president of the American Psychological Association,[19] Martin Seligman and coauthor Mihaly Csikszentmihalyi (Mee-hy Cheek-sent-me-HY-ee) described a new branch of psychology. They defined this new "positive psychology" as "the scientific study of positive human functioning and thriving on multiple levels including the biological, personal, relational, institutional, cultural, and global dimensions of life." The science of positive psychology focuses on the study of factors that increase human thriving, resilience, creativity, and performance.

In short, positive psychology is the science of understanding what makes people happy and helps them flourish.

In the years since the formal beginnings of positive psychology, there has been a major growth in research on human thriving, strengths, and virtues. The findings have had tremendous implications for approaches to wellness, well-being, and population health. The evidence is growing about the connection between physical health and positive psychology constructs such as resilience, optimism, gratitude, and mindfulness. For example, studies have shown that people who embody these positive characteristics have the following traits:

- enhanced motivation to act and be productive[20-23]
- less stress and anxiety[24]
- less frequent illness and quicker recovery from disease[25,26]

As a result, people who embody such positive characteristics ultimately cost employers less in healthcare spending and lost productivity.[13,27-29] They are also likely to be more creative,[30] provide better customer service,[31] and have better relationships with their work colleagues.

Physical Health

In 2008, Martin Seligman announced a new area of study he calls positive health. Our conceptualization of physical health closely parallels Seligman's concept of "positive health."[32] Ongoing research in positive health is exploring whether individual strengths like those studied by positive psychologists contribute to longer, healthier lives. According to Seligman, three areas characterize positive health:

1) subjective health

2) biological health

3) functional health

Subjective health is characterized by an individual's sense of energy, vigor, vitality, robustness, the absence of bothersome symptoms, a sense of durability, hardiness, confidence about one's body, an internal health-related locus of control, and optimism. **Biological health** includes factors familiar to the wellness field, including body mass index, blood pressure, temperature, pulse rate, cholesterol, and blood glucose. **Functional health** includes objective measures of physical capacity such as balance, flexibility, grip strength, and the ability to engage in common daily living. It also includes the fit between the physical demands of an individual's chosen lifestyle (work, family, social) and his or her ability to fully engage in his or her preferred way of life.

80% of disease, disability, and premature death in the US is due to what we eat, how we move (or not), and how we think. Employers can and should be the strongest and longest influence on employees, their families, and their communities to address the core drivers of poor health, excessive medical costs, and lost productivity

Michael Parkinson, MD, MPH, FACPM
Past President, American College of Preventive Medicine

Spiritual Health

Spiritual health includes seeking a sense of inner peace and interconnectedness, personal meaning, and a higher purpose in life. Individuals might strive for spiritual health through religious beliefs and practices, nature, meditation, yoga, and other means of connecting with the divine or sacred. Strong spirituality has been positively linked to both mental and physical health.[33, 34]

Spirituality could also be found in an altruistic commitment to a worthy cause that provides deeper meaning or social connections. Expressing gratitude or volunteering and giving back are also fulfilling ways to feed one's soul while benefiting a cause or others in need. Organizations can offer opportunities for employees to volunteer for high-value community or nonprofit projects.

Reminding ourselves often of our spiritual natures truly changes the quality of our lives. It helps us relax, slow down, lighten up, and generally find more space and joy in life.

When we get down on ourselves or life, we can pull back and ask, "How might my soul regard this situation? What am I being invited to experience?

This shift in perspective helps us let go of the resistance that always comes with negativity. As energy once again begins to flow, our outlook brightens.

Spirituality is the sacred center out of which all life comes, including Mondays and Tuesdays and rainy Saturday afternoons in all their mundane and glorious detail... The spiritual journey is the soul's life commingling with ordinary life.

Christina Baldwin[35]

Intellectual Health

Our great human adventure is the evolution of consciousness. We are in this life to enlarge the soul, liberate the spirit, and light up the brain.

—Tom Robbins, Wild Ducks Flying Backward

Intellectual health has little to do with a person's level of intelligence. Intellectual health is highly individual and involves finding ways to engage in personally stimulating and rewarding activities. Bill Hettler describes intellectual wellness as "self-directed behavior, which includes continuous acquisition, development, creative application, and articulation of critical thinking and expressive/intuitive skills and abilities focused on the achievement of a more satisfying existence. Intellectual wellness is also evidenced by a demonstrated commitment to lifelong learning."[36]

Keeping the brain and mind active and healthy is an important part of growing and maintaining strong intellectual health.

Work that is engaging and challenging without being too frustrating can be extremely rewarding and can contribute to positive mental and emotional health.[37] Like developing any other dimension of health, strengthening intellectual health takes discipline and effort. There are no magic bullets. It is important to be challenged intellectually on a regular basis. Learning a new skill or art form, performing thought-provoking activities, and enhancing an existing talent are all ways to accomplish this. Engaging in novel and creative exploration that uses brainpower throughout life is the key to strong intellectual health. Offering stimulating training and development opportunities in the workplace and novel ways to learn new information can improve the intellectual health of employees. There is an obvious connection between enhanced problem-solving ability and new ways of thinking about effective innovation and productivity in the workplace.

> *A musician must make music, an artist must paint, a poet must write, if he is to be ultimately at peace with himself. What a man can be, he must be. This need we may call self-actualization. It refers to man's desire for self-fulfillment, namely to the tendency for him to become actually in what he is potentially to become everything that one is capable of becoming.*

> —Abraham Maslow

Factors That Enable Health

Social Health

While social skills are internal to an individual, social health is about having positive and satisfying relationships with other people. Positive social ties and connections with colleagues and supervisors at work, support from family and friends, and engagement with community and neighborhood can all influence social health. There is a vast amount of literature on the impact of social factors on mortality, physical health, wellness, and well-being. For example, interactions with friends and family have been shown to be positively associated with healthy outcomes in ailments of the elderly, including diabetes, hypertension, arthritis, and emphysema.[38,39] Conversely, there is a growing body of evidence showing that conflict in families is associated with a host of physical ailments in children of those "risky family" environments.[40]

Encouraging social connection and camaraderie during or after work creates an environment where employees can foster social ties, find commonalities, and create a support network.

In Gallup's Q[12] Employee Engagement survey, one of the most interesting and controversial questions asks employees to rate their level of agreement with the statement, "I have a best friend at work." This item is among the twelve traits that predict highly productive work groups and is connected to employee loyalty, retention, engagement, and support for dealing with stress.

Customs and traditions are also a part of social networks. Some types of traditions may influence health by creating a norm that impacts employees' decisions. These traditions are found in social circles such as ethnic groups and religious communities, as well as in workplaces. Workplace traditions around healthy behaviors can help shape positive norms. For example, start a Friday morning tradition of providing fresh fruit instead of donuts and coffee, or celebrate a team goal with a brisk afternoon group walk instead of a pizza party.

Occupational Health

People spend a large percentage of their waking hours at work. Occupational health and social health dimensions are highly related, so it is not surprising that people socialize and form relationships (both positive and negative) with coworkers. Another recent Gallup survey found a strong reciprocal relationship between well-being and employee engagement, although well-being was a stronger predictor of engagement than the reverse. In other words, while engagement in work positively influences well-being, it is more likely that people with strong well-being will become engaged in their work.[41]

Having a fulfilling occupation or career that allows a sense of purpose, flow, growth, and connectedness is critically important to positive individual health.

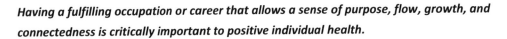

In his book *Positive Leadership: Strategies for Extraordinary Performance*, Kim Cameron (one of the founders of the fields of positive leadership and positive organizational scholarship discussed a little later in this book) outlines four qualities of work that are related to meaningfulness:

1. There is a positive relationship between meaningful work and well-being[42-44]
2. The work is associated with an important personal virtue or value[45]
3. Work that aligns with employee values is related to greater meaning[46,47]
4. Work that builds connections and a sense of community is more meaningful.[48]

The act of work itself can have a very positive influence on personal satisfaction and happiness. Mihaly Csikszentmihalyi coined the term "flow" to describe an intrinsic state that can occur when people engage in activities that have clear goals and provide immediate and ongoing feedback, and when their skills match the challenge of the task. Flow is the state of being completely immersed, absorbed, and engaged in an activity to the degree that the person loses the sense of self and time, and bodily states (e.g., hunger, thirst) are ignored. Artists, athletes, and surfers often experience a state of flow or a sense of being "in the zone."[38]

A sense of flow is deeply and intrinsically enjoyable, so occupations that provide the conditions for flow can be extremely fulfilling and rewarding.

While work can be fulfilling, it can also be very stressful. Finding the right balance between work and leisure time is also essential. Working for a company with corporate values that reflect personal values (shared values) is important for building a sense of meaningful and fulfilling work. Discovering a career or occupation that provides a sense of meaning, opportunities for growth, enjoyable atmosphere, and close connections with colleagues can strongly influence positive individual health.

When people feel good and believe they are doing meaningful work, they do high-quality work. When people feel they are doing meaningful, high-quality work, they feel good.

Environmental Health

Health is influenced by our experience with our environment through exposure, support, and how we make decisions. Environmental factors are associated with varying levels of personal control and are an important consideration for positive individual health. There are at least three levels of environment that can impact health and well-being:

- *The Workplace Environment* encompasses the physical built environment of workplaces (facilities, workstations, break areas, quiet rooms, outdoor space), health-supporting policies (nonsmoking campus, flexible work schedules), benefits and practices of employers (on-site physical activity areas, day-care services), safety practices (protective equipment, emergency procedures), and other workplace factors (noise level, air quality). This also includes the physical environment of home-based and other remote workers.

- *The Home Environment* consists of the physical aspects of the home (air quality, lead exposure, sounds, pollution), safety (secure and protected location), and support (loving and nurturing family life, encouragement for healthy living).

- *The Neighborhood and Community Environment* comprises a wide range of factors in the vicinity where people live, including access to community resources, community centers, health care, parks and shared green space, and access to grocery stores with fresh produce instead of only fast food or convenience stores. Other considerations include walk-ability and bike-ability, clean air, safe drinking water, quality of schools, public safety, low crime rates, transportation, roads and infrastructure, and population density.

Each of these is related to some degree to occupational health, financial health, and many other dimensions of health and well-being. When a person's occupation doesn't provide a comfortable income, it will limit which neighborhood and community he or she can live in. If the workplace is not safe and supportive of health and well-being (an unhealthy culture and environment), it can often negatively impact health.

Our environments can either enhance or hinder our ability to make decisions that lead to health and thriving. Some public-health efforts, such as Healthy People 2020, are designed to identify ways to create physical and social environments that promote good health for all, through programs, practices, and policies. However, individual choices are critical to achieving a thriving way of life.

So much has been written about the importance of culture within an enterprise, especially health and safety. However, mission statements and core values that claim to support any culture are meaningless unless there are genuine commitments from executives, measurable results, and trust that is pervasive throughout the organization. Executives must accept the truth about organizational weaknesses and implement thoughtful, positive changes without punitive actions. Unfortunately, these character traits are not always evident within management ranks.
Joel Bender, MD, PhD
Global Medical Director, General Motors, Retired

Financial Health

Financial health doesn't necessarily equate to having a lot of money. Financial health involves being comfortable with your current and future financial situation by having a clear plan for financial security. Obviously, financial concerns and hardship can be a significant source of stress. In a recent national survey conducted by the Harvard School of Public Health, of those reporting the greatest amount of stress, 53 percent indicated that problems with finances were a contributing factor to their stress level.[49]

Employees can achieve optimal financial wellness by understanding the limits of their income and resources and finding ways to live within their means. Workplaces are beginning to understand the importance of financial health and are offering ways to help employees learn how to build their savings and invest in their future. Resources may include access to financial advisers and workshops, online tools, and seminars, in addition to a savings plan as part of the employer's benefits package.

Providing education and awareness to individuals about the health to wealth connection is the most important first step in the financial-wellness equation. Over the years, we have seen the impact of Health Risk Assessments that help individuals identify personal health risks so that the information can be used as an educational launching pad to promote behavior change to improve physical health. To support individuals in a similar way, the Health Index Calculator (HIC) is a tool designed to help people realize and visualize that they are spending too much on their health, potential savings within their control also based on the promotion of behavior change. Unlike the Health Assessment, the HIC allows individuals to forecast monetary gain based on their behavior changes related to their risk. The reveal of real dollars intrinsically motivates action.

Lisa M. Holland, RN, MBA, CCWS
President StayFit™
Cleveland, OH

Gregory J. Hummer, MD
CEO Simplicity Health Plans
Cleveland, OH

To read the full case study go to appendix B

Clusters of Health Dimensions

Understanding the nature of individual dimensions of health is important to appreciate the complexities of health. We also believe it is important to think beyond individual dimensions to better understand clusters of dimensions and drivers of interactions between and among dimensions. For example, physical health is highly related to many of the other dimensions represented in this chapter. Also, the combination of physical and mental/emotional health is a core part of the success of individual and organizational health. Organizations have engaged the wellness and medical community for physical exams, preventive services, and health assessments, including mental and emotional health. We typically and appropriately view health assessments (by medical or wellness professionals) as prevention and early detection of disease. In addition, we could enhance these assessments by including measures of progress toward thriving and flourishing states of health.

Another example of clustering is the many evidence-based studies in the last decade that have focused on the connection of emotional/mental health (depression, stress, lack of social support, financial burden) to physical conditions like diabetes, heart disease, and asthma. We fully expect that we will soon recognize that all the dimensions of health discussed here result in either positive or negative outcomes in terms of physical conditions.

In our earlier work with health-risk factors and behaviors, we established an important concept: risks travel together within four major clusters.[50] Using that same logic, we can ask the same questions: How do the different positive individual health dimensions travel together? What circumstances influence how and whether dimensions cluster? Wellness and well-being and other fields of study would benefit from a research agenda that helps us better understand the interrelated nature of different dimensions and constructs of health.

The Roots of Our Positive Zeitgeist

Zeitgeist 'tsīt͵gīst —the defining spirit or mood of a particular period of history as shown by the ideas and beliefs of the time.

No examination of health and thriving is complete without paying homage to the early humanistic psychologists who laid the foundation for the "positive" shift in our current sciences and ultimately in our popular society. None is more recognized than Abraham Maslow, who we often credit as being the "grandfather of positive psychology."

Maslow and his fellow humanists broke from what were then the predominant forces in psychology, B. F. Skinner's behaviorism, and Sigmund Freud's psychoanalysis. The humanists were interested in human thriving and our innate human drive toward self-fulfillment, creativity, and self-actualization. Maslow may be best known for his "Hierarchy of Needs." While he never represented his needs hierarchy as a pyramid, it is often depicted that way, with basic human needs as the base, and the highest levels—self-fulfillment—at the apex (see figure 5). Maslow focused on understanding the basic types of human motivation and the most likely order in which they could be met. For example, it would be very difficult for people whose basic needs are not being met (e.g., sustained hunger, chronic lack of sleep, living or working in imminently dangerous environments) to consistently meet their higher-order needs for fulfilling their creative potential. However, Maslow did recognize that the needs hierarchy was fluid, and shifts in levels of motivation could happen at any time.

When we look at Maslow's hierarchy of needs, it is clear how our work and workplaces can help us meet many of our core needs. The money we earn through employment helps us provide shelter and security to meet our physiological and safety needs. Having close collegial relationships and even friendships in our workplaces can help us meet our psychological need for belongingness and love. Meaningful work provides opportunities to meet our esteem needs and ultimately our higher-order needs to achieve our fullest potential.

One important caveat that we want to highlight is that whether and how these needs are met is in the eye of the beholder. One person's safe and secure environment is another person's slum. In our Western culture, many assume that money and wealth are the routes to self-fulfillment and happiness, but there is growing agreement that wealth and power are not the panaceas we once thought them to be.[51,52] Recent data from the Gallup-Healthways Well-Being Index provides valuable information on emotional well-being and life satisfaction and helps answer the question of whether money can buy happiness.[53,54] High income buys life satisfaction but not happiness. Maslow once said, "If I wished to destroy someone, I can think of no better way of doing it than to give him a million dollars suddenly."

Figure 5. Maslow's hierarchy of needs

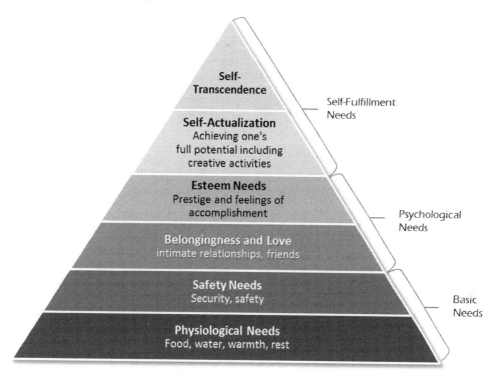

Using data from the Gallup World Poll, Louis Tay, and Ed Diener tested the idea that certain needs are universal to the happiness of humans.[55] They also examined whether those needs follow a hierarchy similar to that originally proposed by Maslow in 1943. They analyzed item responses that represented needs derived from the work of Maslow,[56] Deci and Ryan,[57,58] Ryff and Keyes,[59] DeCharms[60] and Csikszentmihalyi.[61]

- Basic needs for food and shelter
- Safety and security
- Social support and love
- Feeling respected and pride in activities

- Mastery
- Self-direction and autonomy

The data for their study included responses from 123 nations representing 66 percent of the world population. Their analysis supported the idea that there are indeed universal needs that predict well-being. The findings also showed some support for an ordering of need fulfillment. Social support and feeling respected were most strongly related to positive feelings, and lack of respect and low autonomy were most related to negative feelings. They also found that basic needs are strongly related to life evaluations and negative feelings, and more specifically, that deprivation of needs is related to low positive feelings and fulfillment of needs is closely linked to high positive feelings.

Modern Characterizations of Health, Wellness, Well-Being

There are many characterizations of health and well-being. Among the most popular and most relevant to our work are the domains outlined in Martin Seligman's PERMA model and Gallup's dimensions of well-being. In table 3, we map the connection between the health dimensions we use in our work, Maslow's needs, the domains represented by the earliest wellness approaches,[9,7] and several other popular characterizations of the dimensions of health and well-being. We do this not to highlight any one characterization of well-being as the correct one, the most relevant, or the most comprehensive. We are depicting the reality that there are many thoughtful, evidence- and theory-based ways of viewing health, wellness, and well-being. As we said earlier, many have looked into the "cloud" of health (and well-being), and several useful characterizations have been created.

The science and evidence in the area of well-being are evolving. Regardless of our current or future state of knowledge about health and well-being, there is strong agreement that there are universal human needs (both psychological and physiological) that we are driven to fulfill to the degree possible given our personal biology and circumstances. Our workplaces can also help or hinder our ability to fulfill many of those needs and live healthy, happy, meaningful, and fulfilling lives.

Gallup's Five Elements of Well-Being

The Gallup Organization has been researching and measuring well-being for the past sixty-five years. Gallup's most recent construct of well-being is made up of five elements (see table 3). With the exception of physical well-being, the majority of the elements fall into the area that we outlined as more influenced by enabling factors. Social, career, community, and financial well-being are all driven by external forces.

Table 3. Domains from popular wellness and well-being theories

Positive Individual Health (Pitts, Edington)	Wellness (Hettler, Ardell)	Well-Being Elements (Gallup)	Well-Being (PERMA) (Seligman)	Motivational Hierarchy (Maslow)	Psychological Well-Being (Ryff and Keyes)	Self-Determination Theory (Deci & Ryan)
Personal Characteristics						
Mental/Emotional (focus)	Emotional[1,2]		Positive Emotions	Psychological needs	Self-acceptance	
Spiritual (meaning in life)	Spiritual[1,2]		Meaning	Self-transcendence	Purpose in life	
Intellectual (engagement)	Intellectual[1,2]		Engagement	Psychological and self-fulfillment needs	Personal growth	Competence
Physical (vitality)	Physical[1,2]	Physical		Physiological needs		
Enabling Influences						
Social (relationships)	Social[1,2]	Social	Positive Relationships	Psychological needs of belongingness and love	Positive Relations	Relatedness
Occupational/Professional (meaningful work)	Occupational[1]	Career	Accomplishment	Psychological needs of belonging and esteem needs.		Competence
Autonomy				Self-fulfillment needs	Autonomy	Autonomy
Environmental (environment)		Community		Safety needs	Environmental Mastery	
Financial (security)		Financial		Fulfills basic physiological/safety needs		

[1]Hettler, [2]Ardell

For each of the five elements, Gallup distinguishes between two types of well-being. The first emphasizes how we feel at the moment—how we are experiencing our life in real time. The second is more evaluative and emphasizes our satisfaction with the way we are living our life—how we look back on the moments of our lives. These two types of well-being mirror what Daniel Kahneman calls the "experiencing self" and the "remembering self." We talk more about each of these in chapter 12, but for the purpose of discussion here, we merely want to draw parallels between important popular characterizations of human well-being and health.

Seligman's Well-Being (PERMA)

Seligman's theory of well-being is essentially "a theory of uncoerced choice" characterized by five elements that make up the acronym PERMA:

- **P**ositive Emotion
- **E**ngagement
- Positive **R**elationships
- **M**eaning
- **A**ccomplishment

Seligman states that *"each element of well-being must itself have three properties to count as an element."* According to Seligman, an element must have the following qualities:

1. It contributes to well-being.
2. Many people pursue it for its own sake, not merely to get any of the other elements.
3. It is defined and measured independently of the other elements (exclusivity).

Regardless of whether you call it health, wellness, or well-being, and regardless of which set of dimensions resonates most with you, we hope you will take away from this chapter the importance of embracing a far broader and far more positive kind of health.

CHAPTER 3:
Context Matters

Imagine working in a place where the organization and employees all embrace a core set of values, work in a collaborative manner, and fully enjoy their work and their lives.

Would you like to work in a place like that?

Do you work in such a place? If not, why not?

We are at a very scary but exciting crossroads. There is an amazing confluence of evidence and circumstance that provides unparalleled opportunities to either improve or destroy the human condition and the greater economy and ecology of our planet. Our solutions will require holistic, systematic, and systemic approaches and true collaboration among stakeholders worldwide. Improving the health and thriving of employee populations will require a similar level of thinking and true cooperation among stakeholders of organizations.

Poor Health Is a Wicked Problem

While it may sound harsh to characterize poor health as "wicked," it clearly fits into the category of an especially intractable and "wicked problem," as defined by Horst Rittel and Melvin Webber in 1973.[62] The term wicked problem represents a special class of social or cultural problems that are difficult or impossible to solve for many reasons. Wicked problems often have a large economic or social burden, and they are usually interconnected with several other issues or problems. They often have no definitive answers, and enacting solutions to wicked problems requires that many people change their mindsets and their behaviors.

Most organizational wellness programs, as well as medicine, pharmaceuticals and other disease-oriented strategies, have been trying to address employee health using the level of thinking, tools, and methods designed for "tame problems." Tame problems can be clearly stated, they have well-defined goals, and they stay solved. The implicit assumption underlying wellness programs and medicine is that once identified, people with health risks and disease will be motivated to change the behaviors that led to those risks and conditions. Because health is influenced by many factors including social, emotional, environmental, and cultural influences, this is a very simplistic and unrealistic assumption.

Wicked problems, including poor health, are socially complex, so solving a wicked problem is fundamentally a social process and requires highly creative solutions.

To have an effective impact on employee health and well-being will take a greater mindfulness of the influences of the complex social systems, environments, and cultures in which people work and live. We must strive to improve our understanding of the many domains of health, and increase our awareness of the most positive potential levels for each of health's dimensions. Ultimately, we must work to create the conditions that help people become outliers on the positive end of a health continuum that includes vitality, thriving, high energy, and capacity for extraordinary performance. We recommend using principles and methods from systems thinking and human-centered design to improve the environment, culture, and climate for employee health in organizations.

Successful wellness initiatives combine a supportive culture with individual initiatives and healthy lifestyle skills. We can add culture initiatives to wellness programs that had focused almost exclusively on the individual.

—Judd Allen

Systems Thinking—Beyond the Focus on the Individual

Merriam-Webster defines a system as "a group of related parts that move or work together," as "a regularly interacting or interdependent group of items forming a unified whole," and as "a group of interacting bodies under the influence of related forces." Given these definitions, most people would agree that employer organizations are systems. But for most of its nearly forty-five-year history, the wellness industry has adopted the medical model and primarily focused on improving the health and well-being of individuals within the system. We have only marginally recognized the larger set of influences and interdependencies within and surrounding the system.

Systems thinking allows us to use a broader lens to understand the whole system-level impact on health and to map and understand relationships between parts of the whole.

> *The fundamental rationale [of systems thinking] is to understand how it is that the problems that are the most vexing, and difficult and intransigent...come about, and ...to get a perspective on those problems that gives us some leverage...some insight as to what we might do differently.*
>
> *—Peter Senge*

Improving employee health and well-being will take systems thinking on a number of levels. We must think not only about individuals as complex, dynamic systems but also about groups of people and the dynamic interplay of their coexistence and cooperation. We must think about the microsystems within our organizations and about our whole organizations as complex and dynamic systems. We must also think about the place and role of our organizations in the larger ecosystems of our communities and societies.

Organizations must support the health and well-being of employees as a system-wide undertaking.

The five pillars outlined in *Zero Trends: Health as a Serious Economic Strategy* are the product of a type of systems thinking. We used systems thinking again as we developed a strategic, systematic, systemic, and sustainable approach to creating thriving workplaces and workforces. Systems thinking helps us recognize the influences of the workplace, home and community on the health of employees and the health of the organization. We have expanded our knowledge of the impact of the original five fundamental pillars through observing and helping organizations develop healthy, high-performing, thriving, and sustainable workplaces and workforces. We believe that workplace environments and the programs, policies, benefits, and initiatives that organizations offer can help employees truly flourish. But it will take systems thinking and a more "human-centered" design process to create an integrated strategy rather than a series of seemingly unrelated programs.

> A strong and positive culture is essential for companies to achieve their business goals. When the motivation behind that culture is authentic, it is contagious for both employees and the community in which it operates. The result is motivated and positive employees who assume responsibility for their productivity, as well as their health. It is the basis of a system where employees, beneficiaries, and communities thrive. Achieving a positive culture in the workplace is dependent on leadership as it is in any successful system.
>
> Ron Finch, EdD
> Principal, Finch & Associates, LLC

Design Thinking—Collaborative and Empathetic Creative Process

We are in need of meaningful, engaging, and impactful innovations in the wellness and well-being field. We designed many of our solutions with the employer organization in mind, but the true end user of the "product" is the employee. We had the mentality that "if we build it, they will come." Employers built or purchased programs and implemented them, and ultimately, few employees used them as they were intended. So employers have resorted to paying or coercing employees to participate in the programs, which can have counterintuitive impacts in the long run.

Deep empathy with what employees want and need, was often missing from the design of our wellness and well-being approaches.

Design thinking is a type of problem-solving that has been used for many years in the industrial design space and more recently, for attempting to solve some of our most "wicked" social problems. This includes hunger, poverty, and local, regional, and global environmental issues, among others. Design thinking can also provide tools and processes that can help develop courageous and creative solutions to address the "wickedness" of poor health and well-being.

Design thinking is both a method and a mindset that we believe can bring value to the process of evolving more impactful approaches. It emphasizes **strong empathy** with the end user and the ability to see the world from multiple perspectives. It involves **integrative thinking**—striving to see all sides of a potential solution, **optimism and confidence** that workable solutions are possible in spite of the many challenges, and **creativity and fearlessness** to ask out-of-the-box, and even off-the-wall questions to general ideas (ideation). It involves **the will and resilience to "iterate,"** or to try out potential new solutions, learn quickly, throw out what doesn't work and try something new.

There is a tremendous interest among employers who have sponsored wellness programs for many years to broaden the impact of their efforts by focusing more on their culture in addition to their support of individual health habit improvements. Though most wellness practitioners have training in both ecological health and behavioral health approaches, it remains that most of the focus for many years has been on individuals and their lifestyles. As a result, the health risk assessment has been the dominant catalyst for program planning and evaluation, and culture measurement is still in the nascent stages. One thing more troublesome than the lack of integration of environmental and person-level metrics is the segregated approach advocated by some health promotion practitioners. "Start with culture," a few say as if individuals are simply a byproduct of their ecosystems. Worse, a few suggest waylaying individual health metrics in deference to measures of engagement or purpose, as if they represent some transcendent proxy for health promotion.

I can think of few surer ways to make the field of health promotion practice irrelevant than decoupling cultural, psychosocial and health factors. Indeed, if a case is to be made for the benefit of building a culture of health, it will be through the concomitant analysis of environmental metrics and health risk data that encompasses the time-honored definition of health as a state of complete physical, mental, spiritual, intellectual and social health promotion.

Paul E. Terry, PhD
Editor, The Art of Health Promotion: American Journal of Health Promotion
CEO Health Enhancement Research Organization (HERO)

The process of design thinking involves employees directly in a highly collaborative team process. It can be both challenging and frustrating at times, but it is usually fun, and always exhilarating.

Later in the book, we will talk more about systems thinking, design thinking, and other potential solutions to wicked problems and how these apply to employee health and well-being. For now, we want to emphasize that an enlightened approach to improving employee health and thriving must recognize health's complex and multifaceted nature and the many different influences on health. We must ask ourselves what we can all do to make our organizations the most fertile ground possible for supporting and growing positive individual and organizational health. In the remainder of this chapter, we present a model designed to help expand thinking about the context of health and well-being for employees and organizations.

Model for Positive Organizational Health

To guide our work, we have created a high-level conceptual model that outlines many potential spheres of influence on positive individual and positive organizational health. We organized the model (figure 6) from the perspective of the workplace setting, so thriving employees are at the heart of the model, supported by the five fundamental pillars. Strong pillars provide the foundation for Shared Values—Shared Results, and healthy environments, cultures and relationships for thriving employees.

As the issue of rising healthcare costs for employers moved up to the C-suite, the result was much more aggressive and strategic health and productivity management (HPM). Learnings from these experiences, along with the demands of a mobile and multigenerational workforce, are expanding beyond healthcare costs to employee performance. As a result, HPM is becoming an integrated human capital strategy that includes talent management and total rewards, that help to define the employee value proposition and supports a company's business objectives. At the core of this value proposition is ensuring that all employees, regardless of age or position, feel a sense of meaning, purpose, and engagement in their work.

This view of human capital is contributing to how companies will measure success using a triple bottom line: impact on society, impact on the environment, and impact on the economy.

Jack Bastable
National Practice Leader, Employee Health and Productivity
CBIZ, Benefits & Insurance Services, Inc.

Shared Values—Shared Results

We believe creating Shared Values—Shared Results is key to a healthy workplace culture and environment, so it is a prominent part of the model. By Shared Values—Shared Results, we mean that the ideal work culture and environment is one where the employees and the organization share a core set of values (shared values), and what is good for employees is good for the organization (shared results). It should be clear to both the employees and the organization how positive organizational health benefits each in ways that matter to them. When everyone shares the vision, purpose, and values of the organization and recognizes the organizational and personal value it holds for them, everyone, including the organization, wins. We also represent the central place of the employees within the broader context of their environments, cultures, and relationships in their workplaces, with their families and friends, and in their communities.

Figure 6. Model for positive organizational health

Not all employees will have the same values, and not all employees will value the same things at the same level. That's the beauty of the uniqueness that each employee brings to the workforce.

While differences in individual values are inevitable and even welcomed, it is important that a core shared set of values and shared results exists among all employees (for example, a shared sense of meaningful work, shared responsibilities, collaboration, and employee health). Shared values and shared results should be universal enough that they resonate to some degree with every employee, while still being core to the business goals and vision for the organization. Although most organizations would agree that the noble values and results we mention above are universal, there are some organizations that allow economic gain and profit for the organization to supersede these shared values and shared results.

We will return to this model periodically throughout the book as we outline the science that grounds the positive organizational health process and our ideas for practical application in employer organizations.

There are no quick fixes. Just like weight loss, there is no "magic pill." However, organizations need to understand there must be a starting point. You can track costs of claims, and you can track those who utilize your "wellness" programs, but until you are ready to jump in with both feet you will never recognize the total impact that CAN be made by educating your workforce on how our lifestyles impact our claim costs. You won't see the savings overnight, but stay consistent and diligent and in two or three years you will start to see change. By year five you will see such a positive gain that you will wonder why you waited. It will also drive a culture change, so your efforts need to be well-thought-out with involvement from several areas to provide the buy-in needed to be successful.

Judi McMullen, SPHR, RCC, HCS
Vice President, Chief Human Resources Officer, Cuyahoga Community College

Healthy Foundations—The Five Fundamental Pillars

In *Zero Trends*, five pillars were introduced as fundamental to thriving workplaces and workforces. After years of applying these principles in real-world settings, we increasingly believe in the importance of the pillars today, so they have a central place in our model. The five pillars are positioned prominently within the larger context of the employer culture and environment. Their influence even extends beyond the organization to employees' families, communities, and societies.

While the term "pillar" may imply separate standalone structures, the model depicts the pillars as a set of interlocking strengths. The five pillars overlap in ways that are central to the workplace culture and environment and to supporting thriving employees. No single pillar can be at its strongest without strength and support from the other pillars, and any single pillar, no matter how strong, cannot carry the full weight of creating a thriving workplace and workforce.

There are many factors that contribute to the strength of the pillars, and strength in each of the pillars contributes to a more supportive environment, a stronger health culture, and more thriving employees. The stronger the pillars, the stronger the culture, and environment, and the more likely it is the employees and the organization will flourish.

Pillar 1: Engaged and Committed Leadership

For a leader who subscribes to systems thinking, the focus shifts from wanting to control everything to wanting to leverage every relationship.

John Blakely[63]

As we will emphasize throughout the book, executive leaders are crucial to efforts to evolve healthier more thriving environments and cultures. Motivation is key to the level of engagement and commitment leaders must have. Thriving leaders must have "a very passionate, deep and persistent commitment to real learning."[64] They must be prepared to be wrong and ready to acknowledge where they may be part of the problem. They must be willing to bring together people with different points of view from different parts of the system and champion the creation of a truly shared vision of a thriving workplace and workforce culture. Visible and thriving leaders

- have deep commitment to a healthy culture;

- use systems thinking;

- create Shared Values—Shared Results;

- incorporate evidence and practice from other nontraditional areas (e.g., positive leadership, transformational leadership, etc.);

- co-create a truly shared vision.

Committed and courageous leaders are crucial to a thriving work culture and environment.

Engaged leadership is also imperative at all levels in organizations. Leadership from those in formally appointed positions (pillar 1), leadership from individuals with operational or wellness roles related to building healthy environments (pillar 2), and thriving self-leaders (pillar 3) are all part of the larger equation.

Staff Well-being, Performance, and Engagement

Staff morale, attitude and sense of well-being are critical determinants of organizational performance. Ensuring that employees are committed to their organization's goals and values and motivated to contribute to organizational success whilst enhancing their own sense of wellbeing depends critically on their successful engagement.

In the terms of a movement gathering force in the UK it means having managers who present a clear, strong strategic narrative, give their people focus and scope, treat them as individuals, coach and stretch them, with an effective employee voice, and display integrity by demonstrating stated values in their day-to-day behavior.

The Confederation of British Industry, a leading independent employers' organization, found that companies with highly engaged staff report employees taking an average of seven absence days per year, approximately half the fourteen days per year reported in low engagement companies. Employees in high engagement companies also report less workplace stress.

In the National Health Service measures of staff engagement show a high correlation between good scores and a range of desirable outcomes for patients, with greater patient satisfaction and lower standardized patient mortality rates.

Professor Dame Carol Black, DBE, FRCP, FMedSci
Principal of Newnham College Cambridge
Expert Adviser on Health and Work to the Department of Health England and to Public Health England
Chairman of the Nuffield Trust for health policy
Member of the Welsh Government's Bevan Commission on health in Wales
Chair of the RSSB's Health and Wellbeing Policy Group, and a member of PwC's Health Industries Oversight Board

---

Pillar 2: Positive Environment, Culture, and Climate

The environment, climate, and cultures of organizations are designed to provide the rules, norms, and rituals that help keep us safe while we're on the job and help us provide for ourselves and our families. They also help us meet our higher-order needs for creativity, meaning, and life satisfaction, which is increasingly important as knowledge and service workers become a growing proportion of the workforce. Therefore, the model in figure 6 represents the workplace environment and culture as the central and primary influence on thriving employees from the employer-employee win-win perspective.

Each employer organization has its own unique culture shaped by its policies, norms, and values. However, the conditions in which we work can often trigger chronic and toxic levels of stress and fight-or-flight responses once reserved for helping us escape from tigers. Our high-tech, fast-paced, competitive, 24x7, do-more-with-less work style has contributed to high levels of chronic stress and disillusionment, which can lead to poor health behaviors and health conditions. Employers are in an ideal position to have a positive impact, but it will take more than programs to help people counteract the impact of unhealthy work environments, climates and cultures. Relationships with colleagues and supervisors play an important role in employee health and thriving.

It is important to develop positive leaders and managers and help all employees understand the breadth and depth of positive organizational and individual health and the shared values it can provide for both the company and the employees.

The CEO and other organizational leaders should be certain that the individual(s) responsible for creating the environmental and operational evolution share a commitment to continuous and deep learning. This commitment is necessary for the people who represent both internal partners and external partners. Collaboration among all partners is critical, as is

- shared understanding of the problem;
- intelligent dialog about the different interpretations of the issue;
- shared commitment to the possible solutions;
- collective intelligence about how to solve the issue.

To be an effective internal or external partner in this process will require participants to set aside their focus on the goals of their individual department or area (internal partners) or business model (external partners). Operations leaders are core to these partnerships, and can support the process of evolving positive organizational health by

- promoting positive motivation for the organization;
- operationalizing practices that foster development of
  - shared vision and values;
  - positive organizational health;
  - positive individual health;
  - positive personal motivation;
  - measurement and communication of what matters (shared results);

- incorporating practices from other nontraditional areas (e.g., positive organizational scholarship, implementation science, design thinking, organizational development, change management, etc.).

Operations leaders must be attuned to a holistic and synergistic process of serving the ultimate vision of the organization. It is also the role of the CEO and other executive leaders to foster this kind of real collaboration.

None of us is as smart as all of us.

—Ken Blanchard

Pillar 3: Positive Individual Health

There is a mounting body of evidence and a growing recognition among employers and employees that characteristics like resilience, optimism, and mindfulness are important contributors to employee health and performance. Employers are also recognizing that in addition to supporting the physical health of employees and providing a safe work environment, they have an opportunity to create conditions that optimally promote and support self-leadership including meaningful work, resilience, optimism, and creativity in the workplace and their workforce. Some of the ways employers can support positive individual health include,

- revising of wellness and well-being programs to include self-leadership development opportunities for leaders, managers, and all employees. This could include helping employees develop
  - personal vision and purpose;
  - optimism and resilience;
  - brain health;
  - decision-making awareness and skills;
  - mindfulness;
- incorporating evidence and practice from other nontraditional disciplines (e.g., positive psychology, social neuroscience, etc.);
- using human-centered design principles to create engaging organic solutions.

Alignment of environment, culture, climate, programs, policies, and relationships will help self-leaders at all levels of the organization develop a greater capacity to support and encourage each other, and to engage in healthy activities they find personally meaningful and rewarding. This could include involvement in traditional wellness activities, like healthier eating, increased physical activity, or engaging in less traditional approaches like meditation, yoga, spending more quality time with family, and friends, doing volunteer work and being in service to others.

In foresighted companies, community service is not an add-on, but rather a central force, shaping and re-enforcing values vital to the success of the business.

—James E. Austin

Many companies large and small are dedicating time toward community service. One of the most intrinsically rewarding and healthy experiences in life is being in heartfelt service to something greater than oneself.

I slept and dreamt that life was joy.
I awoke and saw that life was service.
I acted and behold, service was joy.

—Rabindranath Tagore

Pillar 4: Positive Personal Motivation

There is increasing recognition of the importance of intrinsic motivation and growing evidence that intrinsic motivation leads to more sustainable behavior change. However, the trend in the wellness and well-being fields has been to promote program participation, and even biometric or behavior outcomes with extrinsic motivators such as financial incentives or healthcare premium reductions. There is persuasive evidence that under some circumstances, external rewards, including money or prizes, can undermine our intrinsic motivation. As part of a strategy to evolve a more thriving environment and culture, organizations can develop an increased capacity for support and recognition that is more likely to foster intrinsic motivation and autonomy within employees. This can include the following:

- strengthening all pillars

- respecting and supporting positive personal motivation

- incorporating evidence and practices from other nontraditional areas including:
    - self-determination theory (SDT)
    - behavioral economics
    - neuroscience
    - social sciences (sociology, social psychology, anthropology, etc.)
    - large and small personal epiphanies

Pillar 5: Measure and Communicate What Matters

To help our organizations evolve more thriving workplaces and workforces, we must embrace a new set of measures and metrics for success. We must also apply new and more creative and appropriate methods for measuring structure, process, and outcomes. Financial metrics will likely remain important, especially to employers. However, we predict they will become less valued as the workplace and workforce find additional ways to share values and results through a shared vision and more meaningful work. While measuring healthcare and productivity costs savings is important, both the employer and the employee will benefit in several ways by attention to outcomes that go "beyond" in several ways:

- incorporating measures that matter to all stakeholders include the following:

    o beyond the outcome measures of healthcare and productivity costs to include the full value of happiness, engagement, loyalty, employee and customer satisfaction, being an employer of choice, and being an organization of caring

    o beyond productivity to the value of an investment in shared values, positive individual and organization health, and investment in supportive environments, cultures, and climates in the workplace

    o beyond physical health measures to include measures of mental and emotional health, spiritual health, intellectual health, social health, and financial, environmental, and occupational health

- incorporating evaluation practices from other nontraditional areas (e.g., social and behavioral sciences)

- engaging in collaborative, comprehensive evaluation planning based on a theory of change and a program theory

- outlining a clearly articulated outcomes framework

- communicating successes and learnings to all stakeholders in an ongoing, responsive and engaging manner

- improving and iterating your approaches

Healthy Environment, Culture, Climate, and Relationships

While people spend much of their waking hours at work, our model acknowledges that employees' homes and families, friends, and communities also play a huge role in supporting their health and well-being. The environment, culture and relationships—in employees' workplaces, in their homes, with their family and friends and in their communities—can all significantly influence employee health and thriving and indirectly impact the health and success of the organization.

Much of the criticism of health promotion stems from the inability to achieve large and lasting behavior change. The individual go-it-alone approach does not produce much in the way of sustained results. Creating wellness cultures makes it possible to: (1) reach those that had been hard to reach, (2) keep healthy people healthy, and (3) increase lifestyle improvement success rates. We need wellness cultures to achieve the magnitude of results that will achieve healthy lifestyles and address the bottom line.

Judd Allen, PhD
President, Human Resources Institute

Home, Family, and Friends

We've all heard the saying that "home is where the heart is." Home is where people should feel safe, secure, loved, and supported. Home is where self-leadership and positive individual health begin. It is where we learn basic health habits in childhood, and it is where we return each day as adults to relax, unwind, and replenish ourselves after a hard day of work. While this is true for some people, for others the home and family environment and culture can be unsupportive, unsafe, and discomforting.

Employers can have a positive effect on the home and family lives of their employees by including family members in health management initiatives. They can also help employees, and their family members develop and maintain **strong relationships** based on solid self-leadership capabilities, including resilience and optimism. An even more important contribution organizations can make is being an energizing and rewarding place to work.

Ideally, employees would leave work more fulfilled than exhausted. Home and family would be the place where we would return each day after a rewarding and energizing day at work. Conversely, work would be the place where we return energized each day after a restful and revitalizing evening and night at home.

Few are those who see with their own eyes and feel with their own hearts.

—Albert Einstein

Family physicians are the leading edge of medical solutions, and we depend on them for everyday pain and suffering. " Keeping the healthy people healthy is something I discuss with my patients, and I also talk with them that it is not my responsibility to keep them healthy. But it is my job to support, guide, and encourage the along the way. With EMR, PCMH and all of the other internal system changes we are making to make this happen I have not been working with my area employers or city to the degree I would like—still on my list of things to accomplish. I do believe I have made great inroads in changing the "culture" with my patients, and it has been rewarding work.

Gregg Stefanek, DO
Family Physician, Alma Michigan

Community

The communities surrounding organizations are important parts of the environment and culture, and can be a source of supportive resources and healthy relationships. Places where we learn, work, play, and worship are all part of the surrounding environments that make up our community. The communities where we live and spend our time can influence the overall well-being of employees, so we have depicted them in the outer circle of figure 6 on page 36. An environment that supports wellness, well-being, and safety in our surrounding communities leads to healthy decisions and healthy lifestyles.

At Henry Ford LiveWell, wellness is seen as a journey taken by everyone rather than a destination achievable by only a few. The aim is to meet people where they are on their journey to help optimize well-being across the lifespan and across the continuum of care.

Sharon Milberger, ScD
Director, Henry Ford LiveWell, Henry Ford Health System

In the remainder of the book, we outline a flexible, collaborative, and inclusive process that organizations can use to build strength in each of the areas outlined in our model for positive organizational health.

CHAPTER 4:
An Executive Summary of the Win-Win Journey Process

Wins for the organization and wins for the employees

To wrap up the "Awakening" section, we provide a high-level view of a win-win journey process. We have based this process on evidence and practice from many different disciplines, combined with our best thinking and experience to help you design your own "how" for creating positive organizational health. It sets the agenda for the rest of the book, where we provide ideas for how you can incorporate the best and emerging next practices for strengthening your organization's environment and culture for health and well-being.

The process outlined here reflects our suggestions for creating strength in each of the five pillars by creating Shared Values—Shared Results, evolving positive individual and positive organizational health, and measuring and communicating what matters in your organization. We describe approaches that represent a more balanced responsibility and accountability between the organization and the individual than the wellness and well-being programs of the past.

Journey of a Win-Win Organization

We call the process of evolving positive health in your organization the "win-win journey." We choose to use the word "evolve" because we believe the process of creating a healthier environment, culture and climate is truly an evolution. Like any evolution, it can be slow. There will be times when growth happens in surges, when many smaller changes converge, and when synergies occur, but, for the most part, the evolution is a slow and measured process.

We emphasize that the journey each organization takes is highly individual and personal; thus, not all ideas or approaches we discuss will be right for all organizations.

There is no one right way to do this work. The journey has many potential paths and many destinations. Much like any individual employee's journey of personal development, there are no recipes, no blueprints for success that apply to all organizations. However, we do believe there are some basic principles, which we discuss throughout the rest of the book along with food for thought and ideas for action that can guide you on your journey.

Whether you are a CEO, another senior executive, or an energized and empowered group of employees from anywhere or at any level of the organization, we believe there is something here that will help you initiate a journey and start a movement.

When I consider the reasons that our industry has not been as successful as it could, I feel that it's due to the fact that we try to make workplace wellness and productivity a commodity; something that we can monetize and sell as a product. However, I feel that we have a strong and bright future if we focus on building relationships and working to align policies, projects and programs toward common objectives.

We need to focus on each workplace and community as a unique culture that has grown organically over time. We have to combat some health issues with the same organic development, which requires patience. Organic doesn't mean happenstance, growing something organically takes more work and more time to develop and learn, but what is cultivated from the process is a much better outcome that has a great depth and breadth of opportunity to impact people's health and productivity, as well as the long-term health and success of the company.

Brian Passon
President, ARCH Health and Productivity, ArchHP.com

The Four Ss: Strategic, Systematic, Systemic, and Sustainable

The journey to becoming a win-win organization, like any great journey, begins by having an inspiring shared vision for where you want to go and by clearly understanding where you are today. We have grounded the win-win journey in four core principles: it is **strategic, systematic, systemic**, and **sustainable**.

- It is **strategic** in that it outlines a process for creating a clear vision for the future based on Shared Values—Shared Results. It helps you create short- and long-term goals and actions to build on strengths and make fundamental improvements if needed in the workplace environment.

- It is **systematic** in that it is a purposeful process designed to strengthen the five pillars and builds upon Shared Values—Shared Results to bring the vision to life.

- It is **systemic** in that it follows the guiding principles of systems thinking and uses human-centered design methods to engage everyone throughout your organization in the process of evolving positive organizational health.

- It is *sustainable* in that it includes a comprehensive process for meaningful and continuous evaluation and feedback on measures that have value for all stakeholders over the long term.

Some organizations will be ready to commit wholeheartedly and embark upon the full journey while others may just want to dip a toe into the water to try it out. As with any journey, it is helpful to have guidance along the way. We provide a flexible template for evolution that follows core principles and provides example practices that may be useful for organizations interested creating healthy and thriving workplaces and workforces.

Win-Win Journey Process Framework

The model for positive organizational health that we described in chapter 3 (figure 6 on page 36) outlines the primary influences on positive organizational health. We introduce a companion process framework that will help organizations attain an advanced level of thriving in each of the areas outlined in our model.

Because the details of the process may be different for each organization, we have outlined the win-win journey process framework (see figure 7 on page 50) at a very broad level surrounding the model for positive organizational health. The process framework is intended to introduce three basic stages, each with several potential substages. While we give detailed examples of how to approach each of the stages, we also provide our suggestions for how every organization can make the process uniquely its own. The three general stages of the win-win journey process follow the three themes of the book:

1) creating Shared Values—Shared Results (engage)
2) evolving positive organizational health (collaborate, co-create, and motivate)
3) measuring and communicating what matters (evaluate, communicate, celebrate, and iterate)

Before jumping into the details of the journey, we briefly outline each of the stages in figure 7, followed by a short description of each on the following pages.

Create Shared Values—Shared Results (Engage)

One of our first great lessons when we set out to help organizations embark upon this win-win journey, was that it is crucial to take the time to purposefully and thoughtfully examine the readiness of the organization. In preparation for the journey, we recommend gathering a core group of leaders who represent all stakeholders throughout the organization. We mentioned earlier in the

Figure 7. Win-win journey process

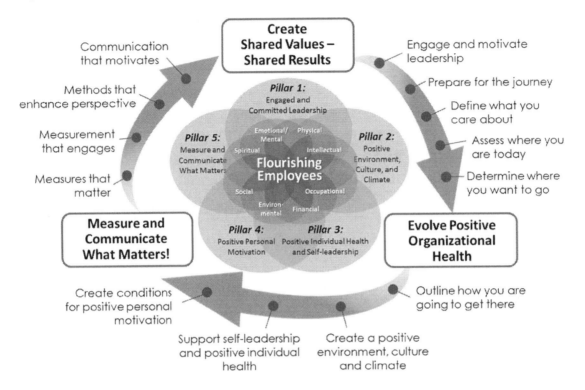

book that when we say "stakeholders," we mean everyone throughout the organization, including shareholders, owners and board members, senior leaders, managers, union representatives, and all employees. It is wise for the core set of individuals who will be engaged in the initial stages of this transformational journey to take some time to reflect on their personal level of commitment and readiness. The main parts of this phase of the journey are as follows;

- Engage and motivate leadership (chapter 5).

- Prepare for the journey (chapter 6).

- Define what you care about (chapter 7).

- Assess where you are today (chapter 8).

- Determine where you want to go (chapter 9).

This phase in the win-win journey helps you understand the collective desire among stakeholders for what the future will look like. Spending the time and effort to understand the personal and professional values of the stakeholders will set the stage for a successful effort in the long run (chapter 7).

What is it that the people in your organization
really care about?

This journey stage also includes assessing the state of the organization with respect to its health-supporting characteristics, as well as employee perceptions of the health and well-being culture. We call this process the Positive Organizational Health Assessment (chapter 8). Information from the early preparation and assessment helps with the process of developing a shared vision built on Shared Values—Shared Results. This phase takes strong commitment and engagement from senior leaders, and later from everyone in the organization (chapter 9).

Evolve Positive Organizational Health (Collaborate, Co-Create, and Motivate)

Evolving a supportive culture and environment for health is an essential and ongoing part of the journey that takes commitment and engagement from all leaders throughout the organization (senior, operations, and self-leaders). It is the heart of any win-win journey effort. We outline a collaborative and inclusive process for developing your strategic plan, and a roadmap for evolving positive organizational health that capitalizes on a clearly defined program This effort requires a great deal of personalization for each organization. The main parts of this journey phase include the following steps:

- Outline how you are going to get there (chapter 10).

- Create a positive environment, culture, and climate (chapter 11).

- Support self-leadership and positive individual health (chapter 12).

- Create conditions for positive personal motivation (chapter 13).

Throughout this section of book, we discuss how to use the model for positive organizational health (figure 6 on page 36) and the win-win journey process (figure 7 on page 50) to develop your own comprehensive framework and methods that can transform your organization. Creating your organization's unique approaches will help you evolve healthy foundations (strong pillars), and healthy environments, cultures, and relationships at the workplace and in the surrounding communities. By building on your organization's current strengths, you can evolve a healthier, sustainable organizational culture and environment.

Measure and Communicate What Matters (Evaluate, Communicate, Celebrate, and Iterate)

A critical part of any journey involves understanding where you are compared to where you want to go. How are you doing? Are you on track? Ongoing measurement and communication of the things all stakeholders care about is an important part of the process from the beginning—and throughout.

- Measures that matters to people (chapter 14).
- Measurement that engages (chapter 15).
- Use methods that enhance perspective (chapter 16).
- Communication that motivates (chapter 17).

We provide detail that will help you develop a plan to evaluate progress and measure and communicate what matters to all stakeholders.

Who Does What?

Throughout all stages of the win-win journey, the process you use must be collaborative and inclusive to be successful and sustainable.

All stakeholders are crucial to the win–win journey, and all have a role throughout. We understand that many different organizational stakeholders will be reading this book. Therefore, table 4 is designed to help you see yourself in this journey, no matter what role you have in the organization. This table is designed to visualize the potential general levels of responsibility, time, and effort for different organizational stakeholders throughout the journey process. The greater the size of the circle, the more responsibility, time, and effort the stakeholder group will have at that point in the journey, but of course that will vary across organizations. There are several things of note in figure 7 on page 50. First, there are no empty cells in this table. The table represents that every stakeholder is involved on some level in every part of the journey. Whether it is by direct involvement or by indirect representation, everyone must have a role throughout the journey if it is to be successful.

Next, the trajectory for roles and level of effort across the journey is different for every stakeholder group. While not all journeys will begin with senior leaders, in cases where senior leaders do initiate the journey process, their role will be most intense in the preparation stage. Their effort and time then waxes and wanes throughout the journey as they are needed to step up and take the reins (waxes), or as others come in to help carry the weight (wanes).

For the purposes of this table we have defined groups as follows:

- **Leadership.** Executive leaders, union leaders, VPs and above
- **Wellness Leadership.** Wellness coordinators, wellness directors, third-party wellness and well-being partners
- **Operations Leadership.** Safety, quality, organizational development, human resources, training and development
- **Managers.** Anyone in the organization with direct reports
- **All Employees.** Includes everyone above plus all other employees throughout the organization

Often wellness efforts take a backseat to more core organizational strategies. To emphasize the importance of employee health and thriving as a business strategy, we have positioned wellness leaders alongside the operations personnel who are more traditionally included in strategic efforts in organizations.

Table 4. The role of stakeholders throughout the win-win journey

Role	Create Shared Values—Shared Results					Evolve Positive Organizational Health				Measure and Communicate What Matters			
	Engage and motivate leadership	Prepare for the journey	Define what you care about	Assess where you are today	Determine where you want to go	Outline how you will get there	Create positive environment & culture	Support self-leadership and positive health	Foster positive personal motivation	Measures that matter	Measurement that engages	Methods that enhance perspective	Communication that motivates
Senior Leadership													
Wellness Leadership													
Operations Leadership													
Managers - Supervisors													
All Employees													

NOTE: The size of the circle represents the amount of involvement. Lighter circles indicate indirect representation. Darker circles indicate direct involvement in the process.

The Ken Blanchard Companies

At the Ken Blanchard Companies, we believe that people matter, and we also believe that everything that happens at Blanchard impacts the well-being of each associate and the company. Our business is all about coaching and coaching to succeed. We are successful when each of us is successful. We maintain an activity space, support a wellness coach, and provide learning opportunities and space for people to share stories of their wellness and personal development activities. We teach—and important, practice what we preach—truthfulness and high ethical behavior, respect and the importance of relationships, continuous learning and excellence for success. We believe the employees win when the company wins, and the company wins when the employees win

The Ken Blanchard Companies' core values are accepted as the overriding "how-to" manual for everyday activities in the organization. Our management team understands our wellness-oriented culture, and we train managers to respect and support employee development. Ken, our chief spiritual leader, sends a morning motivational message every day regardless of where he is in the world. After having many roles in the company, from CEO to my present role of leading our Office of the Future, I continue to support our investment in our people. The return on that investment—outstanding employees—is what the company is about and what we teach in our business.

Margie Blanchard, PhD
Co-Founder and former CEO
The Ken Blanchard Companies

THEME 1:
CREATING SHARED VALUES— SHARED RESULTS

Keep your thoughts positive, because your thoughts become your words.

Keep your words positive, because your words become your behavior.

Keep your behavior positive, because your behavior becomes your habits.

Keep your habits positive, because your habits become your values.

Keep your values positive, because your values become your destiny.

—Mahatma Gandhi

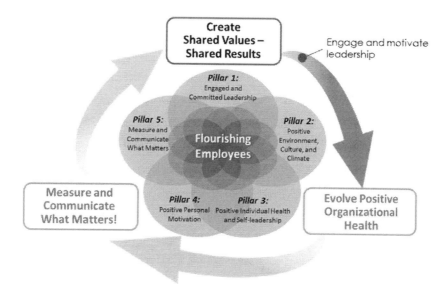

CHAPTER 5:
Engage and Motivate Leadership

People don't mind being challenged to do better
if they know the request is coming from a caring heart.

—Ken Blanchard

Visible and Thriving Leadership

Leadership is the first and arguably the most important of the five pillars of a win-win organization. Committed, engaged, and courageous senior leadership can create a strong foundation for healthier and thriving environments, climates, and cultures. In this chapter, we briefly discuss the current state of best practices for organizational leadership with respect to supporting employee health and well-being. We also describe characteristics of leaders who operate in a manner that transcends best practices to create fundamental and sustainable positive organizational health in the organizations they serve.

There are several types of formal leaders we are addressing in this chapter, including executive leaders and employees in senior-level strategic positions. In midsize and large organizations, these leaders would include the chief executive officer (CEO), CFO, and all others on the C-suite team, senior union leaders, and others with high-level responsibility for ensuring the success of the company. In some organizations, senior vice presidents, and vice presidents may fit in this category. In smaller organizations, these leaders might include the founder, president, and managers with no formal executive title but who still have primary responsibility for setting strategy and ensuring the success of the organization. In very small organizations, this may include everyone.

Envision this...

Imagine a workplace where the leaders actively focus on fostering a positive climate throughout all levels of the organization. In this workplace, each of the leaders exhibits open and honest communication, optimism, integrity, and trust. They emphasize the importance of strong relationships and meaningful work. They genuinely express gratitude and appreciation as naturally and regularly as breathing. A senior leader is seen talking with a line worker about ideas for having a competitive advantage. Another senior leader is breaking a sweat in the company-sponsored lunchtime Zumba class. In company communications, stories of compassion and acts of kindness abound. Daily examples of how company values are lived out are acknowledged. How is leadership perceived in your organization? What are some ways leaders are creating a flourishing culture?

Angela Camilleri
Lead Innovation Strategist, Edington Associates

The second type of leader we are addressing includes any employee who has formal responsibility for leading people. This would include any directors, managers, and supervisors with responsibility for leading other people in the organization. Senior directors and supervisors may fit this category in some organizations while they may be considered executive leadership in other organizations. Anyone who is responsible for overseeing the work of other employees has a crucial leadership position and an important responsibility concerning the environment, culture, and climate of the organization. The highest-ranked person with wellness and well-being responsibility would also fit in this category.

> *Companies whose leaders understand the value*
> *of healthy, engaged, and passionate employees will*
> *have a major competitive advantage going forward in this fast-*
> *changing world.*

Leaders of organizations both influence and are influenced by the culture of organizations. Depending on the age of an organization, its culture may have been passed through several generations of leaders. The original culture was likely established by the organization's founders to meet the demands and market forces of the time. The policies, practices, values, and assumptions that shaped the early years of an organization may not be relevant to the problems and demands of the current times. In today's rapidly changing world, technology, innovation, and social media are generating new frontiers that influence the workplace. To evolve and grow with modern pressures and forces, leaders must help organizations develop cultures that are flexible and open to change. This type of work may require adopting new ways of thinking and operating, and instituting approaches that help employees continuously adapt and change as well.

Adaptability, flexibility, and openness to change are important parts of an organization's culture.

> *Organizational leaders who purposefully talk about how ethics and values are lived out in their workplace seem to enhance leadership skills at all levels. People have clarity, the rules to go by. People can predict how their decisions will be viewed by those above and below them. When performance expectations are clear and specific, people can envision themselves in decision-making situations in advance. Responses can be more automatic because the brain is primed for ethical behaviors. People feel more connected, distress is avoided, and trust develops more easily.*
>
> *Nancy W. Spangler, PhD, OTRL*
> *President, Spangler Associates Inc.*

Evolving a win-win strategy will take persistence, courage and commitment. It will also take inspirational leadership to ignite a movement that catches fire throughout the organization. We are not talking about making marginal changes but real transformation in the way we think about work and the way we support health and thriving in the workplace and workforce.

> *Courage is the enforcing virtue, the one that makes possible all the other virtues common to exceptional leaders: honesty, integrity, confidence, compassion, and humility.*
>
> —John McCain

Creativity and flexibility are strategic imperatives for sustainable, healthy, and thriving organizations. Our most successful organizational leaders will be those who nurture creativity in themselves and in the people they lead. Creativity, engagement, and employee health and thriving are all interconnected.

> *Creativity is not some exotic, optional extra. It's a strategic issue.*
>
> —Sir Ken Robinson[65]

The best leaders will be those who can create the circumstances in their organization environments, cultures, and climates that allow people to be their healthiest, most engaged, and most creative.

> *Good leaders make people feel that they're at the very heart of things, not at the periphery. Everyone feels that he or she makes a difference to the success of the organization. When that happens, people feel centered, and that gives their work meaning.*
>
> —Warren Bennis

Current Best Practices for Leadership

In the past decade, there have been many sets of recommendations, guidelines, and proposed best practices published for wellness and well-being approaches. These are based to some extent on evidence but to a large degree on expert opinion about what constitutes the best wellness and well-being approaches. Every published set of best practices we reviewed emphasizes the role of senior leaders in supporting and promoting wellness programs.[66-73] Best practices of relevance for senior leaders mentioned in these sources include:

- vision connected to company strategy and people;
- organizational commitment in which leadership actively participates;
- engaged leadership at multiple levels;
- program objectives linked to business objectives;
- shared program ownership (ownership inclusive of all staff levels);
- adequate funding allocated.

Most of these best practices for senior leaders focus on activities directly related to health management initiatives and programs. *Zero Trends* emphasized that senior leader support is fundamental not only to the success of wellness programs but also for the successful evolution of a healthy and thriving culture.

While effective wellness and well-being initiatives are an important part of a healthy work culture, to evolve a sustainable and thriving health culture it is important for senior and all leaders to do far more than just support and promote programs.

Emerging Next Practices for Senior Leadership

All too often, new management innovations are described in terms of the best practices of so-called leading firms. I believe benchmarking best practices can open people's eyes as to what is possible, but it can also do more harm than good, leading to piecemeal copying and playing catch-up.

—Peter Senge

Senior leaders find comfort in knowing that the wellness and well-being programs implemented in their organizations are "evidence-based" and follow so-called best practices. However, this only means that these approaches have worked in the past in some context. We question whether best practices alone are robust enough to address the swelling wave of poor health and low productivity that are at epidemic levels in this country. We believe that adopting a win-win philosophy and creating a win-win strategy will help organizations gain traction in their efforts to improve the health and thriving of employees.

For those who have been closely involved in the field of workplace wellness, it is easy to forget that the concept of employer support of good health is still an unfamiliar place for many American companies.

Lee Dukes
Chief Solutions Officer
Catapult Health

Table 5 outlines the leader practices and characteristics that will provide the foundation and motivation for a strong culture of health and well-being in an organization. The core senior leader practices originally presented in *Zero Trends* included holding a strong **commitment to a healthy culture, creating a shared vision** for health and well-being, **engaging all leaders in the vision,** and **connecting the vision to the business strategy.** We still believe those are core to the process of evolving a thriving culture. To undertake any of these in an impactful and transformational manner, we urge leaders throughout the organization to deeply reflect on the bigger picture of influences on employee health, wellness, and well-being. We have included **systems thinking** in our expanded leadership practices to help with this process.

Many senior organizational leaders are familiar with systems thinking and give careful attention to the larger systems that continuously influence and challenge the business practices of the organization. Few leaders, however, seem to have applied systems thinking to the health and well-being of their employees. To help evolve thriving workplace cultures, leaders must expand their thinking to include the wide range of issues that converge to influence health in a complex social system such as an employer organization. They must begin to see the bigger picture and work to increase flow and alignment throughout the organization.

Table 5. Current best and emerging next practices for leadership

Pillar 1: Senior Leadership	Current Best Practices	Emerging Next Practices
Commitment to supporting a thriving culture		✓
Apply a systems thinking process and develop a win-win philosophy		
• Understand the bigger picture.		✓
• Adopt a broader view of health and thriving.		✓
• Create a deeper understanding of the many influences on employee health and thriving.		✓
Create a shared vision		
• Engage all leadership in creating a vision.	✓	✓
• Embrace everyone as a leader.		✓
• Create Shared Values—Shared Results.		✓
• Re-conceptualize success.		✓
• Connect vision to business strategy.	✓	✓
Create a Win-Win strategy that connects the dots between the environment and culture, employee success, and the success of the organization.		✓
Create conditions that are good for the health and thriving of both the employee and the organization.		✓
Truly walk the walk:		
• Go beyond senior-leader endorsement and program participation—visibly engage in personal practices that reflect positive individual health and positive personal motivation.		✓
Recognize others for engagement in balanced, healthy work and life practices.		✓
Inspire alignment among stakeholders in support of a win-win philosophy and strategy.	✓	✓
Encourage and support human-centered design practices and employee design teams.		✓
Ensure that all stakeholders are engaged and aligned throughout the organization:		
• CEO and C-suite	✓	✓
• Senior managers	✓	✓
• Middle managers		✓
• All employees as self-leaders		✓

Leaders who ask themselves, "What can I do to make my setting the most fertile ground in the world for the growth of talent?" put themselves in the best position to succeed.

—Robert Kegan[74]

To create a thriving environment and culture, leaders must have strong commitment and be open to seeing how the bigger picture (systems thinking) influences health.

Table 5 above also shows the components of an expanded process for creating a shared vision for health and well-being. Before an inspiring vision can be crafted and lived in the company, leaders may need to redefine success for the organization and better understand success from the perspective of all stakeholders. Ideally, all levels of leadership in the organization would be engaged in this process, and senior leaders would embrace everyone as a leader. Whether they are executives, operational leaders, managers, or self-leaders (and we view everyone as a self-leader), everyone has a stake in the health and well-being of all employees and the organization. So we recommend that an early part of the visioning process include understanding and creating Shared Values—Shared Results.

The dominant view of leadership is that the leader has the vision, and the rest is a sales problem. I think that notion of leadership is bankrupt. That approach only works for technical problems, where there's a right answer and the expert knows what it is. To change the mindset, the people are the problem and the people are the solution. Leadership then is about mobilizing and engaging the people with the problem rather than trying to anesthetize them so you can go off and solve it on your own.

Ronald Heifetz
Professor of Leadership, Harvard's Kennedy School

Understanding Shared Values—Shared Results involves asking all stakeholders about their values and about the results that matter to them. A formal set of shared values and shared results can then be outlined. It is important that the vision of the organization reflect these shared ideals.

Everyone is involved in the process of evolving a healthy workplace culture. Senior leaders have both formal and informal roles to play with respect to creating a healthy organizational environment and culture. By definition, leaders cannot evolve a culture on their own. Formal and informal leaders at all levels of the organization have crucial roles. Next practices for health and well-being cannot be successful if they are the brainchildren of a just a few. Systems-level solutions embrace the involvement of all stakeholders throughout the organization and from stakeholders outside of the organization (e.g., families, local and regional communities, suppliers, partners, etc.).

Leaders must "walk the walk" when it comes to health and well-being. They must do more than give speeches and attend health fairs. They must engage in both personal and work practices that embody a healthy, balanced life and positively recognize others who do the same.

When you're the CEO, everyone is paying attention to every word you say, every motion you make. If you're ever not feeling good about yourself, whether emotionally, physically or sleepwise, it's very difficult to mask that. But you sometimes have to keep a stiff upper lip, and frankly, it's a lot easier when you are feeling good about yourself, and that reflects in how you treat people.

People listen to what you say, look at what you do, and they will forget what you said, but [remember] how you made them feel. So the job of a CEO is to make sure that your people feel good and want to do good. People love coming up with new ideas and feeling that they are valued and welcomed and listened to. At CEA, everyone is valued, and we're always looking to move forward and try new things.

Gary Shapiro
CEO, Consumer Electronics Association (CEA)
(as interviewed by David Faust, Pinkston Group)

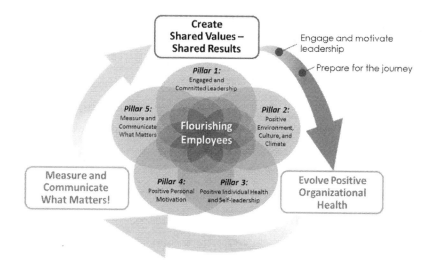

CHAPTER 6:
Prepare for the Journey

*It's not the will to win, but the will to
prepare to win that makes the difference.*

—Bear Bryant, University of Alabama

This chapter discusses the initial work CEOs and other senior leaders can undertake in preparation for a purposeful and successful win-win journey. These leaders are core to generating the momentum it will take to initiate and evolve health and thriving as part of the organization's core values. Senior leaders have a great deal of influence over the organizational culture, but they cannot evolve a culture single-handedly. We mentioned earlier in the book that "it takes a village" to evolve a culture. That village is made up of all employees throughout the organization, and ideally, all segments of the village would be represented from the earliest seeds of the cultural evolution.

To prepare for your win-win journey, you may want to consider the following steps. Again, we acknowledge that every organization is different, so these steps may not all resonate or be relevant to your organization. However, we encourage you to consider them, and if they are applicable, make them your own as you begin your journey:

- **Gather and inspire a core team.** Collect a trusted group of advisers, and inspire them to start a movement.

- **Assess readiness.** Discuss individual and organizational readiness with the core team.

- **Map the system.** Adopt a systems-thinking mindset to outline and better understand the full range of possible influences on employee and organizational health and thriving.
- **Engage design partners.** Create an empowered steering committee, and encourage the formation of employee design teams.

CEOs and other senior executive leaders are a core part of an organization's culture, and they can bring a tremendous amount of legitimacy to the effort. They also have the authority to realign resources and bring budget dollars to the table. But we recognize that not all journeys will begin with the senior executives.

If your journey is being initiated by someone other than senior leaders, the steps in this phase may need to be modified to meet the needs of the team, but many, if not all, will still be relevant.

Envision This...

When you first enter this workplace, you feel a subtle underlying excitement. The first thing you notice is warm eye contact and a pleasant greeting with almost every worker you pass. An open floorplan lends itself to team collaboration, and natural light fills the workspace with energy. Employees are seen working at standing desks and treadmill workstations. Colleagues congregate in common areas to share ideas and brainstorm on writeable walls. One employee is adding a comment to a strategic plan posted on an idea board in the breakroom. A manager and an employee head outside for a one-on-one walking meeting, grabbing an apple from the fruit bowl on the way out. In a nearby conference room, training is taking place to onboard new employees, where the CEO highlights the company vision around health and the organization's commitment to encourage well-being. What are some examples from your organization that paint a picture of a thriving and supportive workplace?

Angela Camilleri
Lead Innovation Strategist, Edington Associates

Everyone has a role in evolving a culture of health.

If your journey is being initiated by the wellness leaders in the organization, or if it is a grassroots employee project, the amount and type of effort will differ for each stakeholder group. We emphasize again that the win-win journey process is intended to serve as a flexible template to guide the development of your unique journey—not a recipe, blueprint, or one-size-fits-all approach.

Gather a Core Team

Before formally embarking on the win-win journey, it is advisable to gather a group of trusted advisers to collaborate during the early conceptualization of the journey process. This shouldn't be a group of yes-men and -women. These individuals should be willing to be candid, open, and honest with each other, and leave their egos and individual agendas at the door. This will require that they participate in this process with open minds and hearts in service of the overall good of the organization and all of its employees. The common interest of this team is that they understand the value of evolving an environment, culture, and climate that recognizes the value of health and well-being to the organization and the employees. They are also aware of the competitive advantage that the enhanced culture will provide to the business objectives of the organization.

Core Team Members

This stage of the journey is very important for developing a healthy, high-performing, and thriving organization. Creating a shared understanding about the value of Shared Values—Shared Results and positive individual and organizational health as a win-win philosophy will help increase the inspiration and motivation of the leaders involved in this process. It's important that the leaders who convened the team share information about the value or the "why" of positive individual and organizational health. It is also critical that everyone involved is allowed to voice their concerns, and feels heard by the team.

The group must come together in the spirit of creating a collective perspective that is greater than their individual viewpoints taken separately. It is especially critical that each member of the core team is given respect and consideration throughout the process.

Ideally, the CEO would be involved in this core team process, and if at all possible, he or she would lead the team. While we understand that CEOs are very busy individuals, the health and well-being of employees is core to the success and ultimate survival of the organization. Regardless of who initiates the journey it is best if that person leads the core team. The initiator of the journey likely has the most commitment and enthusiasm for the effort, and this energy and excitement are important for inspiring the rest of the team.

The time and effort invested in creating meaningful movement at this point will reap tremendous rewards throughout the win-win journey.

The members of this core team should represent people with many different viewpoints, understand the different parts of the system within and surrounding the organization, and be able to identify key leverage points.

Senior leaders play an important role in inspiring this team and in helping team members understand the importance of the work they will be undertaking. They will also be key to setting the tone for an ego-free, unbiased, and honest process. Senior leaders can also help the group understand the potential systems-level influences that can guide the strategic planning process.

For many best-practice wellness program efforts, the CEO and senior leaders approve and endorse the program then pass it off to the human resources department or the most appropriate unit for implementation by a wellness program director or manager. However, the win-win journey is a much more strategic and cultural evolution, and it deserves continued support and engagement from senior leaders throughout the process.

Instead of a handoff from senior leaders to operations leaders, this will involve more of a handshake and joining of forces among senior and operational leaders and all employee representatives.

Operations leaders often have the deepest understanding of the organization as a system. They will be core to the group's discussion and play a critical role in guiding the effort to bring the vision to life in the organization. In these early stages, they should be encouraged to think beyond the usual modes of operation and remain optimistic about the potential for real and positive evolution. Their understanding of the organization will improve the odds of success for the initiative by helping identify and negotiate potential political tangles throughout the process of the journey.

Wellness and well-being leaders have the most direct responsibility for the health and well-being of the employees. It is their job to have a deep understanding of the needs and wants of the employee population when it comes to wellness and health and to make sure the organization is meeting those needs. They can play a pivotal role on the core team.

Outside expertise of an unbiased and skilled moderator may be helpful during this process, especially during the early dialogue among the members of this team. Third-party viewpoints can also be helpful, especially if they bring a view from a discipline not already represented in the group. One caveat: if you include external advisers at this early stage, ensure they do not have a strong self-interest in selling a product or service (including ongoing consulting) that can bias the direction of the discussions.

Medium and Small Companies

The members of the core team may differ greatly depending on the size of the company. In some medium-size organizations, the core team may not all be senior leaders. In very small organizations, the core team may be all of the employees in the company. Regardless, the general nature of the objectives and processes remain the same: to create an environment and culture that emphasizes caring for the health and well-being of the organization's employees, their families, and the community.

Inspire the Team

Your organization likely has historical documents of relevance to any current wellness and well-being approach you may already have in place. These documents could include a full organizational chart, mission, vision, and values of the organization, any descriptive information about wellness programs, healthcare benefits, and any known initiatives, either homegrown or purchased through an external services provider or partner. These materials should be distributed as advance preparation for the first meeting and be discussed early in the preparation process. It is possible, and even likely, these will be revised or even replaced, but this history is an important part of understanding where your organization is today with respect to its support of the health and well-being of employees.

Regardless of the place of the individual in the organization, each will come to the core team with a preexisting opinion of what wellness and well-being are all about. Many will believe it is all about physical and metabolic capabilities; others will understand that it is much broader. If, however, the overall objective is to take a more holistic view of health, this will require some early discussion to expand the collective thinking and gain the agreement of the core team. Without this early agreement, the core team members will not be seeing the same picture of the future.

Everything that happens in the organization impacts the health, wellness, and well-being of the organization and the employees.

Assess Readiness to Begin a Win-Win Journey

Depending on the organization, creating a thriving culture may involve reexamining the way work is organized and reevaluating the reporting structure of the organization.

The change we are proposing in this book is about how the organization and stakeholders view the value of healthy and thriving individuals and organization. It is about more than avoiding sickness. It also includes supporting thriving individuals as core to positive organizational health. It may be necessary to question even the most basic assumptions about the organization and its employees. In this book we are suggesting an evolution of health, wellness, and well-being into the environment, climate and culture of the organization. This is similar to what Robert Quinn from the University of Michigan's Graduate School of Business calls "deep change."

Deep change differs from incremental change in that it requires new ways of thinking and behaving. It is change that is major in scope, discontinuous with the past and generally irreversible. The deep change effort distorts existing patterns of action and involves taking risks. Deep change means surrendering control.[64]

If leaders undertake this process without strong commitment, people will see through the effort as insincere, and it will be unlikely to succeed.

A Wolf in Sheep's Clothing

When is a wellness program not a wellness program? Because wellness is not always an organizational priority, it is imperative to find ways to infuse healthy behaviors into the preexisting culture. Not all wellness programs have to be wellness focused to be successful, and having the best, most robust wellness resources does not necessarily drive people to participate, especially in a sustainable and meaningful way. The people and culture of an organization determine which initiatives will be most successful. To build a culture of health, a strategy of inclusion and intent must be developed based on the psychographic needs of the people and the priorities of the organization.

In some cases, in order to create a healthy culture and keep it sustainable, it is necessary to cognitively and behaviorally connect health and wellness to safety or quality. The learnings and strategies gleaned from conducting a culture audit will produce measurable results and provide long-term, meaningful health, wellness, and safety strategies.

Steve Chevarria
CEO, Pansalus Consulting, LLC

Quinn recommends that leaders considering the type of evolution we are discussing ask themselves tough questions and seriously reflect on their answers. He outlines several questions that we have modified to be about employee health and thriving (see the **Reflect on Personal Commitment Activity** on page 71). It can be helpful for members of the core team to undertake this type of activity early in the process of their work together. Reflecting on the answers to these questions and openly discussing concerns is an important part of the process. Ideally, each individual on the core team would contemplate his or her answers to the questions, and the team would also meet and take the time to openly share perspectives, concerns, and ideas with each other. The following self-administered activity could help individuals assess their commitment to the creation of a healthier, more supportive organizational culture and climate.

Activity: Reflect on Personal Commitment

- I have a deep and authentic commitment to organization and employee health and thriving.

- I have the courage to change our definitions of health and thriving.

- I am open to a new and higher level of thinking and expectations about employee and organizational health and thriving.

- I am prepared to acknowledge our shortcomings and embrace new points of view.

- I am willing to adjust my vision for the future.

- I am willing to play an active role throughout the process.

- I am ready to engage in personal changes to set an example of and align with a new way to define well-being.

If you agreed with most of these questions, take a moment to think about some positive attributes that made your agreement possible. Draw on these strengths to set the stage for a new way of thinking and to generate momentum for the journey ahead.

If you disagreed with any of the above, reflect on why. What are possible barriers? Could you identify any assumptions or traditions that need to be challenged? What would it take for you to move closer to agreement?

For any of the exercises we outline, the most important thing is the conversation it generates.

Only when all leaders and core team members are truly committed will the initiative have the best possibility of succeeding.

Organizations that excel in developing healthy and thriving cultures will be those whose leaders can inspire passion and commitment from all levels of leaders throughout the organization. Otto Scharmer, economist and senior lecturer at the Massachusetts Institute of Technology (MIT), and co-founder of the Presencing Institute, quotes Bill O'Brien, the former CEO of Hanover Insurance, to emphasize this point:

> *The success of an intervention depends on the interior condition of the intervener. Our effectiveness as leaders depends not only on what we do and how we do it, but also on the inner place from where we operate, both individually and collectively.*[75]

According to Scharmer, the most effective leaders work to cultivate the inner place from which they operate as a leverage point through deep personal reflection, commitment, and awareness achieved through a disciplined effort. This may be the most important factor in leading the effort to develop a thriving and healthy culture in an organization.

Collaborative, Open-Minded Leadership

The process of evolving a healthy and thriving organizational culture will be much more effective if everyone involved has a clear sense of themselves as leaders and valued contributors to the process. Participating in the process with a collaborative mindset, letting go of their egos, and continuing to participate with an open mind is essential. Depending on the nature of the health and well-being issues the organization is facing, and the historical working relationships between the members of the team, this is not always easily done. It may be advisable to engage a specially trained moderator to provide an unbiased viewpoint and help negotiate the team through any tensions that might arise during this part of the process.

Map the System

Systems thinking is a critical part of our approach to creating a supportive and thriving organization. It is necessary for understanding potential solutions that can lead to a real and sustainable evolution of health and well-being in the fabric of the organization. Meetings with the core team are a good place to start the deeper-level systems-thinking process.

When we say leaders should engage in "systems thinking," we mean that they should undertake a collaborative process that allows everyone involved to see and explicitly outline the larger set of influences on the organizations and employees.

> *Systems thinking is a discipline for seeing wholes. It is a framework for seeing interrelationships rather than things, for seeing patterns of change rather than static "snapshots." It is a set of general principles—distilled over the course of the twentieth century, spanning fields as diverse as the physical and social sciences, engineering, and management. And systems thinking is a sensibility—for the subtle interconnectedness that gives living systems their unique character.*

—Peter Senge[76]

Undertaking a systems-thinking process means coming together as a group of people all committed to understanding the truth of where their organization is or isn't working, outlining a compelling vision as their reference point, and committing to do whatever it takes to help the organization evolve toward that goal. It is more important to embrace new viewpoints, think bigger about health and well-being, and explore new methods to help expand your understanding of the many factors that influence the health and well-being of employees and the organization than to follow strictly a formal systems-thinking process.

An initial part of the process will involve outlining the many parts of the whole, and the interrelationships between the parts as the team considers an evolution of health and wellness into a core position within the organization. Questions worth reflecting on at this point might include the following:

- What is the existing "landscape" of the organization?

- What political tangles will the core group likely encounter?

- What is the realm of influence that we can reasonably impact?

- Will the focus be purely within the walls of the organization, or will we consider health-related features of the home and family and the larger community?

In addition, the team may want to consider the competitive advantage locally or with their competitors more globally. When outlining the system, all participants should be encouraged to provide all viewpoints, collaborate with all stakeholders, think about parts only in relation to the whole, think bigger (and broader) about health and well-being, embrace new disciplines, and experiment with new methods for exploration.

Visualize the System

A core part of understanding the landscape involves visualizing the larger system and how its component parts influence positive health and well-being of individuals and the organization.

The model for positive organizational health in chapter 3 (page 36) visualizes important areas of influence on positive individual and organizational health. However, we cannot represent all the possible small but important nuances that make each organization unique. There are many ways to represent the numerous influences on your individual system and outline the relationships between the many parts of the whole. The simplest method is to list the components and draw a picture of how they interact. Make it visible for the group. Outline the components of the comprehensive system within and surrounding the organization. Don't worry about making it pretty; just get it out and on paper. If possible, someone with an artistic flair can bring the broad ideas to life in a diagram, a "bigger picture" drawing, or some other representation of the important components and their interrelationships later. Creating a beautiful picture at this stage is not as important as engaging in an inclusive and collaborative process that represents the voice of all stakeholders throughout the organization.

Brief Inventory of the Five Fundamental Pillars

The brief pillar assessment is another helpful exercise the core team can do to prepare for the win-win journey. We introduced this at the beginning of the book (chapter 1, page 5) to guide readers to the most relevant parts of the book to meet their interests. It is also useful for the core team members to go through this assessment together. The inventory can be completed as a team exercise to generate thoughts, create discussion, and inform understanding and perceptions about the current strengths of the pillars. It can also highlight areas needing the most focus.

Reflect on the Information Collected So Far

At this point, the core team will have likely done a great deal of legwork and will have gathered or created quite a bit of information. They will have discussed the definitions and objectives of the initiative, reviewed appropriate historical documents, assessed commitment, and visualized the system, and will have gathered information from the brief pillar assessment. This preparation and information will be helpful in the next part of the core team's work together, so it will be useful to take the time to review and digest the information so far. It will ensure that most of those deeply involved up to this stage have a general agreement and understanding of the win-win journey and feel some ownership.

Expand the Circle

Create a Steering Committee

Senior and operations leaders and other members of the core team understand that no matter how committed they are to evolving wellness and well-being into the culture, they cannot do it alone. To support the evolution of a thriving environment and culture, they may opt to create and even participate in a high-level steering committee to help shape and shepherd the journey process. We recommend the steering committee report directly to the core team and be charged with overseeing evolving positive organizational health.

Depending on the size of the organization, this steering committee may have the same participants as the core team, so a separate committee may not be necessary. Medium and small companies will adjust the committee membership in accordance with their needs and perceived effectiveness. As shown in figure 8, there are many potential layers of support that can be engaged throughout the journey. In the rest of this section, we discuss various ways that stakeholders can help create effective initiatives for improving employee health and well-being.

Figure 8. Stakeholder groups involved in the journey

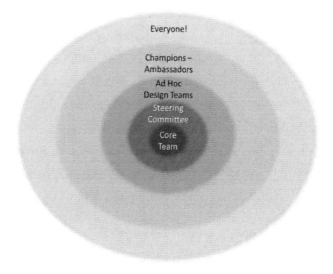

Engage Design Partners

As the journey process unfolds, you will likely undertake specific efforts to strengthen the conditions for positive health in your environment and culture. You may "buy" your health, prevention, wellness, or well-being program from a commercial wellness "partner," or "build" your program using in-house resources. Either way, we recommend at least some components be developed as grass roots efforts that involve your employees in creating, shaping, implementing, measuring and communicating the aspects of the program.

Whenever possible, we encourage you to convene participatory design teams made up of employees from throughout the organization.

Values Exploration Design Team

Some organizations use third-party partners to do their large survey efforts. For example, in addition to asking employees to complete health assessments, many organizations also conduct engagement surveys and satisfaction surveys, among others. For some of the smaller, quick-turn-around inquiries that we outline in this section, it might be good to convene an ad hoc values exploration design team to handle this process.

*This team can design a culturally relevant approach to collecting information from employees about their values. This might be a simple brief information-gathering effort like the exercises outlined above, or other qualitative inquiry methods may be useful. See the **Qualitative Inquiry** section in chapter 8 for more ideas about gathering rich and useful information from organizational stakeholders.*

These teams can use human-centered design principles and ethnographic research methods to gather information directly from their peers to better understand their unique needs and preferences and bring them more directly to the design process. This will help build empathy, trust and engagement in the process from employees throughout the organization. The teams can then work collaboratively with other employees to iteratively prototype and test solutions and ultimately develop successful and sustainable approaches.

The principles that can guide the design teams include:

- **empathy:** the ability to imagine the world from multiple perspectives;

- **integrative thinking:** the ability to see all aspects of a confounding problem;

- **optimism:** the ability to see a potential solution even with all the challenges;

- **experimentalism:** the posing of creative questions that could take the design in entirely new directions; and

- **collaboration:** enthusiastic interdisciplinary collaboration to replace the lone genius.[77]

They can also benefit from following design-thinking practices:

- creating multidisciplinary teams;

- using nonlinear processes;

- taking a different view of things, of what might be;

- thinking visually, telling stories, role-playing;

- experimenting, improvising, taking risks, failing often and early;

- exercising trust and optimism; and

- having empathy.

We acknowledge that not all efforts to evolve cultures will be formal, and they won't all begin with strong buy-in from senior leaders of the organization. We mentioned earlier in the book that anyone can start a movement that influences and shapes the culture of health in an organization: senior leaders, operations leaders, managers, or even frontline workers.

Leadership Strategy at NextEra Energy

Leadership has been fundamental to the program's success. Since its inception in 1991, the program has enjoyed strong support from senior leaders. In fact, leadership constitutes three of the five pillars that support NextEra Energy's corporate culture of health:

1. *Senior leadership demonstrates its support by incorporating employee health into the company culture and including health as a potential core competency for senior management, operational leaders, and employees.*

2. *Operational leaders add further support by encouraging employee participation in wellness programs and being flexible with employees who want to participate in programs during work hours.*

3. *Management encourages employees to practice self-leadership in health matters by assuming responsibility for their own health and the health of their families.*

4. *The company reinforces employees' self-leadership and positive health behaviors through well-placed program incentives.*

5. *Measurement across all aspects of the program—risk status changes, costs, engagement, participation, vendor performance, health claims data, and performance indicators—drives future program growth and direction.*

With senior leadership support, NextEra Energy has ingrained wellness into all aspects of the work environment. The company has tobacco-free policies in all facilities, and cafeterias offer subsidized wellness meals. On-site exercise opportunities thrive even in moderate-sized work sites, and signage and coworker watchfulness reinforce safety policies.

Andrew Scibelli
Manager Health and Well-Being
NextEra Energy

To read the full case study go to appendix B

We also recognize that many organizations have existing wellness, well-being or other such initiatives and may not want to launch another initiative. We recognize this and have designed the journey so organizations can easily join in at any stage of the journey as they see fit in relation to their existing situation.

Regardless of who starts the movement, or where they start, inclusion and collaboration are imperative.

Where and how we live, learn, work, and play largely determines how long and how well we live. Organizational purpose, visible passion, and an aligned environment together create esprit de corps which gives meaning to work. Where my contribution and effort matters—health will be valued and improved.

Michael Parkinson, MD, MPH, FACPM
Past President, American College of Preventive Medicine

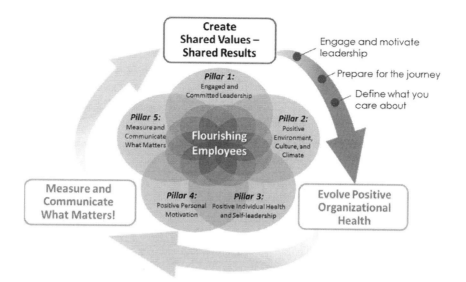

CHAPTER 7:
Define What You Care About

Engagement happens when the organization and the employees are doing what they value and results happen when the organization and employees are engaged.

We are born into this world full of possibilities, and as newborn babies, we are open to everything. We quickly begin to be shaped in response to our surroundings. As we grow, our brains, minds, and bodies become organized around our experiences, hopes, and plans for our futures. We begin to form a vision of the person we hope to become. As we enter the educational system, we start our formal preparation for the future. Our current schools are designed to shape us for careers, vocations, and professions, and unfortunately, our creative spirit is sometimes lost in the process. As we venture into the workforce, many of us begin to see ourselves as our jobs: "I am an engineer," "I am a school teacher," "I am a forklift operator for ABC Construction Company." We often lose sight of the things that once inspired us, the things that made us happy.

> *When I was five years old, my mother always told me that happiness was the key to life. When I went to school, they asked me what I wanted to be when I grew up. I wrote down "happy." They told me I didn't understand the assignment, and I told them they didn't understand life.*

—John Lennon

How can we bring back that spirit of possibility and opportunity? How can organizations create conditions that foster purpose and joy in both our personal and work lives? Answering these questions is what the win-win philosophy is all about. Both organizations and individuals win when we tap into the power of personal vision and purpose, our inherent creativity, our capacity for joy, generosity, and other personal abilities that help us live full and meaningful lives. We believe that positive individual and positive organizational health increase our capacity for a meaningful life.

Envision This...

On any given day at the workplace, several diverse examples of well-being are observed that are as unique as every individual with common interests freely shared. One employee is leading a stretch break for others working on the loading dock. Another employee sends out an instant message to her department for anyone who wants to meet at noon for a lunchtime power walk. Some colleagues are taking a break with a playful game of indoor bocce ball, changing the rules slightly to use their nondominant hand to toss the ball. In the breakroom, one employee takes a moment to ask a colleague about how it's going with his mom's recent declining health. In solving work problems, there's a general openness to exploring unconventional ideas. Taking thoughtful risks is encouraged, and failures are seen as stepping-stones for learning. Teams are encouraged to learn new skills, which is supported through corporate sponsorships. Employees develop their personal interests and relationships outside of work, which help them bring a renewed energy to their work. And their excitement about their work brings energy to their home and community. How does your organization cultivate self-leaders?

Angela Camilleri
Lead Innovation Strategist, Edington Associates

This chapter provides guidance on how to understand the preferred Shared Values—Shared Results of your company stakeholders. These are the backbone of the win-win journey.

- What do we care about? What are the values of the employees and the organization?

- What results matter most to both the organization and the employees. Investigate whether you are living your values?

- Are your current results those that matter most to you? Do your environment, culture, and climate align with your shared values and results?

We believe that having shared values and shared results will help organizations create conditions for meaningful work and productive energy and help organizations and employees thrive. We are often asked for details about how to do this type of work in organizations, so we have provided as much detail as possible given the space constraints of this book. However, as we have mentioned repeatedly, we do not intend for this to be a blueprint or a fixed recipe—just a guide for a process and some examples you can use to create your own Journey process. As with all stages of the win-win journey, the process you use must be collaborative. All stakeholders have a role throughout. Whether you are the CEO, a manager, or an individual contributor, you are integral to the process of defining and creating Shared Values—Shared Results.

Values That Matter to Everyone

At the most fundamental level, the win-win journey is about creating outcomes that matter to the organization and all stakeholders. This process, therefore, should begin with a collaborative exploration of what we care about. What do we value? Also, what are the values by which we must live to create the results we intend? What are our shared values?

The shared values we are referring to are the values the organization and its employees truly embody. The written values of the company are only relevant to the degree they reflect the values lived by the individuals who make up the organization. Outlined below is an example of a very nice set of written values; however, they did not translate into acceptable organizational behavior.

OUR VALUES

Communication: We have an obligation to communicate. Here, we take the time to talk with one another...and to listen. We believe that information is meant to move and that information moves people.

Respect: We treat others as we would like to be treated ourselves. We do not tolerate abusive or disrespectful treatment.

Integrity: We work with customers and prospects openly, honestly, and sincerely. When we say we will do something, we will do it; when we say we cannot or will not do something, then we won't do it.

Excellence: We are satisfied with nothing less than the very best in everything we do. We will continue to raise the bar for everyone. The great fun here will be for all of us to discover just how good we can really be.

These were the values of energy giant Enron before its bankruptcy in 2001. Enron is now the poster child for fraudulent business and accounting practices. Clearly, the actions of at least some leaders and employees within the organization were not aligned with the written values of the company. Some analysts believe that a certain level of complacency among many others within the organization also contributed to the company's downfall. While the organization's leaders are responsible for whether the stated values are lived within the organization, it also takes everyone to embody the values on a day-to-day basis.

We are not saying companies should be completely built around the values of their employees. But we do believe that employees and companies should share a certain set of core professional values, and employees should be able to live according to their personal values in the workplace. Ideally, the work of aligning values begins with the leaders. It can't be a hollow exercise. It has to be a genuine and committed effort between employers and employees to develop a shared set of meaningful shared values.

Understand Employee Values

To help you better understand what stakeholders value, we outlined several exercises designed to collect information for the core team and steering committee to use in the process of creating or aligning formal values and results that matter to everyone.

The best way to understand the values and results that matter to employees is to ask them.

Give employees a chance to be heard, and let them know you've heard them. Also, ask employees about the values that percolate throughout the organization. Most important, listen carefully to what they have to say.

The first exercise (see **Assess Employee Core Values** on page 83) can be conducted regardless of whether the organization has formal values. Ask employees to reflect on things they believe are important in their lives, list their values, and then prioritize them. These are deeply held driving forces that guide constructive decisions and behaviors. This simple exercise can serve at least two purposes. First, it can give the organization valuable information about the values of its employee population. Second, it can help employees be intentional about their values, which is a valuable part of other activities related to individual purpose that we will outline in chapter 12. The open-ended question in this assessment can also be used to gain additional insights.

These values exercises can be done in a number of ways. Senior leaders can engage the whole organization in a values-gathering exercise, or leaders and managers of smaller groups or units can assess and discuss values as a team. With modern technology and social connectivity tools, there are many ways to involve the employees in real-time conversations and ongoing dialogue about values.

Activity: Assess Employee Core Values

Understand and Prioritize Your Personal Values

Personal values reflect the principles you believe are important for how you live your life. They are deeply held driving forces that guide your constructive decisions and behaviors.

- Step 1: Write down ten values you strive to live by in your life (see Appendix A for a list of values)

- Step 2: From this list of ten, select the five values that have the most meaning for you in your life.

- Step 3: Rank these five values in order of importance.

Your Values and Your Work

Please indicate how often your current work and workplace allows you to live by the five values you listed in step three.

Values List	Not at all	Rarely	Sometimes	Often	Always
a. Value 1	❏	❏	❏	❏	❏
b. Value 2	❏	❏	❏	❏	❏
c. Value 3	❏	❏	❏	❏	❏
d. Value 4	❏	❏	❏	❏	❏
e. Value 5	❏	❏	❏	❏	❏

Please provide any specific examples that come to mind when your work or workplace allowed you to live out a personal value, or did not allow you to live out a personal value:

_____

_____

For very low or no cost, this activity can be introduced using one of many available online survey tools like Survey Monkey or Zoomerang. It is also possible to use even lower-tech approaches. For example, in 2005, Zappos sent the following message to its entire employee population in an e-mail:

Companies have core values, and we're working on defining them explicitly for Zappos so everyone is on the same page…

But the purpose of this e-mail is to ask what everyone's personal values are…please e-mail me four or five values that you live by (or want to live by) that define who you are or who you want to be…(do not cc everyone)…each value should be one word or at most a short phrase (but ideally one word)…please email me the values that are significant and meaningful to you personally, not necessarily having anything to do with the company's values.[78]

Ideally, you will share the collective results of the personal values exercise with the entire employee population. When discussing the topic of personal values with employees, be sure to emphasize that there are no preferred answers, and embrace diverse values and the unique contributions of individuals. On another level, looking at which personal values are shared helps tells the story about the current culture of an organization.

Understand the Organization's Core Values

For organizations that already have formal values, it is important to review them and reflect on whether they are aligned with a workplace culture that supports health, wellness, and well-being. It may also be helpful to assess the degree to which the values are actually being lived in the organization. The first step in this next activity will be to list those values (see **Assess Organizational Core Values** below). Then give all employees the opportunity to indicate how much the values are lived in the organization. Providing an ongoing opportunity for employees to give open-ended commentary is a way to gain deeper insights into what they are experiencing on a daily basis.

Activity: Assess Organizational Core Values

1. Listed below are the core values of your employer. For each of these values, please indicate how much they are lived within the organization.

Values List	Not at all	Rarely	Sometimes	Often	Always
a. Value 1	☐	☐	☐	☐	☐
b. Value 2	☐	☐	☐	☐	☐
c. Value 3	☐	☐	☐	☐	☐
d. Value 4	☐	☐	☐	☐	☐
e. Value 5	☐	☐	☐	☐	☐

2. Please provide any specific examples that come to mind for how a specific value is or isn't demonstrated regularly: _____

_____

Results That Matter to Everyone

With a Shared Values—Shared Results approach, the vision is also shared, so our measures should reflect what matters to all stakeholders both inside and outside of the organization. Understanding and measuring what matters to both employees and employers is crucial to developing healthy and thriving workplaces and workforces, as is communicating about successes and failures along the way. The most commonly used measures today are designed to inform senior management, operations personnel, and the people responsible for delivering the wellness program. We contend that it is also important to measure what matters to employees, their families, and other external stakeholders, including the community and the larger society in which the organization operates.

Senior executives and union leaders, leaders of operations, managers, and especially individual employees all have different perspectives on what matters to them. They have different roles in the company and in their lives, so they will find different kinds of information meaningful. They are all individual human beings who have unique preferences for relevant information that they can use in their personal and professional lives. Measuring and communicating what matters includes taking these individual preferences and professional needs into account when designing ongoing evaluation and communication processes.

Results That Matter to Employees and the Organization

Understanding the results or outcomes that matter most to all employees is a partner exercise to understanding employee values. If employees were able to live their values, what would that look like? What would the results be in terms of outcomes that matter to them? The activity below may help you understand the types of outcomes your employees care most about.

Activity: Identify Results that Matter to Employees (Part 1)

Organizations measure many things to be sure they are improving or meeting their business targets. We want to make sure we are also measuring things that matter to our employees so we can be sure we are making continuous improvements in things that everyone cares about.

Imagine your ideal place to work. Imagine that you are able to live fully according to your values and purpose. What are three or four characteristics of that workplace?

1. _____
2. _____
3. _____
4. _____

Please list three or four characteristics of the people at your ideal workplace:

Your manager				
Your colleagues				
Yourself				

Activity: Identify Results that Matter to Employees (Part 2)

What is most important to you in the workplace in order to live fully according to your values and purpose? Check the box to the right of your top 5 in the list below, then rank those five in order of most to least importance to you in the space to the right of the box.

	Top 5	Rank
Organization's vision	☐	_____
Organization's values	☐	_____
Job security	☐	_____
Meaningful work	☐	_____
Health-care benefits	☐	_____
Ethics	☐	_____
Organization's revenue	☐	_____
Manager support	☐	_____
Growth and development	☐	_____
Being heard by leadership	☐	_____
Career advancement	☐	_____
Feeling valued and respected	☐	_____
Fair compensation	☐	_____
Strong team collaboration	☐	_____
Flexibility in work, when appropriate	☐	_____
Autonomy in how I do my job	☐	_____
Other: (please list)_____	☐	_____

Results That Matter to the Organization

We have also provided a companion exercise that senior and operations leaders can use (with the findings from the employee exercise in hand) to identify results for health and well-being that most matter to the success of the organization and employees. The activity below will help you capture and prioritize specific outcomes that matter to both the organization and employees.

Activity: Summarize and Prioritize Results That Matter to the Organization and Employees (Part 1)

You can conduct this exercise with senior and operations leadership. For each of the areas in the table below, please indicate on a scale from 1 to 5; 1 = Not at all, 2 = A little, 3 = Moderately, 4 = Quite a bit, 5 = Extremely, how important it is for the success of your organization.

Assess the Strength of the Pillars:	Matters to the Organization	Matters to the Employees
• Engaged leadership		
• Positive organizational health		
• Resources for self-leadership and positive individual health		
• Conditions for positive personal motivation		
• Comprehensive approach to "measure what matters"		

Activity: Summarize and Prioritize Results That Matter to the Organization and Employees (Part 2)

You can conduct this exercise with senior and operations leadership. For each of the areas in the table below, please indicate on a scale from 1 to 5; 1 = Not at all, 2 = A little, 3 = Moderately, 4 = Quite a bit, 5 = Extremely, how important it is for the success of your organization.

	Matters to the Organization	Matters to the Employees
Assess Environment for Health and Well-Being		
Assess Health and Well-being Culture and Climate		
Assess Process:		
• Participation in programs		
• Program implementation quality and integrity		
Assess Engagement:		
• Employees' engagement in work and life		
• Organization's strategic engagement		
RELATIONSHIPS—ENGAGEMENT AND SUPPORT		
• With supervisor		
• With colleagues		
• With family		
• With friends		
• In the community		
SHARED VALUES		
• Company Values—Are they being lived?		
• Employee Values—Can employees live by their own values?		
SHARED RESULTS		
Positive Individual Health:		
• Mental/emotional		
• Spiritual		
• Intellectual—engagement		
• Physical health*		
• Social—relationships		
• Vocational—meaningful work		
• Financial— security		
• Healthy behaviors		
Positive Organization Health Success Markers:		
• Productivity and Performance		
• Utilization of medical services		
• Recruitment		
• Stories of organizational outliers, positive deviance		
• Meeting organizational profit-related goals and		
Other non-monetary goals (i.e., shared value brought to the community and society		

*In addition to biological functioning, measures of physical health may include subjective self-reported measures of functional status (Can you do the things you want in your life?) and objective physical indicators of flexibility, muscular strength and endurance tests.

Muscular strength is the new vital sign of worksite health in the twenty-first century. The impact that sedentary lifestyle and severe and morbid obesity are having on muscle loss (sarcopenia) has reached a level whereby companies now see greater costs associated with health plans, and higher costs for workers' compensation and disability claims due to poor strength to body weight ratio. Muscle is made to work and is critical to the health and safety of all workers. Loss of muscle puts workers at a greater risk of injury and disease. Focusing on programs to help employees maintain a healthy muscle mass throughout their life span will dramatically lower medical and injury costs

Tom Gilliam, PhD
Founder and President, IPCS

These exercises are examples of what you might use to gather the important information about the values and results that matter to employees and the organization. We provide them with the hope that they will be helpful, but they may not be suitable for the culture of your organization.

The most critical thing at this stage of the journey is to open up the process of defining values to all the stakeholders throughout the organization.

In chapter 9, we provide more detail about using the information you have collected to create or align the values and vision of your organization to match what matters most to your stakeholders. But first, chapter 8 discusses how you can gather additional information about where you are today that will also be helpful to the vision-building process.

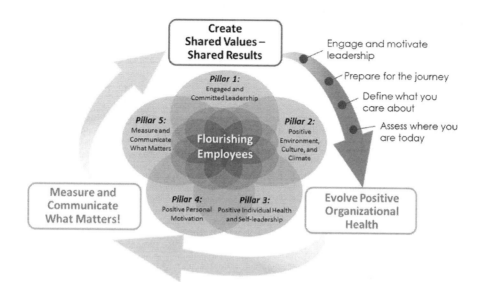

CHAPTER 8:
Assess Where You Are Today

Begin with context and strengths.

In chapter 6, we outlined some of the initial preparation work for the core team of leaders to help with the early planning for the win-win journey. We described methods for mapping the system and capturing preferred employee and organizational values and results. To complete this picture, we also recommend that you conduct a more detailed and formal set of assessments to evaluate the current health-supporting characteristics of the organization.

The Positive Organizational Health Assessment we describe throughout this chapter includes many useful exercises and assessments. You may choose to go through all or only a few of them. You may want to customize any or all of these. However you go about it, we recommend that you gather comprehensive information that helps you answer the following questions:

- What supportive or unsupportive features for health and thriving currently exist in the work, home and community's environment and culture?

- What do employees currently think and feel about the environment and culture in which they work and live?

Positive Organizational Health Assessment

The Positive Organizational Health Assessment is designed to help organizations take inventory of their current health environment and culture and identify strengths and areas of opportunity for supporting the health and well-being of the employees and the organization. There are four parts to the Positive Organizational Health Assessment:

1. Assess wellness and well-being programs and initiatives:

   a.   Interview wellness leaders and stakeholders.

   b.   Review program content and documentation.

   c.   Complete Wellness Program Landscape Assessment.

2. Conduct an audit of the environment:

   a.   Assess what exists in the current environment and culture.

   b.   Interview operations leaders and human resource representatives.

3. Survey all employees about culture and climate:

   a.   Assess employee perceptions of supportive environment and culture.

4. Conduct qualitative inquiry to provide opportunities for all employees to share their voice (focused interviews or direct observation methods).

We describe each of these components of the Positive Organizational Health Assessment in the sections that follow.

Assess the Wellness Landscape

Earlier in the journey (chapter 6), we recommended that you create a brief inventory of your organization's programs, policies, and initiatives designed to support the health and well-being of your employees. At this point, it may be wise to examine more completely the programmatic support for health and well-being currently provided to employees, dependents, and retirees. Figure 9 depicts the major categories of support that can be provided across the health continuum.

Figure 9. Support across the health continuum

We created an activity to help the core team understand the breadth of the current components of the organization's wellness and well-being efforts by taking a deeper dive into programmatic support and services. (See an abridged ***Wellness Program Landscape Assessment*** below. For the full assessment, see appendix C.)

Activity: Wellness and Well-Being Program Landscape Assessment (Abridged*)

Indicate with an "X" or "✓" whether you offer each type of resource outlined in the table below.

Type of Support	Employees	Dependents	Retirees
Manage disease	❑	❑	❑
Case management	❑	❑	❑
On-site screening – Including biometrics, physical health, mental health and positive health	❑	❑	❑
On-site Health Equipment for Self-help (e.g., BP Kiosk, Scale)	❑	❑	❑
On-site Medical Management	❑	❑	❑
Reduce Risk—Help Healthy People Stay Healthy, Wellness Programs	❑	❑	❑
Preventive services	❑	❑	❑
Programs to help employees thrive—development opportunities for self-leaders	❑	❑	❑
Development opportunities for leaders and managers	❑	❑	❑
EAP programs	❑	❑	❑

*A detailed version of this assessment is available in appendix C.

The activity lists many of the traditional types of programs and topics, along with some newer next practice resources that may be offered. The activity also helps capture information on whether your organization provides ongoing support not only in the traditional wellness arena but also for leadership and management development opportunities. A truly win-win organization would offer opportunities to strengthen positive individual health in the broadest sense possible. These offerings can create goodwill toward the organization and support strong and authentic human populations inside and surrounding the organization.

Most countries aside from the United States are not as cost-focused with the development of workplace health promotion strategies. The workplace has not been utilized as a setting to promote health to the degree as it has in the United States due to differing cultural attitudes and system drivers. The main drivers are improving productivity, reducing sick leave and improving employee morale. Health promotion programs at the workplace continue to be fragmented on average, do not follow a systems approach, and are not evaluated.

Wolf Kirsten
Co-Founder and Co-Director, Global Centre for Healthy Workplaces
President, International Health Consulting

Conduct an Audit of the Environment

We recommend conducting a comprehensive audit to understand the tangible health-supporting workplace features of an organization that influence the health of employees. This type of audit is broader than the Wellness Program Landscape Assessment. It assesses such workplace features as policies, procedures, services, and facilities that influence the health of employees. Perhaps the most effective way to gather this information is a guided interview with a small team of individuals who are well familiar with the organization and its policies and procedures. There are now several good tools designed by reputable organizations for this purpose (see Additional Resources in appendix D). The tool we use most extensively at Edington Associates is the Health Environment Check (HECheck) designed by Tom Golaszewski, Professor Emeritus SUNY Brockport. It is based on more than thirty-five years of experience assessing organizational environments.[79-82]

The HECheck yields scores in four primary areas: organizational health foundations, risk management, medical care management, and each of the five pillars outlined in *Zero Trends* and in this book. Each is briefly described below.

A. Organizational Health Foundations analyzes workplace features that should support any health initiative. As the name implies, these components provide the necessary foundation on which any program activity can best improve and sustain employee health behavior and risk modification. Components include:

1. **The Human Resources Function** is an overview of key organizational constructs that impact the personnel management process and relate to employee health.

2. **Commitment** addresses the level of organizational seriousness applied to the health initiative with respect to resource allocation, assignment of authority and accountability, and the relationship of the health initiative to the overall organizational mission.

3. **Culture Change** assesses organizational characteristics that have an impact on the perceived social atmosphere surrounding virtually all health issues in the workplace. These factors include group norms, values, and social supports.

B. Risk Management analyzes the specific intervention activities surrounding prevalent health topics addressed in most workplace health initiatives, including mental health issues.

C. Medical Management assesses an organization's efforts to control medical costs through improved consumer behavior, progressive health-insurance services, and proactive management of disease conditions. In addition to the insurance available, the organization needs to be sure that the healthcare is focused on the issues that matter to the individuals.

D. Five Pillars of a Champion Company are assessed in addition to the factors outlined above; the HECheck yields scores for each of the pillars:

- pillar 1: senior leadership—shared vision and values
- pillar 2: operations leadership—positive organizational health
- pillar 3: self-leadership—positive individual health
- pillar 4: recognition—positive personal motivation
- pillar 5: quality assurance—measure and communicate what matters

Whether you use this tool, or another one of the available well-validated tools, the key is to gather comprehensive information about the health-supportive features of your organization's current environment.

In health care, there is a need to focus on root cause. This is where we can have the greatest impact. The overwhelming evidence tells us this is in the area of lifestyle. A healthy lifestyle is the key component that is not being discussed enough. Yet, it drives the nearly 70-80 percent of annual healthcare costs that are likely preventable. A healthy lifestyle encompasses physical activity, sleep, stress management, and the move toward a more plant-based whole foods diet, for the prevention, and in some cases for the treatment of chronic disease is the trend of the future.

The greatest long-term health benefits will occur through changes in health habits instead of modern medicine. More research is needed in these important areas related to lifestyle medicine, prevention and the treatment of chronic illness. Through additional research, I believe the data will show that lifestyle medicine has only scratched the surface of the true value to improve employee health and well-being.

Dexter Sherney, MD
Chief Medical Director/Executive Director Global Health/Wellness, Cummins Inc.

We propose that, in the future, medical examinations be expanded to include an evaluation of the positive attitudes such as resilience, gratitude, mindfulness, etc.

Basic preventive care is still ignored by millions of Americans, allowing undiagnosed diabetes, hypertension, heart disease, and cancer to fester undeterred until treatment options are complex or futile. We have to use creative approaches to engage those who today seem unreachable.

Lee Dukes
Chief Solutions Officer, Catapult Health

Survey Employees about Their Perceptions of Culture

In addition to an audit of the environment, we recommend surveying all employees to assess their perceptions of the workplace environment, culture, and climate regarding organizational support for a healthy and high-performing workplace and workforce. As "culture of health" approaches have become more popular over the past decade, we have seen measures of health culture come into more frequent use. Edington Associates has developed a culture survey as part of our more comprehensive Living and Thriving Assessment. The LTA is modular and contains subscales in the following areas:

Subscale/Module	Example Content Areas
Mental/emotional health	gratitude, happiness, meaning in life, optimism, perceived control, resilience, values, life satisfaction, stress, anxiety, depression
Spiritual health	values, purpose, meaning in life
Intellectual health	engagement in lifelong learning
Physical health	activity level, perception of health, cholesterol, blood pressure, chronic conditions, tobacco use, safety belt use, alcohol use, illness days, body weight, stage of change, self-efficacy
Social health	relationships with friends and family, community, society
Environmental health:	
• Home culture	supportive home and family
• Community culture	safe neighborhoods, available resources, walk-ability, bike-ability, parks and green space
Occupational health	
• Workplace culture	health support, growth, autonomy, connectedness, balance, fairness, satisfaction with work, meaningful work
Financial	sufficient income, savings, security

Findings from this type of survey can provide valuable information during the early design and strategy discussions. In chapter 16, we discuss how items and subscales from the LTA can be used periodically to evaluate progress over time in areas of importance to employees and the organization.

Qualitative Inquiry

Take a walk in their shoes.

In addition to gathering quantitative information on health-supporting characteristics of your organizations, we recommend the use of at least one or two qualitative inquiry methods. Qualitative research methods provide insights that foster deep empathy for the employees—the people for whom we design the initiatives. We have based our philosophy for evolving win-win organizations on positive concepts, and our recommended approach for evaluating the current state of the organization builds on the positive as well. We recommend identifying the positive assets, skills, strengths, capacity, and knowledge of individuals throughout the organization by using a combination of positive deviance and appreciative inquiry methods.

This approach is designed to gather and publicize stories and experiences that represent extraordinary passion, teamwork, creativity, or other positive characteristics that the employees and the organization highly value.

Appreciative Inquiry

Appreciative inquiry (AI) is a qualitative way to assess feedback about the strengths and positive traits of an organization or group. David L. Cooperrider, PhD, from Case Western Reserve University, developed AI as a methodology to initiate change by focusing on the positive core of an organization through exploring assets instead of deficits.[83-85] AI is a broad model for transforming an organization and has the potential for direct application to an organization's wellness efforts.

This approach is worthwhile to consider (for example, in lieu of an employee interest survey) by identifying the organization's health culture as the topic to explore with unconditional, positive questions and envisioning what unique aspects of positive organizational health would look like in a specific workplace. Unconditional positive questions are used to spark dialogue as a means of transformation. These types of questions include topics about the life-giving aspects of an organization, peak experiences, and exceptional achievements. Fully understanding the collective strengths and merits helps build creativity and the capacity to elevate foundational elements of an organization or community to a higher level.

Rather than conducting surveys of employees, the AI philosophy gains insights and boosts morale by gathering and sharing positive stories from employees throughout the organization. This process acknowledges and restores what employees believe about the organization, builds confidence and conviction, and raises energy and participation for constructive change. Using this method of inquiring about strengths can lead to greater employee engagement. From a culture standpoint, acknowledging these strengths creates the potential and commitment needed to achieve a higher level of results by tapping into the positive core of an organization.

This cycle perpetuates a system that nurtures and supports even more enthusiasm, leading to productive change and innovation. Ultimately, strengths are multiplied, and deficiencies become less relevant.

A core part of appreciative inquiry includes exploration into experiences throughout the organization that represent the best it has to offer—positive examples of how the values are being lived in the organization. It provides a representation of what is working well in the organization by highlighting examples of organizational and individual health and thriving. It is designed to gather and publicize exemplary ways the organization and the people in it have promoted and supported health and thriving.

This process serves several important functions. It provides an account of positive stories of health and thriving in the organization, as well as positive grassroots examples of how the people in your organization are living healthy lives (in the sense of full positive individual health) and supporting others in their own healthy living. Because these are often homegrown successes, they are more likely to resonate strongly with all stakeholders than prepackaged, one-size-fits-all wellness and well-being platforms. Cascading the use of similar approaches may meet with less resistance than canned approaches brought in from the outside.

A second important function is that the process of positive inquiry can also have a positive influence on the climate in the organization, especially if a significant proportion of employees is involved. Humans tend to focus more strongly on negative events than on positive ones. We are also prone to what psychologists call the "recency effect" or the tendency to have better recall of more recent events or information than for earlier events. Over time, examples of positive behaviors and events may fade into the background, and negative events and behaviors may more easily surface in our thoughts and feelings about our workplaces. Recalling positive examples and sharing those stories can bring those experiences back into our more recent thinking and can influence how we view our workplaces and our colleagues in the present.

Appreciative Interviews

A helpful method for gathering positive stories during the appreciative inquiry process is the appreciative interview. The appreciative interview process involves one-on-one conversations among the organization's stakeholders designed to uncover experiences that represent the organization at its best. Applying AI begins with selecting a positive topic to explore, such as customer service or teamwork. In this case, you will likely be exploring examples of healthy and thriving employees, managers, and leaders, and examples from the environment that contribute to employee health and thriving. Then you can apply a 4-D exploratory model:

- In the *discovery* phase, time is first spent identifying examples of excellence and appreciating aspects of the current state.

- The *dream* phase envisions the organization in other ways in which it could flourish as an ideal state.

- In the *design* phase, conversations shift to ways in which to achieve that ideal state.

- In the final *destiny* phase, you aim to uncover innovative ways to create and sustain that preferred future state and define action steps for short- and long-term goals.

Throughout these phases, inclusion is critical; it is accomplished by tapping into as many people as possible for these dialogues. Once the notes from these conversations are compiled, themes that lead to peak experiences are identified.

Common topics in AI interviews include what employees value most about themselves, the work they do, and their organizations. Employees can be asked to describe an example of a time when they were able to do their best work or when they were at their healthiest. Other questions that can be asked include the following:

- What are the core factors that foster positive health and thriving in your organization when it is at its best?

- Imagine your organization ten years from now, when everything is just as you always wished it could be. What is different?

- How have you contributed to this dream organization?

- How often do you engage the members of your organization in a dialogue about the features of the organization that support their positive health and thriving?

Appreciative interviews can be conducted with local experts throughout the organization as well as with employees. People with strong relationships, respected leaders, and people with a reputation for intelligence or fairness are good candidates for these interviews. However, care should be taken to get information from a representative sample of employees from all levels and all areas of the organization. There is a great deal of helpful guidance readily available on how to use the appreciative interview process.[84]

Focus Groups

Focus groups are another useful method for gathering rich information about how individuals feel about an issue, and they can add a more human dimension to survey and audit data. They capture a deeper level of information, feelings, perceptions, and opinions and can be a good source of stories and personal quotes (used with permission, of course). They can also allow clarification of questions and opportunities to drill in with further follow-up.

Moderating a focus group takes skill, so ideally someone with expertise would be used to conduct them. There are many good sources of information on how to conduct focus groups, so we don't provide detailed instruction here. But some potential topics include perceptions and examples of

- role modeling by leaders, managers, and colleagues;

- examples and stories of wellness and well-being practices;

- wellness traditions and symbols;

- rewards and recognition—perceptions of the kind of practices that are used or could be used in the organization;

- pushback—comfort level with healthy practices at the workplace;

- relationship development—on teams, between colleagues, and with managers and leaders;

- recruitment, selection, and orientation;

- microcultures across the organization; and

- the value of wellness and well-being initiatives.

Collaborative Sensemaking

At this point, depending on which of these methods you have used, you may have a lot of information from several quantitative and qualitative sources. Synthesizing this amount of information can be a challenging but valuable and rewarding process that can lead to truly deep insights and understanding of your workforce and workplace culture. Table 6 lists the various types of evaluation methods we have described in the process of the win-win journey to this point. This information can be used to inform the creation of the vision and values, as well as the strategic planning process. The methods outlined here can also be used in the evaluation of progress toward the vision, which is outlined in chapters 14, 15, and 16.

There are many potential evaluation resources that can be engaged to assist with the different components of the positive organizational health assessment process. Larger organizations may have research or analytic staff they can enlist and sophisticated data systems that can be mined. Small or medium-sized organizations may have fewer internal resources, but third-party partners are often willing to aid in the process. For example, many local insurance brokers are looking for additional ways to provide value to their clients, so they may be happy to help you with this kind of work.

Synthesize Information

Much of what has occurred so far in the positive organizational health assessment process has been relatively transparent to the stakeholders involved. Evaluators often take the data from the discovery phase and incubate the material in a synthesis process that is opaque to the end-user of the reporting.[86] In the spirit of inclusion and engagement, it is helpful to involve employees and other stakeholders in the process of synthesizing the information. While we do not intend to provide a detailed tutorial on data synthesis, we do highlight some basic practices and point to some additional valuable resources.

Table 6. Summaries of evaluation methods

Method	What to look for
Prepare for the journey • Assess readiness • Reflect on personal commitment • Assess support for employee thriving	This assessment conducted with your core team members comes very early in the process of evolving your health-related culture and environment. It is important to look for any trends in responses that could indicate concern or low levels of support or commitment from respondents. It is also important to acknowledge these in the feedback of the information and include methods that will allow employees to voice concerns and help build support for your development approaches.
Map the territory • Visualize the system • Brief pillar assessment	This process can help highlight any areas throughout the system that might create bottlenecks or hot spots that may need special care.
Define Shared Values—Shared Results • What do we care about? • Assess organizational core values • Outline personal values • Assess ability to live personal values • Outcomes that matter	This exploration and its findings are of central importance to the win-win journey, or even to any less formal effort to improve the health and well-being of employees. It is also core to the overall long-term success of the organization. Look for common themes that represent values employees throughout the organization share. Also, look for any discrepancies between the strongly held personal values of employees and the organization's core values.
Positive Organizational Health Assessment • Wellness Landscape Assessment • Environmental Audit • Perception of Culture Survey • Positive Qualitative Inquiry • Experience sampling • Appreciative Inquiry • Insights, stories and quotes	Depending on the extent of this assessment, there may be a lot of information to digest. It is important to look for trends or patterns across the different assessments that indicate a particularly strong finding.

If at all possible, it may be a good opportunity for a group of employees to participate in an ad hoc design team to help synthesize the information.

Making sense of it can be time-consuming, and time is often limited for the people in your company who would be involved in this process. We have adapted a framework for quickly making meaning of complex data created by Jon Kolko, founder and director of the Austin Center for Design. We recommend the following six techniques for making meaning of the information collected in the positive organizational health assessment outline six techniques:

1. ***Get your data out into the open***. Spread it out. You may have photographs, survey item responses, environmental and wellness program audit responses, interview transcripts, focus group findings, and other artifacts you have collected during the positive organizational health assessment. If you have a big conference table or a room with a large blank wall, spread the information out; tack it to the wall. Now stand back and squint, both literally and figuratively, and begin the process of "selective pruning and visual organization." Post-it Notes in various colors and a set of colored markers may come in handy during this process. This will help highlight patterns, relationships, or even discrepancies in the information. Kolko points out that often the conversation during this process is more important than the data itself.

2. ***Organize the data into content groupings***. This process may take several iterations.

   a. ***Quantitative Information***—Numerical data or data collected in neat categories or with defined response options can be relatively straightforward to summarize. Look for patterns, themes, and relationships across the different sources of information.

   b. ***Qualitative information***—Qualitative information is a bit messier than quantitative data. Select key information that stands out to you. Look across the stories and edit out extraneous information. Choose the information you find surprising, interesting, or worth pursuing. Aggregate big thoughts if they are linked. Review information for consistencies, inconsistencies, themes, and areas that stand out as priorities. For each, include recognition and celebration of strengths and ideas for how to make improvements. Stay away from blame, finger-pointing, or trying to second-guess who said what in any of the findings.

      Extract revelations and key insights. Insights bring visibility and clarity to previously hidden meanings:

      i. ***Revelations.*** Does anything surprise you? Are there any revelations in the findings? Do you see anything you were not expecting? Is there anything missing that you expected to see?

      ii. ***Insights.*** Extrapolate individual stories to overarching truths.

3. ***Organize to produce "semantic relationships."*** This means to use what you have done so far to generate a credible and logical story of the reason for the relationships between the types of information. "The activity of defining and forging connections actively produces knowledge."

4. ***Prioritize to emphasize what is most important.*** Comparing the findings is a highly subjective process that can contribute to objective uses for the information in later planning stages.

5. ***Judge the data and reduce the quantity.*** Sift through the data to determine what is most significant and pare away the excess.

6. ***Enhance the data through intuitive leaps.*** This is where you ask and try to answer the question "why" regarding what you see in the data. It might help to visualize the answers in sketches and diagrams. But don't get too fancy here or spend too much time as you sketch, or you may have a hard time discarding those sketches that don't work well to explain what you're seeing.

In the next section we discuss ways to bring this information to life in meaningful communication to stakeholders throughout the organization.

Communicate to the Organizational Stakeholders

Compelling and meaningful communication can provide important information and learnings throughout the entire journey process. Perhaps the most obvious function at this stage is to inform the stakeholders involved in the early preparation phase. Another important function is to increase the motivation of all stakeholders to engage in the process of the win-win journey. If you have convened employee design teams to help with collecting, consolidating, or analyzing the information for the positive organizational health assessment, it might also be good to involve the team members in the reporting process as well. It could give these employees some visibility with senior leaders and managers, and can make the findings more relatable for employees.

In table 7, we summarize ideas for how to synthesize the information collected throughout the positive organizational health assessment process and outline our suggestions for output. Reporting should tell a persuasive story about your organization's health-related environmental and cultural practices. You will want to adopt the perspective or frame of the story for each of your stakeholder audiences. Table 8 outlines some content framing you might want to include in your reporting message for specific stakeholder groups across the organization. In chapter 9, we help you take all the information gathered during the preparation phase, from the values-exploration activities, and during the positive organizational health assessment, and create a meaningful vision, shared values, and shared results that can guide the rest of the win-win journey. In chapter 17, we provide more extensive information about a strategic reporting approach.

Table 7. Elements of the synthesis process

Input →	Synthesis Process →	Output
Quantitative data	Statistical analysis	Comparisons (between groups, change over time, etc.) Graphs, plots, response frequencies for multiple choice
Qualitative data	Incubation/reflection Look for relationships, themes	Summarized information, themes, stories, case studies of positive outliers
Observational data	Incubation/reflection Look for relationships, themes	Narrative that provides a credible and logical story to explain the patterns and themes within and across the different kinds of information.
Artifacts	Look for hidden meaning in behaviors	Examples and summary of the types of artifacts Lists and examples of prominently featured artifacts—how are they used, not used?

Table 8. Reporting content

Audience	Message
Core team	The core team has the responsibility to report to the senior leaders and to feed the information to the middle managers, union leaders, and all employees. Tailor the messages specifically for each of the different audiences.
Operations leaders	Operations leaders have a very hands-on role in the company, so reporting to them can be more detailed and tactical than for other audiences.
Leaders and managers	All leaders and managers have a responsibility to report to those in their direct line or in some cases to all such titles in the organization. These middle managers have unique responsibilities by serving both the people under their responsibility and the needs of those at a higher level. They also play the role of matching what matters to those more senior leaders with what matters to most employees. The messages may not be identical for the two groups, but clearly they have to be consistent.
Everyone	What you communicate to all employees is as critical as the messages to the middle and senior managers. Every stakeholder in the organization has a need and a right to know if engagement and motivation are to remain high.

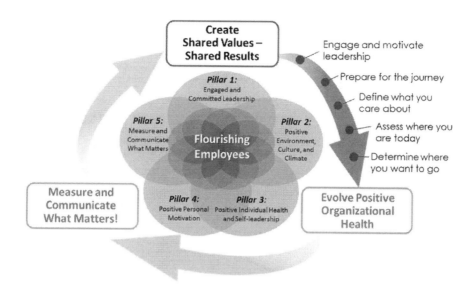

CHAPTER 9:
Determine Where You Want to Go

A truly shared vision emerges from
shared values and shared results.

The word culture has the same root as the farming word, cultivate. Creating supportive cultural environments is a lot like the good farming practices of preparing the soil, planting the seed, nurturing the crop and then harvesting the fruits of our work. First we examine the existing culture. Then we plant the seed by communicating the vision of the desired culture and how people can contribute to this. The third step is to shape cultural influences such as rewards. Finally, similar to a harvest, we celebrate the new culture and prepare for a new cycle of culture change. In this way, a wellness culture evolves with the changing needs of people and their organizations.

Judd Allen, PhD
President, Human Resources Insitute

At this stage of the journey, you have likely gathered a lot of information about the values and results that matter to employees and the organization. The Positive Organizational Health Assessment has been summarized and shared with all organizational stakeholders. It is now time to create a shared vision, shared values, and a set of shared results that matter to all stakeholders. These will be used to guide a high-level strategic plan, objectives, and strategic imperatives.

Importance of a Shared Vision

Efforts and courage are not enough without purpose and direction.

—John F. Kennedy

Ken Blanchard and his associates have been studying leadership and coaching for more than four decades and conclude that three critical factors are common to world-class organizations:[87]

- clear vision and direction championed by top management
- trained and equipped people focused on implementation of the agreed-upon vision and direction
- established recognition and positive-consequence systems that sustain the behaviors and performance that the vision and direction require

While most organizations have a formally stated vision, few have explicitly included health, wellness, and well-being in the corporate vision statement. Some organizations may want to revisit their corporate vision, but others may not be quite ready to jump in at that level. We believe that to have a world-class approach to evolving positive organizational health, organizations should have some level of expressed shared vision for organizational and employee health, wellness, well-being, and thriving.

Envision This...

In this organization, the vision for well-being and health goals are clearly defined, and progress toward achieving the vision and demonstrating values are often communicated to all employees. In particular, leadership is transparent with these results. In a company-wide email, the CEO shares the most recent results of an employee culture survey. The results indicate areas of strength for the organization, such as a generous health-benefit plan. But scores were dismal in work-life balance. Additional data on the lack of vacation time used is coupled with the findings. The CEO recognizes the strengths and acknowledges that improvements are needed. She initiates an open forum to ask for feedback on ways to promote a healthier workplace. As a start, employees are invited to share ideas for fostering vitality, and responses are posted on the company intranet. The CEO promises to set new goals, monitor progress and keep employees informed. How is your organization using metrics to learn about the true climate of health, hear stories surrounding those metrics, and evaluate progress toward an overall vision of health?

Angela Camilleri

Lead Innovation Strategist, Edington Associates

Create a Shared Vision, Shared Values, and Shared Results

In chapter 6 we shared an exercise for assessing the values and results that matter to employees and the organization. Once all stakeholders have had the opportunity to share the values and results that have meaning for them, there are many ways to distill the information to make it useful for the individuals charged with crafting the formal vision and values of the organization. The simplest and most direct method is to list the most-mentioned values and results in order of the number of mentions from highest to lowest.

Senior leaders and the core team should take the time to reflect carefully on the values and results employees said were important to them.

If what rises to the top of this list of values is not in alignment with the organization's values (either formally stated values or widely understood unstated values), leaders and the core team will need to find common ground and create alignment. This could involve restating or rethinking the organization's values to reflect the importance of healthy and high-performing employees. It might even mean engaging in a process of creating better alignment among stakeholders throughout the organization. It is also possible both will be necessary.

It is important to feed back the summarized information to everyone throughout the company. This feedback should explicitly outline how the information will be used to make improvements in the workplace. General steps in creating shared values include

- creating a draft set of shared core values;

- sharing with all employees and senior leaders for comment;

- incorporating comments and finalizing;

- collecting and reflecting on what you have heard;

- reviewing by the core team and the senior leaders (organization and unions) in addition to a representative set of employees from throughout the organization;

- sharing final values with all organizational stakeholders, including all employees; and

- highlighting in your communications that you built these values on what you heard was meaningful and important to all stakeholders.

Levels of Vision

A vision must be woven into everything and repeatedly promoted!

By definition, a shared vision is shared and informed by individuals throughout the organization. There are at least three levels of shared vision for health, wellness, and well-being organizations can consider:

- ***Good***: create a shared vision for any wellness program or initiatives

- ***Better***: create a shared vision for a positive organizational health culture—how you operate overall as a company with respect to the health of our employees

- ***Best***: include the importance of healthy and thriving employees in a shared corporate vision

Regardless of which level of vision is created, it should follow some basic principles. According to Blanchard, a shared vision exists when the following takes place:

- People are inspired by the purpose of the effort

- People feel their values and ideas are incorporated into what the organization is trying to achieve

- People can easily communicate the direction of the effort

- People recognize that both individual and organizational needs are being addressed

- People see how their day-to-day activities can support the overall goals of the effort.

Vision for Wellness and Well-being Initiatives

We recommend that organizations have, at a minimum, a stated vision for their formal wellness and well-being initiatives. This level of vision is often created collaboratively with the internal and external partners who are responsible for developing and implementing the initiatives. It may also accompany a thoughtful branding effort for the wellness and well-being approach. Wellness programs are intended for all stakeholders, so all stakeholders should be asked to participate in creating the vision for the initiatives, and should have input into the design and content. To increase stakeholder engagement, the vision for an initiative should be strongly communicated to all stakeholders. It is important to communicate how the input heard from employees and leaders was incorporated into the vision. Whether or not senior leaders were deeply involved in developing the vision, their visibility and input during the process is desirable.

At a minimum, senior leaders should fully understand and wholeheartedly embrace the vision for the formal wellness and well-being strategies and frequently communicate about them.

The future will be all about moving whole populations regarding their health. The paradox is the only way to move whole populations will be through extreme personalization of services, incentives, and communication within the context of a culture of health. Think Amazon.

Neal Sofian
Director, Member Engagement, Premera Blue Cross

Organizational Vision for a Healthy and Thriving Culture

Some organizations may choose to create a shared vision for the overall culture as it relates to employee health and thriving. This might include providing supportive programs, but it would also be much broader. Ideally, this vision would reflect the shared values of the stakeholders throughout the organization and follow the principles outlined above. Active senior leader involvement in creating and communicating this vision is important. The vision for culture below is from the University of California, Riverside (UCR) and is communicated on the university's website by its chancellor.

UCR is committed to a campus culture that promotes wellness through healthy lifestyles that enhance the quality of life for our faculty, staff, and students.

—Kim A. Wilcox
Chancellor, University of California, Riverside.

This is a clear vision that explicitly addresses the larger health culture of the university and mentions health, wellness, and quality life of all stakeholders. As a constant reminder of the overarching aspirations of your organization, you can post your vision for a healthy organizational culture on your organization's website, in prominent locations in the built environment, in business communications, and in contact information such as e-mail salutations. Calvin College in Grand Rapids, Michigan leverages the values, purpose, mission and vision of the college to build the wellness program into the core of the college.

Calvin College: An Example of Having a Strong Base for Building a Healthy Culture.

Calvin College (a faith-based, private, liberal arts institution in Grand Rapids, MI) initiated a limited employee health promotion (wellness) program in 2000. In 2007, the college made the decision to commit fully to building a healthy culture and hired a full-time wellness director for their Healthy Habits program. The vision of Healthy Habits is to become one of the healthiest workplaces in the United States, defined as a thriving, healthy, and productive workforce. Living out this vision means integrating wellness into all areas of the organization. As this occurs, wellness is becoming the "lifestyle of the community" rather than just a "program."

Calvin's overall goals for building a healthy community include: Providing opportunities...that promote healthy living from a holistic perspective.Creating a supportive environment...for pursuing wellness goals. Encouraging employees and their families to consider health a priority...for lifelong faith-based service.

- *Healthy Habits is committed to making wellness the norm at Calvin*

- *Where there is a community committed to pursuing and supporting each other in healthy initiatives*

- *Where healthy personal and group habits are being practiced daily*

- *Where healthy choices are available and accessible. Where work-life balance is encouraged*

- *Where employees enjoy their work and are highly productive*

- *Where leaders are engaged in wellness initiatives*

- *Where health is being maintained and improved, and risk is being reduced.*

- *Where Healthy Habits is more than a program...it is a community lifestyle*

Roy Zuidema
Director of Campus Wellness, Calvin College

To read the full case study go to appendix B

Another example of a vision for health is from Henry Ford Health System. As they are a provider of healthcare services, it is not surprising that they value health and wellness and include it in their corporate vision. Many of our clients have been hospital systems and health plans that have realized that healthy and thriving employees will be better able to deliver quality health care to their patients.

Henry Ford Health System

MISSION: To improve people's lives through excellence
in the science and art of health care and healing

VISION: Transforming lives and communities through
health and wellness—one person at a time

VALUES: Each Patient First
Respect for People
High Performance
Learning and Continuous Improvement
A Social Conscience

Henry Ford Health System

In July 2009, HFHS CEO Nancy Schlichting and Senior Vice President of Community Health, Equity & Wellness, Kimberlydawn Wisdom, MD, convened a wellness steering committee comprising senior leaders to review the wellness practices of other major US health systems, and discuss potential strategies for wellness and prevention initiatives. HFHS named Dr. Wisdom as chief wellness officer and announced its new vision statement: "Transforming lives and communities through health and wellness—one person at a time." The core functions of Henry Ford LiveWell are coordination, collaboration, and innovation across three areas of focus: engaged and empowered people (including HFHS patients, employees and community members), clinical preventive services, and healthy environment. Underpinning all of the Henry Ford LiveWell strategic objectives is the goal of eliminating health disparities.

Kimberlydawn Wisdom, MD, Chief Wellness Officer
Senior Vice President of Community Health & Equity, Henry Ford Health System

To read the full case study go to appendix B

Employee Health in the Corporate Vision

The strongest representation of commitment to the health and well-being of employees would be to mention it explicitly in the vision or mission and values for the entire organization. We were in the process of looking for good examples of visions or missions that explicitly included employee health, wellness, and well-being. While shopping one day at a local market, I (Jennifer) happened to notice their mission posted near the entrance to the store. It reads as follows:

Mission of the New Frontiers Natural Marketplace in Solvang, California

The Desire to Inspire

At the heart of New Frontiers
is the desire to inspire
personal growth and positive change.

We do this by providing healthy choices,
by educating others and ourselves,
and by creating a delightful experience.

We embrace every opportunity
to improve the quality of life
in our relationships, in our communities, and in our world.

Together, we can make a difference
by enhancing everyone's well-being,
one person at a time.

New Frontiers' values clearly make the connection between the health and well-being of their employees and the service they can deliver to their customers.

- customer delight
- education
- creating abundance
- taking care of our team members
- supporting our communities
- supporting our earth

Their more detailed description of the "***Taking Care of Our Team Members***" value is listed below:

Our Team Members are the heart and soul of our business.

New Frontiers believes that looking out for each other and caring for one another provides a wonderful energy in our stores, which in turn inspires each of us to provide exceptional customer care. We realize that our success depends upon each Team Member every day. By empowering each Team Member with information, education and skills, and providing the best possible Team Member benefits, we seek to foster an environment of excitement, creativity, mutual caring, motivation, and yes—a FUN place to work.

These statements and values are exceptional because they connect shareholder value to products and service, and ultimately to people. The mission starts with people, and with healthy, high-performing people you get creative products, and with creative and quality products you improve shareholder value.

Developing a compelling and inspiring shared vision can be quite an undertaking. We are not experts in this area, but there are many terrific resources that provide practical wisdom and guidance about creating an inspiring and meaningful shared vision. Ken Blanchard and Jesse Stoner's now classic book *Full Steam Ahead*[88] provides concrete assistance on how to create clear and meaningful shared visions for organizations and individuals. Other good resources on visioning are available through the Society for Organizational Learning (www.solonline.org) and the Society for Human Resource Management (www.shrm.org).

When developing your vision, whether for the wellness program, a larger cultural initiative, or for the organization, it is important to consider carefully the shared values and reflect the collective aspirations of all organizational stakeholders.

New Frontiers Natural Marketplace

To be successful in today's society, it is so important for a business not to become stagnant. Businesses must always be evaluating how they treat their team members and customers. When we created our mission statement, we had five stores and over five hundred team members. We invited everyone who wanted to participate in creating our mission statement to write down what key points were important to them regarding our company and customers. We then compiled the points and keywords that were mentioned the most by everyone. Then the president, marketing director, and I started putting thoughts and phrases down on paper using these key points. The whole process from start to finish took a few months. Because we involved the whole team in the process, the finished product rings true in the hearts of everyone at New Frontiers.

Jake Collier
Vice President, New Frontiers Natural Marketplace

The vision must always serve the needs of the stakeholders
plus the needs of the organization:

Stakeholders only win when organizations win and organizations
only win when stakeholders win.

The example ***Vision for Employee Health and Flourishing*** below is modeled after the vision for one of the earliest clients of Edington Associates. The overall vision and its five subcomponents closely map to our five pillars.

Vision for Employee Health and Thriving

We are widely recognized as having a healthy and supportive work environment with passionate, thriving employees, driven to contribute to their fullest potential in their work, their communities, and their families.

- *Our leadership demonstrates commitment to employee well-being by their visible efforts to develop a healthy culture and environment and actively engage in the company's health promotion efforts.*

- *We have an aligned and supportive organizational culture and environment that encourages healthy, creative, and high-performing employees.*

- *We provide effective and engaging health promotion programs that are richly supportive of our entire employee population across the health continuum.*

- *Our employees are self-leaders who understand how to thrive in all areas of their life, including their health, their work, their communities and their families.*

- *We support our employees in their efforts to maximize their health and well-being.*

- *We are committed to collecting, evaluating, and internalizing the information needed to drive continuous improvement efforts and become an employer of choice.*

This vision nicely reflects the company's commitment to creating strength in all five fundamental pillars. Plus, it is consistent with the company's overall business model. In chapter 10, we build on this example vision to demonstrate how you can "connect the dots" between your vision and your goals, objectives, measures, and metrics for the win-win journey.

A truly shared vision emerges
from shared values and shared results

THEME 2:
EVOLVING POSITIVE
ORGANIZATIONAL HEALTH

Everything that happens in the organization has an impact on employee health, and everything that happens to the health of employees has an impact on the organization.

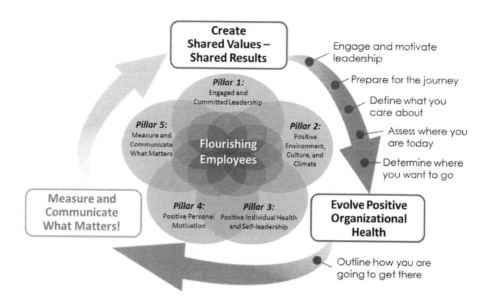

CHAPTER 10:
Outline How You Are Going to Get There

Collaboration, engagement and synergy among individuals who have wellness, well-being, and other operational roles will make or break any effort to create a positive, healthy, and flourishing organization.

Every organization is unique; therefore, in this section we outline a general and flexible process that can be tailored to help you create positive individual and organizational health in your organization. This process is the heart and soul of the win-win journey process, and wellness and well-being, and operations leaders play a key role.

This chapter is about how operations leadership can create the environmental and cultural backbone upon which to build a healthy and thriving workplace and workforce.

Chapters 11, 12, and 13 are companion chapters that build on the work that wellness, well-being, and operations leaders and other stakeholders do to outline the strategic plan for health and well-being in your organization:

- Chapter 11: Create an Environment, Culture, and Climate for positive organizational health

- Chapter 12: Support Self-Leadership and Positive Individual Health

- Chapter 13: Create Conditions for Positive Personal Motivation

Together, these three chapters outline how you can evolve strong and sustainable positive organizational health in your organization.

After years of researching and evaluating best-practice models, there appears to be no cookie-cutter approach to designing the perfect wellness program within the healthcare industry. The unique and dynamic healthcare environment challenges us to look for new and innovative approaches. At St. Jude Medical Center, rather than presenting a calendar of activities throughout the year, we have adopted a philosophy and commitment to intentionally integrate wellness into the fabric of our culture.

Jane Wang
Manager at St. Jude Medical Center
Fullerton, CA

To read the full case study go to appendix B

Operations Leadership

Over the past two decades, we have come to believe that creating a thriving, healthy, high-performing and sustainable workplace and workforce requires an "it takes a village" mindset. The people living and working in the culture and environment represent that village. Individuals must understand that working together as one is greater than the sum of the individuals working alone. Cooperation and collaboration are characterized by everyone working toward a shared objective based on Shared Values—Shared Results.

Operations leaders are any individuals who play an official leadership role in evolving the health environment and culture of an organization. This may include individuals with formal operational positions in the organization (e.g., human resources, organizational development, safety, wellness, well-being, and training and development personnel, etc.). Operations leaders may also be employees and leaders throughout the company in non-operational roles who take on purposeful activities that contribute in a formal way to creating a healthy and thriving organizational culture (e.g., wellness and well-being champions and members of formal work teams).

Operations leaders have a tremendous amount of influence over the ultimate outcomes associated with any effort to evolve a healthy and flourishing organizational culture. Ultimate success will depend on collaboration and leadership from everyone with an operational role, no matter how limited in scope it may seem.

Empowered and passionate operations leaders are crucial to creating a healthy and thriving workplace and workforce, or as we refer to it, positive organizational health.

Over the past several years, we have asked hundreds of people in the audiences of our talks to tell us the words they would use to describe their ideal workplace. The word cloud in figure 10 depicts the words we hear. We trust this book will encourage organizations to discover and develop examples like these within their workplace and workforce.

Figure 10. Descriptions of ideal workplaces

Note: The size of each word is relative to the frequency of its mention.

Current Best Practices for Operations Leadership

Many organizational consultants and program providers have published their views on the best practice recommendations and guidelines for wellness and well-being initiatives. In chapter 5, we outlined the practices that most directly relate to the role of senior leaders. Below, we have listed the current best practices[66-73] most relevant for operational leaders:

- clearly identified plan of operations

- conceptual framework that reinforces an integrated approach to health management for the population involved

- human-centered culture

- assigned program accountability

- comprehensive, integrated programs

- implementation management system

- integration of policies into the health culture of the organization

- integration across multiple organizational functions and departments

- work with all partners to align policies and procedures and develop comprehensive, integrated programs

- wellness champion network

- cohesive wellness teams

- effective ongoing comprehensive communications and program branding

The workplace is the ideal environment for transforming health care. As leaders of their organization, CEOs need to create, encourage, and support an environment that recognizes the hectic lives of their employees and provides easy, convenient access to quality care, including worksite and/or retail health centers that are integrated with a person's primary care provider (PCP) and other corporate sponsored well-being offerings.

Duane Putnam
Walgreens Co.

While these practices were designed to increase the effectiveness of wellness and population health management programs, they were not necessarily intended to help organizations evolve a thriving culture. Without a systematic framework to help guide the evolution of broader health cultures in workplaces, many of the published best practice recommendations read like laundry lists.

Some stakeholders in the wellness industry still take a relatively narrow view of what constitutes a healthy culture in employer organizations. Many "culture of health" efforts today are focused on strengthening or increasing the scale and scope of wellness and well-being programs within organizations. Often, the result is that the responsibility for creating a culture of health falls to the wellness, human resources, or medical director in an organization. These individuals are highly educated and dedicated people who have pursued their careers in service of creating opportunities for making a positive difference in the lives of others. Even so, evolving the culture of an organization will take much more than what human resource, wellness directors, or coordinators can do alone, no matter how well-meaning or effective they may be.

It will take a village working in service of positive organizational health, guided by Shared Values—Shared Results.

Emerging Next Practices for Operations Leadership

The best practices outlined above are necessary but not sufficient for building strong cultures of health that include impactful wellness and well-being initiatives and programs. To guide this work going forward, we need a broader conceptualization of culture and an expanded sense of how to cultivate health and thriving in organizations. Instead of solely focusing on creating stronger wellness or health management programs, we recommend a broader lens be applied to the way organizations are structured in support of positive individual health.

Employees spot gimmicks quickly. If health and well-being are a top priority for the organization, then they need to see the CEO and leadership team take an active interest. When senior leadership is engaged, people pay attention and take notice. Leadership must understand, believe and actively speak about how a healthy lifestyle will improve well-being and how this is beneficial to both the company and individual employees. At Cummins, our leadership wants to provide the tools and resources to empower change.

Dexter Sherney, MD
Chief Medical Director/Executive Director Global Health/Wellness
Cummins Inc.

Broader systems thinking and a more comprehensive strategic framework are required to evolve more supportive workplace cultures and create sustainable improvements in employee health and flourishing.

In the remainder of this chapter, we outline emerging next practices for evolving healthy and thriving cultures in employer organizations. We also advocate for a much bigger way of thinking about what constitutes a healthy culture. We believe an expanded approach to developing a thriving culture is necessary to support positive organizational health. Organizations must have a more comprehensive understanding of what influences the fullest kind of health to support and develop thriving, creative, and high-performing employees. We then must do whatever it takes to align the culture and environment in support of positive individual and organizational health.

Why is it that we often design organizations as if people naturally shirk responsibility, do only what is required, resist learning, and can't be trusted to do the right thing? Yet, most of us would argue that we believe in the potential of people and that people are our most important organizational assets. If that is the case, why then do we frequently design organizations to satisfy our need for control and not to maximize the contributions of people?

—Abraham Maslow

Expanded Role of Operations Leaders

Strong collaboration between senior and operations leadership is essential throughout the process of creating a healthier environment and culture. Operations leaders play an important role throughout the process of engaging in developing shared values, creating a shared vision, and outlining a strategy for bringing the vision to life in the organization. To be maximally effective, undertaking the purposeful evolution of positive organizational health also requires close collaboration between senior and operations leaders and leaders throughout all levels of the organizations. Table 9 outlines current best practices and emerging "next" practices of relevance for operations leadership.

Envision This...

The vibe of this workplace is an enthusiastic hub of contributing individuals and engaging interactions. The excitement of meaningful work and individual autonomy is the underlying drive that sparks employees to get to work each day. The unique talents of employees are used and appreciated. An account team exchanges high fives for their high customer satisfaction scores and take some time to reflect on what specific actions they can take to continue their success. They're surprised at the recognition they receive by the CEO at the next company meeting. Good news travels fast! The CEO then announces that she has a personal goal to walk the stairs more and invites others to a friendly team competition to do the same. The winners choose a local nonprofit organization for a company donation.

What are some ways your company motivates employees in a personal and genuine way?

Angela Camilleri
Lead Innovation Strategist, Edington Associates

Table 9. Current "best" and emerging "next" practices that help support and create positive organizational health

Positive Organizational Health Concepts	Current "Best" Practices	Emerging "Next" Practices
Beyond Programs		
• Comprehensive population health-management programs	✓	✓
• Healthy organizational workplace environment and culture	*	✓
• Approaches built on Shared Values—Shared Results		✓
• A strategic, systematic, systemic, and sustainable ongoing positive transformation process that		
○ is guided by a comprehensive theory-based conceptual model that embodies the vision and guides the process;		✓
○ empowers creative employee design teams to develop innovative, native solutions;		✓
○ encourages systems thinking—nothing happens in isolation; everything is connected;		✓
○ focuses on building a positive future built on current points of strength;		✓
○ involves enterprise-wide collaboration with all stakeholders (internal and external);		✓
○ Work roles aligned with individual values and competencies.		✓
Beyond Individuals		
• Engaging and meaningful population approaches	✓	✓
• Approaches designed to build connections, strengthen relationships, and reinforce team collaboration		✓
Beyond the Organization		
• Include family and friends	✓	✓
• Build connections to the community	*	✓
• Participate in the larger economic and ecological context		✓
• Contribute to the larger ecology and economy—green company practices, community engagement, and value		✓

These practices have become more popular with more forward-thinking employers and service providers.

Before Zero Trends, Bendix Commercial Vehicle Systems LLC had a long-standing wellness program comprised of various annual initiatives but lacked an overall strategy that considered wellness as a key company metric. Zero Trends provided the foundation and rationale to begin thinking of wellness in the same way as the business injury rates and safety metrics that reflect the company safety culture.

Bendix realized that a wellness culture has to be created and driven with the same level of detail, focus, and support as any other critical business strategy. It is difficult to say which Zero Trends pillar is the most important as all pillars are required for success, but the lessons learned in the operational leadership pillar were the most important for driving employee engagement at Bendix. Holding supervisors and managers responsible for the wellness engagement of their employees is essential, and Bendix would not have taken this approach without Zero Trends.

Ed Casper
Occupational Health and Safety Manager
Bendix Commercial Vehicle Systems LLC

To read the full case study go to appendix B

We encourage readers, and especially individuals with operations roles, to think beyond current practices in several ways. First, think **beyond programs,** and beyond the historical focus on wellness and disease management initiatives. Even think beyond the recent influx of popular challenges and "game-ified" programs. These are all indicators of a company's commitment to employee health and well-being, and they can provide education and guidance for those who need and want it. However, they are not sufficient to create a sustainable impact on health and well-being in the long-term. There are often many competing forces in the environment and culture working against the good that existing programmatic wellness and wellness approaches alone can bring. A much more comprehensive approach will be needed.

CHE Trinity Health.

Recognizing a need to build a healthier internal community for employees and their families, CHE Trinity Health, began its journey into workplace wellness in 2008. The goal was to create a culture of health, wellness, and fulfillment, to effectively manage benefit plan costs and increase the productivity and competitiveness of the organization. The purpose statement of the initiative, called Live Your Whole Life, is "to nurture a culture that supports its employees' ability to care for themselves as well as they care for the patients they serve." Unlike many workplace wellness programs that focus solely on physical health, Live Your Whole Life leads with the concept of a healthy spirit. This is defined as "the capacity and ability of people to seek, experience, and express meaning and purpose in their lives often through love, hope, gratitude, forgiveness, peace, and community in order to enjoy a sense of the Sacred (as they understand it)."

Tammie Hansen, RN, COHN-S
Manager Total Rewards Benefits, Health Productivity & Wellness, CHE Trinity Health

To read the full case study go to appendix B

We also encourage organizations to think **beyond individuals** by engaging the total organization. As outlined in table 9, we encourage organizations to evolve healthy and thriving workplace environments and engage leaders throughout the organization in a systems-thinking process that emphasizes organization-wide connections and synergies.

Effective work teams and collaboration are needed to implement approaches that build strong connections among colleagues and to evolve a thriving culture of health. Collaborative and connected teams are also imperative for a healthy company bottom line.

Finally, to create positive organizational health, we encourage organizations to make connections with and add value to families and communities by thinking **beyond the organization.**

Collaboration Is Key to Success

It should be apparent at this point in the book that we believe collaboration between everyone within and associated with the organization is imperative for evolving a healthy workplace culture. Involvement and representation of all stakeholders are critical to the success of any important development effort, and it is crucial that everyone involved is highly cooperative. Both internal and external stakeholders will likely be part of the process.

> *Very often organizations are inflexible because there is too little communication between functions; they are too segregated. A lot of people in organizations are disengaged—there's a lot of research to show that. They turn part of themselves off when they get to work.*
>
> —Sir Ken Robinson[89]

Operations leaders are core to the process of developing positive organizational health, but one of the most important roles they will play is as facilitators for the kind of true collaboration that will be needed. While we challenge employer organizations to take their approaches to the next level, we are also challenging the health, wellness, and well-being industry to play a bigger role in this process. Organizations often have multiple third-party suppliers, vendors, or partners that help provide health and wellness services to their employees. In some ways, these players may have unknowingly contributed to the problem, but they are in a position to be a big part of the solution. We have witnessed a great deal of territorial behavior among these external vendors. To take our employees, our organizations, and our country to the next level of health and thriving, we urge a greater degree of collaboration and the mindset of a partner. While we challenge employer organizations to take their approaches to the next level, we are also challenging the health, wellness, and well-being industry to play a bigger role in this process.

Ultimately, the value of external suppliers should hinge on their willingness to think beyond their narrow business model and collaborate as real partners in service of their clients.

American Express hired Dr. Wayne Burton to achieve the financial services company's goal of improving the health and performance of its service centers' employees, leading to gains in productivity. Internal research indicated that investing more in the overall well-being of employees would translate to higher performance, better customer service and result in an increase in card member retention.

Health is not "one size fits all." Internationally, participation in the HRA has varied and depends on many factors including cultural factors, said Burton. "The incentives and rewards have to be carefully thought out. In India, there is a thirst for better health. Employees there realize the significant value of programs and services which are not otherwise generally available."

Healthy Living is tailored to be culturally relevant and attractive to local populations, so the program varies across geographies. For instance, in Mexico, medical claims data showed that a high incidence of gastrointestinal problems in the workforce was impacting performance. An emphasis on food safety and education has helped to address the problem. Strategies include an on-site cafeteria that offers fresh foods, a clean water supply, and education on proper refrigeration and food storage.

Today, the Healthy Living initiative results in an annual estimated productivity savings of $483 per participating employee in the United States. Burton meets with the global compensation and benefits team to discuss metrics and top management at American Express is regularly updated. Burton also shares results with senior leaders in major US locations, providing them with specific reports on their employees' health and productivity at least annually.

Wayne Burton, MD
Medical Director and Global Leader for Health and Productivity
American Express

To read the full case study go to appendix B

External Stakeholder Partners

To ensure true collaboration, it is important that all stakeholders, internal and external, operate as true partners throughout the process. With respect to third-party service providers, operating as a vendor, consultant, or partner is distinctly different. As defined by Merriam-Webster.com

> *vendor:* a person or company offering something for sale, especially a trader on the street, a business that sells a particular type of product

> *consultant:* a person who gives professional advice to companies for a fee

> *partner:* a person [or entity] who takes part in an undertaking with another or others, especially in business or company with shared risk and/or profits

In addition to operating as true partners, the appropriate leaders in the organization should require external partners to work in a fully collaborative manner with each other. This involves putting what is best for the organization first. While this may seem counterintuitive in the short-term, in the long run, service providers that become known as effective collaborators will have a competitive advantage over those who are more self-serving.

The foundation of a strong partnership is built on trust and transparency. Both parties are working strategically and collaboratively to achieve a common goal. Success happens when the lines between vendor and customer begin to blur and merge as one team with shared vision and results. It's a win-win for both organizations. We help each other succeed.

Lisa M Beck
Group Strategic Health Manager
Parker Hannifin Hydraulic and Filtration

Margaret D Bredehoft, DrPH
Managing Director, Vitalae
Wellness and Corporate Services

We believe that collaboration
will be the new competitive advantage.

Depending on how many third parties your organization works with, careful management of the complex third-party relationships may be required. There are many ways to promote and support wellness and well-being. No one partner or service provider we are aware of has all the answers, plus there is a rich collective wisdom in multidisciplinary or multi-sector partnerships that no one partner can bring. The list on the next page outlines just a few of the potential third-party partners your organization may have:

- wellness companies
- on-site, near-site medical clinics
- health systems
- benefits consultants
- health plans
- community resources
- fitness centers
- other external consultants

We understand third-party partners have to make a profit, but we encourage bigger thinking—systems thinking—thinking about the impact the longer term viability of their clients brings to society, the sustainability of the organization, and the value of their partnership in the long term. For organizations, we strongly encourage thinking about whether you intend for your current or prospective vendors to "teach you to fish" or just work to become your permanent supplier of fish. The health and wellness of organizations and employee populations are too important to be compromised by the profit motive of third-party consultants and service providers.

Internal Stakeholders Partners

In addition to senior and operations leaders, there are many other internal stakeholders that should be involved in the process of designing approaches for evolving positive organizational health. It is important that all internal partners understand the importance of the process and the stakes associated with continuing with business as usual. Below is a partial list of possible internal partners:

- business development
- wellness coordinator
- unions
- human resources
- communications
- organizational development
- training and development
- strategy
- quality
- safety
- marketing and sales

Collaborative relationships between internal partners with respect to health and well-being are core to ensuring the success of the overall effort.

An Experience

"...we like working with you and to continue, here is what we need..."

During an early experience with Steelcase (The mid-1980s), the benefits director at the time, Marshall Beard, called a meeting of their healthcare insurers in the Grand Rapids area. His opening remarks went something like this: "We at Steelcase really value working with each of you but to continue our relationship going forward, we want you to provide all of Steelcase's healthcare claims data to the University of Michigan Health Management Research Center, where they will integrate the data combination with other data in their integrated database.

This will allow us and you to get a bigger picture of health and wellness at Steelcase."

Of course, each of the organizations agreed, but it took us three additional meetings and three years before the data arrived in a usable format (although each organization had their own format). In the meantime, each of the insurers was convinced that they had the answer to Marshall's question, and they individually tried to up-sell to Steelcase. Marshall was firm in his commitment to work with all the insurers, and he prevailed. To the defense of the insurers, at that stage in the history of healthcare claims their data systems were set up as transactional systems to facilitate payments from patients and Steelcase. It took them three years to transform the systems to ICD-9 format by individual interaction.

PostScript. The Steelcase study continued for twenty years (1982–2002).

Collaboration Between External and Internal Partners

Ideally, full collaboration would exist between all partners within an organization, between internal and external partners, and between external partners (see figure 11). As a marker of early success, all partners must work together to develop a shared understanding of the opportunity and shared commitment to the collaboration. They must all ultimately engage in open-minded dialogue about the different interpretations of the opportunity and collective intelligence about how to contribute to a win-win journey.

We believe collaboration is the new competitive advantage, and highly proprietary service providers will eventually fall by the wayside. Agility, open-mindedness, foresight, and the ability to learn and incorporate new ideas as they emerge will be the hallmark of successful collaborations.

Figure 11. A sampling of internal and external partners with potential impact on the health and well-being of the organization and employees

External stakeholders who do not fully collaborate
with the organization's best interests in mind
are not true partners—they are only vendors.

The Value of a Program Theory and Framework

There is nothing so practical as a good theory.

—Kurt Lewin

As you undertake efforts to enhance or develop your approach to evolve your culture and environment, we believe it is critically important to outline your explicit theory for the approach. Some people hear the word "theory" and think of esoteric academic ramblings with little real world value. But theory is crucial for developing effective approaches to activate real world change. There are several different types of very practical theory for enhancing and guiding practice:

1) ***Big-Picture, or System-Level Theories***—These theories attempt to explain the larger system-level influences on health and well-being.

2) ***Change Theory***—Change theories explain why you would expect the program or approach to have an impact on the outcomes you intend to improve. Change theories provide the grounding for interventions in many wellness programs today.

3) ***Program or Action Theory***—The overall theory of intended operations and expected effects on outcomes is the third type of theory important for any initiative. How is the program intended to support the change process?

We briefly discuss each type of theory, and why it is important to your efforts to evolve a healthy environment and culture. These types of theories should be considered together to provide the highest value for helping ground your overall effort to develop positive organizational health.

> *NOTE: As we discuss "programs" in the context of theory, we have adopted the CDC's very broad definition of a program as "any set of organized activities supported by a set of resources to achieve a specific and intended result."*

Big Picture, or System-Level Theories

Recognition of the importance of the influence of organizational culture and environment on health has grown over the past decade. Theories that help us make sense of these broader influences are gaining recognition in the wellness field. These bigger-picture theories emphasize the influence of context on health. Socioecological models, including person-environment fit and systems theory, attempt to explain and improve the relationship between people and their surrounding environments. They consider multiple levels of influence on specific health behaviors. This can include intra- and interpersonal factors like knowledge, demographics, attitudes, social networks, social supports, families, and friends. Organizational influences like organizational environment, culture, climate, leadership and management styles, work groups, organizational structure, and communication networks are important. Societal influences, community resources, and neighborhood organizations are also relevant in these bigger-picture theories.

A thoughtful general framework for understanding the environmental, cultural, and human factors that can influence individuals across a population can be very useful for guiding the development and evaluation of approaches designed to evolve healthy and thriving workplaces and workforces. Bigger-picture theories usually represent some level of systems-thinking.

The model of positive organizational health introduced in chapter 3 is our representation of a very broad theory about the influence of employer organizations and the internal and external social, cultural, and environmental context on the health and thriving of employees.

Change Theory

Most health improvement programs are based on the idea that changing poor lifestyle habits can result in better health and reduce the risk and costs of chronic illness. There is increasing recognition of the value of grounding health improvement programs in sound behavior change theory, and there have been many theories proposed to explain health behaviors. The most utilized type of theory for wellness programs to date has been theories of individual change. Examples include James Prochaska's transtheoretical model,[90] the health belief model,[91] social learning theory (especially self-efficacy, social cognitive theory),[92] and motivational interviewing.[93] While these theories often include larger contextual influences, the use of these theories in the wellness and well-being field has been focused primarily on influencing individual motivation, attitudes, and ultimately behaviors.

When developing approaches, stakeholders can discuss their individual and collective ideas about how the initiatives and programs will create the expected outcomes or change. This could involve describing all the various elements of the overall effort and how they are expected to lead to the outcomes that matter to stakeholders throughout the organization.

In short, a change theory explicitly outlines why you think your program or strategy will lead to the change you expect.

Program Model or Action Theory

Between good intentions and great results lies a program theory—
not just a list of tasks but a vision of what needs to happen, and how.

—Sue Funnell[94]

Another important theory for any kind of program is the overall theory of its intended operations and effects. Outlining the overall program theory is an important component of designing, implementing, and evaluating your program. Leonard Bickman, Professor of Psychology, Psychiatry and Public Policy, Peabody College at Vanderbilt University, defines program theory as "the construction of a plausible and sensible model of how a program is supposed to work."[95]

Huey Chen, director for the Center for Evaluation and Applied Research in the College of Health Professions at Mercer University, provides a more detailed definition of program theory as "a set of explicit or implicit assumptions by stakeholders about what action is required to solve a social, educational, or health problem and why the problem will respond to this action." A program theory includes the identification of program resources, activities and expected program outcomes, and the specification of a chain of causal assumptions linking program resources, activities, intermediate outcomes, and ultimate goals.[96]

Theory has many practical applications including as a planning tool during the design of the program and the outline of an intervention pathway, and to shape both the evaluation processes and outcomes reporting strategy. Ultimately, program theories can be valuable tools to help program planners and stakeholders better understand how their programs and initiatives are expected to work and comprehend the full impact of their efforts.

As part of your program design efforts, explicitly outline the program theory—or the expectations of how the program(s), initiatives, policies, benefits, and so forth—will actually operate. How will they be implemented? Who is the target audience(s)? This process can help stakeholders understand the full range of impacts and the expected time frame for generating the ultimate desired outcomes.

The framework provided by the program theory can help set the agenda for a comprehensive evaluation-reporting plan that can provide useful information on outcomes at relevant points throughout the lifecycle of the program. It will also provide opportunities to demonstrate early program successes and determine if the program is working as expected in enough time for corrective action by program implementers.[97] As part of building your program theory, it may be important to work collaboratively with organizational stakeholders to develop explicit success metrics for short-, intermediate-, and longer-term program outcomes. Please see appendix D for helpful resources on using theory in your planning.

Co-Create a Win-Win Strategy

As you embark upon developing your overall strategy for positive organizational and individual health, it may be helpful to engage a group of key stakeholders to outline the broad boundaries of your health-related efforts in each of the five pillar areas. This process can be undertaken either before, following, or concurrent with your efforts to outline the relevant theories for your overall approach.

Gather Your Support Material

As you begin to develop your strategy, gather your summarized material from the preparation phase of the journey and findings from the Positive Organizational Health Assessment (see chapter 8). This will provide invaluable information about previous successful local approaches that can be scaled throughout the organization. It will also contain information and insights that can point you to high-priority opportunities for improvement. Also, keep in mind the values that your employees and organization share (shared values), and the results that matter to all stakeholders (shared results).

The strategy grid in figure 12 might be a helpful tool as you consider the boundaries of your efforts and the types of initiatives to use in your organization. Our goal here is to provide a tool to help stretch your thinking as you shape your strategic plan. As you outline your general strategy for evolving a healthier environment and culture, you may want to consider how far out into the larger system of influence you intend to reach for each pillar—either to impact or access resources from that level. Are there initiatives that can influence each of the levels in each pillar (individual, organizational, home and family, community, and society)? For some pillars, you may want to focus solely on your employees and the organization. For others, you may want to extend your strategy to include influencing the home and family, or community.

Figure 12. Strategy grid for the win-win journey

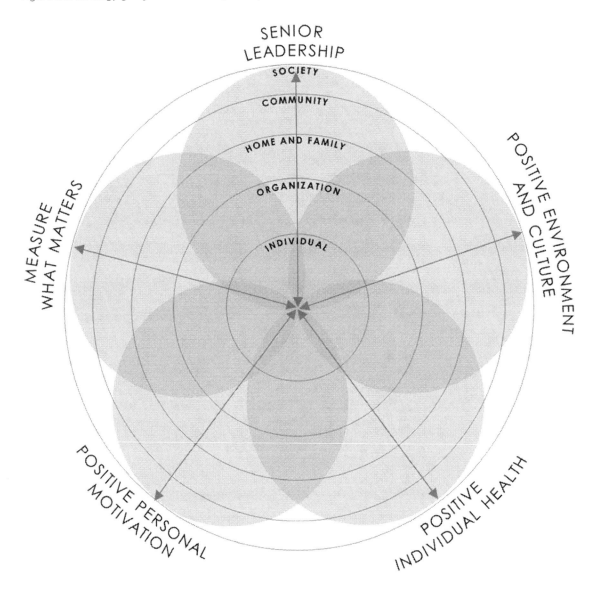

We encourage thinking beyond, whenever possible, to the community as well. General questions at this stage can include the following:

- Will your efforts include the families of employees?

- Will you consider surrounding communities in your approach? Ask the following questions:

    o   How can the health and vitality of your organization and employees bring value to your community?

    o   How can your community and its resources bring value to your employees?

- What are the relevant influences on each area related to health and well-being?

- What potential initiatives can be created and implemented for each pillar at each of the levels you intend to impact or access?

There is no one way to do this, no right way, and it is not required. It is just a resource you can use if you think it would help with the strategy development process. As you work through this process, you may want to consider the following three things for each of the ideas you identify in the exercise above:

- How much do you care about it?

- How much can you influence it?

Figure 13 depicts the "sweet spot" representing the overlap between those two things. You will not be able to do everything at once, so you will need to prioritize the efforts and implement the high-value initiatives that are most likely to succeed and generate enthusiasm and engagement. You can phase in other efforts over time.

Figure 13. What do you care about, and what can you Influence?

This is a good example of where a design team can help with the process. For the general strategic planning, this could involve a group of senior leaders from throughout various areas of the organization with a variety of backgrounds. Once the general strategy is outlined, employee design teams could be convened to brainstorm ideas for the initiatives that will bring the strategy to life.

Connect the Dots Between Your Vision, Goals, and Objectives

In chapter 9, we presented an example vision that reflects a company's commitment to creating strength in all five fundamental pillars (see Vision for Employee Health and Thriving, page 114). We provide an example (specifically for the senior leadership sub-vision) for how you might connect the ideas you generated using the strategy grid with specific goals and strategic imperatives that directly serve your vision in table 10.

In this example, the specific vision for leadership serves the overall vision for employee health and thriving. Plus, each of the listed objectives and strategic imperatives provides guidance about how leaders can operate on a day-to-day basis to help bring the organization's vision to life. Some companies we have worked with ask their individual leaders to outline tangible personal goals they can work toward to be part of this process.

Journey Roadmap

As you develop your strategy, you may find it useful to create a visual roadmap that outlines the stages of the journey, the roles of the people throughout the company that will be part of the journey process, and the general time frame for the stages. At a minimum, we recommend that you outline the general phases of a win-win journey, a general depiction of the effort required of stakeholders in each phase in the journey, and a brief description of what occurs during each phase.

Your roadmap will depend on the design sensibility of your organization's culture and the character of your organization's win-win journey. There are many potential designs that can be used for your roadmap, and we won't presume to prescribe what that should look like for your organization. The purpose of the roadmap should be to provide a high-level guidance and generally inspire others to see themselves as part of the journey and engage in the ongoing process.

Table 10. Example vision, objectives, and strategic imperatives for pillar 1: visible and thriving leadership

Overall Vision for Employee Health and Thriving

We are widely recognized as having a healthy and supportive work environment with passionate, thriving employees driven to contribute to their fullest potential in their work, their communities, and their families.

Specific Vision for Leadership

Our leadership demonstrates commitment to employee well-being by their visible efforts to develop a healthy culture and environment and actively engage in the Company's health promotion efforts.

Leader Objective(s)	Strategic Imperatives for Leaders
Adopt a vision for a thriving culture	Create and promote a health culture vision
	Adopt and formally communicate a culture vision to complement and support employee health in the corporate vision
Manage the vision as a business strategy	Emphasize employee health as a business strategy through the use of health and well-being metrics alongside other core business metrics
	Indicators of employee health, quality, safety, and bottom-line all belong together in the forefront of executives' thinking
	Implement continuous improvement strategies informed by regular reporting on all components of the comprehensive evaluation strategy
Wellness leadership training	Promote wellness leadership throughout the organization
	All leaders (executives, directors, and managers) will participate in wellness leadership training
	Make your wellness goals visible
Become a positive role model	Walk the walk
	Share your enthusiasm for adopting a health and wellness philosophy in your own life
	Talk informally about personal efforts to adopt healthier lifestyle practices
	Participate in organizational health and wellness activities
	Integrate fitness activities at work, for example, by having walking meetings
	Demonstrate a healthy work-life balance and healthy methods for dealing with stress—Employees will follow senior leader examples

Inspire and Lead a Movement

Imagine an entire movement to bring about a vibrant culture of well-being at your organization, where people are drawn together for the very reason of encouraging and living full and energetic lives filled with gratitude and purpose.

Once you have a vision for what it would look like to be part of a thriving and healthy workplace, what motivates you to run wholeheartedly towards this vision?

The movement toward a thriving culture of health can begin from the top-level management, or from a frontline team. Senior leaders, operational leaders, wellness champions, and self-leaders— **anyone can start a movement**. Think of Rosa Parks as an example of a self-leader who helped to advance the famous civil rights movement. Small actions are powerful when they represent taking risks that go against the norm in support of a larger cause. The most important point about a movement is that it's not about things. It's not about building a comprehensive wellness program. It's not about a beautifully branded communication plan for wellness activities. It's not about having more participants than last year. It's not about wearable devices or gadgets, or even the number of "likes" on a social network website.

Movements are about connecting people who share something they deeply care about to be part of something bigger than themselves. Being inspired by a movement stems from an intrinsic desire for people to share what they love by whatever means they have at their disposal.

In the last ten years or so, company health programs that encourage fitness and good habits among employees have become something of a trend. But one of the greatest influences I've seen is when I first announced that I was planning to run a 100-mile race in India. Almost from the moment I announced my race, I noticed a change in the office. My colleagues were interested in my progress as well as their own fitness routines. Employees began signing up for races, CrossFit classes, and even kickball. It became natural to talk about things like weekend exercise excursions, stretching, injuries and gear. It seems my fitness goals unexpectedly engaged the imagination of the office.

David W. Fouse
Partner, The Pinkston Group Public Relations

Movements are not a temporary fad. They shake things up to produce a long-lasting change in the existing culture. A movements is exactly what we're hoping to achieve: prevailing transformation for positive organizational health. What would it be like if every workplace with a wellness program shook up the status quo and started their own homespun and authentic movement toward positive organizational health within their organization? This energy of shared well-being spreads through families, to communities, faith organizations, and other places where people congregate. Little by little, as momentum builds, those positive outliers of health would be joined by those hovering around the norm and everyone along the continuum of health benefits. The collective result would be one of astonishing, life-giving, genuine, widespread change.

> *The role of traditional branding is to influence behavior. The difference with movements is to inspire behavior. So don't try to influence; get out of that business. Now is the time to inspire. People don't want to be influenced. There is a negative connotation associated with that, like you're trying to control their minds and actions. But people long to be inspired. And inspiring them to action is a win-win.*[98]
>
> —Justine Foo, PhD of Complex Systems and the Brain Sciences
> Brains on Fire

In the remaining chapters, we outline how to lay the groundwork and create the conditions that will help ignite and spread a movement of health and well-being in your organization.

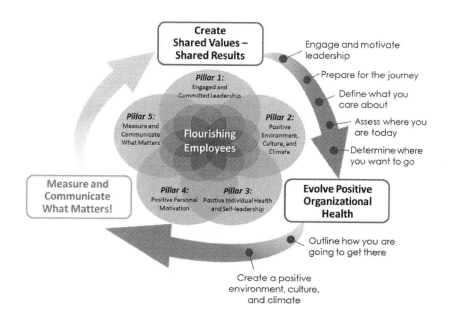

CHAPTER 11:
Create a Positive Environment, Culture, and Climate

Creating positive organizational health is not just a cost containment or human resource issue, it is also a strategic enterprise-wide issue.

Fully-employed Americans spend a large percentage of their waking hours at work,[99] so the workplace environment and culture play a very significant role in our health and well-being. The importance of integrating positive individual and organizational health into the work environment and culture is one of the most significant recent trends in workforce health management. Thomas Golaszewski, Judd Allen, and other colleagues have been promoting the value of healthy organizational environments and cultures (respectively) for several decades. But it has only been in the past several years that organizations have begun to embrace the central role that environment and culture play in health and vitality in the workplace. A 2011 survey showed that while only one-third of the responding organizations indicated that they had a culture of health, 80 percent said they intended to make efforts to improve their health cultures in the next year.[100] Some studies indicate that the culture of an organization has a potentially larger impact on the health of the employee population than the health, wellness, and well-being program-ming offered by that organization.[101-103]

Culture isn't the most important thing in the world; it's the only thing.
It is the thing that drives the business.

—Jim Sinegal
Costco CEO (retired 2012)

In *Zero Trends,* we embraced organizational environments and cultures of health as core to supporting and sustaining the health of employees. While providers of wellness and well-being services are beginning to adopt methods to help employers improve their cultures with respect to health, the health culture of an organization is not something that can be "fixed" by programs alone. Before diving into the nuts and bolts of how we suggest you begin to evolve a healthy environment, culture, and climate, we describe what we mean by each.

Healthy Environment, Culture, and Climate

For our purposes, we consider the environment to be the workplace features that support health and well-being that are measured as part of the environmental audit we discussed in chapter 8. This includes, but is not limited to, the personnel management process, policies, and employee benefits. It also includes the physical environment of the workplace (e.g., the grounds, the building layout, the interior design, access to natural light, etc.), organizational structure, and the developmental resources available within and surrounding the organization. Basically, these are tangible features of the workplace and job characteristics that impact employee health and thriving.

We define well-being as the overall welfare of an employee. This goes beyond fitness to include physical, nutrition, mental, emotional and spiritual wellness. We choose the programs we offer based on the idea of enrichment in all these areas.

Andrew Scibelli
Manager, Employee Health & Well-Being
NextEra Energy

While there is growing agreement that a culture of health is important, there is less agreement on what constitutes a "culture of health" and even less about how to purposefully cultivate a healthy workplace culture. In fact, the term organizational "culture" is often used to describe what could more accurately be called organizational "climate." Although culture and climate overlap to some degree, organizational climate is related to employee perceptions of the organization's practices and workplace.[104] In an organization with a positive health-related climate, employees would value health and well-being, have an optimistic and positive outlook about health and thriving, and strive to live according to their personal values and purpose.

Just like the lizard changes color to reflect its surroundings, people similarly change behavior to reflect their environments (the chameleon effect). Thus, with respect to worksite health promotion, to create healthy employees, create healthy environments; the site where employees will inhabit thirty-five, forty or more hours per week. A healthy environment contains structural features that make healthy behaviors convenient and easy, such as the presence of a fitness center, walkable stairways, and healthy food choices; but also a culture that collectively values personal health, normalizes healthy choices, believes in the tenets of health promotion and socially supports its practice. Last, a healthy work environment utilizes administrative practices that tie these multidimensional features into a coordinated and efficiently working whole.

A workplace health initiative that relies on employee programs is destined for mediocrity. Programs are useful, and most times necessary, but hardly sufficient for long-term and widespread population behavior change. Humans don't learn negative health habits by completing programs; they learn them through a confluence of experiences from living in unhealthy structural and social environments. Therefore, reverse the process. If healthy employees are desired, first create and then maintain healthy workplaces.

It is unthinkable that a responsible company would not utilize its best administrative practices to ensure the success of any major initiative. If workplace health is taken seriously, it would apply the same administrative framework that any other major workplace initiative enjoys.

Tom Golaszewski, EdD
Retired Professor SUNY Brockport, President/CEO, Golaszewski and Associates

Organizational culture runs deeper than climate and includes the shared values, norms, and practices of the individuals in the organization. This distinction is important because evolving a healthy culture takes a true marriage between the artifacts, customs, norms, and practices in organizations and the collective spirit in which they are operationalized and lived over time. Both culture and climate are critical to cultivating a thriving and healthy place to work. Regardless of any purposeful efforts to evolve a culture, what matters in the end is how the culture is perceived by employees. In effect, you could say that evolving a culture can influence climate (employee perceptions) both locally and globally in the organization. Patterns and fluctuations in the organizational climate will ultimately determine the true long-term culture. As employees live the values and engage in norms and rites related to health and thriving, the culture is strengthened, and climate improves. It is a virtuous cycle.

The Centers for Disease Control and Prevention defines a culture of health as follows:

> Culture of health is the creation of a working environment where employee health and safety is valued, supported and promoted through workplace health programs, policies, benefits, and environmental supports. Building a culture of health involves all levels of the organization and establishes the workplace health program as a routine part of business operations aligned with overall business goals. The results of this culture change include engaged and empowered employees, an impact on healthcare costs, and improved worker productivity.

We applaud the effort of the CDC to provide a working definition of a culture of health, and we agree culture is partially influenced by programs, policies, benefits, and environmental support. However, culture is also about relationships throughout the organization and how people respect, trust, and interact with each other, guided by a core set of shared values.

> For decades, there has been an effort to try and control the cost of health insurance. Whether it was the HMO, consumer-driven health plans, medical home, ACO's, or the Affordable Care Act, none have been able to achieve this goal. Health insurance costs have outpaced inflation rates for over 25 years and they continue to increase. Wellness programs have proliferated the marketplace with small effect. The only way to manage costs is for employers to actively manage the health of their employees. The company of the future is going to be intimately involved with creating the healthy and engaged workforce of the future.
>
> Alan Wang
> President, UBF Consulting

The workplace culture can impact our health and well-being on many levels, including physical, mental, social, and spiritual. Ideally, our workplaces would be a source of positive impact and at the very least not erode our health and well-being. Even the most beautifully designed wellness programs won't be effective in a toxic workplace culture. However, effectively and purposefully shaping a culture cannot be undertaken lightly. It takes a clear shared vision and shared values created and embraced by all employees throughout the company—from the CEO to the front line workers. It also takes a strategic, systematic, systemic and sustainable approach that is about more than just increasing the visibility of wellness programs, or pushing harder on employees to participate in them.

Chipotle Creates Well-Being as Part of Their Culture

Chipotle Mexican Grill, a restaurant provider of "food with integrity," wanted to develop a well-being program and change its company culture. The "plug and play" wellness program the company was using through its healthcare provider had no leadership support and garnered dismal employee participation and engagement. The company wanted to build a culture of well-being that matched the culture it had built around food; that is, with integrity and with a program that everybody would believe in and value. This required an innovative, multifaceted strategy that would increase engagement in the well-being program; create a culture of happy, healthy, and highly productive employees; reduce lifestyle risk factors such as obesity, sedentary lifestyle, and stress; and save on healthcare costs.

Colleen M. Reilly, MBA/MSM
President, Total Well-Being

To read the full case study go to appendix B

Incorporating health into a culture does not happen overnight. It is an evolution. Like any evolution, creating a thriving workplace and workforce culture will take time—time to create a shared vision, time to communicate and live the vision consistently, time to evolve shared accountability, and time to build trust, and the patience and acceptance to persist while the evolution unfolds.

The Whitehall Study of British civil servants and other similar studies in Europe have shown that having a miserable job is a big risk for mortal hazard, and in turn, high health spending. The culture of an organization can make workers lives better or worse. Probably the biggest thing an employer can do to improve the health of its employees is to make significant improvements in its management style. Here's an example. When something goes wrong, as will inevitably happen in any organization, there are two contrasting ways to deal with it. Alas, the first, easiest, and most common approach is it to find someone to blame, which is punitive, creates fear, and adds to workplace misery and poor health. The superior approach is for management to look for defects in processes and then set about fixing those. This second style creates a culture of teamwork and productivity, and de-stresses the workplace, all of which in turn leads to a healthier environment. I've led process-improvement initiatives in one of the world's largest corporations and seen first hand how such improvements in management style lead to fewer workers comp claims, fewer sick days, and less turnover...all signs of improved health and well-being of workers.

Tom Emerick
President, Emerick Consulting

Current Best and Emerging Next Practices for Evolving Your Environment, Culture, and Climate

In chapter 10, we outlined current best and emerging next practices that operations leaders should attend to when working to develop a plan for a win-win strategy. We emphasized thinking beyond programs, beyond individuals, and beyond the organization. Here we build on those emerging next practices by going deeper into the specifics of what both organizations and individuals can do to create better health-related environments, cultures, and climates (see table 11 for a summary).

Table 11. Current best and emerging next practices for evolving a healthy environment, culture, and climate

Positive Organizational Health Concepts	Current Best Practices	Emerging Next Practices
What can organizations do to create better health-related environments, cultures, and climates?		
• Inspire engaged and passionate leaders.	✓	✓
• Develop and support all leaders and managers.		✓
• Encourage positive leadership practices.		✓
• Foster transformational leadership.		✓
• Enhance positive energy networks.		✓
• Foster collaboration:		
o Encourage and develop "design thinkers."		✓
o Provide conditions for group flow.		✓
o Foster collegial connections.		✓
• Design health into the environment:		
o Architect healthier workplace choices.		✓
o Working environments that nurture our evolutionary roots.		✓
What can employees do to create a better health-related environment, culture, and climate?		
• Be Part of the Solution—engage in employee design teams.		✓
• Find your element.		✓
• Re-design your job.		✓
• Curate your personal culture.		✓
• Personal choice architecture.		✓
• Architect a healthier social milieu.		✓

Throughout the rest of this chapter, we outline the science and philosophies that have most influenced our thinking. We also provide practical methods you can use in your organization to make a positive difference in the health-related environment, culture and climate.

Positive Organizational Fundamentals

Positive organizational scholarship (POS) aligns particularly well with our philosophy of positive organizational health, so our approach draws heavily from POS tenets and practices. Soon after the positive psychology movement began studying how individuals flourish and thrive, the field of positive organizational scholarship (POS) purposefully began to extend the research of optimum functioning to the workplace. Kim Cameron, Jane Dutton, Robert Quinn, and others from the University of Michigan's Ross School of Business began POS as a field of study in 2003. POS is based on the scientific study of the positive attributes of an organization and seeks to understand how the vitality of organizations contributes to human strengths and cultivates resilient individuals and groups.[105,106] For example, how can teams excel to their full potential and achieve extraordinary performance? How can organizations learn to become virtuous and flourish in the most positive ways possible?

Organizational research has traditionally focused on wealth capital and financial acumen as the main way to define success, but organizations are composed of both economic and human capital. POS explores the human side of organizational success on a social and psychological level. At the core of human capital is the concept of virtuousness. Virtues are those ennobling traits, such as compassion, caring, creativity, gratitude, and growth. In organizational settings, virtuousness is found through the dynamics of work relationships, team interactions, job output, management styles, and structural processes.

Just as individuals may possess virtuousness at varying levels, these same traits are displayed by an organization as a collective entity. Virtuousness within an organization is intricately woven into its culture. A virtuous organization has a positive impact on individuals, exhibits moral goodness, and benefits society on a larger scale without expectation of reward. This organizational embodiment of goodness goes beyond corporate responsibility since there is no implication of reciprocity, but instead it is intrinsically motivated to do good.

Research findings from the field of POS have shown that organizational virtuousness and positive dynamics within organizations are significantly related to improved outcomes including productivity, quality, innovation, employee retention, customer satisfaction, and profitability.[107,108] POS offers valuable empirical insights into what types of organizational functioning and practices contribute to human vitality in a workplace culture. This, in turn, impacts the health and well-being of a workforce. Intentional practices that embrace optimism, abundance, and gratitude have tremendous potential for making a positive impact on individuals and organizations.

What Can Organizations Do?

Perhaps we should begin to seek out the creativity and innovation killers in our organizations instead of trying to fix the people within?

—Abraham H. Maslow

Inspire Engaged and Passionate Leaders

Everyone in the organization contributes to a culture, but senior leaders often have the most direct responsibility for it, and the most capacity for strong influence. While their time and effort toward the journey will likely be greatest in the preparation stage, their ongoing engagement can be incredibly powerful throughout the win-win journey. What does this leadership look like? How can leaders embrace and live the vision and generate enthusiasm in others? They must, at a minimum, support and endorse the wellness program and initiatives. Ideally, leaders throughout the organization will do everything in their power to ensure the organization's environment and culture support and create healthy and thriving employees. Leaders can embody several levels of support when it comes to employee health and thriving:

- *Talk the talk*—When leaders give lip service to health and well-being, yet ignore unhealthy behaviors, the positive evolution of culture likely will not occur.

- *Walk the talk*—When leaders speak out about the importance of health and well-being, and visibly live the principles they are espousing, they make an intentional effort to connect action to the communication plan about wellness.

- *Walk the walk*—When the support for positive organizational health becomes completely ingrained in the way leaders operate throughout the organization (systemic and sustainable), it is truly woven into the tapestry of the organization. The genuine way leaders embrace is naturally and spontaneously observed and communicated.

The following from Abraham Maslow's essential work on management perfectly expresses the core meaning and implications of an engaged leader who truly walks the walk:

It is important to remember that corporations are a large collection of human beings connecting with each other. It is all very personal. We are people talking to people—human beings sitting next to one another trying to accomplish a goal. When the alignment we speak of works, the human part of the organization is very well connected. This also changes the role of the leader. The leader has to believe in these concepts. It has to be dripping from his or her pores, or people will know (and they always do) that it is nothing more than talk. And the charisma of the leader is not what it's about. The stirring speech is not what it's about. The beautifully written mission statement is not what it's about. It sounds trite, but it's leading by example, meaning what you say, standing for something, and being willing to take action when what the company stands for is violated. How does this concept of the leader you have described fit with the alignment of personal and organizational goals? If alignment really exists throughout the organization, when the company runs into hardship, you don't have to look to that one visionary leader for the strategy or the answers.

Leaders who walk the walk are truly engaged. By engaged, we mean more than participating in programs. We mean engaged in the business of evolving positive organizational health. We also mean engaged in living a healthy and balanced approach to work and life. If the senior leaders are engaged, others in the organization are more likely to become engaged as well. Leaders can engage on both professional and personal levels. On a professional level, senior leaders can demonstrate engagement by actively participating in the work of developing a comprehensive strategy for improving their organization's environment and culture. According to Edgar Schein, leaders help create a culture based on:[109]

Talented people leave work environments, voluntarily or involuntarily, when they know their supervisors don't share their values, demonstrate an emotional heart, or show any interest in their personal growth.

—Rose Gantner
Author, Workplace Performance With a Purpose

- what they pay attention to, measure and control;

- their reaction to critical incidents;

- their criteria for resource allocation;

- role modeling, teaching, and coaching;

- their observed way of allocating rewards and status;

- their observed criteria for recruitment, selection, promotion, retirement, and excommunication.

Leaders can also express their engagement and commitment by participating in—or ideally leading—the core team, attending strategic planning meetings, attending meetings designed to communicate information from the positive organizational health assessment process, and generally being visible and available to shepherd the overall journey. It is their job to

- remind people of what's important;

- stay focused on the vision;

- remove obstacles;

- encourage action;

- empower others to take action.

On a personal level, leaders can engage by being visible and active with their personal practices to maintain or improve their health and well-being. This includes not only physical health, but also mental, spiritual, social, and intellectual health, or any dimensions of health they personally value.

The task of organizational leadership is to create an alignment of strengths in ways that make a system's weaknesses irrelevant.

—Peter Drucker

Nelnet, a provider of innovative educational products and services, was looking to reenergize their wellness program. Since 2006 they had decreased their healthcare costs by ten percent and wanted to sustain the savings and keep the trend flat. In partnership with Total Well-Being, a corporate well-being consulting company, Nelnet focused on simplifying their offerings, creating a more fun and culturally relevant tracking tool as well as increasing their leadership and operational engagement in the program. This program also included the introduction of a consumer-directed health plan that also built-in a level of health awareness and personal accountability among all employees. They saved 20 percent in the first two years and have kept their costs flat over the past six years even with population growth. They truly have built a sustainable culture of well-being on all levels, and it is an integral part of the way they do business, recruit, and retain the right type of people, and sustain a great place to work!

Colleen M. Reilly
President, Total Well-Being

Develop and Support All Leaders and Managers

Ideally, at this stage of the win-win journey, leaders and managers will have embraced their role in this process and understand the value it will bring to themselves and the organization. Even so, it is important to provide them with opportunities to develop their abilities to support their team members in ways that contribute positively to both their own and their team members' their health and well-being. Earlier we mentioned the quote from Bill O'Brien, the former CEO of Hanover Insurance: "The success of an intervention depends on the interior condition of the intervener." In his book, *The Fifth Discipline,* Peter Senge talks about "personal mastery" as a core discipline to help leaders develop their "interior condition."

People with a high level of personal mastery are able to consistently realize the results that matter most deeply to them—in effect, they approach their life as an artist would approach a work of art. They do that by becoming committed to their own lifelong learning.

Personal mastery is the process of continually engaging in practices that support a sense of individual purpose, values, and vision. Senge's concept of personal mastery is strongly related to our concept of self-leadership. Practicing the art of seeing things through a combination of lenses (objective, subjective, and intuitive) is an important part of this process.

In every organization we have worked with so far, the middle and frontline leaders have been the least enthusiastic about efforts to support positive health and thriving. It is not because they don't care about the health and well-being of the people they supervise. Asking managers to add responsibility for the health and well-being of their team members can seem overwhelming at first. They have full-time "day jobs" with full-time pressures and stresses. Many have not developed the specific skills it takes to support employee health and well-being. Also, the behavior of midlevel leaders is influenced by what senior leaders allow and expect. It is dictated by their job design and perhaps by their personal beliefs, as well as by the internal culture. When expectations and job design in organizations include responsibility and accountability for supporting health and thriving in direct reports, and when organizations give leaders and managers opportunities to develop their leadership skills in this respect, they will be more likely to evolve their support in a genuine manner.

I see why people participate as a subtopic of why people don't. I think the biggest challenge for the field is the unremarkable stats related to engagement. We haven't been successful in moving a critical mass of a target population to committed, sustained action that is linked to a defined outcome.

If I was going to write a book for the practitioner/employer communities it would be on this topic. Creating a "culture of health" is critical, but something is still missing and incentives are not the answer either. We talk of intrinsic motivation and self-leadership, but I see this only in a small minority of individuals. I believe the literature defines the attributes of this group: self-efficacy, confidence, goal focused, enjoyment/self-satisfaction, etc., but we haven't been very successful in getting others to drink the Kool-Aid.

George J. Pfeiffer, MSE, FAWHP
President, The WorkCare Group
President, International Association for Worksite Health Promotion

Over the past few decades, many important theories have surfaced to explain leadership and its impact on others. There is a growing amount of research on organizational factors and leadership styles as they influence job satisfaction,[110] employee engagement,[111] employee passion,[112] and employee well-being.[113] The good news is that the evidence is converging to support the idea that positive organizational practices, positive leadership styles, and positive psychology interventions can help employees thrive not only in their work but physically, mentally, emotionally and spiritually in all aspects of their life.[114,115] Positive leadership and transformational leadership are among the more popular leadership approaches, and they are in keeping with our positive philosophy for organizations. There are many more leadership theories and strategies that can be used to develop effective leaders, but due to space limitations, we will only summarize these two.

Encourage Positive Leadership Practices

The relatively new field of positive leadership is gaining traction and facilitating positive deviance in the world of business. It was founded by Kim Cameron (also one of the founders of positive organizational scholarship discussed earlier in this chapter), Robert Quinn, and Jane Dutton, and others at the University of Michigan's Ross School of Business. Positive leadership is the study and practice of what is going right with organizations, and particularly, what is extraordinarily positive. It is built on principles arising from the emerging fields of positive organizational scholarship,[116] positive psychology,[117] and positive change[118] to help organizational leaders enable "positively deviant performance."

The tools, techniques, and practices of positive leadership have three characteristics:

1) They have been confirmed by empirical and valid research.

2) They are grounded in theory.

3) They have been applied in a range of organizational settings.

Positive leadership practices in organizations emphasize the things that currently work rather than focusing on what is going wrong—the negative. The practices recommended by positive leadership are heavily evidence based.

Positive leadership is about more than making sure everyone is happy. It is about strategies that help create positive organizational climates. Positive leaders don't necessarily seek to avoid or eliminate the negative but work to transform it into opportunities for thriving. In his book, *Positive Leadership: Strategies for Extraordinary Performance*, Kim Cameron explains that positive leadership does not ignore negative levels and conditions. It does, however, have three core positive orientations:

- It emphasizes positive deviance, or positive performance that far exceeds the norm—extraordinarily positive performance.

- It focuses on strengths and creating conditions for human and organizational thriving.

- It is based on the assumption that human systems are predisposed toward goodness for its own sake. It emphasizes fostering virtuousness in individuals and organizations.

Develop Transformational Leaders

Another popular leadership theory that aims for extraordinary performance through positive practices is transformational leadership. This theory was introduced in the seventies by James MacGregor Burns[119] and later elaborated on by Bernard M. Bass.[120,121] Transformational leaders build human capacity and enhance human potential by inspiring followers to achieve goals toward a higher vision, thereby achieving more than they thought was possible. Transformational leadership relates to the impact of leadership qualities such as charisma, intellectual stimulation, and developing employees, all with the aim of improving organizational functioning. Many research studies have shown evidence connecting transformational leadership with a higher level of organizational functioning,[122,123] greater employee commitment[124,125] and improved employee performance.[126,127] Bass outlined four components of transformational leadership:

- *Intellectual stimulation* challenges the status quo and promotes creativity among followers.

- *Individualized consideration* offers support and coaching to individuals, with an open communication style.

- *Inspirational motivation* promotes a clear vision and instills passion in others to achieve goals.

- *Idealized influence* recognizes the leader as a role model, garnering respect and trust from followers and helping them internalize the organizational values as their own.

Transformational leadership practices and characteristics can be learned, so training provided to managers and leaders of organizations aims to stimulate employees to cultivate awareness and adoption of the group's purpose and mission. This results in a greater overall contribution to the organization while challenging and advancing the culture toward a unifying purpose. These general concepts of cultivating constructive leadership traits, aligning values, and building organizational culture all ring true for our current model of positive organizational health.

Provide Leader Development Opportunities for Supporting Health and Well-being

We believe that managers should be given access to developmental opportunities and resources that can help them evolve as health-supportive leaders and to:

- comprehend the value for themselves, their direct reports, and the organization;

- understand how to live it;

- appreciate how to support it in others.

Kim Cameron developed a positive leadership assessment that can be a helpful diagnostic tool to help leaders identify potential areas to work on (see Assessing Positive Leadership Practices below). This assessment, and many others assessments and resources can be accessed at the University of Michigan Center for Positive Organizations at the Ross School of Business website (http://positiveorgs.bus.umich.edu).

Positive leadership has four primary strategies that align perfectly with creating a win-win organization: cultivating a positive climate, positive relationships, positive communication, and positive meaning.[128] Outcomes of interest to positive leadership include thriving at work, interpersonal thriving, virtuous behaviors, positive emotions, and energizing networks.

Activity: Assessing Positive Leadership Practices

This is a quick assessment of practical leadership activities that enable positive relationships.

Use the following scale for your answers: 1=Never, 2= Seldom, 3=Sometimes, 4=Frequently, 5=Always

As a leader, to what extent do you

- ensure employees have an opportunity to provide emotional, intellectual, or physical support to others in addition to receiving support from the organization?

- model positive energy yourself, and also recognize and encourage other positive energizers in your organization?

- support and utilize individuals in energy hubs as well as help develop peripheral members?

- provide more feedback to individuals on their strengths, than on their weaknesses?

- spend more time with your strongest performers than with your weakest performers?

- establish positive targets rather than focusing on solving problems or getting rid of obstacles?

Reprinted with permission from Kim Cameron.

Outlined below is a set of questions we designed to help leaders assess their perceived level of personal mastery for supporting the positive individual health of employees. Findings from this self-assessment can be shared and discussed with other leaders and managers, or they can be kept private. In any case, encourage leaders and managers to reflect honestly on their responses, share their strengths with others, and examine how they might improve.

Activity: Leader Commitment to Employee Health and Thriving

Please indicate your level of agreement for each of the questions below using the following scale: 1=Strongly disagree, 2=Disagree, 3=Neither agree nor disagree, 4=Agree, 5=Strongly agree.

- I am enthusiastic about supporting employee health and thriving and actively promote it at the workplace.

- I recognize how encouraging employee health supports the vision and purpose of our organization.

- I feel confident that I can explain our organization's vision for employee health and well-being.

- I understand the importance of my role in supporting the health and well-being of employees in the organization.

- I clearly see the connection between the positive health of employees and their peak performance.

- I celebrate employees' lifestyle changes or maintenance efforts in ways that have meaning for them.

- I actively participate in the health-promotion activities in our organization.

- I positively recognize and support employees' attempts to adopt healthier lifestyles.

- Working for this organization is having a positive impact on my health.

- I am clear about my personal values, purpose, and vision.

- I am a positive role model for work-life balance and mindful and healthy living.

For those items that are strengths, how could you build on these to advance the wellness efforts?

For those items that need improvement, what are some steps you could take to develop a deeper commitment in that area?

Enhance Positive Energy Networks

There are two important areas supported by the research in the area of positive leadership where leaders can make a tremendous difference; building positive energy networks, and reinforcing individuals' strengths.

One of the simplest yet most powerful concepts in positive leadership is the concept of energy. We have all likely experienced interactions with people who just drain the life out of us. Often, this is because they have very negative attitudes. We leave interactions with those people less energized and feeling somewhat depleted. Kim Cameron and his colleagues have found that a person's level of energy is four times more important to performance on the job than his or her title and role in the organization. Their research has shown significant positive relationships between positively energizing leaders and the job satisfaction, well-being, engagement, enrichment of families, and performance of employees in the unit. They also found that energizing leaders also have a significant positive impact on group cohesion, experimentation and innovation, team learning, and performance.[129]

People can be identified as energizers or de-energizers[130] based on the perceived impact they have on the people around them. Table 12 lists the major attributes of energizers and de-energizers.

Table 12. Attributes of energizers and de-energizers

Energizers	De-Energizers
They connect with others as people.	They don't show concern for those around them.
They solve problems.	They create problems.
They see opportunities.	They mainly see roadblocks and have criticisms.
They fully engage in conversations and are heedful.	They don't create opportunities for others to be valued.
They are trustworthy, have integrity, and are dependable.	They often don't come through on commitments.
They express gratitude and humility.	They are often inflexible in their thinking.
They use abundance language.	They just get louder when people don't listen.
They smile.	They seldom smile.
They are genuine and authentic.	They are superficial and insincere.
They help others flourish.	They ensure that they get credit.

Reprinted with permission from Kim Cameron.

The good news is that people can learn to be positive energizers, and organizational leaders can play a role in making that happen. Leaders can be positively energizing by how they behave, by what they recognize, and by how they support the people on their team. Identifying and building on people's strengths can produce a greater benefit than finding and correcting their weaknesses.[131-133]

Shifting the Responsibility for Health and Well-being

Marathon Health, Inc. is a Vermont-based company founded in 2005 based on the principles of patient empowerment and a holistic approach to health. Its primary focus is on creating trusting relationships between the clinicians and the patients they serve.

Zero Trends' business concept that excess costs follow excess risks encapsulates Marathon Health's population health risk management model. Population risk management looks at all the factors impacting an individual's health, including genetic predisposition to disease, environmental conditions such as the quality of the air and water, and, in particular, lifestyle risk such as tobacco use, alcohol, and substance abuse, eating habits and levels of physical activity.

The key to population health management is working with patients of all risk and disease levels, not just the medium- and high-risk patients. Healthcare should be thought of in the same way as production, distribution, and other business systems: a set of interdependent parts that can be measured, benchmarked, and improved. But improvement will not occur without managing a total population's health—from the fit and healthy to the obese—and providing a lasting health and wellness culture.

Marathon Health has found that a successful worksite healthcare program is dependent upon a shared vision for health and a passion for influencing change on an organizational and individual level. The attributes and values that characterize the Marathon Health client base include:

- *Management, operations, and culture are aligned around health as an important business driver.*

- *Leadership actively demonstrates support for innovative health programs.*

- *A long-term interest in the health and well-being of employees and their families is demonstrated.*

- *To become or maintain a status as an "employer of choice" in the community is a desired goal.*

- *There is a fundamental belief that the current healthcare system is broken, and that new, innovative solutions are needed.*

Tracey Moran
Vice President of Marketing, Marathon Health | For Life.

To read the full case study go to appendix B

Foster Collaboration

Encourage and Develop "Design Thinkers"

So far, in this book we have spoken about using the principles of design thinking as you have contemplated the overall vision and goals for your organization. Here we discuss design thinking as a means to engage stakeholders from throughout the organization in the process of co-creating their own native solutions for improving the health and well-being of employees and the organization. IDEO, an international design firm founded in Palo Alto, California, originally popularized the use of design thinking in the design of commercial products. Design thinking has also been used as a means to understand and help resolve difficult and sometimes "wicked" organizational and societal problems. Design thinking combines empathy, creativity, and rationality to gain deep perspective about the daily lives of employees.

Activity: Form a Design Team: Getting Started

It is ideal if you have an area that can be dedicated for design sessions, but it isn't necessary. Just as design teams are dependent on creativity, you can get creative about where and when you convene a design team. During the design-thinking process, ideas are expressed in visual, tactile, and experiential ways. Materials used during these meetings help the collective thinking process and provide a flexible forum for thinking about new ideas. The most basic supplies needed for design meetings include the following:

- pens and pencils
- markers (different colors)
- paper
- Post-it Notes
- additional helpful supplies include:
- construction paper
- foam-core boards
- scissors
- mobile-phone cameras

For the team's workspace, a blank wall can be used to post notes, thoughts, or images from your exploration. This ongoing visual display will help your team become absorbed in the ideas and stay engaged. If a wall isn't available, then large pieces of foam-core board could be used. Later in the process, additional materials for prototyping are used, which will depend on the visual representation you'll be creating. This could include foam, fabric, felt, cardboard boxes, paper plates and cups, Velcro, duct tape, hole puncher, glue sticks or a hot glue gun, string, aluminum foil, popsicle sticks, and pipe cleaners. The construction of a rough prototype provides an opportunity for the end user to interact with the concept in more than just words. Observe actions and ask the user to think out loud during the interaction.

Brainstorming leverages the collective thinking of the group and requires listening, open-mindedness, and building on ideas regardless of the source.

IDEO recently made available their "human-centered design" toolkit (www.designkit.org) that outlines their approach to design thinking. In their view, human-centered design (HCD) begins with desirability. What are the needs, desires, hopes, and dreams of the people whom the solution will be designed to serve? It is next concerned with what is feasible given the resources available, what is "technically and organizationally feasible?" Third, human-centered design is concerned with "viability," or what is financially practical. We recommend this toolkit and the HCD process for any organization whose people are game for engaging in inclusive, creative, fun, and efficient ways to quickly develop relevant solutions for their employees and even their customers.

Throughout the book, we will be highlighting times when design teams can be especially useful. However, the design-thinking mentality is helpful in nearly any kind of creative process. Some areas where design thinking can help with the process of better supporting health and well-being in the workplace include:

- New initiatives for wellness and well-being
- Enhancement existing initiatives and programs
- New employee onboarding
- Employee training
- Products/technology
- Work environments
- Work policies
- Work culture
- Employee appreciation/recognition
- Communication and feedback

The activity below will help you prepare an area that employees can use for the design team process.

Provide Conditions for Group Flow

Earlier in the book (chapter 2), we discussed Mihaly Csikszentmihalyi's concept of "flow," and how achieving a state of flow can be incredibly satisfying and deeply meaningful. Csikszentmihalyi found that individuals are more likely to experience a state of flow when their environment has four important characteristics:

1) *Match between skill and challenge*—The individual's level of skill must match the challenge of the task. If the challenge is too great, the individual will be frustrated. If the challenge isn't great enough, the individual will be bored.

2) *Clear goal*—Flow is more likely to occur when the end goal is clear.

3) **Feedback**—Feedback about progress toward the goal must be constant and immediate.

4) **Concentration**—Flow occurs when full concentration on the task is possible.

Csikszentmihalyi and others have also explored the concept of "group flow." There are several ways a group can work together so each member achieves flow. Some environmental conditions that support group flow include the following:

- Much like the ideal work arrangement for the human-centered design process, group flow is fostered by creative spatial arrangements: chairs, whiteboard walls, and flip-charts. Standing and moving is encouraged.

- Include whiteboards, corkboards, flip charts for scribbling information, flow graphs, and diagrams. It is a safe place to be a bit wacky and say what you think without negative repercussions.

- Design physical arrangements that provide conditions for interaction and collaboration among employees and opportunities to concentrate.

Working practices of groups that facilitate flow to some degree mirror conditions that foster individual flow. Having a clear collective goal, a compelling vision, a shared mission, full engagement, "deep listening" by each group member, and complete concentration all contribute to group flow. In his book, *Group Genius: The Creative Power of Collaboration*, Keith Sawyer describes moment-to-moment interactional dynamics that contribute to group flow and draws parallels between successful group dynamics, jazz performance, and improvisational theater.

Group flow happens when many tensions are in perfect balance: between convention and novelty, between structure and improvisation, between the critical, analytic mind and the freewheeling, outside-the-box mind, between listening to the rest of the group and speaking out with your own individual voice. The central paradox of group flow is that it can only happen when there are rules, and the participants share tacit understandings, but with too many rules or too much cohesion, the potential for innovation is lost.[134]

You may recognize the parallels between these conditions and the principles and practices of design thinking we described above.

Foster Collegial Connections

Social network analysis has revealed interesting patterns of health-related factors among friendship networks. James Fowler, a political scientist from the University of California in San Diego, and Nicholas Christakis, a physician and social scientist at Harvard University, examined patterns in the Framingham Heart Study data.[135] They found the risk of obesity was 45 percent higher in a person with an obese friend. If friends of friends are obese, the risk is 25 percent higher, and obesity in friends of friends' friends (three degrees of separation) is associated with a 10 percent higher risk of obesity. To explain this phenomenon, the researchers looked at three possibilities:

1) Weight gain in one person somehow causes weight gain in the other person.

2) "Birds of a feather flock together"—in other words, people tend to hang around other people who have similar body size.

3) Socially connected individuals have common exposure to something that causes weight gain or loss.

They found support for all three, and also found evidence that social norms about appropriate weight in friendship networks likely had an influence on the body size of others in the network.[136,137] Fowler and Christakis have also found similar patterns of relationships for happiness[138] and smoking cessation.[139] The implications from this and other research on the positive health impact of social connections have profound implications for thinking beyond the individual when designing interventions to improve health and well-being.

Architect Healthy Choices

Choice architecture is a part of the field of behavioral economics, which developed from the work of psychologists Daniel Kahneman and Amos Tversky. Daniel Kahneman won the Nobel Prize in Economics in 2002 for the pioneering research he conducted with Amos Tversky on human judgment and decision-making under uncertainty. Behavioral economics examines the systematic errors and biases that humans make in our everyday judgments and decisions. We would like to believe we are rational decision-makers, but in many ways this is not the case. We would also like to think that our intuitions are largely accurate and that we are aware of how our emotions influence our moment-to-moment choices.

A strong body of research indicates we are subject to errors in our thinking and our emotions, and we are often unaware of how they influence our judgments.

The popularity of behavioral economics is evidenced by the many best-selling books that have used its core principles to help people shape their thinking and environments to support the kind of life they intend to live. Books like *Sway*,[140] *Switch*,[141] *Nudge*,[142] and many other good books—some with more than one word in their titles, including Kahneman's seminal book, *Thinking Fast and Slow*[143]—have become popular best-sellers.

The basic tenets of behavioral economics can help us better understand why it is that change is so hard for us, and provide practical guidance that we can use to make better decisions in our everyday lives.

We discuss the relevance of behavioral economics in two places in this book. In this chapter, we outline ways that organizations can create environments and cultures to help employees live healthier lives while they are at work. In chapter 12, we present ways that individual employees can better understand the influences, both internal and external, that shape the large and small behaviors and decisions that make up their lifestyles (see **Behavioral Economics: To Err Is Human** on page 185).

The principles in Zero Trends have proven to be among the most useful I've encountered in public health. Practical, data-driven, applicable, the Zero Trends adage "Just don't get worse" has become one of the guiding teachings in my course, Go Sugar Free, which serves groups all over the world. Go Sugar Free guides adults to intelligently reduce, if not eliminate, added sweeteners and refined grains from their diet to gain freedom from mental and physical health problems and unwanted habits. The adults who take my course go through a period of intense withdrawal, often characterized by frustration, doubt, and substantial effort, then ultimately: exhilaration, ease, and far-reaching success.

It's in the entirety of this process that both Zero Trends and Shared Values—Shared Results truths come into play. Members move from high risk to low risk. Simultaneously and naturally, when they remove added sweeteners and refined grains from their lives, optimism, gratitude, vitality, and openness arise, uncovering human beings radiating positive health. The longer I lead groups in changing habit, the more I see Zero Trends' sensibility and Shared Values—Shared Results positivity reinforce and propel each other.

Jacqueline Smith, MPH
Founder and CEO of Go Sugar Free

Create Healthier Workplace Choices

The idea that someone might purposefully craft our environments to subconsciously shape our decisions and actions has raised many eyebrows and even more questions. While some people frown on any such paternalism, the reality is that marketers have been purposefully architecting our environments for decades. In the United States and other Western countries, there is a massive marketing machine that uses everything in its power to exploit the quirks in our decision-making to sell products. Some of these products have even negatively contributed to the public-health crisis we are now facing in the United States and abroad. Choice architecture is everywhere. It's in our popular media and on our product labels. It has shaped the layout and the content of our grocery stores, cafeterias, and restaurants. It is used during the design of the materials and forms we use when applying for health insurance, signing up for savings plans, and applying for driver's licenses.

Purposeful choice architecture is already in use everywhere.

Harvard University professor Cass Sunstein argues that "choice architecture…is inevitable, and hence a form of paternalism that cannot be avoided." Sunstein makes the case "that there are profoundly moral reasons to ensure that choice architecture is helpful rather than harmful—and that it makes people's lives better and longer."[144] According to Sunstein, "There are many opportunities for improving human welfare through improved choice architecture."

Sunstein also states that "a key question is whether the relevant choice architecture is helpful and simple or harmful, complex, and exploitative." He recommends using the mildest forms of choice architecture that preserve the individual's choice, which he calls "nudges." Sunstein describes a nudge as any aspect of choice architecture that alters people's behavior in a predictable way without forbidding any options or significantly changing their economic consequences. According to Sunstein, "To count as a mere nudge, the intervention must be easy and cheap to avoid. Nudges are not mandates. Putting fruit at eye level [to attract attention and hence increase the likelihood of being chosen] counts as a nudge. Banning junk food does not."[142] Table 13 outlines examples of nudges that organizations can implement to encourage healthy practices or discourage unhealthy practices. Later in this chapter we discuss nudges that employees can design for themselves.

Table13. Examples of externally imposed nudges

Encourage Positive Practices	Discourage Negative Practices
Post a sign near the elevator to use the stairs instead.	Post a sign in a conference room to discourage multitasking during meetings.
Use footprints to point people toward the stairs instead of using the elevator.	Place calorie counts on food choices in the cafeteria, with healthier options highlighted, to discourage eating unhealthy foods.
Opt-out approaches: Activate enrollment in an employer savings plan unless intentionally disenrolled.	Place a mirror near unhealthy food choices in the cafeteria.
Automatically schedule preventive screenings.	Place a red sticker on unhealthy foods choices in the cafeteria.
Send automatic mailers for dental appointment reminders every six months.	Place unhealthy foods in non-central locations in the company cafeteria.
Label a food product "fat-free" among other choices that contain fat.	Have the signage on a waste bin labeled "landfill" instead of "trash" next to a recycle bin to discourage throwing away recyclable items.
Simplify application processes for signing up for employer-sponsored savings programs.	

This is an especially good application for an employee design team. Encourage employees to create a team to design healthy nudges in their work environment.

We recommend that as much as possible, you involve employees in the process of choosing or designing healthy nudges. If employees are engaged in the process of choosing the nudges in their environment, they are much less likely to see them as controlling. We worked with a hospital system that removed all chocolate from the cafeterias in their hospitals with no notice. While this was a good faith effort to improve the health of its employees, there was a tremendous backlash. The employees resented that they weren't asked about the change—it felt controlling, it was sudden, and it left employees with no choice. Plus, you just don't mess with someone's chocolate!!! A better approach may have been to position the chocolate in an inconspicuous area in the cafeteria rather than right next to the cash register in an "impulse buy" position, or include healthier chocolate products (darker chocolate versus milk chocolate). Most important, involve employees in deciding how to create healthier offerings in the cafeteria.

At the University of Michigan, we have recognized the critical importance of creating healthy workplace cultures and environments to achieving and sustaining population health. We are systematically embedding the value of employee health and well-being in our leadership expectations, development programs, employee engagement surveys, policies, practices, and traditions. We have also made significant progress through the development and support of over 550 wellness champions across the University, who work with their supervisors and co-workers to implement healthy activities and positive workplace cultures in their units. Our goal is to support members of the U-M community to lead healthy and fulfilling lives and contribute to the U-M being a great university.

LaVaughn Palma-Davis, MA
Senior Director for Health and Well-Being Services at the University of Michigan.

Working Environments that Nurture Our Evolutionary Roots

Many modern workplaces and office buildings are designed more for efficiency than for the comfort and well-being of employees. Workplaces can be busy, noisy, artificially lit places designed to minimize unnecessary movements. All of these can contribute to poor employee health and well-being. Insights from the field of evolutionary psychology are highlighting ways to enhance employee and workplace health and thriving.[145] Not all employers can design a campus from the ground up like Google or Apple, but nearly any workplace can incorporate elements into its environment to create a more supportive environment for its employees. There are many ways to improve the experience of work and the health and well-being of workers. Some examples include the following:

- Natural sunlight in the work environment has been found to be positively correlated with employee well-being and job satisfaction.[146] To the extent possible, invite the sunlight into your workspace. Open the blinds or curtains, position workstations near windows and natural sources of light.

- Rather than purchasing desktop printers for employees, encourage them to get up from their desks and walk to the shared printer to retrieve their printed documents. Provide standing desks, hold walking meetings, promote parking farther from the office, encourage taking the stairs to use restrooms on another floor. Allow, and even encourage, exercise breaks.

- Provide nap areas, or pillows and encourage employees to lay their heads down at their desks for time-out rest, relaxation, and rejuvenation.

- Promote connections and social interaction. Provide plenty of areas where employees can convene informally.

- Allow employees to bring pets to work, especially dogs.[147,148]

- Include a generous amount of greenery in and around the office—position plants and potted trees throughout the workplace.

- Reduce noise exposure and include sounds from nature.

Research is showing the importance of everyday contact with nature.[149] Exercising outdoors in a pleasant setting, such as in a park, is associated with improvements in depression to a greater degree than jogging through urban environments.[150] If at all possible, create pleasant surroundings around your work environment such as safe walking pathways or comfortable places to gather, work and exercise outdoors. Physical activity in those pleasant settings also improves cognitive functioning.[151] Simply viewing images of natural settings and sitting in a room with live plants can increase prosocial behaviors.[152]

Consider including small water features in and around the workplace to create a soothing environment. A small koi pond or even a desktop waterfall can promote a peaceful atmosphere. A place to sit and relax with a view of nature—or ideally within nature—can be rejuvenating, and provided places for social interactions, engagement, and impromptu gatherings with colleagues.

Changing Workplace Expectations—A Millennial Perspective

We are in the midst of a workforce shift, and different generations are being combined in the workplace, creating a new dynamic. Millennials [generation Y] are joining the workforce and it is said that they are going to be the largest generation, passing the baby boomers and other previous generations.[153] The ideal workplace for millennials may be much different from that of other generations. Today's technological advancements and mobile capabilities create a whole new work culture.

Eternal Optimists

Despite the economic and environmental plights passed on from the baby boomers to Millennials, this generations' optimism and technological savvy is positively changing workplace dynamic. In a piece by Jessica Brack, "Maximizing Millennials in the Workplace" she states, "Despite the setbacks millennials experienced as a result of the recession, the bad times, according to the Pew study, did not trump this generation's optimism."[154] These characteristics shape the types of organizations where millennials seek employment. Companies like Google, the technology giant, have a work culture that fosters this generation's needs. The philosophy at Google is "to create the happiest, most productive workplace in the world."[155] With this philosophy, they delve into the employee's mindset and tailor the workplace to foster creativity, innovation, and productivity.

Flexibility and Fun

Employers like Google, with a high number of millennial employees, work hard to bring the ideal workplace to life. This is what millennials want—a place where they can be creative, be appreciated—a more relaxed, flexible work environment. "Millennials want fun and a less formal atmosphere may help foster it."[154] It is apparent that not every company can afford things that Google has at their offices, but they can adopt their same principles in terms of a culture that promotes creativity and productivity. The advancements in technology can also help foster this, making it easier for employees to work from home if they need. This gives employees more freedom, creates more flexible hours, and promotes creativity without micromanaging.

Millennials are the workforce of the future so organizations should prepare for higher volumes of workers seeking flexible, fun, creative places to work. With time comes change. This is true in all aspects of life, including the workplace. If companies don't embrace the millennial ideals, they will likely not employ fresh minds and will find their company in an increasingly stagnant business model, while others prepare for a millennial workforce and flourish.

Jaclyn Richardson
Lead Research Associate
Edington Associates

Other Useful Disciplines and Perspectives

The current wellness and well-being field is bursting with webinars, conferences, blogs, research studies, and vendors eager to offer advice and solutions. Even so, we can learn a lot about how to create and apply innovative solutions by being open to ideas from many diverse disciplines outside the traditional wellness field. We can begin to appreciate different perspectives and perhaps adopt seemingly unlikely solutions to improve overall health and well-being in our organizations. We outline here examples of disciplines somewhat removed from wellness and well-being that can push our thinking:

- **Architecture:** What new ideas in architecture and physical design could contribute to the built workspace? Are open floor plans more conducive to teamwork and collaboration? Assessing the needs of the team's physical space could identify changes to improve workflow and help make healthier choices more likely.

- **Education:** What could we learn from childhood education as it relates to creativity? How could we change conference rooms and meeting places to encourage out-of-the-box thinking? Incorporating playful and tactical items could help trigger our brains to respond in new and different ways.

- **Spirituality:** How could practices from spiritual disciplines help bring a sense of mindfulness to the workplace? Try starting a meeting with one minute of silent contemplation to set intentions on the objectives, visualize how to achieve goals, embrace collaboration, and focus the team's energy on the tasks at hand.

- **Community:** What are examples of activities in the community or urban planning that foster health and well-being? Just as safe walking paths are forming in communities, how could a similar approach be installed near the workplace?

- **Art:** What role could art have in your workplace? How could a work of art start a different kind of conversation about a team project or illustrate a vision? Incorporating art into the workplace, either temporarily or permanently, can support a creative mindset. Displays of creative projects of employees or their children can contribute to a fun and fresh atmosphere.

- **Music:** What genre of music inspires a different kind of thinking? Are there lyrics to songs that express an idea that you can apply at work? Are there ways to work with local musicians for hands-on experiences, like a percussion lesson for team building?

- **Movies:** Is there a movie that illustrates a point of view or thought that would be important for the organization or team to view and then discuss? For example, we use *A Beautiful Mind* to illustrate the impact of supportive colleagues and *Money Ball* to illustrate the importance of opening up to innovative ways to look at a common issue.

- **Personal talents:** How could employees with creative talents share them in the workplace? How could these talents be highlighted as examples of personal thriving? What analogies could be made to the team's goals and the organization's vision?

- **Metaphors:** How could metaphors (from sports, movies, nature, cooking, gardening, for example) be used to make connections to work, and open up a new way of looking at issues? What metaphors describe the unique strengths of your team?

- **Technology:** How could new advances in technology help you think about the future of a problem in a different way? For example, how can the "Internet of Things" (IOT) be used to help create more supportive health-related environments and cultures (see chapter 15, page 257 for a description of IOT)?

- **Neurobiology:** What research studies about brain functioning help to determine the cause of certain behaviors? What are some parallels to draw in the organization?

- **Globalization:** What global ideas or solutions have been tried in a different context and culture? How can we learn to think outside of our own industry, or even outside of our society and country?

- **Media:** What are some inspirational stories in the local or national news about paying it forward, simple acts of kindness, and making a difference?

- **Improvisation:** When we think of improvisation, we think of theater, music, comedy. We think of the arts. But improvisation is the art of dealing positively with the unexpected. How can improvisation be used to teach leaders, managers and all employees to listen closely and respond positively ("Yes, and…") in the moment, instead of operating with a closed mind ("No, but…")?

- **Sports:** What does participation in or being around sports teach us? One example is "the play is over," which could be a resilience lesson related to bouncing back after a poor performance or not resting on your laurels after a best performance. "The team, the team, the team."

What Can Employees Do?

As we outlined earlier, evolving an organizational environment and culture takes strong leader champions and alignment among policies, process, and benefits. However, the attitudes and actions of employees also play a huge role. There are a number of ways that employees can get involved in formal efforts to shape and develop positive organizational health. Individual actions lived on a day-to-day basis will ultimately shape and define the culture and climate of the organization. We outline ideas for both in the sections that follow.

Be Part of the Solution—Engage in Employee Design Teams

We've outlined many areas of the win-win journey that can benefit from direct employee engagement in design teams and other collaborative planning and development efforts (see *Encourage and Develop "Design Thinkers"* and *Forming a Design Team: Getting Started* earlier in this chapter). These teams benefit from having members with many different perspectives and a variety of skill sets. Regardless of the employee's position or role in the organization, joining in these collaborative efforts can be extremely rewarding and fun for the individual and the team. It can also help the employee create an environment and culture that truly resonates on a personal level for design team participants, as well as for other employees throughout the organization.

Find Your Element

Research on person-job fit suggests that when employees see more of a positive fit between themselves and their jobs, they are more likely to experience their work as personally meaningful, as well as respond with enhanced job performance, satisfaction, and retention in their organizations.[156] [157]

Sir Ken Robinson begins his book *Finding Your Element* with a fitting story for this point in the book:

> *Two young fish are swimming down a river and an older fish swims past them in the opposite direction. He says, "Good morning, boys. How's the water?" They smile at him and swim on. Farther up the river, one of the young fish turns to the other and says, "What's water?"*

Sir Robinson describes your "element" as the place "where natural aptitude meets personal passion." It means doing something for which you have a natural feel—something you are good at…and something that you love to do.[158]

> *It is vitally important, especially when money is tight, for organizations to have people doing what is truly meaningful to them. An organization with a staff that's fully engaged is far more likely to succeed than one with a large portion of its workforce detached, cynical, and uninspired.*
>
> —Sir Ken Robinson

Self-leaders actively seek and know how to ask for what they need to be in their element. They work at being positive outliers.

Choose a job you love, and you will never have to work a day in your life.

—Confucius

Redesign Your Job

One way employees can help themselves excel in their work and careers is by actively changing some aspect of their job so it better suits them. Amy Wrzesniewski, a professor at the Yale University School of Management, refers to this as "job crafting." Wrzesniewski defines job crafting as "the physical and cognitive changes individuals make in the task or relational boundaries of their work" and encompasses a vast range of bottom-up moves made by employees to create a more optimal design of their jobs. Job crafting is an ongoing and active process where employees redefine and reimagine their job designs in ways they find personally meaningful.[159] By meaningful, we refer to work employees believe is significant and serves an important purpose.[160] The extent to which employees can proactively change aspects of their jobs will obviously depend on the role in the organization and stage in their career,[161] as well as the social context in which they do their work.[162] Job crafting is a bottom-up approach initiated by employees rather than directed by their managers. This process enables employees to craft their jobs in ways that create more personal meaning and fulfillment and may not even involve formal "permission" from a supervisor or manager.[163] Wrzesniewski suggests several ways to improve the quality of work life:[164]

- *Task crafting*—Employees shape the responsibilities of their formal job requirements, adding tasks, removing tasks, and changing the nature of tasks, or when and how the tasks get done.

- *Relational crafting*—Changes in where, when, how, and with whom employees relate with others in the course of their job.

- *Cognitive crafting*—Changes in the way employees think about their job, how they see the bigger picture of the purpose and value of their job, and how their job it fits into delivering on the vision and mission of the organization.

Wrzesniewski collaborated with Justin Berg from the Wharton School at the University of Pennsylvania and Jane Dutton from Ross School of Business at the University of Michigan to create a "Job Crafting Exercise" toolkit that can help employees redesign their jobs to align with their personal values, purpose and passions and better utilize their unique strengths.[165] This can help employees create a better fit with their jobs and improve their happiness and productivity at work.

The chances are good that at some point, you have changed an aspect of your job so that it better suited you. Whether you took a different approach to a task you were responsible for, changed an interaction pattern with someone at work, or refined how you thought about the job in a more general sense, you were engaging in job crafting

Amy Wrzesniewski,
Professor Yale University School of Management

Curate Your Own Personal Culture

We mentioned choice architecture earlier in this chapter as a way for employers to create conditions that lead to healthier choices in the workplace. We can each curate our own healthy cultures, in much the same way that a museum curator collects and displays the material, artwork, or artifacts that reflect an artist, period, or discipline.

Personal Choice Architecture

One way we can be culture curators is by architecting our own nudges. Table 14 outlines examples of self-imposed nudges that either encourage healthy behaviors or discourage unhealthy behaviors. Many of these nudges involve planning ahead to help your future self behave in ways that support your values and goals. The more you can curate your surroundings to be supportive, the more likely you will be to meet your goals or live by your values in the long run.

Table 14. Examples of self-imposed nudges

Encourage Positive Practices	Discourage Negative Practices
Use an alarm on a mobile phone as a reminder to take daily medication.	Keep spare change in the car for parking meters, to avoid getting a parking ticket.
Keep a notebook by the bed to recount daily gratitude.	Only purchase small amounts of non-fat frozen yogurt or sorbet instead of ice cream to keep in the freezer.
Join a personal goal-oriented website and agreeing to donate money to charity if goal isn't reached.	Enrolling in an automated refill program for medications to help remember to pick them up.
Place healthy fruits on the kitchen counter to encourage healthier snacking.	Enroll in an automated bill payment option to avoid delinquent payments.
Meeting a friend for a morning walk; choose not to let the friend down by not showing up.	Use a smaller plate so that smaller portion sizes seem larger.
	Remove the TV from the bedroom to avoid late-night watching as a way to improve sleep.

Create a Healthier Social Milieu

Milieu: the physical or social setting in which people live
or in which something happens or develops

We spend much of our time in our places of work, but after work we go back to our homes and into our communities. Depending on the kinds of stresses and frustrations we experience at work, we may leave the workplace tired, frazzled, and generally sapped of any energy to resist temptations or stick to any promises we have made to eat healthier, be active, spend quality time with our families, or other positive behaviors. To effectively support the health and well-being of employees, we must also think beyond the workplace to homes and families, local and regional communities, and national and global societies. It is important for employees to have positive, supportive people on whom they can rely to help them navigate difficult changes. As part of any more formal wellness or well-being program offered through the organization, encourage employees to create positive experiences with family or friends, or in the community:

- Have a family discussion each week on a topic of choice—family members take turns choosing the topic.

- Design family togetherness goals—eat together three times a week, at least one physical activity as a family each week, weekly movie night.

- Engage in one activity each day to make your living space a healthier place to live

- Rotate household chores.

Judd Allen's book, *Bringing Wellness Home: How to Create a Household Subculture that Supports Wellness Lifestyle Goals*[166] could serve as a great resource. As we learned from the research of James Fowler and Nicholas Christakis (see **Foster Collegial Connections**, page 160), the actions and behaviors of the people we surround ourselves with can make a big difference, either positive or negative, to our health and happiness. Our own behaviors also affect the people around us, so introducing purposeful, healthy practices in all areas of our lives is not only good for us, it is good for the other people who we care about. This can create a positive upward spiral that has far-reaching benefits for our social networks.

Central High School

The Wellness program is a winner for Central High School. The staff's participation in a wellness program has not only improved their waistlines and the school district's bottom line, it also has gained them some national recognition. Administrator Scott Pierce said as of

March 1, the district was ranked second in the nation among all of the businesses, schools, and other entities that participate in the Humana Vitality wellness program.

In addition to organized activities, such as walks and blood drives, participants can earn points on their own by logging their activity, teacher Melissa Bahnson said. "I actually set a goal to obtain enough points to purchase some nice pots and pans off of Amazon," Bahnson said, adding she recently met that goal. She said teachers often get together to help each other meet their fitness goals, such as walking 10,000 steps per day. "I notice staff members walking the halls during their lunch breaks," she said. "It is cool to see the school culture changing as a result of participation in the program."

Jill Tatge-Rozell, Kenosha News

To read the full case study go to appendix B

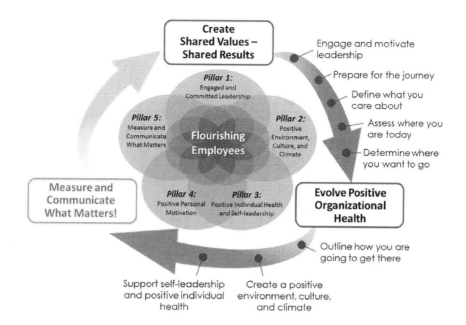

CHAPTER 12:
Support Self-Leadership and Positive Individual Health

You must be the change you wish to see in the world.

—Mahatma Gandhi

Individual employees have been the focus of wellness programs for the past several decades; most specifically, individuals who were deemed to be at high risk for disease and medical costs. The prevailing strategy for wellness programs in organizations has been to try to get employees to reduce health risks and minimize the impact of disease. The thinking presented in *Zero Trends* shifted the strategy to include helping low-risk people stay low risk and helping those at risk improve their health or at the very least, not get worse.

In this chapter, we briefly describe current best practices and propose emerging next practices that can be used to support and develop thriving and engaged self-leaders. We also outline the science that most influenced our current thinking about how to support employees so they can live in a manner true to their personal and professional purpose, values, and vision. Developing positive self-leaders is core to creating positive organizational health, and crucial to the thriving and positive functioning of organizations. Both the organization and the employees share the responsibility and accountability for developing positive individual health and self-leadership. We suggest practices for both organizations and individuals to enhance self-leadership.

People are an organization's most important resource.

Positive self-leaders and positive organizational health are the next frontier for healthy and thriving individuals and organizations.

Dr. Dee Edington's decades of pioneering research published in his earlier book, Zero Trends, *has been the cornerstone of our employee wellness program. Dee is a visionary who has provided insight and direction as we move from a "wait for disease—fix it" model, to one encompassing a lifestyle and work life that focuses on health and the whole person.*

Lynn Skordahl   *Cindy Vander Well*   *Rick Maursetter*
Wellness RN   *Benefit Manager*   *Risk Manager*

Duininck Companies

What Is Self-Leadership?

Self-leadership is everyone's responsibility, as is supporting others in their ongoing efforts to become self-leaders. By "everyone," we mean all employees in the organization, including senior and operations leaders, managers, and all other employees throughout the organization.

Self-leadership is the process of purposefully engaging in positive personal change, making thoughtful decisions, working on resilience, building on strengths, and continuously learning and growing.

We use the term self-leadership to represent the ways people purposefully engage in positive personal change, make thoughtful decisions, work on resilience, build on strengths, and continuously strive to learn and grow. Self-leaders constantly aim for high levels of the positive individual health we described in chapter 2.

Employers are beginning to recognize the importance of fostering characteristics related to self-leadership in their employees. Figure 14 depicts self-leadership as made up of many different qualities, including being resilient, purposeful, mindful, optimistic, autonomous, confident, connected, and competent. These are all important, but this is far from an exhaustive list of self-leadership characteristics. **Perhaps most important to self-leadership is continuously striving to be at your best.** Self-leadership is not a destination, but a lifelong process—a journey. It is a journey best taken with the support of others, and it is more successful when taken in a positive and supportive environment. Self-leadership helps us maintain and strengthen the many domains of positive individual health.

Figure 14. Selected descriptors of self-leaders

The Impact of Self-Leaders on Positive Organizational Health

I've learned that you shouldn't go through life with a catcher's mitt on both hands; you need to be able to throw something back.

—Maya Angelou

In many ways, evolving a thriving organizational culture, parallels the process of becoming what Peter Senge calls a "learning organization." One of the five disciplines required for such an evolution, personal mastery, is closely related to our concept of self-leadership.[167] While we could paraphrase Senge, perhaps his words best reflect this discipline:

Personal mastery is the discipline of continually clarifying and deepening our personal vision, of focusing our energies, of developing patience, and of seeing reality objectively. As such, it is an essential cornerstone of the learning organization—the learning organization's spiritual foundation. An organization's commitment to and capacity for learning can be no greater than that of its members.

The discipline of personal mastery starts with clarifying the things that really matter to us, of living our lives in the service of our highest aspirations. Here, I am most interested in the connections between personal learning and organizational learning, in the reciprocal commitments between individual and organization, and in the special spirit of an enterprise made up of learners.

This type of mastery and self-leadership are related to Maslow's need for self-actualization, or the drive to fully realize one's potential.

"Good Health is Good Business" has always been our focus when working with clients. It's difficult to call ourselves healthcare benefit consultants if we are unable to significantly affect the $0.85 of every premium dollar going towards the delivery of healthcare services. We achieve that by assisting our clients in managing the health of their workforce. This can only be done with a focus on vision and environment—a vision from leadership that supports the principle that "good health is expected—not hoped for"; and an environment that focuses on and is supportive of the workforce's ability to do their job and manage their lifestyle. Without this support at the workplace, home, and community; success in health risk mitigation is very difficult. Also important are strategic benefit design decisions that minimize barriers toward medical self-care compliance, and emphasize accountability of personal health and its related costs.

Finally, today it isn't about wellness—it is about well-being. We need the objective data like biometrics, but high blood pressure or BMI is often the result of an unhappy marriage, someone with an abuse problem, financial insecurity or mental illness—these are the root causes and human resource challenges that every health enhancement strategy must look for and address.

David Rearick, DO, MBA, CPE
Chief Medical Officer
Marsh & McLennan Agency LLC

Stephen Cherniak, MS, MBA
Wellness Director

Current Best Practices for Supporting Individual Health and Thriving

Let the beauty of what you love be what you do.

—Rumi

We reviewed the best practice recommendations and guidelines that have been published and promoted for managing the health, wellness, and well-being of employees. Most best practices have understandably focused on programs; particularly on how to implement and manage the program operations, and how to identify and engage individuals in the programs. The best practices for programs mentioned in the sources we reviewed[66-73] include the following:

- comprehensive, integrated programs

- effective implementation

- integration of program components at the point of implementation

- effective targeting of and outreach to high-risk individuals

- effective screening and triage

- assessment of health risks with feedback (health assessments, biometrics screening)

- use of data to target and tailor program design and communications

- state-of-the-art theory and evidence-based (or evidence-informed) interventions

- program accessibility

- access to a full continuum of care

- wide variety of program offerings

- dedicated onsite staff

- connected to families and community

- multiple program delivery options and modalities

- multilevel programming (individual, group, management/organizational, environmental, policy)

- shared data among all programs to promote cross referrals, transfers, and enhanced program effectiveness

- linkage (i.e., linkage to related programs such as employee assistance programs, disease management, case management, safety, quality, etc.)

- provides a seamless and coordinated experience to the end user

- health education (i.e., skill development and lifestyle behavior change, along with information dissemination and awareness building)

Currently, the content of programs is primarily geared toward helping individuals change the unhealthy behaviors and health risks that can lead to disease and high healthcare costs. We recommend including practices that support and enhance employee thriving and self-leadership.

We believe the next generation of approaches should not only be to reduce risks and disease but also to increase our capacity for engagement, energy, flow, vitality, creativity, empathy, love, and happiness.

Emerging Next Practices for Self-Leadership

You are the sum total of everything you've ever seen, heard, eaten, smelled, been told, forgot—it's all there. Everything influences each of us, and because of that I try to make sure that my experiences are positive.

—Maya Angelou

There is a wealth of evidence converging about the physical health benefits of resilience, optimism, and having a positive outlook. In table 15, we outline some of the emerging next practices for self-leadership. Organizations can offer these resources and practices along with more traditional wellness topics to help support and strengthen self-leadership.

Table 15. Emerging next practices for supporting and developing self-leaders

Example Self-Leadership Resources

Example development opportunities for self-leaders
- Self-leadership principles
- Change
- Resilience
- Decision-making
- Mindfulness
- Emotional intelligence
- Brain health
- Relationship building
- Work-life integration efforts
- Mind, body, spirit
- Stress management
- Yoga
- Meditation

Example opportunities to develop meaningful work
- Job crafting[159]
- Values in Action[168]
- Personal conditions for flow

In the next several sections, we discuss the evidence and practice from several of the disciplines that have most influenced our thinking about positive individual health and self-leadership.

Science of Positive Outlook

For many years, we have bought into the belief that we are born with a certain hardwired outlook that is difficult or impossible to change. It is not uncommon to hear people say "I'm just a glass-half-full (or empty) kind of person. It's just who I am. You can't change nature." We commonly believed that it was not possible to make meaningful change in our disposition. However, one of the most important findings from the study of human thriving is that while our disposition does have a genetic component, with effort and attention we can develop stronger positive attitudes and dispositions.[169,170]

There are a number of simple evidence-based practices that can lead to increases in happiness and optimism, such as recalling three good things that happened during your day, or taking the time to express gratitude to someone in your life. Findings from many disciplines have improved our understanding of how to cultivate a positive outlook. Insights from social and cognitive psychology, philosophy, neuroscience, behavioral economics, leadership studies, organizational studies, and many more, all provide collective evidence that a positive outlook has important implications for employee thriving.

International Business Machines (IBM): "Commit to Health"

IBM is a multinational technology and innovation company with over 400,000 employees across approximately a hundred countries. Addressing the health needs of such a dispersed, diverse population relies on a steadfast commitment from senior leadership and an integrated strategic approach. The specific goal of health promotion at IBM is to reduce health risk and build vitality among employees and their families to enhance well-being, enable high performance, and mitigate avoidable health-related costs. IBM has embraced WHO's Healthy Workplace guidelines to help refine company health priorities and objectives.

IBM's "Commit to Health" approach begins with long-standing corporate support with an integrated strategy that reflects a shared commitment and responsibility for health between both the company and employees. All IBMers are encouraged to commit to healthy living and vitality, building engagement with regular preventive care, and active involvement in healthcare decisions. In turn, IBM commits to helping employees succeed by making the healthiest choice the easiest choice, by putting the required resources directly in their hands. IBM has leveraged innovative social analytics technology to capture "mini pulse" feedback from employees as they interact with health programs. This real-time, practical input is invaluable when serving such a large dispersed population such as IBM's.

Stewart Sill
Manager, Global Health and Vitality,
IBM Integrated Health Services

Megan Benedict
Global Health and Vitality Manager,
IBM Integrated Health Services

To read the full case study go to appendix B

New Insights about the Mind-Body Connection

For hundreds and even thousands of years, the relationship between the mind and body has been a topic of debate among great philosophers—since long before Descartes outlined his dualistic notions of mind and body. Modern characterizations of the mind-body relationship have nearly universally accepted that they are inseparable, yet we still do not fully understand the intricacies of their relationship. Most current theories characterize the mind as having an important impact on the body; however, recent research has also demonstrated that the human mind and body have a greater reciprocal impact than was once believed. Not only does the mind influence the body in important ways, but the body can make significant changes in the brain and mind. Some evidence of this comes from research in the field of embodied cognition, an outgrowth of the fields of social and cognitive psychology. This field is providing valuable information about the directional relationship between the body (our motor system) and how a person feels emotionally and spiritually. Studies have shown that the manner in which we carry ourselves, the facial expressions we make, the energy we give out, and how we receive the energy of others and our surroundings can all influence our emotions and attitudes. In one classic study, while participants held a pencil in their teeth forcing them to use the muscles of a smile, they were quicker to understand positive sentences than negative sentences. The reverse was true when they held the pencil between their nose and upper lip, forcing more of a frown.[171]

Live as if you were to die tomorrow.
Learn as if you were to live forever.

—Mahatma Gandhi

Business education researchers are embracing the importance of this body-mind relationship. The research of Amy Cuddy, a Harvard Business School professor, is further improving our understanding of the link between body language and our physiology, our emotions, and our behavior. Her work is providing evidence that "faking" body postures that mimic positions of power (she calls these "power poses"), even for short periods of time, can impact levels of testosterone and cortisol, increase performance in some situations, and help us better cope in stressful situations.[172] This work and other research on the reciprocal relationship between mind and body have important implications for the practice of population health management in employer settings.

Advances in Brain Science

Modern brain research has discovered that the brain is much more malleable or "plastic" throughout life than we once thought. This brain plasticity runs counter to our long-held belief that the brain cannot substantially change after a critical period in childhood, except to deteriorate as we age. This belief has shaped our notions about the structure and function of the brain itself, as well as our ideas about human nature, brain injury, and aging. New discoveries about the brain have led to some of the most revolutionary and important ideas in science today.

> *More widely accepted now is the practice of training managers and employees about brain health and resiliency, and showing them how to become more hopeful and optimistic, which leads to being more productive.*

—Rose Ganter
Author, *Workplace Wellness Performance With a Purpose*, 2013

Of particular relevance to health and thriving is our improved understanding of how our attention physically shapes our brains. There are two basic rules governing changes in the brain. The first rule, "use it or lose it," refers to the "competitive nature of brain plasticity."[173] If we do not regularly use a skill or perform a behavior, the area of the brain responsible for that activity will be taken over by brain activity for other skills that we do practice. The second rule is that "neurons that fire together wire together." This refers to the tendency of brain cells that are active at the same time to chemically wire together, resulting in a greater tendency for one cell to fire when the other is active.

Forming Good Habits—Replacing Bad Ones

Many of the behaviors we undertake on a daily basis, the behaviors that make up our lifestyles, are a result of habits formed early in life. William James wrote, "We are what we repeatedly do… Could the young but realize how soon they will become mere walking bundles of habits, they would give more heed to their conduct while in the plastic state."[174] If James were alive today, he would undoubtedly be excited by the discoveries of modern neuroscience and their implications for the advancement of the human condition. While the brain is indeed more plastic in our early years, research on neuroplasticity is shedding light on how we can effectively shape our brains and rewire old unhealthy habits throughout our lives. More than 120 years ago, William James discussed the plasticity of our brains in his seminal text *The Principles of Psychology*. While his description of the physiology of brain plasticity is not completely accurate, his general characterization of the process is quite prophetic.

> *If habits are due to the plasticity of materials to outward agents, we can immediately see to what outward influences, if to any, the brain-matter is plastic. The only impressions that can be made upon [it] are through the blood, on the one hand, and through the sensory nerve-roots, on the other; and it is to the infinitely attenuated currents that pour in through these latter channels that the hemispherical cortex shows itself to be so peculiarly susceptible. The currents, once in, must find a way out. In getting out they leave their traces in the paths which they take. The only thing they can do, in short, is to deepen old paths or to make new ones. A path once*

traversed by a nerve-current might be expected to follow the law of most of the paths we know, and to be scooped out and made more permeable than before; and this ought to be repeated with each new passage of the current. Whatever obstructions may have kept it at first from being a path should then, little by little, and more and more, be swept out of the way, until at last it might become a natural drainage channel.

Using the principles of brain plasticity, instead of working to "break" our bad habits we can work to replace them with better ones.

According to Rick Hanson, PhD, a neuropsychologist and senior fellow at the Greater Good Science Center at the University of California, Berkeley, you can:

...gradually replace negative implicit memories with positive ones, just make the positive aspects of your experience prominent and relatively intense in the foreground of your awareness while simultaneously placing the negative material in the background. This process takes awareness of the habit and its triggers, and a concerted effort to actively focus attention on something pleasurable other than the old habit. This will strengthen the brain circuitry and trigger dopamine release which rewards the new activity. Over time and with repeated effort, our old bad habits can be replaced with new more healthy ones.[175]

These rules of brain plasticity can also work to help us build positive dispositions. As Hanson puts it, "If you point your attention toward the good in life, the better your brain will get at fostering goodness, and the healthier it will become." There is an increasing body of evidence that supports the idea that practicing gratitude, mindfulness meditation, and reframing negative thoughts into positive affirmations, all work to physically change your brain and strengthen positive states of mind.[176-178] Helping employees understand the benefits of such practices on health and thriving has important implications for creating positive organizational health. As Hanson points out,

because of all the ways your brain changes its structure, your experience matters beyond its momentary, subjective impact. It makes enduring changes in the physical tissues of your brain that affect your well-being, functioning, and relationships. Based on science, this is a fundamental reason for being kind to yourself, cultivating wholesome experiences, and taking them in.

The plasticity of our brains can help us strengthen our ability to be in the moment, to better encode the information that we attend to, to better recall our information and experiences. It can also help us be more mindful, and less "mindless."

The Empathy Neuron

Another fascinating discovery from neuroscience may help us better understand the hardwired social nature of human beings and other primates. Giacomo Rizzolatti, MD, from the University of Parma in Italy, discovered a unique type of neuron in the human motor cortex. Now known as "mirror neurons," these neurons fire both when a person makes a movement and when he or she sees someone else make a similar movement. Vilayanur Ramachandran, PhD, director of the Center for Brain and Cognition at the University of California, San Diego, believes that these mirror neurons give us an innate capacity for empathy. According to Ramachandran, the mirror neuron "…is truly astonishing. It's as though this neuron is adopting the other person's point of view. It's almost as though it's performing a virtual reality simulation of the other person's action."[179]

The firing of mirror neurons represents a very real connection between people—"there is no real distinctiveness of your consciousness from someone else's consciousness."[179] This discovery has huge implications for our culture, both broadly and within our employer organizations. It brings a new dimension to the importance of modeling healthy behaviors or truly living by the core shared values of a company.

When we experience other people's actions in our employer organizations, especially the actions of leadership and other influential people, it is almost like we are experiencing the behavior or living the values ourselves just a little bit, even before we adopt similar behaviors.

Behavioral Economics: To Err Is Human

We make decisions about our lifestyles from moment to moment every day. Some of these choices have only minor consequences, and some can be quite consequential. When making these choices, we would like to think that we are rational beings and that our brains, like computers, gather information and act on it in a logical way. But the sheer amount of information we face when making decisions is too much for us to process fully. So we use mental shortcuts to help us organize the information, screen out irrelevant things, focus on what matters, and guide our decisions and actions. While these shortcuts, or heuristics, can save us time and sometimes make our decisions easier, they can also influence our thinking in ways we aren't aware of—in seemingly irrational ways. While we prefer to believe we make choices that are rational and largely in our best interest, irrational thinking can sometimes lead to choices that are less than optimal. In this section, we discuss an area of behavioral economics that helps us better understand our human nature.

The work of Daniel Kahneman and Amos Tversky created a new level of understanding regarding the role of emotions and intuitions in shaping and biasing our decision making. While our intuition and emotions can serve important functions, they can also bias our decisions in many important and often unconscious ways, including:

- We aren't always right when judging how a decision will make us feel later on.

- We don't always include or completely process important, relevant information at the time of the decision.

- The emotions we feel while making decisions can make it harder to reason well.

- When we're emotional, we're especially sensitive to the impact of the mental shortcuts and biases that can lead to irrational choices.

These insights from the field of behavioral economics have particular relevance for wellness programs. We can help improve the choices we make from day to day and moment to moment by better understanding the social, cognitive, and emotional influences on our decision-making and behavior.

Our Two Selves

In other work of relevance to population health, Kahneman writes about the important distinction between experience and memory with regard to happiness.[180] He characterizes humans as having something akin to two distinct selves: an "experiencing self" and a "remembering self." Our experiencing self lives in a continuous flow of moments and experiences one after the other. Our remembering self is a storyteller, living just after the moment—creating an almost immediate narrative about what we just experienced. With regard to happiness, there is an important distinction between our experiencing and remembering selves.

Our experiencing self has a certain level of happiness "in" our lives, and our remembering self has a certain level of happiness "about" our lives.

Our remembering self is the one who makes our choices for us. The experiencing self has no say in the decision. According to Kahneman, "we don't choose between experiences, we choose between memories of experiences. Even when we think about the future, we don't think of it in terms of experiences, we think of it in terms of anticipated memories."[181]

The notion of having two selves has important implications for population health, especially with respect to interventions designed to strengthen positive individual health. Improving our happiness and well-being can take two very different courses, depending on which self you are trying to please. The experiencing self finds happiness in things like building connections and spending time with friends, while the remembering self thrives on more tangible things like money and tangible goals.

Employers are beginning to utilize initiatives that can please both of our "selves." The more status- and goal-oriented remembering self is drawn to competitions and challenges that provide tangible monetary or points-based rewards. The experiencing self may gain satisfaction from the connections and relationships these challenges provide.

There is also increasing recognition among employers of the value of practices that strengthen our ability to be in the moment, in the flow, to create the conditions that foster creativity. Over the past several years, there has been a growing influence from the contemplative disciplines in our wellness initiatives. Yoga and meditation are fast becoming staples in the world of wellness and well-being.

To support employees in these efforts, we believe it is important for the wellness field to embrace an eclectic array of concepts both within and beyond our usual comfort zone and to develop approaches for both of our selves. For example, approaches that help our experiencing selves better experience the moments of our lives both at home and at work can increase thriving (see the inspirational work of Mihaly Csikszentmihalyi on flow and creativity).[38,182,183] Plus, incorporating principles from positive psychology, brain science, and behavioral economics in our approaches can help our remembering selves develop stronger tendencies to have positive yet still realistic narratives or stories about those experiences.

What Can Employers Do?

The win-win journey is designed to help organizations evolve healthy and thriving cultures hand-in-hand with developing wellness and well-being initiatives and programs. The collaborative process of developing organic solutions can help drive engagement and passion among stakeholders throughout the organization and strengthen the health-related culture and climate in the organization.

> *An organization can change its environment and policies to achieve a culture of health. However, without individuals contributing by taking responsibility for their own health behaviors—exercising self-leadership—a culture cannot thrive as a collective group.*
>
> —Anne Marie Ludovici-Connolly

Instead of wellness or well-being initiatives being a programmatic end, they can be continuously evolved through a dynamic, meaningful, and creative process to enhance the various dimensions of positive individual health. By supporting employees in their unique growth process toward reaching their potential, the stage will be set for developing thriving self-leaders, and as a desirable consequence, a thriving organization.

Schindler Elevator Corporation: A Call for "Going Stealth"

In 2013, Julie Shipley, Manager of General Training (now Senior Human Resources Business Partner) at Schindler Elevator Corporation, reached out to Motion Infusion to inquire about the possibility of incorporating well-being into an upcoming leadership development program for the company's rising top managers. This initial conversation blossomed into what has now become a multi-year "Odyssey" series that has created a ripple effect of enhanced well-being throughout the organization. The success of the first "Leadership Odyssey" workshop (held in the spring of 2014) has sparked follow-up events including "Safety Odyssey," "HR Odyssey" and additional "Leadership Odyssey" workshops.

Like other wellness providers, I had felt continually frustrated by the lack of time and resources that are typically afforded wellness programs. "Going stealth," I have discovered, may be our best bet in getting around this chronic shortage. A stealth strategy simply calls for embedding wellness and well-being concepts into non-wellness programs, such as leadership development, safety training, culture change initiatives and onboarding, and swapping out wellness language, such as health improvement and stress management, for "stealth" terms, such as energy and human performance improvement. The idea is to allow improved health and well-being to emerge as a result of a broader set of corporate-wide efforts. Sounds sneaky, but it's really just a smarter way to go where the money is and move toward what is deemed "essential" (especially in the eyes of senior leaders) in helping the organization to achieve its core objectives.

Laura Putnam
CEO, Motion Infusion
Author, Workplace Wellness That Works

To read the full case study go to appendix B

For much of the past two decades, wellness programming has been designed to help employees address the threat of poor health, including physical and mental health evaluations, and understand why, what, and how to manage their weight, selected diseases, blood pressure, and cholesterol levels. Behaviors like sedentary lifestyles, poor nutrition, stress, and smoking are among the issues most commonly targeted by wellness programs. Over the past several years, the variety of programs has been increasing to include financial management, anxiety, and sleep, among others. The integration of the wellness and well-being concepts has led to additional programming that helps employees strengthen mindfulness, resilience, gratitude, values, and inner strengths, among other offerings.

We're excited about what the future holds...new technology and enhanced data analytics will broaden our horizon in the quest for better health. We can now integrate wellness and health improvement programs with newly available technology including popular apps and activity trackers and condition-specific medical sensors that track testing compliance in real time and deliver personalized messaging. Leveraging this new technology and the newly available compliance data takes wellness to a new level. Coupled with professional health coaches who add the human touch and the ability to integrate with an employee's care teams, we deliver a seamless experience for members that is personalized, meaningful, and relevant. And with the ability to deliver more targeted interventions during teachable moments, we will improve engagement and results. These latest innovations will take us a step further toward consolidating care, bridging information, and communications gaps in healthcare, and making the member experience more personalized, engaging, and effective.

Arielle Band
Executive Vice President, Health and Wellness Solutions, Accountable Health Solutions

In chapter 10, we provided an exercise that can be used to assess the health-related programming, services, and resources offered by your organization. We also included exercises that can help outline what people care about in terms of their personal purpose and values and the results that matter to them. We provide an exercise below that builds on the earlier exercises to help you prioritize the types of programmatic health-related resources you might consider. For each type of support listed, consider the degree that it serves the values and results of both the organization and the employees. You may find some things that you can stop doing or identify other resources and support that your organization does not currently provide that could provide high value to the employees and the organization.

Activity: Wellness Programming Across the Health Continuum (Abridged)*

Type of Support	Does Your Company Do This?	Is It of Value to the Organization?	Is It of Value to Employees?
Manage disease			
Case management			
On-site biometric screening			
On-site medical evaluation and management			
Reduce risk—help healthy people stay healthy, wellness programs			
Preventive services evaluation and management			
Help employees thrive—development opportunities for self-leaders			
Development opportunities for leaders, managers, and supervisors			
EAP programs and services			

*A detailed version of this assessment is available in appendix C.

We believe there is value in offering development and support opportunities in the areas traditionally served by wellness and well-being initiatives. When employers provide these opportunities for caring reasons, wellness and well-being make a crucial contribution to the way employees think about the vision and sustainability of the organization. So we challenge companies to support the whole person by offering programs and support to help employees develop stronger self-leadership capacity. We recommend involving employees directly in the choice of programs that are made available. Ask them how valuable each type of resource would be and engage them as much as possible in the design and implementation of the approaches.

The secret to workforce wellness is to engage frontline workers in owning it. At Kaiser Permanente, the unions take responsibility for engaging frontline workers in all organizational goals—quality, service—and in establishing a healthy and supportive workplace culture. It works because the Unions and Kaiser Permanente have a labor-management partnership and frontline teams (called "unit-based teams") that have explicit agreements and structures for empowering the staff. The result is a workforce that understands metrics, appreciates the factors involved in health, and has learned how to lead. With frontline teams taking ownership for health and embedding health practices into day-to-day work, we are transforming workplace culture.

Margaret Peisert
Retired, Kaiser Permanente

Coaching for Self-Leadership

Wellness coaching is often designed as a resource to help employees or family members when they have a health problem or condition. However, we know that there is a wide range of rapidly growing coaching skills that could be of high value for the organization such as executive coaching, manager and supervisor coaching, and life coaching, among others. Ideally, it would be beneficial to have resources available to aid the employee population in each of their areas of need.

Health Coaching

Dr. Edington has rightly recognized an important shift in our society—the workplace as a foundation for health and wellness. The workplace plays an important role in melding our personal lives with our work lives in many ways, and wellness is no exception. Wellness programs that reshape behaviors can't help but have an impact on personal relationships. We see this time and again in testimonials from our health coaching participants that underscores the impact that newfound energy, stamina, and healthy habits are having on their relationships and their lives as a whole.

Kailin Carroll Alberti, MS, FACW, CWWPC
Senior Vice President, Health and Wellness Solutions

There are many ways that coaches can be instrumental in helping support health, wellness, well-being, and self-leadership, and evolving a supportive culture for health. Some relevant coaching areas are outlined below:

- *Coaching for peer support or mentoring.* Coaches can support employees in their efforts to support each other. The coaches can teach peer support and mentoring skills or facilitate the use of online training for that purpose. They could also provide feedback to those engaged in mentoring or peer support.

- *Coaching for family and household support.* Coaches can assist employees in their efforts to champion the creation of supportive environments at home and within their families. The coaches can teach skills for household wellness or support online training for that purpose. They can provide ongoing feedback to employees as they work to create wellness cultures at home.

- *Coaching for wellness leadership.* Coaches can assist managers and members of wellness committees in their efforts to support wellness within workgroups. The coaches can teach wellness leadership skills or support online training. Coaches can also provide ongoing feedback.

- *Coaching for self-leadership.* Coaches can increase employees' capacity to manage their health and to make lifestyle changes. Self-leadership skills include a deeper understanding of the process of lifestyle change, how to find or create supportive environments, and how to increase positive thinking and self-efficacy.

- *Connecting people to organizational and community wellness programs.* Coaches can maintain a database of available resources, how they can be accessed, their cost, and information about their quality. The coach can refer clients to these resources.

- *Coaching for life skills.* Quite often the job-related stress or dissatisfaction comes from a lack of personal life skills in such areas as decision-making, change, resilience, and self-leadership. The coach can be the person who helps people build those skills.

- *Coaching for leader skills.* Coaches can assist supervisors and managers in developing positive leadership skills to moderate toxic climates and especially to create positive environments, cultures, and climates. This is especially important since employee health and satisfaction is influenced by relationships with coworkers, supervisors, or managers.

- *Coaches can be a source of referral* for more serious issues such as physical or mental issues, relationship issues, and financial issues. The coach can stay in touch and be a source of encouragement as employees continue to make progress.

Providing training for health coaches to align with these topics would help to reinforce a broader kind of health and provide a context to set overall goals about well-being and thriving.

Specific to the area of corporate wellness programs, we lend our deep expertise in physical assessments and exercise and nutrition, led by a best-in-class coaching approach designed to engage large employee populations. As a component of this, we have incorporated Edington Associates' Self Leadership Project. Today, we offer two methods for our corporate clients to set goals that support lasting behavior change:

The first option utilizes the self-leadership online learning modules as self-directed programs. Each module is easy to understand, engaging and actionable. Participants are able to learn easily the concepts and reinforce their personal development through various exercises that get them applying the concepts to their everyday life.

The second option combines Life Time's exercise and nutrition expertise with Edington's behavior change model. Recognizing that personal responsibility is at the core of taking charge of one's health, our coaches begin every client interaction with an assessment of that individual's Self Leadership aptitude. This provides valuable insights regarding how their values, purpose, and strengths dictate their lifestyle, how they deal with change and difficult decisions, and how resilient they are when distractions and temptations take them off a healthy way of life path.

Andrea Puckett
Director, myHealthCheck Operations, Total Health Division by Life Time

To read the full case study go to appendix B

What Can Individuals Do?

We believe it is important for employees to develop basic life skills that help them live according to their purpose and values. We identified several areas we believe are core to self-leadership and that have evidence-based practices that organizations can offer to employees along with wellness and well-being programs. We created a set of web-based modules that provide information and activities to help employees develop and support self-leadership skills:

- **Self-leadership:** Self-leadership helps people identify and live according to their values, purpose, and vision.

- **Resilience:** Resilience helps employees build a strong positive outlook and enhance their happiness and brain health.

- **Change:** It is important for people to understand how to build on their strengths, frame their experiences in a positive way, and create a meaningful and achievable plan for change.

- **Decision-making:** Choice architecture is being used throughout our environment to shape our attitudes, beliefs, and behaviors. Also, understanding how intuition and emotions can influence decisions, and becoming more aware of mental shortcuts and biases can help people make healthier decisions throughout their lives.

The self-leadership areas listed above represent fundamental life skills for all individuals. We all need to know how to adapt to change, develop decision-making awareness and abilities, become more resilient, and take charge of our lives. These practices help all of us develop basic life skills that have relevance for setting our personal values, building optimism, having a growth mindset, making positive life changes, and understanding important influences on the large and small decisions that make up our lifestyles. Being a self-leader involves the following activities:

- actively seeking out opportunities to reach your highest potential

- defining values that are important to you

- developing a personal purpose statement

- having a clear vision for your future

Clarifying personal values, defining a unique purpose, and establishing a clear vision for the future can help individuals be motivated to engage in healthy behaviors. Understanding these inner motives for taking care of themselves will help employees seek new ways to grow. It is becoming more widely accepted to train managers and employees about brain health and resiliency and show them how to become more hopeful and optimistic, and ultimately, more productive.

We combine our behavioral therapists and wellness coaching staff to truly partner with our employees and their families to understand their "why" for achieving a higher level of well-being. Through the partnership, we help them build self-confidence, intrinsic motivation, and a renewed purpose. Vital to the process is identifying what is most important to them, whether it be finding joy in the little things in life again, building stronger interpersonal relationships, strengthening their spiritual foundation, or running a marathon. By helping those refocus on what is important to them, they learn how to make sustainable changes which lead to happiness in life.

Kris Baldwin
Administrative Director, Integrated Services
Centura Health, South State Operating Group

In the sections that follow, we present selected concepts and activities covered in our modules, along with many other practical ways to create conditions that foster and support self-leadership in employees. A company is more likely to be successful if its workforce is filled with purposeful, resilient, and positive people.

Personal Values

Communicating about examples of how values play out at all levels of the organization demonstrates how teams are moving in the same direction and reinforces the opportunity to be mindful of the organization's core values on a daily basis. In chapter 7, we included exercises to help individuals assess their personal core values and help your organization assess its core corporate values. The activity outlined here builds on those earlier exercises. Once you have defined a clear set of values, identifying actions that are associated with living by those values can reinforce the benefits. Clarifying how these values are a part of your daily living can lead to a sense of satisfaction. Thinking of new ways to live out these values helps bring meaning to your actions. The exercise on page 195 can be used to help employees clarify their personal values (see **Living Out Our Values**).

Values in Action

Everyone has been made for some particular work,
and the desire for that work has been put in every heart.

—Rumi

Martin Seligman and Chris Peterson's work in positive psychology is the basis of a validated, standardized assessment, Values in Action (VIA), to help individuals identify their core character strengths.[168] The system categorizes six overarching virtues: courage, justice, humanity, temperance, wisdom, and transcendence. Within these six categories, twenty-four distinct signature strengths are measured based on a 240-item questionnaire.[184,185] This free, online assessment takes about thirty minutes to complete and produces a personalized profile of character strengths.

Activity: Living Out Our Values (See Companion Activity on Page 83)

For each value identified, think of actions you have taken or could take that support that value, and complete this sentence:

- "When I do_____, I am living my value of _____."

- Here's an example of the value of "respect":

  "Whenever I'm on time and prepared when meeting with someone, I demonstrate my value of respect."

Repeat this activity for each value, listing several examples. Think of different scenarios where you may practice these values (in meetings, when working with team members, in your home life, in your relationships). This creates an awareness of how your actions are demonstrating your values. What are some other ways you could demonstrate that value in the future?

Peter Drucker was speaking to a group of senior-level executives, and he asked them to raise their hands if there was a lot of "deadwood" in their companies. Many in the audience raised their hands. He then responded, "Were the people deadwood when you interviewed them and decided to hire them, or did they become deadwood?"

A man [person] should never be appointed into a managerial position if his vision focuses on people's weaknesses rather than on their strengths.

—Peter Drucker

The VIA tool helps individuals identify their core strengths, find ways to utilize what they're good at, and live out their personal values. This increases the likelihood of positive experiences and plays a large part in living a purposeful and fulfilling life. Once identified, these strengths could be applied during daily activities and tapped into as resources when resiliency is needed. Unfortunately, the inclination to focus on weaknesses is in our human nature. This creates a greater need to be intentional about identifying talents and core strengths both personally and in an organizational setting. In the workplace, VIA is a useful tool to help employees and managers learn about the unique talents of individuals on their teams and craft jobs that align with employees' strengths.[186]

Personal Purpose

The two most important days in your life are the day you
are born and the day you find out why.

—Mark Twain

Purpose gives meaning to experiences and challenges. Purpose sets the direction for where you're going. Purpose is about drawing upon your energy and resources to take meaningful action toward your goals. Understanding your purpose has many benefits:

- feelings of control over your fate
- higher self-esteem and self-worth
- a context for making decisions
- positive feelings about personal beliefs, identity, and community

The activity below can help employees define their personal purpose and better understand how to live in accordance with it.

Activity: Define Your Personal Purpose*

Step 1: Defining Your Purpose

Your purpose describes how you want to live your life.

- **Strengths:** Write down some words that describe your strengths. What words have others used to describe you? *(Examples: knowledge, creativity, kindness, resourcefulness, analytic thinking, acceptance, empathy)*

- **Abilities:** What do you do well? What are some of your best and most positive abilities? Write those down as well. *(Examples: synthesize information, organize a team around a task, educate children, project management skills)*

- **Cares:** About what do you care deeply? What are some of the things that give your life meaning? (Examples: Building a supportive and thriving community, improving the quality of health care, helping the elderly feel appreciated, building a sustainable environment, helping children build self-esteem)

Step 2: Putting it all together

Now take words from the previous step and create a purpose statement:

My purpose is to use my (*enter your strengths*) to (*enter an ability*) in order to fulfill my mission of (*enter a care*)

*We owe thanks to Margie Blanchard for introducing us to this exercise.

Change

Many people do not like change, yet change is an ongoing part of self-leadership. There are many ways to learn how to bring about positive results by accepting change, being open to growth, and reframing failures into opportunities. Being open to growth and new experiences are great ways to approach positive change in your life. Here are some ways you can get started:

- Build on your strengths to learn something new, face a challenge, or solve a problem.

- Reframe failures into learning experiences, and see setbacks as growth opportunities

- Create a plan for setting and accomplishing personal goals, and then take action.

One way to build a more positive attitude toward change is to learn how to reframe negative beliefs that follow a minor bad event. Calling attention to negative thoughts and being aware of what we do next can lead to a more positive outlook. It can also provide the opportunity for development that will enhance thriving in work and life, advance the organization, and increase competence, and mastery. We have included an activity below that you can use with your employees to help them develop a growth mindset, and work through change.

Activity: Counteracting Negative Thoughts

1. A Minor Setback? Think of a recent event that didn't go well		2. What were your thoughts? What did you believe caused the event?	3. What were your feelings and behaviors as a result of your thoughts and beliefs?
I got a rejection letter from a company that I really wanted to work for.	Initial Negative Reaction	*I must not be qualified or good enough for that company.*	*I felt rejected, depressed, lowered self-esteem.*
A company that I applied to for work did not see the value that I could bring to them.	Reframed Positive Reaction	*The company may not be ready for someone with my skills, or background. Maybe I was overqualified for the position.*	*I feel OK about the rejection but have reframed my thoughts about the company, and the position I applied for. Maybe it really wasn't right for me.*

Start out by thinking of a bad thing that happened in your recent past. Then, pay attention to events that happen in your day where you can apply these simple steps in the moment.

Decision-Making

I am always wary of decisions made hastily. I am wary of the first decision, that is, the first thing that comes to my mind if I have to make a decision. This is usually the wrong thing. I have to wait and assess, looking deep into myself, taking the necessary time.

—Pope Francis

Even with the best intentions, many people make poor decisions about their health. The core principles of behavioral economics suggest that we commonly make mistakes in our thinking that can drive irrational actions that undermine our true intentions. Understanding how we make decisions can help lead to the best choice of action to take among different options. Here are some ways to improve your decision-making:

- Increase your awareness of how emotions and intuitions affect your decisions.

- Understand the role of mental shortcuts and biases and how they can undermine your ability to accomplish what you desire in life.

- Learn how your emotions and environment can impact big and small decisions that you make every day.

- Shape your environment to support better decisions.

We may know what is required to lose weight and understand why it is important, yet we still eat that second helping and avoid that morning power walk. Better understanding how systematic errors and biases in our judgment can lead to irrational behaviors can help us use deliberate strategies that help us make wiser decisions for our health and well-being.

For example, there are things you can do to shape your environment and the way you operate within it. The activity on page 199 (see **Evaluate Your Environment**) can help you be aware of things in your environment that influence your decisions. This could provide insight into how your environment can help or hinder you reaching your goals, and give you ideas for how you can create more supportive surroundings.

Activity: Evaluate Your Environment

Take some time to think about the different levels of your environment: home, work, and community. Especially notice things that you might have overlooked before. This may include structures that could influence a healthy lifestyle, accessibility, activity level, or how people interact. As examples of positive influences of the environment on health, maybe there are safe biking paths in your community, or you have a work colleague who would like to try a new fitness class with you. On the other hand, for examples of negative influences of the environment on health, there could be a big bag of salty potato chips calling your name from the kitchen cupboard, or there are no changing rooms or showers at work to clean up after a noon workout.

Enter some examples of the positive and negative features of each environment in the table below:

HOME	
Positives—Enter up to three positives of your home environment.	Negatives—Enter up to three negatives of your home environment.
COMMUNITY	
Positives—Enter up to three positives of your community environment.	Negatives—Enter up to three negatives of your community environment.
WORK	
Positives—Enter up to three positives of your work environment.	Negatives—Enter up to three negatives of your work environment.

Once you have observed these environments, begin to think of how you can change the environment or change how you interact with your environment to help you make better decisions based on your goals and values.

For each of the positive features you have listed, outline how you might make them more prominent or noticeable so that you take better advantage of them. For each of the negatives, outline how you can remove them from your environment or restructure your environment to minimize their impact. For negative environmental influences that you cannot control, outline how you might interact with your environment in a way that minimizes their impact. For example, if your route home from work usually takes you past a fast-food restaurant, and you have low resistance to driving through to order a quick snack of french fries, consider taking another route home. This not only minimizes the lure of the french fries, but it is also good for your brain to periodically change your routine.

Resilience

It is a given in life that things will go wrong. When disappointments happen, it is easy to shut down mentally and just want to crawl into a hole. Often our health-related goals are the first to suffer when we get into a low frame of mind. This can lead to feeling down and depressed, which makes it hard to engage in activities and take good care of ourselves. Negative events can trigger a downward spiral that is hard to break. Purposefully cultivating resilience in our daily lives can help us overcome obstacles and bounce back when hard times hit. Learning ways to maintain a positive outlook and developing a practice of gratitude can lead to a greater sense of happiness and well-being. Optimists tend to see setbacks as temporary and see challenges as opportunities.

This doesn't mean having a sugarcoated view of the world. Healthy optimism is genuine and stems from a realistic understanding of capabilities and resources to address the challenge.

Employers are adopting a new attitude toward human capital management: help your employees optimize their potential and they'll take care of your business. In today's business environment, with the sky-high prevalence of stress and overwhelm in the workplace, resilience can have a profound impact by helping people dial up their coping skills to manage the setbacks and adversities that they face daily. Rather than mindfulness, brain focus games and relaxation techniques, resilience coaching helps every employee where they need help by getting to the root cause of their stress and adopt new habits for managing through setbacks and stressful situations. Resilience isn't a new concept, but with the advent of interactive coaching applications we can deliver it scalable, affordable and measurable. meQuilibrium has been pioneering this approach for four years, and the market has been turning in our direction: employers now make the connection between greater resilience and improved engagement and performance, and lower stress and absence.

Janesse Bruce
CEO and Cofounder, meQuilibrium

Resilience is not a fixed trait. People can learn to become more resilient, which has benefits at home and work. Coping with adversity in positive ways has a direct impact on the workplace, both on your performance and your morale when interacting with others. Employees often are asked to be creative with limited resources, learn new skills, and take on additional responsibilities. They may also be concerned about job uncertainty or changing organizational structures. The ability to adapt to these changes, deal with stress, maintain a sense of control, and sustain a healthy lifestyle will all contribute to success. Having a good sense of humor helps, too! Upholding a positive view of the future, taking the time to appreciate the good things that happen throughout the day, and being grateful for and acknowledging the good in others all contribute to a more optimistic outlook.

In a recent study of resilience and conditions that foster a healthy and productive workplace, we found among 157 employees that as individual resilience scores increased, so did passion about work, feeling challenged but not overwhelmed, and having a greater sense of belonging. Highly resilient employees believed that what they did contributed significantly to the organization's purpose, and they were more willing to exert more effort because they believed in the organization.

Highly resilient people were more likely to say that they trust the people they work with, have opportunities to participate in work groups that encourage collaboration, and combine efforts to reach goals working with rather than against each other.

We also found that those who were more resilient and scored high in the areas above were less likely to report depression, stress, and anxiety. Those with the lowest resilience and who scored the lowest on the above items, reported the greatest stress and depression.

Gail Wagnild, PhD
Owner and CEO, Resilience Center

Mindfulness

Mindfulness can be thought of as a mental state of focused awareness and calm acceptance of one's thoughts, feelings, bodily sensations, and surrounding environment in the present moment. Research is increasingly supporting the positive effects of mindfulness practices on both our mental and physical health (e.g., lowered emotional stress, reductions in blood pressure, and improved symptoms of chronic conditions, to name a few).[187-192] Mindfulness meditation is finding a place in work settings to help decrease employee stress and improve resilience, vigor, and overall well-being.[193] There is also evidence that mindfulness can help improve self-compassion and quality of life in healthcare practitioners.[194] Some of the most intriguing work is finding that mindful meditation can change the gray matter of our brains and even change the expression of our genes in ways that can significantly improve our health.[177,178]

Enhance Your Mental Immune System

There are ways to boost your "mental immune system" to prepare for challenges. Just like taking care of your body to ward off disease, you can build brain health to improve resilience during difficulties. Some ways to keep your brain healthy include fueling your brain by eating fruits and vegetables, including omega 3s in your diet, drinking plenty of water, getting enough sleep, taking time to relax, breaking a sweat, seeking challenges, and connecting with others. Close, positive relationships also help nurture your brain and build a support network. There are many ways that you can enhance your brainpower.

Seek Challenges

You can kick things up a notch by experimenting with some simple daily activities to help strengthen your brain's performance. There are many things you can include in your everyday routine that can help:

- *Improve your memory.* Watch a documentary about a topic that is interesting to you or go to a museum. After the movie or when you get home from the museum, try to recap what you watched or saw in an outline, remembering as much as you can.

- *Get coordinated.* Play around with hand-eye coordination with activities like Ping-Pong or juggling. Working to improve this type of sensory-guided movement can have a widespread positive impact on your brain.

- *Develop better balance.* Whenever you have a choice, take the rockier road. Much of our modern world has smooth, even walking surfaces. However, walking on uneven surfaces, like flagstones, hiking paths, or unpaved pathways, can help improve your balance and stability in the long run. Remember to be careful not to lose your footing to avoid slips and falls.

- *Work new regions of your brain.* Try using your nondominant hand. Start by using your opposite hand to comb your hair, open a door, or pick up your fork; then work up to more complex tasks like brushing your teeth or eating. Keep practicing until you feel comfortable doing it. (Something to try now: draw a happy face with your nondominant hand. You can also try using your mouse with your nondominant hand.)

- *Improve your hearing and concentration.* As we age, our hearing ability begins to decrease. Rather than turning up your television or radio, try turning it down a notch. Concentrate more intensely until it becomes easier to follow. Then turn it down another notch.

- *Sharpen your focus.* Memorize a new song and sing along to it while you are learning. This can help improve your ability to focus, understand, and remember. It also releases a brain chemical called acetylcholine that enables plasticity and helps make your memory more vivid.

- *Enhance your visual-spatial ability.* Complete a challenging jigsaw puzzle (at least five hundred pieces). Rotating the pieces in both your mind and in your hand and determining where they belong in the big picture can help strengthen your brain in important ways.

Other longer-term endeavors that are great for your brain include learning to play a musical instrument and learning a new language. This type of training strengthens relationships between different brain functions, including listening, memory, control of refined movements, and translation of written notes (sight) to music (movement and sound).

Slow Down

Another way to strengthen your brain is to slow down and notice things around you that you may have otherwise missed. If you often feel frenzied and stressed in this fast-paced world, consider these ideas:

- *Do one thing at a time.* Stick to one task instead of multitasking so you can better concentrate. Before moving onto something else, try to finish the task or make a plan for when you will come back to it.

- *Take deep, long breaths.* Start out by inhaling through your nose for four counts and then exhaling for four counts, making your inhales and exhales the same length. Eventually, try to lengthen your breaths for six or eight counts.

- *Slow down when driving.* Driving too fast could have worked its way into a habit, even when you are not in a hurry. Try the slow lane. In fact, consider walking, riding your bike, or taking the bus instead whenever possible.

- *Do not answer your phone.* Alternatively, shut it off for periods. Avoid the temptation to have that ring interrupt your workout, meditation, or conversation with a friend.

- *Meditate.* Taking the time to calm your mind can bring a sense of peace. Just a few minutes a day can help.

- *Do a task more slowly than usual.* Take the time to notice things you have not noticed before. Be mindful of the moment.

- *Resist overcommitting.* Realistically assess your ongoing obligations before saying yes to that next request.

- *Know your priorities.* Something may seem pressing, but when you think about it, it is not important for the moment. Do you really need to add that to your day? Focus your energy on your goals and priorities.

- *Get back to nature.* Make time to step outdoors, inhale the fresh air, and look at the colors in the earth and the sky. Exercising outdoors is a great way to bring more nature into your life.

- *Take your time when eating.* Enjoy the smell, taste, and texture of each bite, instead of hurrying through the meal or grabbing food on the run.

- *Be present with people.* Pay close attention to words and body language instead of letting your mind wander or planning what you want to say in response.

We understand that it may not be possible to undertake all of the approaches that we described in this chapter. We do, however, encourage you to start with one or two organization-level efforts that promote self-leadership, and one or two resources and opportunities that help individuals develop their self-leadership capacity.

As Kaiser Permanente was developing our workforce wellness strategy and approach, Zero Trends *was a valuable resource in helping us frame the principles and promote innovation in support of* Total Health *for our employees. Dee Edington expresses his ideas and expertise in actionable ways that have helped drive positive change within our organization.*

Maria Dee
National Director, Healthy Workforce, Kaiser Permanente

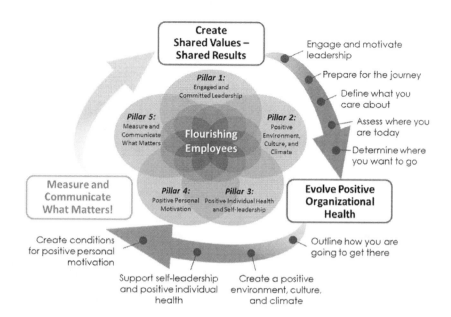

CHAPTER 13:
Create Conditions for Positive Personal Motivation

Positive personal motivation is about striving to maximize energy and motivation in service of a greater positive personal purpose.

What would it be like to wake up each morning with energy and enthusiasm? To have a strong sense of purpose and to operate in an authentic manner that continuously supports and feeds the purpose and vision for your life. In this chapter, we focus on how organizations can better understand and support this kind of energy and purpose in their employees and explore ways employees can nurture it for themselves. It starts by recognizing and embracing that what motivates each individual is unique and very personal. We introduce the concept of positive personal motivation (PPM) to reflect the personal nature of what drives each of us to reach for our best self and to strive to achieve our highest purpose. We believe this is at the core of positive individual health and thriving.

PPM is related to self-leadership but is conceptually distinct. It is what drives the personal mental and physical energy source that allows us to live as self-leaders. PPM is where the why, what, and how of maintaining or improving health and well-being become especially important. The why, or the reason for maintaining or changing our attitudes and behaviors, is deeply personal for each of us, and the how, or the path we take, is also uniquely ours.

Positive personal motivation is our internalized motivation to engage in patterns of thinking and behaviors that move us toward meaning and purpose in our lives.

The wellness industry is exploding with technology, incentive models, physician integration, and social wellness programs all designed to challenge and motivate behavior change. In the end, it is up to the individual to find their motivation to sustain a healthy lifestyle and enjoy a life of wellness.

Cindy Bjorkquist
Director, Wellness, Care Management, and Health Promotion Program Development
Blue Cross Blue Shield of Michigan

Human Motivation: The Basics

Before presenting emerging practices for motivating employees, we briefly discuss the social science research on human motivation that has most influenced our thinking in this area. Ed Deci (pronounced Dee-cee) and his research partner Richard Ryan, together with their colleagues at the University of Rochester, have conducted hundreds of studies on human motivation over the past forty-four years. Deci and Ryan are the founders of self-determination theory (SDT), which is featured heavily in Dan Pink's best-selling popular book, *Drive*.[195] At its core, SDT is about human motivation and a core set of human needs that, when met, contribute to living a full and healthy life. According to Deci, "motivation is all about energy for action. It is what gets you up in the morning and moves you through the day."[196]

Many in the wellness field are making the distinction between **extrinsic** and **intrinsic** motivation with respect to their differential impacts on behavior change. While we agree that this is an important understanding for our field, SDT makes a primary distinction between **controlled** motivation and **autonomous** motivation.

Autonomous Motivation

According to Deci, autonomous motivation is related to having "a true sense of volition, willingness, and choice in this moment. This is what I choose to be doing for myself." Autonomous motivation is a close cousin to mindfulness or any other way of operating that helps us be in the present moment in our lives. If we endorse what we're doing and concur with it, we are operating at a higher level of awareness than if our actions were being controlled by external pressure. When we are guided by autonomous motivation, we live in a much more authentic way. Truly autonomous motivation is what pleases our "experiencing selves"—the part of ourselves that experiences the present moment (see **Our Two Selves** on page 186 of chapter 12). Relative to controlled motivation, autonomous motivation is associated with deeper learning, greater flexibility and creativity, and greater persistence at behavior change efforts. It is also related to more interest and enjoyment in the activity, less anxiety, and better health and well-being. These findings hold true for a broad range of personal characteristics (e.g., gender, age, socioeconomic status) and across different cultures.[197]

Given SDT's primary distinction of motivation as either autonomous or controlled, where does that leave us with respect to intrinsic and extrinsic motivation? It is tempting to equate autonomous motivation with intrinsic motivation and to treat controlled and extrinsic motivation as equivalent concepts. But the alignment between the types of motivation is a bit more nuanced. Deci discusses autonomous motivation as having "two flavors":

1. Intrinsic motivation
2. Fully internalized extrinsic motivation

Intrinsic motivation is truly autonomous when you are engaging in a behavior of your own free will, for the sheer interest you have in it and the pure enjoyment it provides. It is in our nature to interact with our world in a way that we find enjoyable. We are born with that capacity, and engaging in things that we enjoy. It satisfies all three of our basic psychological needs (see page 209). When we function with a high degree of autonomous motivation, we endorse what we're doing and operate at a high level of self-awareness. We understand ourselves in relation to the world at that moment and operate in an authentic way.

Fully internalized extrinsic motivation operates differently. As we all know, the realities of life require that we sometimes do things that are important, but that we don't find inherently interesting and enjoyable. Deci and Ryan use the concept of "internalization" from developmental psychology to explain how external demands can become internalized and integrated into who we are. However, it is not simply a process of just doing something enough times that it eventually becomes internalized. An extrinsic prompt can only become integrated when the person engages in a proactive process that transforms external prompts into internal prompts. In other words, this transformation is an active process that the person must do for him or herself.

Fully integrating extrinsic motivation involves identifying with the importance of the behavior for yourself and integrating it into who you are as a human being.

Controlled Motivation

Controlled motivation involves doing something because of a sense of coercion or pressure, and consists of two types of extrinsic motivation that have not been well internalized.

1. External motivation, which involves doing an activity specifically because it will lead to some external outcome.

2. Introjected motivation, which is motivation that is partially, but not fully internalized.

External motivation is the classic "carrot" or "stick" situation. Providing incentives to employees for completing a health assessment or changing an unhealthy behavior is an example of controlled motivation from the carrot perspective. If you do what we are asking we will give you a reward (the carrot). Requiring employees to take the assessment or change their behavior in order to keep their current health-plan benefit structure (i.e., their copay amounts, their level of coverage, or the amount of their contribution to the cost for their plan) are also examples of controlled motivation, but from the stick perspective. If you don't do what we are asking, we will take something away, or punish you (the stick). Both of these conditions can be experienced as very controlling. Both involve pressure or coercion, and both can undermine our individual autonomy.

Many studies show that using external rewards can undermine intrinsic motivation.[198] This is especially true when the reward is expected as a result of the task. If a task or behavior is performed without the expectation of a reward, and then a reward is given after the fact, it does not have the same negative effect on intrinsic motivation.

The primary reason that the expectation of a reward erodes intrinsic motivation is that it is designed to be controlling. It undermines our basic need for autonomy.

Introjected motivation is a type of *internal* motivation that can be experienced as quite *controlling*. One example of this is guilt. Guilt is an internal motivator, but if we do things because of the threat of guilt (if I don't do it I will feel guilty, so I better do it), it doesn't usually feel very autonomous. It is not "me" making a volitional choice. It feels controlling. So again, just getting a person to do something repeatedly is not enough. We may partially internalize the behavior, but never fully accept it as part of who we are.

The distinction between these forms of motivation has relevance for our efforts to create positive conditions for the health and well-being of employees. This is in part due to the influence of controlled and autonomous motivation on our basic psychological needs—another core aspect of SDT.

Fundamental Human Needs

No one will refute that our survival depends on meeting some basic *physiological* needs. We need air, water, and food to stay alive and healthy. According to SDT, all humans also have basic *psychological* needs that must be met to be fully healthy and to thrive over time. SDT states that there are three fundamental needs relevant to all people:

1. *Competence* is about feeling capable and effective in our social interactions, and in our work and lives, and being able to express our capacities. According to SDT, the need for competence "leads people to strive for challenges that are optimal for their capacities and to persistently attempt to maintain and enhance those skills and capacities through activity."[199]

2. *Relatedness* reflects our need for connection with others and the need for both being cared for and caring for others. It reflects the need for a sense of belonging with other people and with our communities.

3. *Autonomy* refers to our need to feel that we have control over our behavior.[205,206,207] It is about our need to behave in ways that have value for us and that align with our personal values. According to SDT, we are autonomous when our actions reflect our true selves, even when we are influenced by external sources.

As Deci puts it, these needs are "part of the architecture of being human."[201] Satisfaction of these needs leads to greater wellness and deprivation of these needs leads to less wellness. While Abraham Maslow and other humanist psychologists believed this to be true, Deci and Ryan and dozens of other researchers have empirically validated this in thousands of studies. We discuss each type of motivation in some depth below, and then outline ways that both organizations and individuals can work to create better conditions for supporting and nurturing our basic human needs and fostering positive personal motivation.

Current Practices for "Motivating" Employees

Current question: How can we motivate people to participate in wellness programs?

In earlier chapters, we outlined the current wellness and well-being best practices for the pillars of engaged and committed leadership (chapter 5), positive environment, culture, and climate

(Chapter 11), and self-leadership and positive individual health (chapter 12). In each of those chapters, we also outlined emerging next practices. The original *Zero Trends* pillar that most closely corresponds with the concepts of PPM is pillar 4, "Rewards and Recognition." Since *Zero Trends* was written, the practices that wellness providers have been using to motivate people to live healthy lifestyles have evolved, but not always for the better. In this chapter, we even hesitate to use the term "best practices." We intend to make the case that many of the current practices that focus on short-term participation objectives are unsustainable and a fundamentally different approach is needed.

Current practices for "motivating" employees to improve their health are among the most hotly debated topics in the wellness field today. Although the importance of intrinsic motivation is increasingly recognized, the current practice is still to use extrinsic motivators, such as financial incentives or disincentives, to increase program participation, increase behavior change, and decrease health risks or disease. Such practices have become deeply embedded in the way we do things to the extent that the most recent guidance concerning incentives is part of the Affordable Care Act (ACA).[203]

What began years ago with promotional hats, T-shirts, and mugs to excite people about participating in programs, transitioned to larger and larger monetary incentives and disincentives to encourage participation. A 2007–2008 survey conducted by National Association of Manufacturers (NAM) and the ERISA Industry Council (ERIC) showed that 71 percent of employers offer incentives for health and wellness or disease management programs.[204] Even so, a 2012 RAND Employer Survey found that the average participation rates for wellness screening activities were not overwhelming (46 percent for both HRA and clinical screening), and participation in lifestyle management components of wellness programs was even less impressive (between 7 percent and 21 percent).[205]

Each year, often on the advice of wellness providers and benefits consultants, employers spend millions of dollars to incentivize employees to participate in wellness programs. The dollar amounts of the incentives have also increased at an alarming rate. The Third Annual (2011) National Business Group on Health, Fidelity Investments Benefits Consulting survey found that employer spending on health and wellness incentives in 2009 was $368 per employee. In 2011, the amount was $629—a 70 percent increase in two years.[206] This rate of increase (approximately $130 per year) is not sustainable for most organizations. Eventually, the financial incentives could be more expensive than the potentially avoided costs they were designed to address—if that isn't true already.

Commonly used extrinsic incentives and disincentives used to motivate employees to behave in ways employers want, include the following:

Incentives	Disincentives
Cash	Health insurance premium increases
Health insurance premium reductions	Copay increases
Tiered health insurance offerings	Reduced benefits
Copay reductions	Salary reductions
Health-account contributions (e.g., health savings accounts, flexible spending accounts, health reimbursement accounts)	Job sanctions
Paid time off (PTO)	
Gift cards	
Tangible gifts	

What other industry can sell an employer a program or service that employees don't use, and then recommend the employer pay its employees to use it? What is wrong with this picture?

There are many questions surrounding the use of incentives for good reason. While there seems to be no doubt that financial incentives can increase participation in wellness programs in the short-term, their impact on employees' attitudes and longer-term behavior change is not yet fully understood. There is a substantial body of research that suggests that under some circumstances, external rewards and incentives can have counterintuitive effects. Incentivizing people to perform a behavior can reduce their intrinsic motivation to continue that behavior in the long-term.

Emerging Next Practices for Supporting Positive Personal Motivation

New question: How can we help employees flourish by creating conditions that foster positive personal motivation?

Need Fulfillment in the Workplace

Employers can provide incentives or disincentives that might persuade people to participate in wellness programs, but that is not likely to build the deep personal motivation it will take to pursue lasting change over the long-term. Creating conditions that support employee motivation to change will take a thoughtful and strategic approach that combines the best and emerging next practices described throughout the book. There are specific principles related to motivation that deserve purposeful attention along the journey. The key lies in addressing the three psychological needs mentioned earlier; 1) competence, 2) relatedness, and 3) autonomy.

In the long-run, we believe that paying employees to use wellness programs or change unhealthy behaviors will be unnecessary in organizations with alignment in the areas covered throughout the book.

What Can Employers Do?

In some highly structured work environments, employees' experience of autonomy, competence, and relatedness can be diminished, and their motivation to work will likely focus on money, prestige, praise, and promotions.[207] But there is evidence that when work environments are changed to better support the psychological needs of employees, they will better internalize the rules, standards, and procedures of their workplace, come to value the work more, and be more creative, purposeful, and proactive.[208, 209]

> *...a [person] who energizes below his [or her] normal maximum*
> *fails by just so much to profit by his [or her] chance at life;*
> *...a nation filled with such [people] is inferior to a nation run at a higher pressure.*

—William James

The same principles can be applied to how organizations support employee health and well-being. Tying participation in wellness programs to incentives and rewards will likely result in employees doing only what it takes to get the reward or avoid the punishment, and the employees will be less likely to internalize the healthy practices into their personal lifestyles. Honoring employees' competence, relatedness, and autonomy with our wellness and well-being approaches will help them fully integrate healthy behaviors over time. Table 16 outlines some of the things that organizations can do to help create the conditions for positive personal motivation.

> *Workplace organizations are a leading influence often determining the degree to which a person lives a thriving life. In our current thinking, the health messages heard by employees from organizations are to participate in the initiatives to lower cost and the focus has been physical health. Monetary payments are used as carrots or sticks to drive better numbers and our outcomes show little movement on the continuum to better health.*
>
> *Frankly, it is because of the failure to care about the people first, tap into intrinsic motivators and take a whole person approach. It is time for a paradigm shift in our thinking; a shift to truly caring, inspiring and creating a partnership whereby organizational systems are supported and not forced. It is time to approach the initiatives through the lens of the employee.*
>
> *Lexie Dendrinelis, BS, CHPD*
> *Wellbeing Thought and Practice Leader*

Table 16. How can employers cultivate conditions for positive personal motivation?

Create a need-supportive environment and culture

Support and develop competence

- Provide development opportunities for all stakeholders, especially managers, to learn to help employees build competence
- Create alignment between employees' skills, values, purpose, and work or career—Help employees develop meaningful work
- Help people succeed—Small wins—Keep it simple—Help healthy people stay healthy

Foster connections and relationships

- Provide development opportunities for leaders and managers to learn to foster relatedness
- Create environmental conditions that foster connections
- Encourage teamwork and positive energy networks
- Support, encourage group flow, and empower design teams

Provide autonomy support

- Provide development opportunities for managers to learn to be autonomy-supportive
- Engage employees in designing initiatives
- Allow autonomy over how work gets done
- Allow choice over the path to health and well-being. Don't force it—allow it

Develop Need-Supportive Leaders

Self-determination theory is extremely relevant to how we think about our wellness programs and initiatives, but it can also guide leaders and managers in their interactions with the employees they supervise. In every organization we have worked with, middle-level managers and leaders have been the least enthusiastic about efforts to promote wellness and well-being initiatives or to more generally support employee health and well-being. This is not because they don't care about the people they supervise. There are many more likely reasons. Leaders and managers already have very busy full-time jobs and many may not see supporting the health and well-being needs of employees as part of their formal role. However, whether they recognize it or not, the role of leaders and managers is to guide, support, and motivate, their direct reports. This is a form of extrinsic influence that can have negative effects on motivation, health, and well-being if handled poorly. Other reasons that managers may resist such a role can include:

- ***Personality***—Some people have very controlling authoritarian personalities. Make sure you have the right people in management positions. Recruit and promote managers who can operate in a need-supportive manner.

- *Skills*—While some people don't have the skills, need-support can be taught. So provide opportunities for managers and leaders to develop the necessary skills to support the needs and well-being of employees.

- *Situation*—Some organizational practices undermine the ability of managers to provide need-support. Do managers feel unrealistic pressure from above to push on their employees to perform in unhealthy ways? Do they have the freedom to allow their employees autonomy in the way they get their work done? Is supporting employees part of their explicit role?

One of the most important things that organizations can do is help managers and leaders support the health and well-being of employees by attending to the basic psychological needs of both managers and employees. In the next several sections, we discuss the importance of developing leaders and managers to support each of the basic human needs. We also outline ways that organizations, leaders, and managers can best support the needs and positive personal motivation of employees.

Support and Develop Competence

Leaders and managers in organizations are often promoted to their current positions because they were competent at some important aspect of their previous jobs that had nothing to do with their ability to support and manage people. Provide development opportunities for leaders and managers to improve their ability to support employees' basic human needs. Fostering this kind of competence in leaders and managers is a great example of a win-win. Everyone benefits. It not only helps meet an important human need for leaders and managers, it ultimately helps the employees they manage.

Cultivate Meaning and Purpose

> *...as a rule [people] use only a small part of the powers which they actually possess and which they might use under appropriate conditions.*
>
> —William James

In chapter 12, we talked about the importance of personal values, vision, and purpose. One of the most important things that managers can do is help employees understand how their work contributes to their personal values and purpose. Even for jobs that aren't inherently very exciting or rewarding, managers can help people recognize the importance the job has for the larger purpose of the organization.

Help people do things that have meaning for them
and help them find meaning in the things that they do.

In chapter 12, we also described the Values in Action work of Martin Seligman and Chris Peterson. This tool can be a great resource to help managers and employees create alignment between the values and skills of employees and their jobs or careers. Providing just the right amount of challenge, along with opportunities to build competence, can also positively contribute to meaningful work, health and well-being. We also want to emphasize the link between the need-support that employees experience at work, their positive personal motivation, and their overall health and well-being. It is important to apply the principles for creating meaning and purpose to our wellness and well-being programs and initiatives. The more people can see the connection between their health and well-being and their ability to live in alignment with their personal values from day-to-day, the more likely they will be to engage in healthy behaviors from moment-to-moment.

Help people see how health and well-being can contribute to their
purpose and meaning in work and life.

Help them see how meaning in work and life can contribute to their
health and well-being.

Hal Adler, former president of the Great Place to Work Institute, says the secret isn't sushi chefs and Shih Tzu walking services. On the contrary, the formula is pretty simple. "Ever since 1981 [when the "Great Place" lists were started], employees have said and continue to say that a great place to work is one where you trust the people you work for, take pride in what you do and enjoy the people you work with," he says. "Benefits play a role, although it's not the 401(k), it's not lavish benefits but unique benefits that make a workplace great."

As an example, Adler cites Analytic Graphics, where leaders purchased flat-screen monitors for employees after reaching a business goal. "It was a benefit that matched that company's culture and one employees would value. Employees at another company would want a dinner cruise, ski trip or box seats." Adler says employers should remember that "you can't buy employee engagement. Even at Google [2007's Fortune Best Place to Work], while employees appreciate all the perks, they speak most about the relationships, feeling of empowerment, and freedom to make mistakes" as what makes the company special. Relationships, he notes, are "one of the systemic differences between good places and great places" to work.

Quoted in Employer Benefit News August 21, 2007

Foster Connections and Relationships

Positive social relationships and connections are a basic human need. It's part of who we are and how we're wired. In chapter 2, we discussed the social dimension of positive individual health and the strong association between positive relationships and physical health. Our sense of relatedness is heavily influenced by our collegial and friendship connections at work. You may recall the strong association between agreement with the Gallup survey item "I have a best friend at work" and positive workplace outcomes including engagement and well-being.

This is another area where organizations can provide development opportunities to help leaders and managers understand how to foster this kind of relatedness by creating environmental conditions that foster connections (see **Architect Healthier Workplace Choices** in chapter 11). Leaders and managers can also encourage teamwork and positive connections using positive leadership principles (see the sections on **Positive Leadership**, **Positive Energy Networks** and **Foster Collaboration** in chapter 11), and by supporting and empowering design teams (see **Engage Design Partners** in chapter 6, and **Encourage and Develop Design Thinkers** in chapter 11), and by creating an environment that encourages group flow (see **Provide Conditions for Group Flow** in chapter 11).

Fitness Challenge: Texas Department of Transportation (TxDOT)

TxDOT's wellness program began with the 2007 passage of HB 1297, authorizing state government to allow time off for employee exercise, with supervisor approval of thirty minutes during normal working hours three times each week combined with their lunch hour. So far, the wellness program has been developed with very few resources.

Approximately thirty-five hundred employees participated in the Get Fit TxDOT Challenge. Employees pay 100 percent of the costs of any classes, and other than a staff of two, this program has operated with no budget and incurred almost no cost to the agency. TxDOT's wellness program partnered with the Department of Aging and Disability Services which provided an online tracking software and technical assistance. The safety department is paying for voluntary biometric screenings that will be rolled out October 1.

A seven-question survey was given at the end of the challenge to participants. Self-report results indicate that 74 percent had more energy, 70 percent were more productive, and 95 percent planned to continue exercising. Comments from the participants included weight loss and increased energy, and many expressed thanks to the organization for offering the challenge.

Audrey Thompson, MS
TxDOT Statewide Wellness Coordinator

Games and competitions can encourage relatedness. They can be fun, exciting, and engaging, but ultimately, someone or some team ends up winning, and everyone else ends up being "not winners." One way to keep competitions positive, is instead of always pitting people and teams against each other, give each team an award for its most important accomplishment or its biggest improvement. Rather than having teams compete against each other, they compete against themselves or strive to meet an agreed-upon goal, and each person or team can be a winner. This is true for work-related team goals and projects as well as goals specific to wellness and well-being.

Create Conditions That Support Autonomy

There is growing body of research that shows a strong relationship between our well-being and feeling that we have some level of autonomy and control over our work and our lives. However, there are certain things that have to be done in nearly every work setting and times when it is necessary to set limits. There are ways to help employees have a sense of autonomy in even the most regulated work settings. Some practical ways that managers can support autonomy include:

- Offer choices within the structure.

- Include clarification of responsibilities.

- Give employees clear goals for what is needed and then let them decide how to do it.

- Listen actively and acknowledge the employee's perspective.

- Ask open-ended questions that invite supportive dialogue to explore possible solutions.

- Provide authentic, positive feedback that recognizes inventiveness and creativity, and give feedback about problems without judgment or criticism.

Develop Autonomy Supportive Leaders

The practices outlined above may not always be comfortable for managers, so training and practice is important. Most certification programs for health coaches who work in the wellness industry include motivational interviewing as an important part of their training. Coaching managers to use similar approaches with their employees could be a natural extension of the role of these coaches. An important thing to remember is that in order to best support autonomy in others, managers need autonomy support themselves.

Involve Employees in Designing Wellness and Well-Being Approaches

One way to increase employee autonomy, as well as competence and relatedness, is to involve them in creating solutions designed to improve health and well-being in the organization. The more engaged employees are in deciding what and how support is offered, the more committed they will be to the effort, the more satisfied they will be with the offering, and the more likely they will be to engage in the practices. Because the approaches will better reflect the employee culture, they may also be of a higher quality than initiatives implemented without employee collaboration. Involvement in decision-making also improves work engagement for employees who directly participate in designing the efforts.

This kind of involvement also helps when work-related goals and limits must be set. The best way to set goals for employees or work teams is to involve the people in the process. When limits are necessary, help employees understand why limits are needed and involve them in setting the limits. It can also be helpful to have people come up with their own rationale for why limits are needed.

Provide Choice Whenever Possible

Research has shown that providing choice improves autonomous motivation. If it is not possible to involve employees in creating work-related goals, or limits, or designing health and well-being initiatives, at a minimum, allow them some level of choice. There is almost always a way to provide choice or autonomy about how a task gets done. This is also true for our efforts to engage employees in wellness and well-being programs. Giving people some amount of choice always has positive consequences in terms of their motivation. As Deci puts it, "make the limits as wide as possible, and allow choice within them." In a sense, this involves sharing the authority or power with employees. This can be done at both the individual level and the group level.

Communicate and Connect

As a professional in the benefit management business for nearly twenty years I found most employers in the past controlled annual health-insurance rate increases by shifting more of the cost to employees by raising copays and deductibles and/or having employees pay more towards the monthly premium.

What can be done?

Fortunately, there is a solution that will work in the long-term if employers and employees "communicate and connect" and truly become accountable to each other. "Communicate and Connect"—that we're all truly in this together. What helps me successfully assist clients manage the cost of their health plans is my ability to connect with their employees. I spend a great deal of time with their employees educating them on the facts, on the reality of the situation, and on the premise that ultimately they and their families are the solutions to the healthcare cost crisis.

While it's very important to design and implement incentives around employee health improvement programs the real key to driving a culture of health is found in fostering intrinsic motivation. If you as the employer can truly connect with employees, and tap into their intrinsic motivation, you and your employees will both see long-term success and reach your goals.

Daniel J. Elliott
Vice President, Group Benefits Department, Haylor, Freyer & Coon Inc.

To read the full case study go to appendix B

Provide Recognition Without Undermining Motivation

*Praise is infinitely divisible. Give it away every chance you get
and there's always plenty left for you.*

—Donald Berwick

Some work-related tasks don't require a lot of creative thinking, and some jobs are not very interesting. For the more routine types of tasks associated with these jobs, extrinsic rewards can provide motivation without harmful side effects. In some ways, it's just common sense. As Edward Deci, Richard Ryan, and Richard Koestner explain, 'Rewards do not undermine people's intrinsic motivation for dull tasks because there is little or no intrinsic motivation to be undermined.'[210] Dan Ariely and his colleagues demonstrated this phenomenon in several experiments across the world, across cultures, and across many types of jobs. When tasks call for "even rudimentary cognitive skill," a larger reward "led to poorer performance." But "as long as the task involved only mechanical skill, bonuses worked as they would be expected: the higher the pay, the better the performance."[211]

Providing positive feedback, or verbal rewards that acknowledge good work, can build employee competence. When provided after the fact, it typically does not have negative effects, but instead, enhances positive motivation.

> *A person's interest often survives when a reward is used neither to bribe nor to control but to signal a job well done, as in a "most improved employee" award. If a reward boosts your feeling of competence after doing good work, your enjoyment of the task may increase. Rewards, rightly administered, can motivate high performance and creativity. And extrinsic rewards (such as scholarships, admissions, and jobs that often follow good grades) are here to stay.*
>
> *David G. Meyers in his text* Psychology: Eighth Edition *in Modules*

Employers can help employees develop self-leadership skills and positive personal motivation by creating opportunities for more meaningful work that aligns with their purpose values and the values of the organization. We feel this is a critical part of the win-win philosophy. Ideally, employees will embrace the why, what, and how of organizational efforts to support healthy and thriving employees. But we must do more than communicate the organizations' answers to these questions. To foster positive personal motivation, we must ensure that we provide resources and opportunities that address the unique needs and motivations of employees. Help them find their own why, what and how.

Member Quote:

I am in my late fifties, and my wife is close behind. We are a working couple like most households nowadays. I am in the construction industry while my wife works at a high school. Both are demanding in their own sense. We allowed time and space to grow between us and our health as well.

In order to gain better health insurance rates, we were introduced to Accountable Health Solutions. As we started allowing time for evening walks, we discovered we enjoyed the time alone and talking to one another again. The walks got farther, and the talks became longer. Then it was on to purchasing bikes, and we now enjoy our grandkids bicycling with us on weekends.

Thanks for bringing the value of life and spark back to our marriage. Saving money isn't the point but rather the saving of life, health, family, and future for us and the next generation. We are still working toward our goals, and we know it will take work and effort, but the rewards are greater than any cost.

Thank you, enjoy, and until we see you on the trail.

Accountable Health Solutions
Health Coaching Participant

What Can Individuals Do?

Many of us would like to improve some aspect of our lives. Often our goal is to change some unhealthy behavior that isn't working for us—but changing our behaviors and ultimately, our lifestyles can be very hard! Many things wear away our ability to withstand temptations and cause us to behave in ways that keep us from reaching our goals. The positive and negative behaviors and beliefs that make up our lifestyles are strongly embedded in a very personal context. Smoking, overusing alcohol, unhealthy eating, and many other unhealthy behaviors serve a purpose such as stress release, anxiety reduction, and emotional comfort. So making and sustaining change can be difficult. Even so, there are many ways that individuals can influence their own positive personal motivation and table 17 outlines just a few.

Identify What You Care About—Your Personal "Why"

Employees must embrace their own meaningful why, and undertake a quest that suits their unique what and how.

Underlying most positive personal motivation is a meaningful "why"—something you care deeply about. Earlier in the book we spoke about the importance of identifying your personal purpose and vision (see the sections on **Personal Purpose** and **Personal Values** in chapter 12). What do you care

Table 17. How can individuals create and nurture positive personal motivation?

Nurturing Positive Personal Motivation

Identify what do you care about—your personal "why"

- Identify your personal purpose and vision
- Identify your personal and professional values

Set yourself up to succeed—Build your competence

- Understand the nature of willpower
- Create and celebrate small wins
- Heighten awareness of the link between personal practices and energy (how)
- Strengthen your willpower "muscle"
- Understand and nurture epiphanies (how)

Exercise your autonomy

- Create a healthier job—job crafting
- Architect your own healthy environment —work, home, and community

Strengthen your connections

- Foster relationships and connections
- Create a supportive personal social milieu
- Support others in their journeys

about? What do hope to achieve in your life? This is your big "why"—this can guide the smaller "whys" in your day-to-day life. You may want to increase your energy so you can keep up with your children or grandchildren. You may want to learn to speak another language so you can travel abroad. You may want to get fit so you can run a marathon, play softball after work with your friends, or just so that you will feel better about yourself. You may want to meditate so that you can better cope with stressful situations in your life. There are as many reasons (or "whys") as there are people, but something they all have in common is that they all can influence health and well-being in some manner.

Cultivating positive personal motivation is ultimately the role of each individual. Successful behavior change begins with a genuine interest and strong personal motivation. You must ask yourself why you are trying to change and think honestly about your answers. Then you can identify and engage in practices that will make it easier to think and behave in ways that serve your values and life purpose.

Set Yourself Up to Succeed—Build Your Competence

In recent years, there has been a convergence of discoveries from several fields including psychology, neuroscience, medicine, and behavioral economics that can help us better understand the social, psychological, and physiological influences on our behaviors and our self-control. In chapter 12, we spoke about the influence of our social networks (see **Foster Collaboration** on page 158), and the importance of creating a healthy and supportive social milieu (see **Create a Healthier Social Milieu** on page 172).

We also discussed environmental and cultural factors that can influence our behaviors and shared ideas for how to create more supportive conditions for health and well-being (see the sections on **Curate Your Own Personal Culture**, and **Personal Choice Architecture**, on page 171). In this chapter, we discuss recent thinking about the physiological and psychological influences on our self-regulation and self-control. We tip our hats throughout to William James for some older wisdom that mirrors the "new" insights we are gaining from recent scientific advances.

Understand the Nature of Willpower

Everyone knows on any given day there are energies slumbering in him [or her] which the incitements of that day do not call forth, but which he might display if these were greater.

—William James

Self-control and self-regulation is also known as "willpower." Willpower can be thought of as the energy or will to do the positive things that some part of us doesn't really want to do, or resist doing negative things that some part of us really wants to indulge in. There are a number of current theories about willpower. One of the more popular theories is that willpower is a bit like a muscle that can become fatigued if it is overused, but can also be strengthened over time through exercise. Roy Baumeister, a social psychologist from Florida State University, and Mark Muraven, a psychologist from the University at Albany are among the researchers who have been studying this "muscle model" of willpower for the past two decades. Research in this area has demonstrated that willpower is a finite resource that can be depleted by exertion,[212] and replenished to some degree with glucose and rest.[213] According to Baumeister, "choice, active response, self-regulation, and other volition may all draw on a common inner resource." In other words, we use a common, limited source of energy for willpower and other types of purposeful thinking and behaviors. There are many things that deplete that source of energy on a daily basis, including resisting the temptation to snack, focusing on a difficult mental task, fighting the urge to fall asleep, concentrating on self-presentation during a meeting, and many other mental and social behaviors that require self-control.

Health psychologist, Kelly McGonigal, distinguishes between three types of willpower in her popular book, *The Willpower Instinct*:[214]

- *I will power*—the ability to do what you need to do, even if part of you doesn't want to.

- *I won't power*—the ability to resist doing things that part of you wants to do.

- *I want power*—the ability to tap into what really matters when you are tempted. For our purposes, this means accessing your positive personal motivation for inspiration when you need it most.

Understanding willpower gives you strategies for developing self-control and greater strength to pursue what matters most to you. According to McGonigal:

> *people who have better control of their attention, emotions, and actions are better off almost any way you look at it. They are happier and healthier. Their relationships are more satisfying and last longer. They make more money and go further in their careers. They are better able to manage stress, deal with conflict, and overcome adversity. They even live longer. When pit against other virtues, willpower comes out on top. Self-control is a better predictor of academic success than intelligence (take that, SATs), a stronger determinant of effective leadership than charisma (sorry, Tony Robbins), and more important for marital bliss than empathy (yes, the secret to lasting marriage may be learning how to keep your mouth shut).*

The more you know about your own willpower the better equipped you will be to exercise and strengthen it. You can work to understand your willpower and then choose your willpower battles wisely. Plus, if willpower is like a muscle, you can work to build it over time and gradually develop stronger self-control and willpower.

Create and Celebrate Small Wins

Many wellness goals can set people up to fail if they are too ambitious. Good examples are setting a starting goal to walk 10,000 steps a day or pledging to lose twenty pounds. Many of us find these types of goals to be specific and compelling, but walking 10,000 steps for someone just starting out is a huge undertaking. Once we start working to achieve such large goals, the difficulty often leads to lapses in our progress, which can be experienced as disheartening failures. William James put it very eloquently more than 100 years ago, "The need of securing success at the outset is imperative. Failure at first is apt to damp the energy of all future attempts, whereas past experiences of success nerve one to future vigor."[175]

Make It Easier On Yourself—Keep it Simple. The importance of keeping it simple and celebrating small wins was emphasized in *Zero Trends*. Instead of setting unrealistic goals that will likely lead to failure, start with smaller goals that will lead to smaller wins. Create a more manageable goal to add steps to your day by walking to the printer on the far side of the office, or parking further from your shopping destination or workplace. Losing two, three, or even five pounds is far easier than maintaining the long-term effort and perceived sacrifice it would take to lose twenty pounds. Better yet, heed the *Zero Trends* challenge to not get worse on some outcome of importance to you. The natural flow for most of us over the course of our lives is to get worse—for our weight to increase, for our activity level to decrease, and for our physical health to deteriorate. Depending on your situation (i.e., your age, your current health, etc.), it may make sense to create a goal to maintain your weight over the next thirty days, or even six months, or to maintain your cholesterol values over the next six months or year. You can then set small manageable shorter-term goals to achieve this maintenance. Be sure to take the time to congratulate yourself for your wins, no matter how small. These are well-known health coaching strategies but we can work to be better coaches to ourselves on a daily basis.

Heighten Awareness of the Link Between Personal Practices and Energy

> *...the human individual thus lives usually far within his [or her] limits; he possesses powers of various sorts which he habitually fails to use. He [or she] energizes below his [or her] maximum, and he behaves below his [or her] optimum...We live subject to arrest by degrees of fatigue which we have come only from habit to obey...Excitements, ideas, and efforts, in a word...are what carry us over the dam.*

> —William James

Before making any goal to change your behavior, Kelly McGonigal encourages people to become willpower scientists. Start by just noticing the moment-to-moment decisions you make. Pay attention to your impulses. When do they happen and what is going on internally and externally if you give into them? What does that process of giving in look like? Are there certain situations, feelings, and patterns of thinking that make it more or less likely that you will give in to your impulses? Just pay attention for a period of time; one day, three days, a week.

After the initial noticing period, start to catch yourself earlier and earlier in the process. Work to purposefully connect to your purpose and values in the moment of temptation and bring to mind the short-, moderate-, and longer-term consequences of your actions. Eating the donut may feed an immediate emotional craving (short-term), but sap your energy for spending quality time with your family later in the day or (moderate-term). It may also undermine your goal to finish that long overdue project, or shed the two pounds you have been trying to lose so that you will feel better in the long-run.

Strengthen Your Willpower "Muscle"

In chapter 12 we talked about the power of mindfulness (see **Mindfulness** on page 201), and our abilities to strengthen our brains through mindfulness (see **Forming Good Habits—Replacing Bad Ones**, page 183). It turns out that one of the best things you can do to strengthen your willpower is to meditate. As we mentioned earlier, people who meditate regularly have more gray matter in the prefrontal cortex, the part of the brain responsible for self-control, as well as regions of the brain that support self-awareness. Studies have found that meditating, even for relatively brief periods of time, can lead improvements in measures of self-directedness (which is related to autonomy, self-efficacy and self-esteem), cooperativeness (related to the ability to make social connections), and self-transcendence (associated with the concepts of spirituality and creativeness). Longer-term meditation practice can significantly increase neural connections between regions of the brain important for staying focused, ignoring distractions, and controlling impulses.

Understanding and Nurture Epiphanies

The word "epiphany" probably has a million definitions. It's the occurrence when the mind, the body, the heart, and the soul focus together and see an old thing in a new way.

—Maya Angelou

Commonly referred to as an "aha moment," an epiphany has the potential to be a surprising catalyst for positive change. These spontaneous insights trigger a realization, typically profound but sometimes trivial, where a connection is made that alters our perspective and allows us to see things in a new light. Many substantial health behavior changes are preceded by a personal epiphany. Unfortunately, this is often triggered by a serious health event. Epiphanies are sometimes about aspects of people's lives other than health, but health, vitality, and energy are often required to support the turnaround motivated by the epiphany. Whether it is a change in career, marriage, the birth of a child, the passing of a relative or close friend, or any other profound realization, these more profound epiphanies are simple yet powerful discoveries that can be life-changing.

If you have read *Zero Trends* or attended any of Dee's many talks over the past twenty-five years, figure 15 may look familiar to you. It is the natural progression of a heart attack or other major negative health event. Every person can think of himself or herself as being on one of the lines in that graph. Many individuals with no or low risk will stay on the dotted or dashed lines throughout their lives. But many others are traveling through time on the solid line. Unfortunately, their epiphanies about the need to seriously change their lives often happen at the top of the spike or shortly after—in other words, near or at the point of a serious and deadly health issue. While this graph shows healthcare costs related to a serious event on the y-axis, you could also replace "medical costs" with "misery," "pain," or "suffering." These all likely travel together.

Be open to unexpected insights when something meaningful clicks in your mind and tugs at your heart about workplace culture and advancing your organization's vision toward health. With a listening and intuitive sense, cultivate an awareness of possible associations and an intention to learn from new perspectives. Avoid distractions and resist the temptation to disregard your newly found truth. Share your realization with others so that you're held accountable to act on it, and your new understanding will undoubtedly lead to tangible results.

Figure 15. The natural progression of a serious health event and leading to high cost

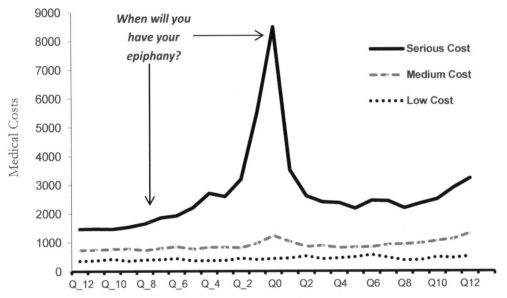

In any case, we believe it is possible to make major health-related epiphanies less necessary. We can work to downsize epiphanies through regular practices of gratitude, wonder, and appreciation of the small but profound things that your health allows you to do; practices that create a flow of micro-epiphanies while you are still on the dotted line. These more trivial micro-epiphanies can add up and shape our lives in profound ways.

We don't always take the time to think about extraordinary moments in our lives and what they really mean. We miss the experience of awe that comes from listening closely to others, to ourselves, and to the signs in the world around us.[215]

—Elise Ballard

Are You a Wellness Champion?—I Wasn't—But I Am Now

I am the vice president of human resources for my company. In 2011, I attended the Health Benefits Conference in Clearwater, Florida. Upon returning from the conference, I assembled a group of enthusiastic human resource professionals whose initial responsibility was to design a wellness program that included a mission and values statement, goals, activities and a budget for the following year.

Our 2012 and 2013 wellness initiatives were a complete success. Ninety-three percent of our employees completed all of the programs and activities that were a part of our wellness program and that far exceeded our goals and expectations. With these achievements, I truly considered myself to be a "Wellness Champion."

When I introduced our company's 2012 and 2013 Wellness Initiatives, I was a whopping eighty pounds overweight. I had no sustainable exercise program, my eating habits were atrocious, and my blood pressure was through the roof. I was brought back to reality during my August 2013 physical. My doctor told me that my blood tests revealed that I was prediabetic (impaired glucose tolerance). I was in total shock. My diagnosis of being a prediabetic was a life-changing event for me.

I immediately decided to change my life. (Go to appendix B to see how Randy did it)

So I ask you: Are you a Wellness Champion? I wasn't—but I am now.

Randy Millard
Vice President—Human Resources, Elecmetal

Exercise Your Autonomy

In the acquisition of a new habit, or the leaving off of an old one, we must take care to launch ourselves with as strong and decided an initiative as possible. Accumulate all the possible circumstances which shall reinforce the right motives; put yourself assiduously in conditions that encourage the new way; make engagements incompatible with the old; take a public pledge, if the case allows; in short, envelop your resolution with every aid you know. This will give your new beginning such a momentum that the temptation to break down will not occur as soon as it otherwise might; and every day during which a breakdown is postponed adds to the chances of it not occurring at all.

William James, Habit

There are many ways to exercise autonomy over your work and life. Throughout the book, we talked about how you can create more ideal conditions for yourself so you aren't constantly tempted to think and behave in unhealthy ways. From the perspective of autonomy over your physical health and well-being, this can include creating your own healthy micro-culture and being the personal architect of your own healthy environment (see the sections on **Curate Your Own Personal Culture** and **Personal Choice Architecture** in chapter 12).

From the perspective of occupational health and intellectual well-being, we also discussed how to re-invent at least some meaningful parameters of your job (see **Redesign Your Job** in chapter 11, page 170). From the perspective of spiritual well-being, you can choose healthy practices that help you connect to your life's purpose and your ability to operate in a manner consistent with your personal values (see the many exercises that can strengthen self-leadership in chapter 12, in the section **What Can Individuals Do?** beginning on page 192).

It is often hard to find the motivation to do things we don't find immediately satisfying. Earlier in this chapter we quoted Ed Deci as saying that autonomous motivation is "a true sense of volition, willingness, and choice in this moment. This is what I choose to be doing for myself." The better you understand what energizes you—your volition, or your purpose and personal why, and the more aware you are of what depletes your energy and willpower, the more likely you are to make choices in the moment that serve your greater purpose.

Participation in Health Risk Assessments without Financial Incentives

Senior management at Fortune Business Solutions, a human resource company in Tampa, recognized the challenge of participation in Health Risk Assessments even when financial incentives were offered, and they wanted to create a culture of self-leadership.

So how did they achieve a 93.3 percent participation in completing the health risk assessments biometrics without any financial incentives? They implemented a system designed by the Institute of Benefits and Wellness Professionals. We first made sure that management participated, supported and understood the business case for wellness. This was absolutely essential. Without it, we would have walked away.

They then took steps to create an environment of trust. Their health risk assessment process was absolutely confidential, handled by a third party, and not tied to their health insurance carrier. No names, no social security numbers—100 percent confidential. Even though their health Insurance provider offered free resources in this area, the company felt the additional trust gained by using a third party was more important than a free resource. It was voluntary, and offered to all employees regardless if they were on the health plan or not.

We created an experience—employees feel comfortable and empowered, not penalized or talked down to. We talked about what was in it for them, not what was in it for the company.

Kimberly Eckelbarger
Owner, Tropical Benefits and CBWA certified by IBWP, Tampa Florida

To read the full case study go to appendix B

Strengthen Your Connections

Human beings are fundamentally social creatures, so throughout the book we have discussed the need for social solutions to improve health and well-being. Fostering supportive relationships and connections can be one of the most powerful strategies you can use to be successful in your efforts to gain or maintain motivation and realize stronger positive personal health (see *Create a Supportive Social Milieu* in chapter 12). It is important to spend time with other supportive people, especially those who make you feel better about yourself and share similar values and goals. We also described the findings of Nicholas Christakis and James Fowler (see *Foster Collegial Connections*, page 160) on the power of social networks to influence our health and well-being. The actions and behaviors of the people we surround ourselves with can make a big difference, either positive or negative, to our health and happiness. Supporting others in their journeys can also be a powerful and rewarding way to develop deep and meaningful social connections. You can also create a sense of social connectedness by doing something nice for someone else; you might even consider checking out organized volunteer opportunities.

Disengaging From Incentives and Rewards

So where does this leave us with how we approach any current wellness programs we may have in place? The contract or agreement you have with your wellness program provider may not look anything like what we have been talking about here. You may be immersed in tactics that rely on paying people to participate in programs. How can you effectively change direction?

One of the things we hear from employees of organizations that use significant incentives to gain program participation is that they think those dollars could be better spent. We also hear that the most effective ways to gain engagement—not just participation, but real engagement—is through word-of-mouth and face-to-face contact. Creative, locally designed, grass-roots efforts to inspire and engage employees are among the most effective ways to excite people about health and well-being initiatives and create a healthier workplace culture.

For employers who want to move away from incentives, we think the best way to change direction is to be transparent with employees. To stand up and say "We don't think we have been doing this right and we think there is a better way to do things here—and we think you can help us create that better way. So we are going to take the money we are paying in participation incentives and put it toward supporting local efforts to engage in healthier practices in the workplace." Then support employee-led design teams and other locally evolving home-grown employee-driven efforts throughout the organization.

People are an organization's most important resource.

We are not saying that you should get rid of your wellness and well-being programs. There is an important, central place for wellness and well-being programs in our vision for positive organizational health in the workplace and workforce.

We feel strongly that programs and initiatives designed to promote wellness and well-being are critically important. They are not "decorations" or add-ons to be used in organizations only after more comprehensive health cultures have been developed, or instead of working on the environment and culture at all.

But going forward, we may want to rethink the way that programs have been offered to employees. Approaches should support voluntary participation that allows for employee autonomy, choice, and preferences. At a minimum, allow people a choice of what they do, and how they participate. Ideally, employees would be offered the opportunities to participate but not be pressured to do it.

In the future, these initiatives will be about listening to the aspirations of those in the organization and designing a structure (using systems and design thinking) for a thriving workplace and workforce.

The bottom line is to create the most supportive environment, culture, and climate possible to support employees' motivation to flourish.

Important note: We want to acknowledge that we have barely scratched the surface of the advances in our thinking and understanding in the area of motivation and willpower. There are many terrific people and resources that have influenced the ideas in this chapter and beyond. Please see appendix D for a list of additional resources that most significantly shaped our thinking.

THEME 3:
MEASURING AND
COMMUNICATING
WHAT MATTERS

Measure what matters
because you will inevitably become what you measure.

CHAPTER 14:
Measures That Matter

*What matters to individuals and organizations
drives motivation, engagement, and positive individual and
organizational health.*

Measuring and communicating what matters is about evaluation and feedback for decision-making, motivation, engagement, momentum, and sustainability. It is about generating and distributing meaningful information that demonstrates to all stakeholders how the organization is progressing toward the vision. It is also about using measurement to achieve what you seek. Giving employees a voice in what is measured leads to their engagement in the process.

When deciding where in the book to discuss our third theme, "measure and communicate what matters," we faced a dilemma. We feel measures and measurement are important enough to be a core theme in the overall win-win philosophy. However, positioning the topic last in the book may lead some readers to believe that evaluation is something that is planned and executed after the initiatives are in place. Nothing could be further from our intention. Developing a strong approach to measuring and communicating what matters begins when the journey begins, and it continues throughout.

- When defining shared values and shared results, we discussed that it is important to identify and build on measures that matter to all stakeholders and the organization.

- When developing positive individual and organizational health, we highlighted the importance of creating intuitive, engaging, and seamless mechanisms for the ongoing collection of meaningful information from all stakeholders.

- Most obviously, measuring and communicating what matters is important for evaluation and continuous improvement purposes. It is essential that you measure in areas that your employees care about and communicate about progress in ways that resonate with the organization and all stakeholders.

The health of individuals and populations are often the stated objective of wellness and well-being initiatives. Over time, the purpose of the programs has become focused more on their economic value to the employer than on the value to employees. It is not surprising that cost savings and financial return on investment (ROI) have been the outcomes of choice in the past.

The Intel-GE Validation Institute states, "US Preventive Medicine (USPM) is the first, and as of now, only wellness company to achieve a sustained and significant reduction in wellness-sensitive medical events (41% overall decrease in Hospitalizations and ER Visits) for asthma, cardiac events (CAD and HTN), COPD, congestive heart failure and diabetes) across that portion of its entire book of business for which comprehensive claims data was available (N=33,459). The reduction achieved by USPM significantly outpaced the much smaller national decline in these events, as evidenced by both the database maintained by the Disease Management Purchasing Consortium and the federal Healthcare Cost and Utilization Project (HCUP) database."

Ron Loeppke, MD, MPH
Vice Chairman, US Preventive Medicine, Inc.

To read the full case study go to appendix B

In the chapters of this section, we outline some current best practices for evaluating health management initiatives. We then discuss emerging next practices for evaluating the impact of the health-related environment, culture, and wellness and well-being approaches in organizations. We provide our recommendations for putting the most meaningful measurement and evaluation approaches into practice.

Current Best Practices for Assessing the Impact of Wellness and Well-Being Initiatives

How to best evaluate the impact of wellness and well-being programs is a highly debated area in the wellness field. There is no shortage of strong convictions about right and wrong ways to measure the value of the initiative and the included programs. While most of the published best practices for programs acknowledge that evaluating effectiveness is indeed a best practice, few provide many other details. The "best practice" publications often focus on processes that help improve program operations and offer less advice on how to effectively evaluate the impact of the programs. For example, the published resources we reviewed[66-73] included the following practices related to evaluation:

- ongoing assessments that drive quality improvement processes
- evaluation of effectiveness (outcomes)
- generation of sophisticated ongoing and outcomes-oriented reports
- integration of data systems
- secure, efficient, and effective data practices
- relentless focus on safeguarding personal health information privacy and confidentiality

Until recently, the focus has been primarily on measuring clinical health risks and disease, randomized controlled trials are considered the "gold standard" method, and biostatistics are the most commonly used analytics. There is a very rich profession of program evaluation research in the social sciences that can tremendously enhance the approaches we currently use to evaluate wellness and well-being programs.

Emerging Next Practices for Evaluating Impact

The next practices we outline here are designed to help organizations understand and implement useful approaches for evaluating the impact of their efforts to create healthier and more thriving workforces and workplaces. Table 18 summarizes some of the current best practices and proposes emerging next practices and measures for evaluating the effectiveness of our efforts.

Table 18. Current best and emerging next evaluation practices

Practice	Current Best Practices	Emerging Next Practices
Measure what matters to all stakeholders (current chapter)		
Use a broader lens on what is measured.		✓
• Strength of leadership support		✓
• Environment for health and well-being	✓	✓
• Health and well-being culture and climate		✓
• Program process	✓	✓
• Relationships—engagement and support		✓
• Shared values		✓
• Shared results		✓
○ Positive individual health:		✓
▪ Mental/emotional	✓	✓
▪ Spiritual—meaning in life		✓
▪ Intellectual—engagement		✓
▪ Physical health	✓	✓
▪ Social—relationships		✓
▪ Vocational—meaningful work		✓
▪ Financial—security		✓
▪ Healthy behaviors	✓	✓
○ Positive organizational health success markers:		✓
▪ Productivity and performance	✓	✓
▪ Utilization of medical services	✓	✓
▪ Recruitment		✓
▪ Retention		✓
▪ Accounts of organizational outliers and positive deviance		✓
▪ Organizational profit-related goals and	✓	✓
▪ Other non-monetary goals (i.e., shared value brought to the community and society)		✓
Ask better questions (Current Chapter)		
• Beyond the question of "Does wellness work?" to "What approaches works for whom and why?"		
○ Do wellness programs save money/reduce costs for employers (return on investment—ROI)?	✓	
○ Do wellness programs provide value to employers and employees (value of investment—VOI)?	✓	✓
○ Do caring organizational environments and cultures provide value to employers *and* employees (value of caring—VOC)?		✓
○ What works, for whom, under what circumstances?		✓

Practice	Current Best Practices	Emerging Next Practices
Use measurement that engages (See chapter 15)		
Represent all stakeholders in the design and execution of the ongoing evaluation process.		
Qualitative methods:	✓	✓
• Experience sampling		✓
• Organizational ethnography		✓
• Focus groups	✓	✓
• Interviews	✓	✓
• Observation		✓
Use methods that enhance perspective (See chapter 16)		
• Randomized controlled trials	✓	
• Quasi-experimental designs	✓	✓
• "Realistic evaluation" methods		✓
• Create a guiding framework for evaluation		✓

We discuss these topics in the following chapters as indicated in the table.

HealthNEXT™

This case study chronicles our work with an international manufacturing company with approximately three thousand employees in the United States. We were approached by the Head of Human Resources in the Americas in 2009 to assist them with their strategy to control a double-digit increase in their healthcare costs. Historically they had tried to stem these increases through benefit design as many others have done without success. After initial discussions, it was clear that their human resource team was receptive to a new approach that would foster a culture of health and elevate the health status of their workforce.

Our approach was to assist this employer three ways. Increase the accountability of the employee population, enhance the corporate approach to wellness, and facilitate closer relationships with the popular primary care providers who care for the majority of the covered lives. There were clear connections between identified health risks such as hypertension and hypercholesterolemia and higher incidences of cardiac and stroke-related disease in their high-cost claims and disability reports. Making these connections were essential to obtain buy-in from leadership, management, and ultimately the covered population.

Ray Fabius, MD
Chief Science Officer, HealthNext

To read the full case study go to appendix B

Measures that Matter to Everyone: Using a Broader Lens

Shift our thinking to a higher level
of outcome measures for individuals and organizations.

Throughout the book, we discussed how the industry's approach to wellness programs in America has been shaped over time by an increasing focus on lowering healthcare costs. We also emphasized the need for a solution that provides employees with a positive and healthy organizational culture and environment. It is now time to reconsider our view of the measures and metrics of success.

Lifestyles and corresponding disease trends are converging globally, and countries can learn from each other with regard to what works. However, major differences persist in health infrastructure with numerous countries facing serious challenges. Some countries, especially in Europe, have taken a more holistic approach to improving health and well-being by addressing psychosocial risk factors, such as role ambiguity, poor communication, and low levels of support for problem-solving.

Wolf Kirsten
Cofounder & Codirector, Global Centre for Healthy Workplaces
President, International Health Consulting

Nearly five decades ago, Robert F. Kennedy spoke of his vision for a new kind of metric in his presidential campaign speech at the University of Kansas. He spoke of a metric that reflects the values upon which this country was founded:

Even if we act to erase material poverty, there is another greater task, it is to confront the poverty of satisfaction—purpose and dignity—that afflicts us all. Too much and for too long, we seemed to have surrendered personal excellence and community values in the mere accumulation of material things. Our Gross National Product, now, is over $800 billion dollars a year, but that Gross National Product—if we judge the United States of America by that—that Gross National Product counts air pollution and cigarette advertising, and ambulances to clear our highways of carnage. It counts special locks for our doors and the jails for the people who break them. It counts the destruction of the redwood and the loss of our natural wonder in chaotic sprawl. It counts napalm and counts nuclear warheads and armored cars for the police to fight the riots in our cities. It counts Whitman's rifle and Speck's knife, and the television programs which glorify violence in order to sell toys to our children.

Yet the gross national product does not allow for the health of our children, the quality of their education or the joy of their play. It does not include the beauty of our poetry or the strength of our marriages, the intelligence of our public debate or the integrity of our public officials. It measures neither our wit nor our courage, neither our wisdom nor our learning, neither our compassion nor our devotion to our country, it measures everything in short, except that which makes life worthwhile. And it can tell us everything about America except why we are proud that we are Americans.

—Robert F. Kennedy

Kennedy's speech is as relevant today as it was those many decades ago. In the decade following Kennedy's historic speech, the small country of Bhutan enacted a development philosophy that reflected the spirit of Robert Kennedy's vision. For the past forty years, instead of measuring their gross national product (GNP), Bhutan has measured their gross national happiness (GNH). Today in Bhutan, "GNH is the bridge between the fundamental values of kindness, equality and humanity, and the necessary pursuit of economic growth. GNH acts as our national conscience guiding us toward making wise decisions for a better future."[216] The philosophy of psychological well-being in Bhutan nicely illustrates the principles of measuring what matters. The country tracks and reports on nine component measures of their GNH:

- psychological well-being
- health
- education
- cultural diversity and resilience
- time use
- good governance
- community vitality
- ecological diversity and resilience
- living standard

An official explanation of the country's approach said the following:

What a society chooses to measure will in turn influence the things that it seeks. If a society takes great effort to measure productivity, people in the society are likely to focus more on it and sometimes even to the detriment of other values. If a society regularly assesses well-being, people will give it their attention and learn more about its causes. Psychological well-being is, therefore, valuable not only because it assesses well-being more directly, but it has beneficial consequences.[217]

It does take not a great stretch of the imagination to see how measures like those used in Bhutan could be translated and used in our employer organizations. We need a new vision of "what matters" to our organizations and to the people who are the lifeblood of the organizations, families, communities, and our larger society. We propose embracing an expanded set of measures and metrics for success and a new set of methods for evaluating impact.

It is not possible to learn without measuring, but it is possible—and very wasteful—to measure without learning.

—Donald Berwick, 1998

We need measures of positive individual health that more broadly reflect the many dimensions of health as we understand it today. We also need health-related measures of culture and environment that reflect the highest possible levels of positive organizational health.

As we evolve our approaches to support a broader kind of health, we need to move beyond the outcome measures of healthcare and productivity costs to measures that represent the full value of health, performance, happiness, engagement, and a life well-lived.

The next generation of measures must reflect what it takes to be an employer of choice and embody the characteristics of positive organizational and positive individual health. The next generation of data must help us demonstrate the full value of an investment in evolving shared values, healthy and supportive environments and cultures, and healthy and thriving workforces. We must look beyond physical health measures to measures of mental health, social-emotional health, workplace environment and culture, family/friends and community. Later in this section we describe the evolution from a focus on the financial return on investment (ROI) to the broader value of investment (VOI). We also introduce measurement practices that help demonstrate the value of caring (VOC).

As we evolve what we intend to impact,
we also need to evolve what we measure.

Living and Thriving Assessments

Just as it is time to think beyond risk and disease, it is time to think beyond traditional health-risk assessments. Going forward, it is necessary that we ask new questions. What keeps us healthy? What helps us thrive? With the increasing emphasis on helping healthy people stay healthy and helping people thrive, we now need additional tools to measure the known influences on and outcomes associated with thriving individuals and organizations.

Our twenty-first-century health assessments must take into account recent learnings and additional determinants of health. Following years of consultation and research, we developed the Living and Thriving Assessment (LTA) which includes a new set of dimensions that represent the fuller spectrum of health we outlined in chapter 2. Such measures are more often seen in social-science research than in biomedical research. Some of the major areas of a Living and Thriving Assessment are listed below.

- Physical health, energy, vitality
- Mental/emotional health
- Intellectual health
- Spiritual health
- Financial health
- Social health—includes friends, family, and community health
- Environmental health
- Occupational health
- Workplace and community culture

In addition to rethinking the content of our health assessments, we must also rethink how they are used. The response rates for health-risk assessments (HRA) completion are often very low. This has been a major concern since most wellness programs begin by administering an HRA to determine an individual's risk status and recommend follow-up actions based on the findings. Often the HRA serves as a "gatekeeper" of sorts for the rest of the program. If you don't complete the HRA, you don't get into the full program. It's time to evaluate whether and how to make an LTA integral or optional to the wellness program of your organization.

The most commonly used other measures of the health of employees are from administrative sources like medical claims data, or information collected as part of operating the wellness programs and biometrics screenings. This includes data on program participation, lab values and other measurements, and self-reported information from health assessment question-naires. These measures primarily reflect the medical model and what matters to employers.

What my board is asking for is current local data to prove we're making a difference. As you've always said, are we at least breaking even? If so, our investment in wellness is free. When you're a local cooperative nonprofit funded by taxpayers, the stakes are quite high. If we can prove that a wellness culture improves performance and cost, we're set for life because everyone knows it's the right thing to do intuitively. Then we have to give them the skills to make it happen in reality. That's where the rubber meets the road.

Bottom line…People are still very much willing to invest in people as long as it's done well.

Gillian Pieper
Health Promotion Specialist, Vermont School Boards Insurance Trust

---

Meaningful Measures of Structure and Context

As we have increased our focus on creating more positive environments and cultures, we have had to create better measures of structure and context. Current process measures primarily focus on information collected as part of the operation of programs while outcome measures largely represent a biomedical mindset and the perspective of the employer. Information about employee productivity (e.g., lost work time) is now being measured more commonly. While many managers and leaders care about productivity metrics, most employees likely care very little about them or even understand them, unless their job depends on a productivity quotient.

What Measures Matter to Your Stakeholders?

In earlier stages of the win-win journey, we outlined ways to better understand the results that matter to stakeholders throughout your organization (see activities to *Identify Results that Matter to Employees* and *Summarize and Prioritize Results That Matter to the Organization and Employees*, chapter 7) and create shared values and a shared vision built upon those "shared results" (see *Create a Shared Vision, Shared Values, and Shared Results*, in chapter 9). We also discussed designing wellness and well-being approaches that reflect your shared vision and shared values and create approaches most likely to impact "shared results" (see chapter 10, *Outline How You Are Going to Get There*). Your ongoing evaluation and communications should include the measures and metrics that reflect these important stakeholder preferences.

> *My lesson learned from over three decades working with the C-suite is they are data driven. Through various mergers and acquisitions, having data including outcomes data on health promotion and disease management programs resulted in continuing C-suite support even in challenging economic times. Creating a culture of health from the top down is essential to drive outcomes.*
>
> *Wayne Burton, MD*
> *Chief Medical Officer and Global Well-Being, American Express Inc.*

Figure 16 is an impact framework that represents the many different dimensions that you might expect to influence as you evolve a healthier environment, culture, climate, and employee population. In this framework, it is important to represent the employee's and the organization's objectives and clearly identify them. When everyone understands the win-win philosophy, nearly all the dimensions are of interest to both employees and the organization.

Having an explicit impact framework can be beneficial for many reasons:

- The impact framework guides interpretation of outcomes findings:
  - improvement in various dimensions
  - patterns of findings across dimensions
  - relationships between and within dimensions
- This framework can help set expectations for how the impacts will unfold over time.

Depending on your overall efforts and priorities, your impact framework may look a lot like this, or somewhat different. It is helpful, though, to outline your ideas for how you expect your impacts to unfold.

Figure 16. Outcomes framework for shared results

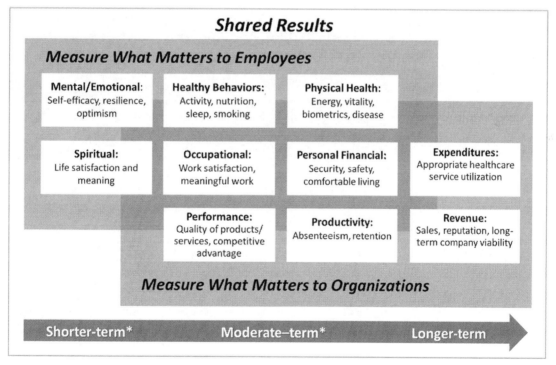

These are general estimates only. Depending on your approach and your population, some outcomes could happen earlier or later than their position in this framework indicates.

Ask Better Questions

Historically, many of the evaluations used to assess the impact of wellness programs can be thought of as tests of "main effects." Testing a main effect is statistics-speak for testing the effect of an intervention on a single outcome of interest. This is the simplest question we can ask about the relationship between those two things. For example, "Do wellness programs reduce employee healthcare costs?" But are we asking the right questions? Wellness and well-being programs and initiatives are designed to influence human beings, and by our nature we are very complex. Both humans and the programs we design are embedded within very complex social systems. Because of this, main-effect-type questions provide answers that have very limited value.

The HRA-screening-checkups-incentive approach currently described as a preliminary element of wellness is not providing the maximum economic value to organizations. In particular, the ROIs are clearly baseless given the narrow range of data utilized in the calculations. Until organizations realize the false sense of economic value they are being sold by many of the third-party providers, consultants, and evaluators, the investment they are making will underperform. Additional tactics, such as social connections and challenges, may prove to be valuable in terms of team building. However, in the final analysis, companies will likely have to expand their wellness and well-being initiatives including implementing environmental and cultural changes, even to the extent of changing the way work is done in the organization. Clearly appropriate outcome measures will have to have a mutual agreement between management and all stakeholders. What is a success for one organization is not necessarily a success for another organization.

Al Lewis
Author, Surviving Workplace Wellness
Founder and first president, Population Health Alliance

From Return on Investment (ROI) to Value on Investment (VOI)

For most of the past three decades, return-on-investment (ROI) analysis has been the most commonly relied upon analytic tool in research designed to determine the financial effectiveness of wellness programs. Most often, the R in return on investment has focused on cost avoidance, largely related to reductions in healthcare utilization. In a very real sense, ROI studies have been used to answer a main-effect-style question:

Do wellness programs save companies
more money than they cost?

As organizations embrace the view that health and well-being are multidimensional and have a more far-reaching impact than purely financial return, the trend in analysis is shifting to value on investment or VOI. The question then becomes the following:

Do wellness programs provide value
to employers and employees?

Outside of the United States, employer-based health insurance doesn't exist and yet globally, wellness programs are more popular than ever. This tells us that the value of having a wellness program extends well beyond saving healthcare costs.

As our Western culture continues to promote an unhealthy diet and sedentary lifestyle, the need for effective wellness programs will continue to grow.

It has taken 40 years for the obesity and diabetes trends to reach their current state. It will probably take twice that long to reverse them. That also means worksite wellness programs are here to stay.

Steve Aldana
CEO, WellSteps

While this is still a relatively simple question, it is a more thoughtful question that can provide more meaningful answers. Instead of focusing on the impact in terms of monetary value for the organization and management, this broader question includes other "shared results" for organizations and employees.

The 2013 RAND Workplace Wellness Programs Study concluded that healthcare cost savings from workplace wellness programs are insignificant—implying that from an ROI perspective, wellness programs don't work. But assessing wellness program success or failure based solely on ROI for healthcare expenses is the problem; it paints an incomplete picture. Yes, organizations need to manage healthcare costs and consider health and productivity as assets, just as they do equipment and buildings. But unlike bricks and mortar, people are not static, interchangeable parts that fit a neat mathematic formula. And while some employers have done an admirable job of attempting to honestly measure the true financial impact of wellness, the average workplace doesn't come remotely close to having the resources to measure ROI with any degree of confidence. Nor should they.

Employers don't typically evaluate ROI for pensions, paid time off, family leave, adoption assistance, long-term care insurance, casual days, contraception benefits, legal assistance, sports team sponsorship, or retiree medical. Organizations make these investments because they think it's good for business; yet in almost all instances they have no proof-positive financial justification. They offer these benefits because they think they'll attract and retain the best employees to make their organization successful. And that's the rationale we need again for workplace wellness.

Dean Witherspoon
Founder and CEO, Health Enhancement System

The following is an example of an organization that measures value in areas beyond averted costs. Manatee County, Florida, uses the measures of success listed below for their wellness initiative:

- negative cost trend with no cost shifting to employee
- ninety-eight percent of exit interviews give highest marks for benefit and wellness program
- reductions in out-of-range values for biometrics and labs
- high usage of primary care
- eighty-five percent generic prescription usage
- seventeen percent less than PBM book on PMPM Rx costs
- employee feedback

This VOI includes measures of cost reductions, but it also represents appropriateness of care and measures that indicate how well the organization supports its employee health and thriving.

Manatee County Government

At Manatee County, we have a much different view of ROI than some in the industry. For us, the return on our investment is first knowing that we are doing everything we can to help our employees first find what works for them and their family members to move to a higher level of well-being and health status; doing the right thing is important to us. Second, we see that our employee exit interviews give highest marks for the benefit and wellness programs. In terms of our financial ROI, we have a negative 2.5 percent trend since 2009 on our self-funded health plan without shifting costs to our employees. We believe that our trend is a direct result of the plan design paired with the on-site clinical programs and supportive Advocates who work together with the member to help them achieve better health and a higher level of well-being.

Our success has been fostered by our leadership's commitment to a culture of health and all of our members who have struggled to find what works for them. All of this results in lower costs to the county, lower costs to our members and taxpayers and a higher level of service provided to our community.

Kim Stroud, MA, LMHC
Benefits, Manatee County Government

To read the full case study go to appendix B

From Value on Investment (VOI) to Value of Caring (VOC)

What is the value of caring?

While we emphatically support the growing trend toward VOI, we believe it is important to even more strongly highlight the "caring" component of value.

There is growing agreement that positive relationships and social support from colleagues, friends, and family can have a hard financial return for employers. We concur with this statement made by Deborah C. Stephens and Gary Heil, in the foreword to Abraham Maslow's posthumously published book, *Maslow on Management.* [218]

> *People spend too many hours in organizations and institutions that do not support them in reaching their true potential. We believe this should be as much a driving force as financial management, product development, return on investment, and all of the other indicators we put into place to measure success. Without this force, our successes will be short lived, our plans nothing more than short-term, and our ability to continue to compete in a global world severely restrained.*

Organizations are realizing, or will soon realize, the workforce, especially the evolving workforce, deeply values non-monetary compensation and a people-friendly workplace. The value of a caring organization, in our opinion, will soon eclipse the value placed on ROI or VOI by the employees and the employer. Currently the metrics are more qualitative and self-report, which makes them even more valuable because they get to the emotional connection of employees to the organization and the organization to the employees.

Wellness at ACT

When we launched the wellness program at ACT in early 2012 one of our guiding resources was Zero Trends: Health as a Serious Economic Strategy. *It has provided much of the research, rationale, and philosophy for designing and implementing our program.*

We began to offer a variety of onsite convenience services to alleviate the work/life "imbalance" and foster work/life integration. These services included onsite nurse practitioner (two days/week), prescription delivery twice a week, dry cleaning pickup/delivery twice a week, on-site chair massage (one ten-minute massage free each month), on-site H&R Block office during tax season, and a weekly "food box" delivery (a pay-as-you-go CSA program).

Our leave time policy provides generous time off to improve personal well-being, including ten sick days, three personal development days, three floating holidays, three personal days, and one volunteer day. ACT encourages community "social" well-being by providing a paid volunteer day for team members to contribute their time locally to an organization of their choosing. We also have ten paid holidays and three weeks paid vacation, and healthcare benefits (medical, dental, and vision) beginning on day one. There is no waiting period.

Sandy Stewart, MEd, CWWPM
Wellness Manager, ACT, Inc.

To read the full case study go to appendix B

The Anatomy of a Better Question

As we mentioned above, many of the current and best practices evaluation questions have been framed as tests of main effects. For example, "Do wellness programs reduce employee healthcare costs?" To really understand the value of our investment in wellness and well-being initiatives or the value of caring, we must think beyond main-effect questions.

In social contexts like employer organizations, the impact of a program or initiative depends on a combination of emotional, social, and environmental influences. It is rare that main-effect questions provide terribly useful answers. There is a thriving evaluation tradition in the social sciences that can enhance the approaches currently being used to assess the impact of wellness programs—as well as broader efforts to evolve healthier organizational environments and cultures.

With the proliferation of new, dazzling, and different technical/pharma medical applications, it will be increasingly important to gauge the value of such remedies. Value is, of course, benefit over cost (V=B/C). Staying healthy and out of the remediation game is, of course, the winning solution.

Tom Welsh
Director and Plan Administrator, Retired
PPG Industries

Methods used for research in the social sciences are more geared toward tests of interactions. This is statistics-speak for looking at the relationships between an intervention and an outcome given the influence of another factor or factors. For example, what is the effect of a wellness program (the intervention) on cost savings (the outcome) given different levels of implementation quality (a third factor)?

Another interaction question might be, what is the impact of a self-leadership development course on employee job satisfaction, given the level of leader support for the program. Factors that might have an impact on programs and initiatives (interventions) also include the strength of the health-related culture in the organization, the quality of relationships between managers and employees, and the intrinsic motivation of employees to engage. Other examples of more complex but useful questions include:

- What is the impact of leadership support on the evolution of a healthy environment and culture in an organization?
- How does the culture of the organization influence the participation in and effectiveness of wellness and well-being programs?
  - o   Sub-question: What does it mean to participate in the program?
- Which unhealthy behaviors (or combinations of behaviors) are the most important influences on physiological outcomes? On quality-of-life outcomes? On functional outcomes?
- How much change is required, and for how long before a meaningful impact on physiological outcomes can be expected?
- How do we measure meaningful impact? Does statistical significance represent a meaningful change? What constitutes a meaningful clinical and functional difference?

Ideally, your evaluation questions would help you

- understand not only whether your efforts worked, but for whom, and why;
- identify the most effective organizational wellness and well-being initiatives and program components, and for whom they worked;
- evaluate what worked the way you expected, and what didn't;
- understand the importance of unintended side effects, and what can they teach you;
- demonstrate links between what was done and the outcomes that matter to your stakeholders;
- look for positive and negative deviance and outliers.

We wrote earlier in the book about becoming better health explorers and the fact that the true nature of health "is in the clouds." We want to emphasize again that all of the questions we are attempting to ask and answer here are couched within the realm of what we can currently measure and understand with the imperfect assessment tools, methods, and analytics that we now have available to us. All these things limit our ability to understand the true nature of health. We encourage the use of a broader set of methods that help us answer the following types of questions:

- How strong are your foundations (the five fundamental pillars)?
- How supportive are your leaders?
- How well are your values being lived in your organization?

- How supportive are your approaches to creating a healthy and thriving environment, culture, and climate?

- How strong are your approaches to support positive individual health and self-leadership?

- How strong are your approaches to foster autonomous motivation?

- How relevant and valid are your evaluation methods? Are you using the information to make continuous improvements in your culture?

From the first to the last page in this book we emphasize the critical importance of people in the organization, including all stakeholders. The following are some of the performance and engagement questions that will likely matter to both the organization and employees. Including questions in our evaluation agendas like all those discussed above and below can help advance our understanding of how to best support the health and performance of employees and organizations.

- What is the performance of the organization?

- Do employees want to come to work each day?

- Do all stakeholders like working there?

- Do they feel engaged in meaningful work?

- Do they believe in the organization and what it stands for?

- Are the employees and work teams optimistic, collaborative, and resilient?

- Do all stakeholders have opportunities to have fun and be creative at work?

The complexities of the lives of individuals are often deeper than some of the measures used in the past. There are circumstances when these deeper issues arise to impact performance at work and at home.

The Messy Reality of People's Lives

Three things are important to me when it comes to employee health, well-being, and productivity: treating employees with dignity, beautiful, elegant solutions that work, and the messy reality of people's lives. For the sake of this opinion piece's length, I will focus on our messy lives.

I often draw upon my life experiences for inspiration. In that vein, I received a great deal of reader response from a column I wrote about my mom's death. While people were sympathetic to my loss, the avalanche of emails, tweets, phone calls and handwritten notes I received told story after story about the impact caregiving had on people's work and home lives.

Having been immersed in this topic already, it felt like a validation to talk with Alexandra Drane, cofounder of the Eliza Corp. and EngageWithGrace.org, about what she's called "the Unmentionables"—five life obstacles that make employees more vulnerable to certain health conditions and, in turn, spend as much as five times more on healthcare.

What are these life challenges? Well, there's a reason they're called the unmentionables. They are real-life issues that begin with caregiving, financial difficulties, and relationship issues, and end with two topics that make employers very uncomfortable: workplace stress and an unhealthy sex life.

Two sets of coping factors magnify or buffer employee vulnerability to these life stressors. Negative coping factors (or magnifiers) are sleep difficulties, substance use, and feeling sad or worried. Positive coping factors (or buffers) include strong peer support, a sense of spirituality, and exercise. Too many magnifiers coupled with too few buffers makes the best employees more vulnerable to the unmentionables.

How worried should employers be about their employees and the unmentionables? The Eliza Corp.'s survey conducted with the Altarum Institute pointed out 94.4 percent of respondents experienced at least one negative life issue.

Drane isn't the only one to cite non-medical causes of employees' self-perception of well-being, health and healthcare utilization. Aetna Inc. published a study in August 2012 on the nonmedical drivers of disability and found many of the same factors, which the company headlined as the physical, mental, emotional, and financial demands of work, childcare and elder care. And, in 2010, Cigna's review of family medical leave claims found employees who use FML to care for a family member are 50 percent more likely to eventually submit a behavioral-health-related short-term disability claim.

I believe we're at a crossroads when it comes to our employees. Either we develop elegant solutions and benefits that treat workers with dignity and give them the help they need at the time they need it, or we accept that employee health and productivity will increasingly be challenged. As Drane said in a Health 2.0 presentation, "Empathy is [our] single biggest missing ingredient."

Carol Harnett
Health and employee benefits consultant, speaker, and writer

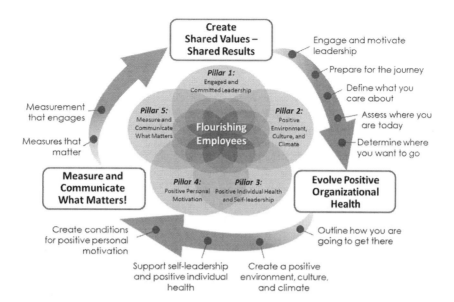

CHAPTER 15:
Measurement That Engages

...Tell me and I will forget, show me and I may remember,
involve me and I'll understand.

—Chinese proverb

Collaborative and Comprehensive Measurement and Evaluation Planning

As with most other parts of the win-win journey, we recommend that the evaluation planning process be collaborative. It is imperative to engage senior leaders in the planning. What is their bottom line interest? What do they care most about? Depending on the nature and structure of your organization, other stakeholders for this effort might include the employees responsible for safety and quality initiatives, human resources, or organizational development. Most of all, involve employees! Include their voice, engage them as researchers, as distributors of the findings, and as brainstormers about potential solutions.

If your organization has individuals with evaluation and measurement expertise who can help with this kind of planning it would be ideal to involve them from the beginning of the journey as well. While it would be nice to have a team of PhD-level analysts on your staff to run sophisticated analyses, it isn't necessary. If you rely on third-party partners for this kind of work, involving those partners from the start may also be helpful—but be aware of any bias that this might bring to the process.

If your organization has a wellness program partner, it is important that they are at the table for these discussions. Depending on the breadth and level of integration of existing programmatic wellness and well-being approaches, and the level of trust that exists in your relationship with them, they may substantially guide or even drive this process.

Involve All Stakeholders in the Evaluation Process

Asking for input through surveys and focus groups can increase employees' feelings of engagement in the process of designing and evolving positive organizational health. However, there are several other inclusive methods that can take engagement to an even deeper level. We recommend engaging employees in the assessment process to collect stories and other relevant information from their peers about how working for the organization influences their health and well-being. Recruit employees to participate in the assessment as interviewers, to collect information, or even serve as project leads.

In this chapter, we describe several engaging methods that can be used to capture rich and timely information about how you are progressing toward your vision. Regardless of which methods you use, we recommend an eye toward creativity, and deep representation of the employee experience of culture in the organization overall, as well as within their own work groups, departments, or units.

Experience Sampling Method

Formal ethnographic research can be very resource intensive and it is usually done by an outside party. However, it is possible to capture information about employee perceptions in a real-time and ongoing manner with a process called "experience sampling method" (ESM). In his early research on flow, Mihaly Csikszentmihalyi used the experience sampling method to capture periodic self-reported information from people as they went through their daily lives.[219] While study participants in Csikszentmihalyi's research carried beepers and diaries, the modern version of ESM makes use of modern technology (smartphones and other personal communication devices) to deliver periodic real-time prompts to capture information from people in the moment as they go through their lives. People's personal experiences can be sampled at various times of the day, on certain days of the week, and across many settings (home, work, play, etc.). When they are given a signal, participants reflect on what they are experiencing at that moment.

Depending on the purposes of the inquiry, people can respond to a brief set of yes/no questions, choose from a brief checklist, answer multiple-choice questions, or provide open-ended commentary about what they are doing, whom they are with, how they are feeling, and so on. Using ESM and related methods like event sampling, individual employees (randomly sampled volunteers) can share rich information about their experience of the organization's culture and climate. There are several freeware ESM applications that can be easily downloaded onto smartphones, and there are also more sophisticated and flexible ESM programs that can be licensed. There is even a new business model making its way into the wellness arena that specializes in taking the pulse of a random set of volunteer employees with one or two questions each day or so.

Culture Journalism

Among the more engaging approaches that can be used to capture information about the organizations' current culture is the use of what we call "culture journalism." This can be done using either written journals or photo journals or through the collection of any materials, artifacts, stories—especially oral or written traditions and folklore. Employees throughout the company can volunteer or be recruited (willingly) to document their experience of the company culture from their perspective. Using disposable cameras, cell-phone cameras, written journals, or even the voice-recognition feature of their cellphone, employees can capture photos of moments, collect artifacts, write or speak about interactions, or any other aspects of the organization's environment that represent what the organization's culture means to them, especially with respect to their health and well-being. With permission, stories, journal entries, photos, and other information collected using this process can be used in feedback reports to stakeholders and shared on bulletin boards or on the organization's intranet.

Organizational Ethnography

Another potentially valuable method that has been underutilized in culture-of-health efforts is ethnography. The word "ethnography" conjures up images of explorers in khaki outfits immersing themselves into the lives of indigenous cultures in exotic and distant parts of the world. However, ethnography is just "the study and systematic recording of human cultures."[220] Ethnography can be extremely helpful for better understanding our culture and the cultures and subcultures of our organizations. It is conducted from the viewpoint or lens of the group being studied. It can add deep and rich qualitative information to the other more quantitative data gathered in the positive organizational health assessment.

Ethnography is usually conducted by someone from outside the culture—in this case outside the organization—who immerses him- or herself into the context as an observer in an unobtrusive manner. A formal ethnography captures and describes the culture's traditions, rites, and rituals. The goal is to improve understanding of behavior on a day-to-day basis.

Capturing and uploading images with photos has become remarkably easy with mobile phones and could be incorporated into various ways to communicate about healthy cultures in an organization. In a previous public health initiative, photos were used in a grassroots health promotion program called "Amigos en Salud" (or "Friends in Health)[221] which trained lay community health workers to provide peer support to Hispanics with diabetes in underserved locations. In this example, teenaged youth that were part of an inner city photography program were asked to capture images of "what health means to them" in their local community. The results included photos from diverse and unique perspectives, and captured life that was real and relatable—physical activities that they actually had access to, healthy foods that were familiar to them, and support through family gatherings. These images were then used (with the proper permission) in health education materials in the specific community. This led to a greater connection with the health content, enhanced a sense of pride in their community, and promoted creativity. Organizations can use a similar approach to promote a unique, personal, and meaningful message about shared values, different ways to experience well-being, and the importance of supportive relationships.

Angela Camilleri
Lead Innovation Strategist, Edington Associates

This kind of observation can be especially valuable since what people say can sometimes be very different from what they do. It also gives the observer a deeper sense of empathy for the individuals in the culture—in this case, the employees.

While a true formal ethnographic study would be difficult and expensive, there are elements of an ethnographic approach that can be used to understand an organizational culture. We can learn a lot from incorporating principles from ethnographic method in the observation of our organizational cultures. Some third party partners may want to demonstrate a deep level of commitment by intensely immersive observational approaches. It can provide important knowledge and insights that can guide those partners in their efforts to provide value to their clients.

From Big Data to Full Data

Most of our big data sets do not include some of the most relevant data necessary to solve today's most pressing issues.

Gathering and synthesizing quantitative data and qualitative data can be done on a rolling basis to create a fuller picture of our organizations. All of the methods described above can be used to continuously evaluate your programs and initiatives. To the degree that the methods involve employees in capturing, synthesizing, and reporting on the findings, they will help employees take ownership of the findings and solutions that emerge from them. This is all part of a different kind of big data that we call full data that can help you tell a compelling story with all the information that you have available. This fuller kind of data can also help determine the "value of caring" from the voice of the employees.

Internet of Things

In recent years, the "Internet of Things" (IoT) has infiltrated our surroundings and will continue to grow exponentially as possibilities are rapidly developing. The Internet of Things (IoT) refers to the interconnectivity of everyday objects through technology such as data sensors, biochip transponders, actuators, and global positioning systems (GPS). These sensors are embedded into various things throughout the environment and are commonly found today in mobile phones, automobiles, homes, and city streets. "Things" are broadly defined as items, appliances, machines, buildings, vehicles, plants, the ground, animals, and people. The placement of sensors in things allows for remote monitoring and manual or automated adjustments based on detecting changing conditions like temperature, lighting, or capacity. Examples of this technology are found in thermostat readers in homes and offices, or lighted indicators in a busy parking lot to assist in locating a vacant parking spot. By transferring data over an Internet IP address, these various objects are networked together to communicate to larger networks, creating a "system of systems" for transferring data. In short, the IoT is a way for these devices to "talk" to each other and perform more sophisticated tasks. This larger infrastructure adds greater possibility to improve efficiencies, lower costs, save energy, or even prevent a health crisis by sharing data across multiple systems.

The mind-boggling potential of technologies increasingly being interwoven into ordinary objects will change our lives as we know it. With the IoT already underway, the predicted growth will revolutionize most every aspect of our daily life. By the year 2020, it's expected that the number of devices connected to the internet IoT will be about 50 billion, comprising a hundredfold increase since 2003.[222] As this technology becomes more refined and accessible, the decrease in component costs will allow for greater ease of built-in capabilities. This explosive growth means that just about everything will be connected through the IoT, with seemingly boundless potential to improve the quality of our lives. Safety and security will improve, through tracking and monitoring of possessions. The finance world will continue to transform through automated modes to securely exchange funds. Fitness devices have already expanded to include clothing or body implants. Medical technology will be more automated and connected, home health more feasible, and health data more integrated. The IoT will cross-pollinate systems of transportation, utilities, industry, and agriculture. Along with all of these benefits come the concerns about personal privacy and surveillance, where policies and standards around security will need to pave the way for this imminent new field. Overall, the advancements in embedded technologies creates tremendous opportunities and impacts the future culture in our homes, workplaces, and communities.

Angela Camilleri
Lead Innovation Strategist, Edington Associates

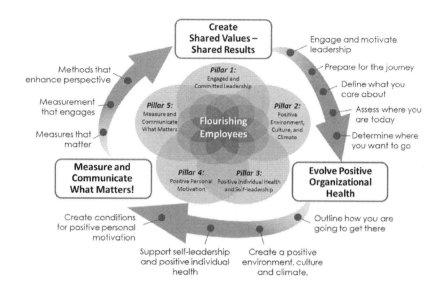

CHAPTER 16:
Methods That Enhance Perspective

When you change the way you look at things,
the things you look at change.

—Wayne Dyer

Randomized Controlled Trials—All That Is Gold Does Not Glitter

The randomized controlled trial (RCT) has long been considered the gold-standard method for evaluating the efficacy and causal impact of many types of treatments and interventions. However, unless they are combined with other methods that we will discuss a little later, randomized trials are still designed to answer main effect questions like those we discussed in chapter 15. For wellness programs, RCTs are expected to answer the question:

Do wellness programs cause...?

Examples of outcomes that can be inserted into the sentence above could include fewer health risks, increased performance and productivity, and decreased healthcare costs, just to name a few. Figure 17 outlines the logic of RCTs: first you measure (O_1), and then you randomly randomly assign (R) some people to receive the intervention (X) and other people to a control group that does not receive the intervention (C). Randomization is done to ensure that the two groups are equivalent. After the intervention, you measure again (O_2). Finally, you compare the findings for the groups and report any differences.

Figure 17. Common Notation for Randomized Controlled Trials

$$O_1 \rightarrow R \nearrow X - O_2 \searrow C - O_2$$

To assess the purest possible effect of the intervention, RCTs often control for differences in personal and contextual factors as much as possible. Unfortunately, this limits external validity and generalizability of findings and reduces the utility of RCTs when used as the sole evaluation method. Plus, better understanding the personal and contextual factors that influence health and well-being is badly needed in our evaluation studies. When RCTs are used to evaluate complex, population-based programs, the results are often ambiguous, and study authors often conclude that "more research is needed." The findings often provide little other information unless supplemented or replaced with additional, more appropriate methods for evaluating complex social programs.

Some still believe that RCTs are the gold standard for evaluating social programs and have heralded lackluster findings from RCTs as definitive proof that wellness programs don't work. A 2014 meta-analysis of the ROI for wellness programs found a negative relationship between the rigor of the study design and the strength of the ROI for the program.[223] The analysis showed that the more rigorous the design, the lower the ROI, and the most "rigorous" design (randomized trials) showed the lowest return. Randomized trials may be the gold standard for testing the *efficacy* (i.e., performance under ideal controlled circumstances) of some types of very well-defined medical treatments (e.g., medications and some very highly controlled medical procedures). However, they are rather blunt instruments for measuring the *effectiveness* (i.e., performance under real-world conditions) of complex, population-based social programs designed to improve complicated social issues.

In a commentary in the Journal of the American Medical Association, Don Berwick (co-founder of the Institute for Healthcare Improvement and former Administrator of the Centers for Medicare and Medicaid Services, or CMS) makes the following statement about using RCTs to evaluate social programs:

> *With social changes—multicomponent interventions, some of which are interpersonal, all of which are nonlinear, in complex social systems—then other, richer, but equally disciplined, ways*

to learn (such as CMO [Context, Mechanisms, and Outcomes] designs) are needed. It is possible to rely on other methods without sacrificing rigor. Many assessment techniques developed in engineering and used in quality improvement—statistical process control, time series analysis, simulations, and factorial experiments—have more power to inform about mechanisms and contexts than do RCTs, as do ethnography, anthropology, and other qualitative methods. For these specific applications, these methods are not compromises in learning how to improve; they are superior.[224]

In 1998, the World Health Organization also recognized that "the use of randomized control trials to evaluate health promotion initiatives is, in most cases, inappropriate, misleading and unnecessarily expensive."[225] To better understand and improve the impact of our efforts we must begin to expand our evaluation methods to reflect the full character of the impact we intend to make in the health and thriving of our employees and our organizations.

During thirty-four years at the University of Michigan Health Management Research Center we never designed a randomized controlled trial because we believed the requirements and assumptions needed to conduct a research trial could not be fulfilled in a worksite environment; they were too limiting to allow valid scalability, thus not real for use in other situations; the data needed most often do not meet the assumptions necessary to conduct the analyses; contamination exists across the experimental groups; important data are not often available to ensure equality of the groups, group bias often contaminates the results or increases the variance; and, it is too expensive for most organizations without government or foundation funding.

More Realistic Evaluation Methods

To address the complexity of evaluating programs in a social context, Ray Pawson and Nick Tilley suggest an alternative approach to evaluation, which they call "realistic evaluation."[226] For complex social programs, realistic evaluation methods can be superior to standard randomized controlled trials for understanding the mechanisms, contexts, and outcomes associated with change. They assert that "Programs work (have successful 'outcomes') only insofar as they introduce the appropriate ideas and opportunities ('mechanisms') to groups in the appropriate social and cultural conditions ('contexts')."

The Common Notation for Realistic Evaluation is C + M = O

Realism holds that both context and mechanism must be systematically researched along with the intervention. Realistic evaluation does not prove or disprove a theory. Rather it produces explanations that plausibly account for observed patterns in the data and accommodate the range of contingencies and exceptions found. It builds on current best understandings of the field.

Context Matters

Wellness and well-being programs are interventions that often have many components that may act both independently and interdependently. The programs are part of the context, along with many other characteristics of the employment setting and the larger system in which the organization operates. These programs are highly context-dependent: the impact of the same intervention will vary considerably depending on who delivers it, to whom it is delivered, under what circumstances, and with which tools and techniques.

Applying the Program Impact Measure at Premera Blue Cross

Employers expect more than efficient claims administration from their health plans. Based on that opportunity, employers want a roadmap for making it happen. Zero Trends *provides a conceptual framework to do this. We translated the five pillars into an actionable and measurable roadmap that we could use to structure targeted services for our customers.*

Unlike many modeling tools, this Program Impact Measure, or PIM, ties traditional healthcare data (claims, health risk, demographics, etc.), cultural data (policies, communication strategies, corporate support, etc.), and levels of participation for the services previously delivered.

The PIM demonstrates the impact a "culture of health" strategy can have regarding the health of a workforce population based on the best employer health research:

- *provides the employer a strategic and tactical roadmap (programs, policies, communications, and incentives) for achieving the health and productivity improvement*

- *helps employers make informed purchasing decisions around health and productivity initiatives*

- *provides an ongoing objective mechanism for measuring progress and for fine tuning implementation*

Neal Sofian
Director, Member Engagement, Premera Blue Cross

To see the complete case study go to appendix B

Understanding Mechanisms

Pawson and Tilley define mechanisms as "underlying entities, processes or (social) structures that operate in a particular context to generate outcomes of interest."[226] Mechanisms include things like perceptions of the company's purpose for the programs, personal perceptions of the need to lose weight or participate in the program, intrinsic motivation to make the recommended change, and perceptions of the ease of use of the program. These can all contribute to whether employees participate in programs or are influenced by their context. Mechanisms are not inherent to the intervention but a function of the participants and the context. The mechanisms by which an intervention works are varied across individuals. There may be many mechanisms, some that are intended by the program designers, and some that are unintended.[227]

Programs do not directly change employees. Employees' reactions to the opportunities provided by the programs trigger the change. The decisions and actions taken by the human components are what generate the outcomes.

According to Berwick, "the effectiveness of these systems is sensitive to an array of influences: leadership, changing environments, details of implementation, organizational history, and much more. In such complex terrain, the RCT is an impoverished way to learn."

Outcomes

Any outcomes associated with the wellness program are not simply linear or deterministic. Providing employees with resources or time off to participate in them does not cause employees to become healthier or change their behaviors, but it may make behavior change more likely.

There is no single way to conduct a realistic evaluation, since this type of evaluation, by its nature, includes multiple methods and measures with the goal of creating a broader and deeper perspective. Some principles to keep in mind are as follows:

- Keep context, mechanisms, and outcomes in mind when designing the evaluation.

- Use both quantitative and qualitative methods to
  - o collect rich information about the way the program is intended to operate;
  - o identify mechanisms, both intended and unintended, that support or interfere with the intended outcomes.

- Use information collected throughout the evaluation in "real time" to continuously refine your approaches.

- As themes emerge, engage in conversations with stakeholders to get their perspectives on the findings, and make any needed refinements to approaches in real time.

- Conduct small tests to validate or invalidate interpretations of information as they emerge.

- Synthesize all information collected throughout the continuous evaluation process to convey a compelling narrative to stakeholders at many time points and tell the story as it unfolds to stakeholder groups.

In chapter 15, we described many different methods for capturing qualitative and quantitative information about positive individual and positive organizational health. These methods can be continued as a way of conducting realistic evaluation over time and as a means to keep employees engaged in the process. They provide invaluable information about the evolution of your organization's environment and culture related to health and thriving.

Treatment Fidelity

Treatment fidelity refers to how well the program is implemented for each eligible individual. It is possible to create an index of treatment fidelity using objective indicators of the program's process and structure. Mark Lipsey of Vanderbilt University's Peabody College has conducted many meta-analyses,[228-230] and even meta-meta-analyses (a meta-analysis of many meta-analyses)[231] and has co-authored a seminal book on meta-analytic methods.[232] Findings from his 2009 review of characteristics of effective programs designed to reduce recidivism in juvenile offenders highlight the importance of the quality of implementation.

> *In some analyses, the quality with which the intervention is implemented has been as strongly related to recidivism effects as the type of program, so much so that a well-implemented intervention of an inherently less efficacious type can outperform a more efficacious one that is poorly implemented.* [232]

> *Mark W. Lipsey, PhD*

While the intervention in this example is not in the wellness and well-being arena, the finding does highlight the importance of the integrity and fidelity of programs, and emphasizes the need to include measures of treatment integrity or fidelity.

Using Indicators of Implementation in Analyses

Indicators of fidelity can be reported over time as metrics or used as control variables in more formal analytics performed by evaluators:

- Develop a measure or index of implementation and define a measurable implementation continuum that can be used as a variable in the analysis.

- Break treatment into activities or components to consider their individual contributions to treatment effects and their interactions with each other.

- Block different implementation levels together and compare differences in outcomes.

Create a Guiding Framework for Evaluation

Throughout the book, we have emphasized the value of organizing frameworks to help make sense of complexity, whether that means simplifying rich and sometimes overwhelming amounts of information, or better understanding and mapping the many potential influences on outcomes of importance to our organizations.

We highly recommended using organizing frameworks but acknowledge that too narrowly framing things could be limiting. Don't let your framework result in a constricted mindset through which you see the world. Always be open to seeing things that you might not have thought of before or that you have not included in your framework.

Don't let your "framework" become a limiting mindset. Always be ready to change your mind and your framework.

In chapter 11, we discussed program theory as way to outline how your programs and initiatives are supposed to operate. For example, is your program designed to reach all your employees, or just a subset? Are participants expected to attend a workshop, read materials online, or go through a health-screening event? The program theory outlines the flow of the program and how people are supposed to interface with it. Change theory helps outline the mechanisms that influence change in individuals and organizations. For example, are your approaches designed to increase employee awareness about health risks, improve self-efficacy for changing behaviors, create stronger relationships and support systems, and develop resilience, optimism, and mindfulness?

In figure 18, we provide an example of a general model that can be used to guide a comprehensive evaluation plan. Creating a model that combines the program theory with a conceptual outcomes framework can help manage expectations while continuously delivering important information about leading and lagging indicators related to the initiative. The win-win evaluation framework combines the high-level model that we introduced in chapter 3 with the outcomes framework for share results we introduced in chapter 14. Your program model and outcomes framework will likely be more detailed than this. It will represent the main components of your unique set of efforts to evolve your health-related environment and culture, as well as your wellness and well-being approaches. In any case, a comprehensive evaluation should include assessment in each area that your approach is intended to impact.

Figure 18. The win-win evaluation framework

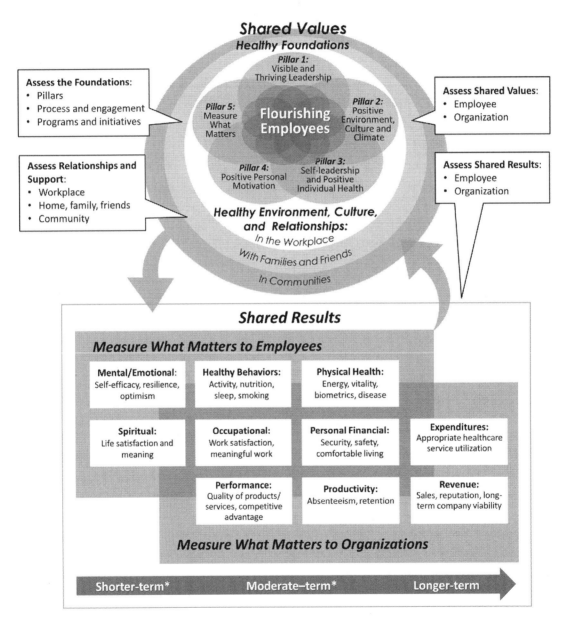

These are general estimates only. Depending on your approach and your population, some outcomes could happen earlier or later than their position in this framework indicates.

Assess the Foundations

In chapter 8, as part of the positive organizational health assessment, we described methods for assessing the foundations. Our measure of culture assesses the five foundational pillars, as does the environmental audit that we commonly use with our partners. You may have outlined a different (although hopefully somewhat related) set of foundations. Whatever it is that provides the grounding for your efforts to evolve a health-related environment and culture, you will want some indication of its strength.

It is important to re-administer an environmental audit at least biannually, to understand the evolution of the health-supportive features of your organization's environment, climate, and culture. Depending on which audit your organization uses, this process can be relatively brief and should not take a huge amount of company resources to complete. In addition to annual or biannual measurement, we recommend periodically reviewing and representing any midyear changes that were made in the organization's environment (newly implemented programs, construction, policies, benefits, etc.). We recommend that you periodically ask employees about their perceptions of the environment, climate, and culture in the workplace, home, and community.

Assess Shared Values

We have emphasized the importance of Shared Values—Shared Results throughout the book, and chapter 7 provided some examples of how you might assess values as part of beginning the journey and creating a meaningful set of shared values. This assessment can be repeated periodically to evaluate whether your employees believe the values are being lived in the organization over time. This is a great way to capture and share stories from employees about how they are impacted by—and live according to—the values of the organization.

Assess Relationships and Support

In our model, relationships are core to employee health and well-being, so we recommend assessing perceived support from and connectedness with colleagues, family, friends, and community. These are all related to how we perceive our extended environment and culture, and their evaluation could be included with the organizational environment and culture assessment. You will want to highlight the importance of their measurement for the success of the individual, the work team, and the organization.

Assess Shared Results

The win-win evaluation framework depicts many dimensions of health that matter to both employees and the organizations. As shown in the framework, these dimensions overlap to a greater or lesser degree, with some being more important to organizations, and others being more important to employees. Assessing meaningful shared results over time is core to the win-win philosophy. It may not be necessary to repeat every measure at every time-point, but ideally, ongoing measurement of core and meaningful metrics at key points throughout the journey will help determine how you are doing along the way.

Independent Group Home Living Program, Inc. (IGHL) is a nonprofit organization headquartered in Manorville, New York. IGHL strives to identify ways to meet employees' changing lifestyles by addressing financial, emotional, physical, social, and mental needs. One of the fundamental principles in launching this initiative was a top-down leadership approach—we understood that we must lead by example.

In 2013, in an effort to promote family wellness, we expanded the program to include employees' spouses and adult dependent children. Health is Wealth™ not only requires employees to participate in the biometric screening and health assessment, but also requires their spouses and adult dependents to do the same

Over the years, we also found that for any successful wellness program, communication to employees is key. In 2013, we launched a website that allows employees to view all class offerings, schedule their own classes and track their progress throughout the year.

The transformation of the overall health of our workforce has been incredible. Catastrophic events such as heart attacks have reduced from four to ten percent per year down to three percent in 2013, the lowest ever. While the national average of insurance costs over the last five to six years has gone up 41 percent, IGHL's costs have increased 10 percent, mostly due to administration costs, not claims costs. IGHL has also seen a reduction in claims over a two-year time frame. We have saved money on training because employee retention improved by 4.3 percent.

Doris Geier
Sr. Director, Health is Wealth Program, Independent Group Home Living Program, Inc.

To read the full case study go to appendix B

Assess Short-Term, Moderate-Term, and Longer-Term Impacts

Many things contribute to the ultimate impact of an organization's effort to support employee health and well-being. Explicitly outlining the predicted short-term, intermediate, and long-term outcomes can provide guidance and structure for the program design, implementation strategy, evaluation processes, and outcomes reporting. Most of us have experienced the situation where stakeholders expect a lagging indicator like service utilization or cost avoidance in an unrealistically short time frame. Some dimensions will be impacted early (short-term or leading indicators), and some impacts may come a bit later (moderate-term outcomes). Some of the most commonly measured areas may take years to show an impact (longer-term, or lagging indicators). It is helpful to discuss the expected time frame for outcomes with stakeholders to establish expectations for what kinds of impacts to expect and when. Review outcomes in each domain that contributes to understanding the overall impact of your efforts:

- Did you see changes in psychosocial outcomes?

- Did health behaviors improve?

- Did job satisfaction and engagement improve?

- Did health risks, behaviors, and clinical outcomes improve?

- Were there positive changes in organizational and worker productivity and performance?

- Was there an improvement in the tone of commentary given in "stay" or exit interviews?

Amesbury Well Power

The Amesbury Well Power program created tremendous goodwill and loyalty between MIIA and the city. Success measurements included participation and satisfaction. Incentives didn't seem to increase participation, and, in fact, created frustration when participants didn't know how to redeem their points or didn't receive their award. We will gradually move away from using incentives for any program components, as they are transactional and do not create intrinsic motivation.

We have learned that employee engagement is not the same as employee participation, and in order to have an engaged population, we will work with leadership to help employees feel good about coming to work. In year 3, for the second time we conducted a satisfaction survey via Survey Monkey.

Below are the highlights, and reflects combined responses from 'Agree' and 'Strongly Agree' categories.

- *helped them improve their overall health—82%*
- *helped them make positive behavior changes—85%*
- *lead them to make at least one significant behavior change—90%*
- *helped them to be more productive at work—62%*
- *has been of value to others in their family—56%*
- *has the potential to reduce healthcare costs—90%*
- *is a valuable part of their employee benefits—95%*
- *contributes to better employee morale—86%*

Jayne M. Schmitz, MPH
Wellness Program Specialist | MIIA Health Benefits Trust, Amesbury MA

To read the full case study go to appendix B

Examine Patterns and Relationships

In addition to assessing each of the outcome areas, there is a real benefit to better understanding relationships between the outcome areas. As we previously quoted Michael Parkinson in *Zero Trends*, "Knowledge comes when relationships are connected to outcomes."

- Look at relationships and patterns between shorter-, moderate-, and longer-term impacts:
  - Were changes in shorter-term metrics related to changes in moderate-term impacts?
  - Were changes in moderate-term impacts related to changes in longer-term impacts?
  - Is there an overall pattern of relationships between findings that best explains (fits the patterns of) the data?

The focus on wellness outcomes is appropriately shifting to health improvement rather than financial metrics. Sophisticated employers and brokers realize that while better financial results will likely follow improved health, worsened financial results will certainly follow poorer health

—Lee Dukes
Chief Solutions Officer, Catapult Health

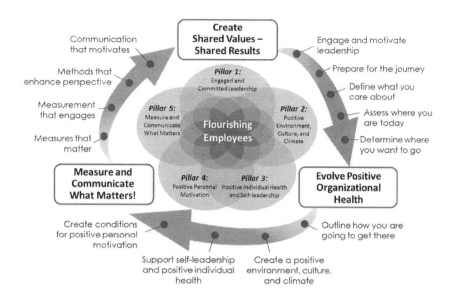

CHAPTER 17:
Communication That Motivates

*Communicate in the relevant language
to get the desired results.*

As the efforts to evolve thriving workplaces and workforces unfold, it helps to demonstrate to stakeholders that short-term outcomes are occurring as expected, and provide early evidence that the approach is on track to deliver a longer-term impact. Conversely, if short-term outcomes are contrary to expectations, early reporting allows for midcourse corrections to the program.

It is critically important to provide meaningful feedback to everyone, every step of the way, to build and maintain movement toward the vision.

The Third Annual (2011) National Business Group on Health, Fidelity Investments Benefits Consulting Survey revealed that 76 percent of companies do not know the impact that their wellness and well-being programs have on employee health or on their healthcare costs. The majority get annual reports of summarized information from health assessments from a variety of third-party vendors. This basically means that for a long time organizations have had little substantial information available to guide ongoing improvements in approaches designed to evolve health and thriving.

Health-risk assessments are often lengthy and completed only once a year or even biannually. Because employers rarely have access to medical and pharmacy claims, they rely on their health plans to report on healthcare utilization outcomes once a year. For fully insured employers, this often accompanies determination of health plan premiums for the upcoming year. Information must be gathered far more often to be useful.

Strategic Reporting to Stakeholders

We are in a truly amazing time when it comes to collecting, analyzing, and reporting our findings. We can clearly recall the days of transferring survey data from the original survey forms to the computer punch cards that were manually fed into mainframe computers the size of a respectable dwelling. Today it is not uncommon for data to be automatically transferred from our Internet of Things to the big data coffers. While that can sound scary, used properly, it can also be exciting and hugely useful to employees and their employers. We emphasize the importance of employee choice and autonomy in this world of stealth data capture and urge employers to make employees aware of how the data will be used and give them a choice over whether it is collected at all.

After becoming inspired by the research included in Zero Trends *and our desire to deliver real solutions to our clients (not just insurance policies) we designed, built, and implemented our own benefits risk-management division at Ottawa Kent. The objective of this 'loss control for benefits' unit was to provide access to wellness coaches to help average 97.6 percent participation in health risk assessment with no financial incentives.*

The process used by Ottawa Kent is nearly identical to the property/casualty risk management process. We start out by identifying our client's risk exposure and then analyzing their loss data and developing strategies to control or eliminate losses. It is only after completing these three steps that we even talk about insurance as one way to finance the costs of risk. The final, ongoing step is monitoring and measuring results.

Randy Boss, Certified Risk Architect
Partner at Ottawa Kent

To read the full case study go to appendix B

Advances in technology make it possible to monitor more frequently and report on these and other important outcomes with minimal burden on the population. Subsets of questions can be frequently administered to random or cohort samples of the employee population.

When it comes to reporting, we can start by following the lead of safety, quality, and sales.

Organizations typically distribute information about safety as well as quality and sales at least monthly if not weekly or daily. It is important to keep everyone informed, not just the senior and operational leaders. Everyone in the organization has value and everyone needs to receive meaningful feedback about how the organization is progressing toward the vision. If only a select group has the information, it will not generate and maintain the momentum needed to evolve and sustain a healthier culture and environment.

Organizational and employee data should be made available frequently to be an effective part of shaping a healthier environment and culture. Measurement is most valuable when meaningful information is provided to individuals, program decision-makers, and management in a timely and user-friendly manner. Employees, as well as senior leaders and managers, need timely knowledge to support good decision-making about how to best move individual and population outcomes toward the vision (see table 19).

Table 19. Current best and emerging next practices for reporting and communications

Measures and Methods	Current Best Practices	Emerging Next Practices
Reporting What Matters		✓
Provide timely feedback of progress toward vision, culture, self-leaders, actions, economic outcomes		
• annual	✓	✓
• semiannual		✓
• monthly		✓
• real time		
Beyond the usual audience for "outcomes" reporting, share tailored information with everyone:		
• senior leaders	✓	✓
• operations leaders	✓	✓
• managers		✓
• employees		✓

An important part of your ongoing evaluation will be continuing communication about results that matter to all stakeholders. Many organizations get periodic outcome reports from their benefits and program partners, but they are often delivered long after the collection of the data represented in the reports. You can ask for information more frequently, but it often comes with a hefty price tag.

Feedback is most effective when it is specific,
actionable, and timely.

—Ken Blanchard

The bottom line is that evaluation must support decision-making with real-time information. The information is too valuable to wait for an annual report or even a semiannual report. Leaders and employees are making decisions every day; they deserve to have the most up-to-date information at the point of decision-making, as with any good decision-support system.

Guaranteeing Savings Based on Employee Participation in Best Practices

Benefit Commerce Group, an employee benefits consulting firm in Arizona, has developed a program that guarantees cost savings based on employee participation. The ROI is not based on actual health outcomes; this is especially important for midsize employers, since their claims experience is not a fully credible reference for insurers when pricing premium rates, and medical trend usually accounts for 50–70 percent of their renewal rate increase.

With 100 percent or even with less than perfect participation, employers win with Trend Neutralizer, because of the sliding scale of credit for each of the seven practices below:

- *consumer-driven health plan enrollment*
- *annual physical with biometric screening*
- *health risk assessment*
- *disease management*
- *healthy lifestyle programs*
- *specific employer-sponsored health events*
- *premium differential for smoker vs. nonsmoker*

Employees then had a clearer picture of their own health conditions and began participating in health improvement programs. They had started a culture of wellness. The result was that within two years the health plan cost increases were halted, and the per-employee cost had been reduced by more than 15 percent from where it had been at its height. By the third year, the Trend Neutralizer and their employee participation achievements were directly responsible for reducing by nearly half, the renewal increase the organization otherwise would have received.

Chris Hogan
Director Trend Neutralizer, Benefit Commerce Group

To read the full case study go to appendix B

Design Engaging and Intuitive Reports

The power of presentations is rooted in our craving for human connection. A shared experience that aligns their minds and moves them forward with unified momentum.

—Nancy Duarte

Throughout the book, we have discussed the importance of collecting meaningful, rich, and timely information about the people, the environment, and the culture of your organization. How you disseminate the information is at least as important to the success of your effort to evolve a thriving environment and culture as the data you collect. Earlier in the book we described what you can do to synthesize the information you have collected as part of your Positive Organizational Health

Assessment (see Synthesize Information and Report on Findings, and Reporting to the Organizational Stakeholders in chapter 8). In the remainder of this chapter, we build on those ideas to help you make continuous improvements and maintain momentum. Ultimately, the information from your ongoing evaluation is intended to inspire your audience, create motivation, and keep your movement alive.

Develop Responsive Approaches to Communicate Results That Matter to All Stakeholders

Ongoing use of the quantitative and qualitative evaluation methods we discussed in chapter 12 can create engagement as well as provide rich information for meaningful and frequent feedback to stakeholders. It can also provide valuable information that can be used to refine your approaches over time. This is another area where an ad hoc design team might come into play. Gather an employee-based design team to brainstorm innovative ways to evaluate, synthesize, and communicate meaningful information to all stakeholders. This is a good way to ensure that the voice of the employee is included in the information that shapes the efforts to evolve the workplace culture and environment. It is also a great way to build engagement and ownership in the evaluation process.

Many organizations frequently report on several types of business metrics on executive dashboards and administrative reports. We believe that progress against goals and objectives for wellness and well-being programs deserve the same level of attention from executive and operations leaders. We recommend that these metrics be included alongside any other corporate performance indicators.

Start with What is Already Working Well

There is always some good news, and there are always opportunities to improve and grow. If you don't have some good news to report to your stakeholders, you probably didn't look closely enough for examples of positive deviance and for illustrations of what is already working well in your organization. Make sure you highlight the positive examples you have found, and encourage celebration among stakeholders about their constructive impact on the organization.

Make it Intuitive and Personal

Many reports of outcomes rely primarily on bar charts and pie graphs to convey quantitative information. While these can be dry and devoid of emotion, they don't necessarily have to be. There are several tools and resources that can be used to help you create more compelling feedback of quantitative information (See appendix D for a list of useful resources). It is important to include personal stories to create empathy and excitement and motivate action. Stories help people see themselves and their colleagues in the findings and create greater meaning and relevance.

Employees typically best respond to messages that are written using language that is comfortable and culturally relevant to them and sensitive to their needs. Why should leaders be any different? Leaders at different levels within an organization may find more meaning, value, and relevance in certain types of metrics and messages. But many times we use a "one size fits all" approach with leaders when it comes to reporting the outcomes from our programs. A front line manager may care more about safety and productivity metrics while a regional vice president or business unit leader may be more interested in metrics related to waste/rework, quality, or customer satisfaction rates. A comprehensive approach to evaluation and value demonstration relies on an array of metrics that appeal to various stakeholders.

Jessica Grossmeier, PhD
Vice President of Research for the Health Enhancement Research Organization and CEO of Verity Analytics

---

Reinforce Connections

We have spoken about collaboration and creating connections throughout the book. Strong connections take time to develop, and the reporting process is one way to help strengthen bonds. So your reports should speak to everyone in the organization. The results should go to as many people as possible. Ideally, everyone in the organization should get some kind of information about successes, ongoing progress, and opportunities to make continuous improvements.

People should see themselves and their role in the feedback. It is important to draw connections between functions with your reporting, to help people in different roles throughout the organization see themselves as important collaborators. For example, there is a growing recognition of the connection between safety practices in an organization and the wellness and well-being of its employees. So the individuals responsible for overseeing the organization's safety protocols may already have a good sense of their influence on employee health. We are also learning that having autonomy and opportunities for doing meaningful work is important to the health and well-being of employees. Managers and supervisors may not see the direct connection between their leadership capabilities and employee well-being. This is an opportunity to help them understand their pivotal role in helping employees do creative, meaningful work that positively affects their quality of life.

Invite Interaction

We hope that you will use at least some of the many creative and inclusive methods we outlined for capturing information over time (see chapters 8, 13, 14 and 15). If you have, it is likely that many employees have been involved on one level or another in that process. As part of the positive organizational health assessment feedback, we encourage the involvement of individuals who participated in the data collection process. This can provide good exposure for those employees and help senior leaders empathize with the message that the employees bring from their own perspective.

Use Multiple Communication Channels and Creative Visual Displays of Information

Given the technology of the times, it is easier than ever to disseminate information. Earlier in the book we encouraged the use of employee design teams at various stages of the planning and evaluation of your approaches to evolve a healthier environment and culture. It may also be advisable to convene a design team to create a creative and comprehensive approach to publicizing your evaluation findings. Depending on the structure of your organization, you may want to consider providing feedback across multiple channels. This might include

- email;
- intranet;
- social media—Twitter, Facebook, Instagram;
- photo collage posted in a prominent area of the organization.

You can even create a low-tech crowdsourced approach where employees collect information over time and display it on a dedicated wall or corkboard in your workplace. The more you can make the information inclusive, empathetic, creative, intuitive, and visual, the more it will resonate across the many stakeholder groups in the organization.

Frequent Feedback to All Stakeholders

Advances in technology make it possible to monitor more frequently and report on these and other important outcomes with minimal burden on the population. We recommend that reporting represent the relationships and interactions (mediators and moderators) between the workplace environment and culture, and the short-, moderate-, and long-term outcomes. This can provide opportunities to demonstrate early program successes and determine whether elements of the program are working as expected in time for corrective action by program implementers.[238]

- Share meaningful information with all stakeholders.
- Use the information to reinforce success and make appropriate improvements.
- Share with everyone how the information is being used.
- Revise and repeat cycle.

Table 20 outlines a very high-level set of measurement and communication timeframes for gathering information over time that will help your organization and all your stakeholders understand how well you are progressing toward your vision. For each of the quantitative measures in the table, traditional measurement timeframes are represented in shaded rows. Incremental measures are also represented for each. Rather than administering the entire measure to your whole employee population at each point, we recommend sampling a representative group of employees and administering subsets of questions at different points. This can make more frequent, incremental measurement more palatable to employees.

Table 20. Potential measurement and communication timeframes for a win-win evaluation

Month	1	2	3	4	5	6	7	8	9	10	11	12	13
Environmental Audit													
Administer full audit	X												X
Record incremental improvements		x	x	x	x	x	x	x	x	x	x	x	
Perception of Culture Survey													
Administer full survey	X												X
Monthly random sample of employees and items		x	x	x	x	x	x	x	x	x	x	x	
Living and Thriving Assessment													
Administer full survey	X												X
Monthly random sample of employees and items		x	x	x	x	x	x	x	x	x	x	x	
Medical Claims	X	x	x	x	x	x	x	x	x	x	x	x	X
Pharmacy Claims	X	x	x	x	x	x	x	x	x	x	x	x	X
Laboratory Data	X	x	x	x	x	x	x	x	x	x	x	x	X
Enrollment Engagement	X	X	X	X	X	X	X	X	X	X	X	X	X

Make Course Corrections as Necessary

An important part of your evaluation will include purposefully using the evaluation information and ongoing feedback from stakeholders to validate the results and make improvements to your approaches. Sometimes these will only be minor tweaks or adjustments to small components of your initiatives or programs. Other times, what you learn from your evaluation and feedback from stakeholders will indicate a need to make a major change or completely change direction.

It is important to maintain the spirit of possibility and optimism throughout the evolution of your health-management, cultural, and environmental initiatives. We recommend that you periodically reconvene your ad hoc design teams as necessary to engage in any redesign efforts or to develop any new approaches to improve health and wellness.

As always, creating and implementing innovative approaches that can help improve positive individual and positive organizational health should include collaboration, open-mindedness, creativity, and fun!

Dee, along with Jennifer Pitts, has done it again. Shared values—Shared Results is a tour de force. The father of Corporate Wellness who brought us initial benchmarking and Health Risk Assessments, shows us how it's not just the measurement and tools to measure that matters, but also recognizes the importance of social behavior, and of social networks, and social pressure to catalyze health activities and outcomes. As we say at Keas "if it isn't fun and social, the consumer isn't going to participate"—Shared Values—Shared Results validates the need to make health fun, social, germane, and most of all easy so that real people and make real change in their lives, to live longer and happier, in good health.

Josh Stevens
CEO, Keas

Communication leads to community, that is,
to understanding, intimacy and mutual valuing.

—Rollo May

FINAL WORDS

Other People Matter
– Chris Peterson

Call to Action: Embrace Disruptive Innovation

When we began our work on this book, we assumed we would include a call to action as part of our Final Words. After completing the book we stepped back and took a broad look at efforts to improve employee wellness over the past several decades. We realized that the call to action is proposed throughout this book.

While much progress in any field is built on continuous improvement efforts, sometimes an innovation comes along that supplants a part of the system and disrupts the normal flow, elevating outcomes to a significantly higher level. Figure 19 illustrates a series of innovations that have influenced employee health and well-being in this manner—a phenomenon sometimes referred to as "jumping the curve." As shown in the figure, the value of innovations or new technologies improves slowly at first. As familiarity and acceptance of the technology increases, the value and performance improves more rapidly. Eventually increases in performance begin to plateau, and may even start to reverse, which stimulates the next disruptive innovation.

Disruptive innovation moves the field forward if, and only if, it displaces dysfunctional processes or even less effective processes and interjects a process that significantly improves performance.

Employee Wellness Programs as a Solution for High Costs of Care

Wellness was introduced as a holistic concept for healthy living in the 1960s. While it took some time to gain traction with employer organizations, workplace wellness took hold when it was tied to the financial pain that companies were experiencing due to costs of medical care for employees. Organizations began to acknowledge and use wellness in the 1970s, seeing it as an opportunity for disease prevention and health promotion for employees and a strategy for healthy living. The primary focus was on improving the lifestyles of individuals to reduce health risks and disease, and ultimately, reduce costs for organizations. Over time, wellness programs focusing on risk reduction began to experience a performance ceiling, due in part to low rates of participation and because "value" was narrowly defined by the financial return on investment to organizations.

Figure 19. Disruptive innovation in wellness and well-being improvement strategies

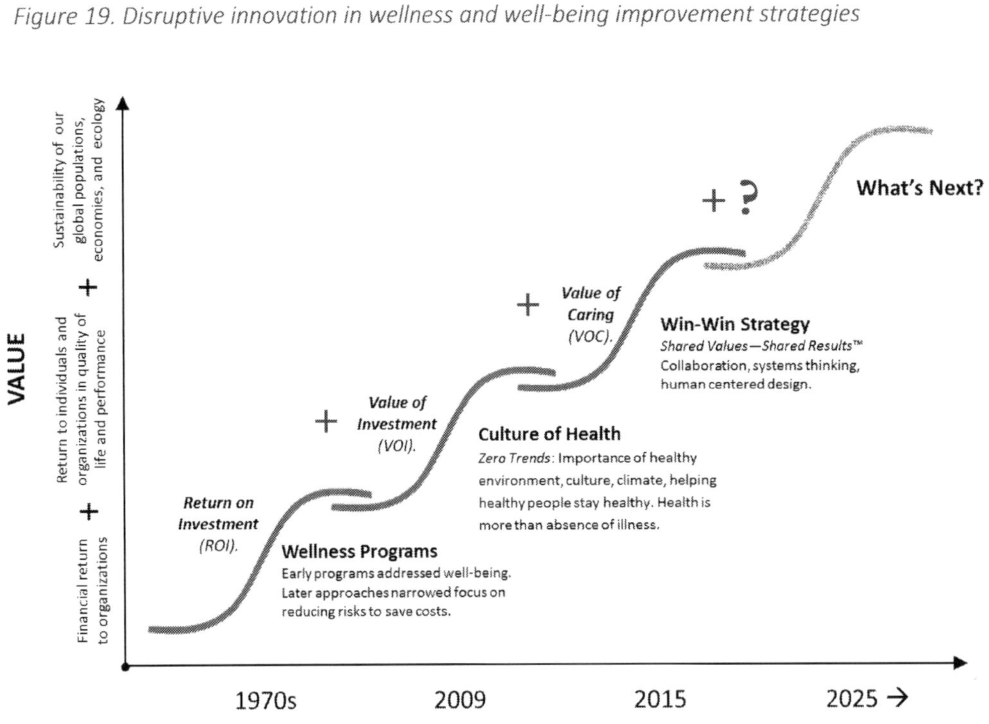

Wellness Programs Plus Culture of Health

Zero Trends: Health as a Serious Economic Strategy (2009) summarized more than thirty years of research and experience at the University of Michigan Health Management Research Center that developed the financial business case for employee wellness. It also introduced an innovative and disruptive framework for integrating individual wellness activities with environmental and cultural considerations to expand the health and wellness impact within organizations, families, and communities. After the publication of *Zero Trends*, we were pleased with the acceptance of the business case for workplace wellness. We were also happy about the acceptance of the five-pillar framework and about how many organizations acknowledged the value of a healthy environment and culture for the health and well-being of employees.

As depicted in figure 19, the early "culture of health" movement began in the 1970s and began to gain traction with wellness providers and organizations in 2009. The wellness field expand how value was measusred and who received the value. "Value on investment" now includes indicators of performance and quality of life for the total employee population, and value to organizations and employees are factored into the equation.

We envisioned that efforts to improve environments and cultures in workplaces, combined with wellness and well-being programs, would add substantial value for both individuals and organizations. However, while evolving a healthier culture takes time, we find that many organizations continue to be focused on short-term solutions to their financial pressures. Quite a few "culture of health" efforts we have seen, focus on adding more programs and initiatives, employing the newest technological gadgetry, or increasing the pressure on employees to participate in initiatives.

We have experienced a great deal of impatience from organizations who say they want to create a healthier environment and culture but continue to ask about the "low hanging fruit," and expect quick programmatic fixes. We are often asked "what is the one thing we can do that will make the greatest difference." We see culture of health providers offering to "install a culture of health," or provide a "step-by-step blueprint" for changing culture. We feel, and experienced practitioners agree, that we can't evolve a culture of health by changing just one or two things or by following a fixed blueprint.

There are no quick fixes. There is no single blueprint that will serve all organizations. We believe this book represents an opportunity and content for another disruptive innovation. We must jump past the plateau that we will see if we settle for the superficial "culture of health" efforts we are seeing today.

Wellness Programs Plus Culture of Health Plus a Win-Win Organizational Philosophy

With this book, we are making a disruptive challenge to merge initiatives around individual health with the efforts to improve the health of organizations. By engaging all stakeholders throughout organizations we can bring a win-win organizational philosophy and serious strategy to life. We know there is no silver bullet that can solve complex social issues like poor employee health and well-being. We also recognize the rapidly changing nature of worldwide competition, the shifting character of the workforce, and the evolving complexity of individual and organizational health. These considerations, and many others, demand that we apply unprecedented innovation and creativity in our approaches to developing solutions. Our approaches will benefit from incorporating systems and design thinking and the integrated contributions of all resources within the individuals and the organization.

Our solutions must recognize the value of caring (VOC)!

We see no downside to the immense possibilities that emanate from healthy, high-performing, and sustainable organizations, employees, and communities. Our challenge to organizations, and the challenge to the world is to transform the common purpose and vision to reality.

We are not proposing an expensive solution,
only a change in attitude.

The Purpose of this Book

Our main message in this book is that healthy, high-performing and sustainable organizations need healthy and high-performing employees, just as healthy and high-performing individuals need healthy and high-performing organizations. This is the basis of the win-win philosophy that we describe. We propose practical methods that help organizations create their own win-win strategies guided by three major themes: Shared Values—Shared Results; positive organizational health; and, measure and communicate what matters. We emphasize a shared and collaborative philosophy for employers and employees in addressing these themes.

Zero Trends was primarily focused on strategies for the workforce and workplace. With Shared Values—Shared Results we build on these strategies and also recognize the central influence of families and communities on employee quality of life, meaning, and happiness. We integrate several concepts and key strategies to deliver on the win-win promise:

- Expand the concept of health: from individual health to positive organizational and individual health. Keep in mind that context matters.

- Encourage a strategy of inspired and shared values, vision, and results for the organization and all stakeholders.

- Develop a functional plan for a strategic, systematic, systemic, and sustainable approach built upon the five-pillar foundation introduced in *Zero Trends*.

- Implement concrete positive organizational health opportunities for the employees and the organization as well as for families and communities.

- Introduce key life-skills for learning and continuous growth.

- Create conditions for positive personal motivation and engagement.

- Engage in collaborative decision making and co-create innovative solutions by utilizing systems and design thinking.

- Measure and communicate what matters to all stakeholders.

The win-win philosophy presented in this book shows how individuals, families, and communities can improve their quality of life, happiness, and higher standard of living while organizations maintain or even increase their revenue and profitability and service to society.

What's Next?

This book comes at a time when the United States is at a crossroads in its role in the world. Will our large organizations and financial institutions continue to serve the financial interests of the few at the expense of the quality of life of the many? Adam Smith (1723-1790) was an early proponent of the capitalist theory and his writings are often quoted in the argument that the self-interest feature of capitalism would be self-regulated by competition. However, he also warned of the dangers of what could happen when self-interest degenerates into greed and when wealth becomes concentrated in the few. His warning has come true in the United States and other countries of the world. While some in the US live at an elite level, the majority of people in the population are losing ground in their financial and quality of life status.

Part of the motivation for writing this book was to support the American values in our Declaration of Independence: "…life, liberty and the pursuit of happiness." America seems to have lost sight of the "pursuit of happiness" or quality of life, while increasing our interest in power and wealth accumulation. National measures such as Gross Domestic Product fall short of measuring what matters most to the citizens of the country. Many organizations have lost their way over the past several decades by focusing more and more on financial ratings, shareholder value, and status rather than the value they bring to their employees, their customers, and to society at large.

We are seeing a large number of social pathologies playing out on our planet, and the need for real solutions is urgent. Along with the growing income disconnect—the top 1 percent of our population now owns more than the bottom 90 percent—we see an increasing consumerism disconnect. We seek well-being and happiness through greater and greater material consumption, which feeds a massive ecological disconnect. We are currently consuming the resources of 1.5 planet earths. Otto Scharmer, senior lecturer at MIT and co-founder of the Presencing Institute, refers to these as disconnects between "ego" and "eco." This is fueling a scarcity mindset and a self-serving scramble for earth's resources that feeds a growing divisiveness in many areas throughout the world. This is especially true within and across political systems and between fundamentalist religious factions, which, According to Scharmer, represents a disconnect between ourselves and others. Scharmer also speaks of a growing disconnect within ourselves—essentially a self-self disconnect. These disconnects drive us, individually and collectively, to positions and behaviors that are diametrically opposed to flourishing, healthy, high-performing, and sustainable lives of our employees, our organizations, and our populations.

In the preface we challenged readers to do more than pay lip service to Einstein's often cited caution, "The level of thinking that got us into the problem will not be the same level that gets us out of it." We must actually think differently and do different things. We must stop looking solely to the solutions of the past for the solutions of the future. We challenge organizations to think bigger—beyond their walls to the surrounding communities, and to the larger society, regionally, nationally, and globally.

On the bright side, the world seems to be gravitating away from a blind focus on Gross Domestic Product (GDP) to a more balanced set of metrics that includes indicators of the quality of life and happiness of its citizens. It is encouraging to observe Bhutan, United Kingdom and other countries developing new metrics including Gross National Happiness (GNH), or the Genuine Progress Indicators (GPI) being utilized in some countries and US states to complement the national GDP or any other financial index (for more on these efforts see appendix D).

The best news is that organizational leaders are waking up to the power and competitive advantage of healthy and flourishing employees. There is real value in fostering creative, energized, collaborative, optimistic, and high performing workforces in high performing and profitable organizations. We invite you to examine the win-win philosophy we presented in this book and embrace any value it may have for your organization and employees.

There is no downside to creating Positive Organizational Health as a Win-Win Philosophy.

Appendix A
Common Personal Values

Acceptance	Credibility	Health	Prestige
Accomplishment	Curiosity	Helpfulness	Productivity
Accuracy	Decisiveness	Honesty	Professionalism
Achievement	Dependability	Honor	Prosperity
Adaptability	Depth	Hope	Recreation
Adventure	Devotion	Humility	Reflection
Affection	Dignity	Humor	Relationships
Affluence	Diligence	Imagination	Relaxation
Agility	Discipline	Independence	Reliability
Alertness	Discovery	Innovation	Resilience
Altruism	Drive	Inspiration	Respect
Ambition	Duty	Integrity	Responsibility
Appreciation	Education	Intelligence	Responsiveness
Authenticity	Effectiveness	Intimacy	Rest
Availability	Efficiency	Intuition	Security
Awareness	Empathy	Joy	Self-control
Balance	Encouragement	Justice	Selflessness
Being the best	Endurance	Kindness	Self-reliance
Belonging	Energy	Knowledge	Serenity
Benevolence	Enjoyment	Leadership	Service
Bravery	Enthusiasm	Learning	Sharing
Calmness	Excellence	Love	Simplicity
Camaraderie	Experience	Loyalty	Sincerity
Capability	Fairness	Making a difference	Skillfulness
Carefulness	Faith	Mastery	Spirituality
Caring	Family	Mindfulness	Stability
Challenge	Fidelity	Motivation	Strength
Charity	Financial independence	Neatness	Success
Cheerfulness	Fitness	Open-mindedness	Support
Clarity	Flexibility	Openness	Teamwork
Cleanliness	Follow through	Optimism	Thankfulness
Closeness	Freedom	Order	Thoughtfulness
Comfort	Friendship	Organization	Tradition
Commitment	Fulfillment	Passion	Trust
Compassion	Fun	Patience	Truth
Confidence	Generosity	Peace	Understanding
Connection	God	Perfection	Uniqueness
Consistency	Grace	Perseverance	Virtue
Contentment	Gratitude	Persistence	Vision
Control	Growth	Perspective	Vitality
Cooperation	Guidance	Play	Warmth
Courage	Happiness	Positive attitude	Wealth
Courtesy	Hard Work	Practicality	Wisdom
Creativity	Harmony	Preparedness	Work

Appendix B
Case Studies: Current and Next Practices

1. ACT, Inc., National Headquarters, Iowa City, IA

ACT, Inc., has about 1,300 employees, with 1,000 working at our national headquarters in Iowa City, Iowa. We are most well known for the college entrance exam, The ACT test. The wellness program at ACT program was approved by our board of directors in December 2011, and a wellness manager was hired in March 2012 to design, implement, manage and promote the program.

When we launched the wellness program in early 2012, one of our guiding resources was Dee Edington's book *Zero Trends: Health as a Serious Economic Strategy*. It has provided much of the research, rational, and philosophy for designing and implementing our program. A copy of the book was provided to our senior leadership team and we began to offer annual health screening and health risk assessments, using aggregate data to stratify risk profiles for participants/non-participants compared to healthcare claims. We began to offer monthly health coaching on a voluntary basis for those individuals in the high-risk category. In the past three years our healthcare costs annual increases have been trending to zero, from 7 percent in 2012, to 5 percent in 2013, and 3 percent in 2014.

We created a brand and logo for 'Wellness at ACT'—with a communication brochure that provided an overview of our program covering five categories: health and physical fitness; convenience services; social and personal well-being; financial well-being and retirement education; and leave time options. We also established a wellness committee with broad representation from across the organization—to help inform the design and offerings of our program, and to help with promotion and advocacy. With input from leadership and our committee we created a mission statement—"To provide a comprehensive and inclusive wellness program to help team members achieve happiness, health, and well-being." In 2013, we began a partnership with the University of Iowa Health and Human Physiology Department to offer students an opportunity for practicum or internship experience. This has been a great "win-win" for us to have additional support and expand our program offerings.

In January 2013, we became a tobacco-free workplace and began providing 100 percent coverage for tobacco cessation counseling. Even without an onsite workout facility or showers, we offered physical activity classes in conference rooms during lunch and after work. Our leadership made a decision in 2014 to renovate 8,000 square feet in our Tyler building to create the ACT Wellness Center, complete with locker rooms/showers, group fitness studio, cardio/weight room, recreation area with ping pong, foosball, interactive games, TV lounge, and lunch break area—which just opened May 26, 2015.

We began to offer a variety of onsite convenience services to alleviate the work/life imbalance and foster work-life integration. These services included onsite nurse practitioner (8 hours per week), prescription delivery 2 times a week, dry cleaning pickup and delivery 2 times a week, onsite chair massage (one 10-minute massage free each month), onsite H&R Block office during tax season, and a weekly food box delivery (a pay-as-you-go CSA program).

Our Social and Personal Well-Being largely involves our organization's commitment and participation in community events such as American Heart Association Heart Walk, American Cancer Society Relay for Life, as well as being a major supporter of our local United Way campaign. We have been, and continue to be, a leader in the Iowa Healthiest State Initiative and the Blue Zones Project, becoming the first Blue Zones Certified worksite in Iowa City. We offer quarterly financial wellness lunch and learns and bring the TIAA-CREF representative on campus every quarter for individual consultations.

Our leave time policy provides generous time off to improve personal well-being, including ten sick days, three personal development days, three floating holidays, three personal days, and one volunteer day. ACT encourages community 'social' well-being by providing a paid volunteer day for team members to contribute their time locally to an organization of their choosing. We also have ten paid holidays and three weeks paid vacation, and healthcare benefits (medical, dental and vision) that begin on day one of employment.

Since 2012, we've had over 90 percent of our team members participate in at least one of our wellness program offerings.

Sandy Stewart, MEd, CWWPM
Wellness Manager
ACT, Inc.

2. AMERICAN EXPRESS (An IBI Case Study)

In 2009, American Express hired Dr. Wayne Burton to achieve the financial services company's goal of improving the health and performance of its service centers' employees, leading to gains in productivity. Internal research indicated that investing more in the overall well-being of employees would translate to higher performance, better customer service and result an increase in Card Member retention.

How They Did It

In 2009, American Express launched its corporate wellness initiative, Healthy Living, in the United States and has since rolled it out to major global locations including India, United Kingdom, Europe, Mexico, Argentina, Canada, and Singapore. Through supportive resources, enhanced access to care, and incentives to foster healthy changes, Healthy Living aims to help employees achieve greater physical, psychological, social, and financial well-being.

In the US, the initiative includes a health risk assessment (HRA) including an eight-question Work Limitations Questionnaire (WLQ), to be completed annually by employees; free onsite biometric screenings; free preventative screenings; and free support programs such as onsite coaching and nutritional counseling.

American Express provided centralized funding for the initiative over the first year as seed money to demonstrate the value of the program to managers and supervisors. With a majority of employees now participating in Healthy Living, funding now is a combination of central and business funding depending on the location and services offered.

Health is not "one size fits all," which is why American Express needed a data-driven approach to understand better how to serve its employees. In 2010, the company partnered with the University of Michigan to create an integrated data warehouse to uncover healthcare gaps among its employees and create tailored health programs to address them. Healthy Living promotional materials incentivize employees to earn Healthy Rewards for completing the HRA and participating in a walking program.

American Express has four major service centers in the United States, and six others around the globe. The company now had an opportunity to better understand the drivers behind lost productivity at its service centers. "There are not many jobs where you can so easily measure productivity," Burton said, noting it is possible to measure productivity and quality in telephone-based service center environments.

The company experienced challenges in acquiring and synthesizing data on a global scale. Burton saw that the best course was to build a data infrastructure based on self-reported sources and in-house biometric and clinic data. The company was looking to accurately measure productivity and presenteeism (the impact of ill-health on performance while at work). The self-reported information from employees' annual HRA and the WLQ provided American Express "a roadmap" for health and productivity, according to Burton. It allows the company to compare populations across locations and gauge program success; especially in countries where insurance claims data aren't available. The WLQ measures the degree to which workers are experiencing on-the-job limitations because of health risks and medical conditions, including mental health. As a result of the cognitive nature of the customer service center duties, research has noted the particular importance of mental health to job productivity. The WLQ asks workers to rate their level of ability to perform tasks necessary to their job demands. The WLQ is an important component of self-reported on-the-job productivity because results can be tracked over time, allowing for a much more complete assessment of impact; it is standardized and has been validated in many employment settings. It is incorporated into the annual HRA, so it is brief and easy for employees to respond. "The WLQ allows us to show management the impact of health on productivity in different countries and the cost of lost productivity due to poor health," Burton said. "It also allows us to show improvements in productivity over time."

American Express offers different participation incentives, customized for each location to encourage employees to complete an HRA and WLQ, as well as to participate in biometric screenings, coaching and other program elements. In India, for instance, the vast majority of American Express' 63,500 employees participate in programs with very little incentive. In 2010, the company offered a $10 voucher for a healthy meal in the onsite cafeteria and got a 70 percent response rate. In the US, HRA participation rose to about 50 percent by rewarding with a $100 contribution to a flexible spending account for workers and a $50 contribution for spouses or domestic partners.

Internationally, participation in the HRA has varied and depends on many factors including cultural factors," said Burton. "The incentives and rewards have to be carefully thought out," "In India, there is a thirst for better health. Employees there realize the significant value of programs and services which are not otherwise generally available."

Results

Healthy Living is tailored to be culturally relevant and attractive to local populations, so the program varies across geographies. For instance, in Mexico, medical claims data showed a high incidence of gastro-intestinal problems in the workforce that were affecting perfor-mance. An emphasis on food safety and education has helped to address the problem. Strategies include an onsite cafeteria that offers fresh foods, a clean water supply, and education on proper refrigeration and food storage.

Disease management is one area that American Express is tackling in the United States. The company had offered telephonic disease management counseling. Participation initially was low, largely due to the nature of workers' jobs. "Most of them are on the phone all day long for work," Burton said.

American Express is now piloting a voluntary chronic disease intervention program for US workers who have been diagnosed with specific common conditions of diabetes, migraine headaches, or asthma. The program offers an onsite registered nurse, dietician, health coach, and biometric screenings. So far, 300 employees have participated in the diabetes intervention program and over 500 in the migraine headache program. No results are available yet, but the company is encouraged by higher than expected participation.

Today, the Healthy Living initiative results in an annual estimated productivity savings of $483 per participating employee in the US. Burton meets with the global compensation and benefits team to discuss metrics, and top management at American Express are regularly updated. Burton also shares results with senior leaders in major US locations, providing them with specific reports on their employees' health and productivity at a minimum annually.

Recommendations

Getting a clear picture of employee health across geographies and cultures can be difficult. But there are tools available that can help put that picture into focus. These include:

- Leveraging self-reported, validated information tools such as health risk assessments and absence and performance questionnaires

- Capturing data through an integrated warehouse system that can provide regular reports and track progress over time

- Tracking metrics closely and utilizing all local resources available, such as public health departments and local immunization campaigns, especially in countries like the United Kingdom with nationalized health systems that therefore don't have claims data

- Getting buy-in from top management and employees on-the-ground in international locations to roll out programs and take ownership

- Being sensitive to cultural differences

Wayne Burton, MD
Medical Director and Global Leader for Health and Productivity
American Express

3. Amesbury, MA.

Well Power

This program was available to all Massachusettes Interlocal Insurance Association (MIIA) employees and their spouses who were subscribers of Blue Cross Blue Shield of Massachusettes (BCBSMA). Amesbury has 436 active subscribers, averaging 38 years old. The group is split nearly even between men (48 percent) and women (52 percent).

In third year of the Well Power program, we conducted a satisfaction survey via Survey Monkey. We received a 17 percent response rate (up from 12 percent in Year 2) with no incentives attached. Below are the highlights, and reflects combined responses from 'Agree' and 'Strongly agree' categories.

- helped them improve their overall health—82%
- helped them make positive behavior changes—85%
- lead them to make at least one significant behavior change—90%
- helped them to be more productive at work—62%
- has been of value to others in their family— 56%
- has the potential to reduce healthcare costs—90%
- is a valuable part of their employee benefits—95%
- contributes to better employee morale—86%

The Amesbury Well Power program was successful in the sense that it increased awareness of good health and appropriate use of the healthcare system. It created tremendous good will and loyalty between MIIA and the city. Success measurements included participation and satisfaction. Incentives didn't seem to increase participation, and in fact created frustration when participants didn't know how to redeem their points, or didn't receive their award. We will gradually move away from using incentives for any program components, as they are transactional and do not create intrinsic motivation. We have learned that employee engagement is not the same as employee participation, and in order to have an engaged population, we will work with leadership to help employees feel good about coming to work.

Amesbury, Massachusettes
Jayne M. Schmitz, MPH
Wellness Program Specialist
MIIA Health Benefits Trust

4. Bendix Commercial Vehicle Systems LLC

Before *Zero Trends*, Bendix had a long-standing wellness program comprised of various annual initiatives, but lacked an overall strategy that considered wellness as a key company metric. *Zero Trends* provided the foundation and rationale to begin considering wellness the same as the business injury rates and safety metrics that reflect the company safety culture.

Bendix realized that a wellness culture has to be created and driven with a the same level of detail, focus and support as any other critical business strategy. It is difficult to say which *Zero Trends* pillar is the most important as all pillars are required for success, but the lessons learned in the operational leadership pillar were the most important for driving employee engagement at Bendix. Holding supervisors and managers responsible for the wellness engagement of their employees is essential, and Bendix would not have taken this approach without *Zero Trends*.

An interesting side note: Site-level wellness teams historically tried to tailor wellness offerings to the perceived unhealthy population and were left feeling unsuccessful when the same "healthy people" were the main participants. The simple statements to "Keep Low-Risk Low" and "Don't Get Worse" completely changed the dynamics of site wellness teams. Wellness teams no longer saw programs as failing when the engaged low-risk population participated.

Ed Casper
Occupational Health and Safety Manager
Bendix Commercial Vehicle Systems LLC

5. Benefit Commerce Group

Guaranteeing Savings Based On Employee Participation In Best Practices

One employee benefits consulting firm in Arizona, Benefit Commerce Group, has developed a program that guarantees cost savings and a defined ROI—all based on employee participation. The ROI is not based on actual health outcomes; it is structured to align with the percentage of employees who participate in each of seven best practices. This is especially important for mid-sized employers, since their claims experience is not a fully credible reference for insurers when pricing premium rates, and medical trend usually accounts for 50-80 percent of their renewal rate increase.

With 100 percent employee participation in each of these best practices, an employer can receive credit of up to 12 percent against their renewal increase, completely negating the influence of medical trend. However, even with less than perfect participation, employers win with Trend Neutralizer, because of the sliding scale of credit for each of the seven practices:

- Consumer-driven health plan enrollment
- Annual biometric screening
- Health risk assessment
- Disease management
- Healthy lifestyle programs
- Specific employer-sponsored health events
- Premium differential for tobacco versus non-tobacco

Even healthcare service providers find themselves caught by rising healthcare costs. For example: an integrated healthcare provider in Arizona operates in twelve locations with over three hundred employees. From 2008 to 2011, this organization's employee health plan cost doubled: from $5,402 per employee per year in 2008 to $10,904 per employee per year in 2011. Management knew it had to take action to reverse these unsustainable increases, and they decided to hit it hard. With the guidance of Benefit Commerce Group, the organization's CEO and a manager, with the title Director of Wellness Services, provided the leadership that they needed to begin motivating and engaging their employees. They began by moving more employees into consumer-driven health plans (CDHPs). They also added biometric screening, annual physicals and health risk assessments to their regular practices. Employees then had a clearer picture of their own health conditions and began participating in health improvement programs. They had started a culture of wellness. The result:

- Health plan cost increases were halted
- 5 percent decrease in cost in 2012
- 1.53 percent decrease for the 2013 plan year (the per-employee cost had been reduced by more than 15 percent from where it had been at its height).

For the 2014 plan year, Trend Neutralizer and their employee participation achievements were directly responsible for reducing by nearly half the renewal increase the organization otherwise would have received. The results have not just been monetary. This organization has been recognized for its results and achievement within its wider community:

- Named one of the 2014 Healthiest Employers by the Phoenix Business Journal
- Recognized for "Process, Progress & Leadership in Worksite Health Promotion" by the Wellness Council of Arizona in 2013

Most groups in this segment are executing on wellness plans in hopes that someday they may receive some type of return on their investment and efforts. This organization—Benefit Commerce Group—is guaranteeing a return.

While the case study above is one example of the program, Benefit Commerce Group has over 30 clients, with a total of more than 5,300 employees, that have saved a total of more than $55 million in benefit costs. That is an average of more than $2,000 per employee per year, yielding an average of more than $10,000 per employee over five years.

Trend Neutralizer RESULTS	
Total Savings	$55,747,374
Employers/Employees	33/5,366
Savings Per Employer (5 years)	$1,689,314
Savings Per Employee (5 years)	$10,389
Savings Per Employee Per Year	$2,078

Chris Hogan

President

Benefit Commerce Group

6. Calvin College

Healthy Habits

Calvin College, a faith-based, private, liberal arts institution in Grand Rapids, Michigan, initiated a limited employee health promotion (wellness) program in 2000. In 2007, the college made the decision to commit fully to building a healthy culture by hiring a full-time wellness director for their Healthy Habits program.

The vision of Healthy Habits is to become one of the healthiest workplaces in the United States, defined as a thriving, healthy, and productive workforce. Living out this vision means integrating wellness into all areas of the organization. As this occurs, wellness is becoming the "lifestyle of the community" rather than just a "program."

Calvin's overall goals for building a healthy community include

- providing opportunities that promote healthy living from a holistic perspective;
- creating a supportive environment for pursuing wellness goals, and

- encouraging employees and their families to consider health a priority for lifelong faith-based service.

Like most wellness programs, Healthy Habits emphasizes individual behavior change and risk reduction, but also realizes the importance of building a community and culture that support and reinforce those positive behaviors. The dashboard metric is engagement; physically, spiritually, emotionally, intellectually and socially. Since 2008, Calvin has raised annual engagement in Healthy Habits—as defined by participation in a minimum of eight activities per year—from 52 percent to 60 percent of their 630 health benefit members.

One advantage that Calvin experiences in its wellness initiatives is its faith-based identity. Building a culture of wellness is greatly aided by a community that shares a common purpose and underlying set of values. At Calvin, this building block is part of the very nature of the college. Maintaining good health (individually, corporately and holistically) is part of their faith-based stewardship. Building meaningful relationships and a spirit of community is an important aspect of authentically living out one's faith.

In addition to typical wellness programs such as exercise classes, seminars, health challenges and health coaching, Calvin offers other, sometimes unique, opportunities for building success, including:

- Paid time off for exercise.
- Support groups: depression caregivers; book clubs and healthy-eating lunch groups.
- Adventure trips: grow spiritually, physically, intellectually and socially with a group of faculty, staff and spouses while hiking the Grand Canyon or the Camino de Santiago.
- State of the art facilities: two fitness centers, climbing wall, Olympic-sized pool, indoor track, dance studios and a variety of gymnasiums and outdoor athletic fields.
- Bicycle friendly campus with over 750 bike rack spaces available.
- Quarterly participation reports ranked by department that go out to 50 department "Ambassadors."

Healthy Habits is committed to making wellness the norm at Calvin…

- Where there is a community committed to pursuing and supporting each other in healthy initiatives
- Where healthy personal and group habits are being practiced daily
- Where healthy choices are available and accessible
- Where work-life balance is encouraged

- Where employees enjoy their work and are highly productive
- Where leaders are engaged in wellness initiatives
- Where health is being maintained and improved, and risk is being reduced
- Where Healthy Habits is more than a program…it is a community lifestyle

Roy Zuidema,
Director of Campus Wellness,
Calvin College

7. Central High School

Wellness program is a winner for Central High School Central. High School staff's participation in a wellness program has not only improved their waistlines and the school district's bottom line, it also has gained them some national recognition. Administrator Scott Pierce said, as of March 1st, the district was ranked second in the nation among all of the businesses, schools and other entities that participate in the Humana Vitality wellness program.

"Many of our staff members have seen significant payback from their efforts beyond increased wellness," Pierce said. "In the two years that the Central staff, their spouses and families have participated in this program, the district has been able to realize a $321,000 reduction in health costs." The district will also get a break in its renewal fee as a result of the participation. "Through their hard work and perseverance, for the coming year we are able to reduce our overall health renewal costs by 8 percent," Pierce said.

In addition to organized activities, such as walks and blood drives, participants can earn points on their own by logging their activity, teacher Melissa Bahnson said. "I actually set a goal to obtain enough points to purchase some nice pots and pans off of Amazon," Bahnson said, adding she recently met that goal. She said teachers often get together to help each other meet their fitness goals, such as walking 10,000 steps per day. "I notice staff members walking the halls during their lunch breaks," she said. "It is cool to see the school culture changing as a result of participation in the program."

Jill Tatge-Rozell
Kenosha News

8. CHE Trinity Health System

Recognizing a need to build a healthier internal community for employees and their families, CHE Trinity Health, the second largest Catholic health system in the nation, and fourth largest health system overall in the United States, began its journey as into workplace wellness in 2008.

The goal was to create a culture of health, wellness and fulfillment, effectively manage benefit plan costs and increase the productivity and competitiveness of the organization.

The purpose statement of the initiative, Live Your Whole Life[SM], nurtures a culture that supports its employees ability to care for themselves as well as they care for the patients they serve.

Unlike many workplace wellness programs that focus solely on physical health, Live Your Whole Life leads with the concept of a healthy spirit, which is defined as "the capacity and ability of people to seek, experience, and express meaning and purpose in their lives often through love, hope, gratitude, forgiveness, peace, and community in order to enjoy a sense of the Sacred (as they understand it)."

"Our hunch is that if we can lead with the concept of spiritual health, the body and mind will follow. The healthy spirit is something we are working to define further by gathering input from our employees," said Tammie Hansen, RN, COHN-S, Manager Total Rewards Benefits, Health Productivity & Wellness, CHE Trinity Health.

To establish a benchmark for spiritual wellness among its employee population, in 2013 CHE Trinity Health worked with the third-party administrators of its employee medical benefit plans to add spiritual health questions to the health assessments its employees and their spouses would take for the 2014 benefit year.

Additionally, the organization partnered with the vendor that administers its employee engagement survey to incorporate questions focused on wellness and spirituality into its 2014 survey. The responses to survey items such as, "I believe that my life has purpose and meaning" and "This organization fosters my sense of spirituality" were quite favorable as reflected in both the employee engagement survey and the health assessment aggregate results.

The organization is continuing to investigate how the results correlate with other engagement and health assessment data.

Tammie Hansen, RN, COHN-S
Manager Total Rewards Benefits
Health Productivity & Wellness, CHE Trinity Health.

9. Chipotle

Creates Well-being as Part of their Culture

Chipotle Mexican Grill, a restaurant provider of "food with integrity" —wanted to develop a well-being program and change their company culture. The "plug and play" wellness program they were using through their healthcare provider had no leadership support and garnered dismal employee participation and engagement. They wanted to build a culture of well-being that matched the culture they had built around food; that is, with integrity and with a program that everybody would believe in and value. This required an innovative, multifaceted strategy that would; increase engagement in the well-being program, create a culture of happy, healthy and highly productive employees, reduce lifestyle risk factors such as obesity, sedentary lifestyle, and stress, and save on healthcare costs.

They partnered with Total Well-Being, a corporate well-being consulting company, to help them create a three-year strategy and build a well-being framework that focused on the key success factors; engaged and visible senior and operations support, creative and culturally relevant incentives, and effective communications. The most effective and engaging challenge thus far has been the Fitness Rally which is now an annual event with strong leadership engagement, support, and participation. It is not uncommon to see leaders encouraging employees to host walking meetings or taking the stairs instead of the elevator.

Overall, the results have been astounding with a 333 percent increase in biometrics, a 62 percent increase in engagement, a zero trend in weight gain over the past three years and healthcare costs have been below industry standard hovering at a 1% increase. Chipotle is committed to well-being and the next three years will be focused on solidifying the framework to support well-being as a business strategy so being healthy, happy and productive becomes the social norm of working at the company.

In 2005, the US Company underwent a transformation that would make its culture as distinct as its food. As stores opened across the US, the company focused on creating a system where promoting managers from within would create a feedback loop of better, more motivated, and more engaged, employees. That year, about 20 percent of the company's managers had been promoted from within. In the recent year, nearly 85 percent of salaried managers and 96 percent of hourly managers were the result of internal promotions. (Source: Chipotle)

Fundamental to this transformation is something Chipotle calls the restaurateur program, which allows hourly crew members to become managers earning well over $100,000 a year. Restaurateurs are chosen from the ranks of general managers for their skill at managing their restaurant and, especially, their staff. When selected, they get a one-time bonus and stock options. And after that they receive an extra $10,000 each time they train a crew member to become a general manager.

The foundation of their culture, on which everything else stands, is the concept is that each person at Chipotle will be rewarded based on their ability to make the people around them better. Now that is a different way to build a culture, isn't it?

Here are the further detailed reasons we feel their culture has been so successful:

Emphasis on people

One of the simple basis for the Chipotle's success in their culture strategy is people. It starts at the top and trickles down. It takes root when you create a culture where people can grow and be whatever they desire to be. You can't create a brand that people love until you build a company your people love. And once that happens, you're going to create a culture of heroes.

Promote from within

Chipotle's has implemented a "hire from within" campaign that has allowed them to promote line employees to be store managers for the new locations. This results in lower training costs and improves morale, engagement, and productivity on the line.

Pride in quality

Maintaining and driving high standards and expectations around food quality, customer service, food safety, and store cleanliness by empowering teams in every restaurant to be accountable and take action without waiting for permission.

Process for hiring and evaluating employees

Chipotle hires employees by looking for 13 key characteristics that they feel, with the right development, will make them what they call the top performer. Employees who cannot become top performers don't last long. Employees either get it or they don't.

Performance based advancement

The company believes that creating a performance based culture leads to the best restaurant experience possible for both employees and customers.

Chipotle embraces its employees' unique perspectives, personalities, and strengths, as it believes these factors are the most significant to the brand's success. Chipotle has a well-defined and transparent advancement structure that encourages loyalty from part- and full-time employees.

On the flip side of this strategy, one of their biggest competitors, Taco Bell and parent Yum! Brands rely heavily on franchised operations, which, we believe, intrinsically hinder advancement. About 86 percent of Yum's employees are part time. And while there is a small opportunity for advancement, promotions are limited to store-specific management. Employee development isn't something that Yum! prioritizes. As such, the fast-food giant risks high turnover and employee dissatisfaction.

Career development

From day one, Chipotle employees learn that if they work hard and do a good job and represent the brand in keeping with the company's vision and mission, they can move up. They can go from a modest hourly wage on the front lines to running the kitchen or running the front of the shop, to assisting the manager, to running a restaurant, to becoming a manager of multiple locations. In other words, you can go from minimum wage to six figures and a company car. This can happen for anyone who wants it and can handle it. It's up to the employee.

Keep customers happy

Chipotle has a unique corporate culture that's constantly reinforced at the local level: Serve good food, fresh and fast. (Chipotle locally sources its vegetables and meats, which mean you'll never see a freezer there.) Keep the place clean and efficient. Pay attention to details. Stay involved in the community. Keep the customers happy.

Have long term goals

Chipotle doesn't want just to serve great food—it wants to change the way people think about and eat fast food. Each local store supports a local farm. Simply by the way it operates, the company encourages consumers to set higher expectations for what they can expect in a quick service restaurant.

Team versus individual success

They desire for employees to understand that their success is based on the success of their teams, and aspire to make the people around them better than they are. I've written numerous blog posts about the value of customer-facing employees, employee engagement and employee empowerment. And I believe the Chipotle culture and employee engagement strategies are one of the best around.

Takeaways

Having the right culture and employee engagement practices are driven by understanding the most meaningful motivators to a company's employees. Committing to an intentional culture like Chipotle, one that's open, transparent, and enables employees to thrive is a very smart investment. Your employees are your business. The better they are, the better your business.

Chipotle gets it and as a result is winning the war of employee engagement and its resulting business performance.

Colleen M. Reilly MBA/MSM
President
Total Well-Being

10. Elecmetal

Are You A Wellness Champion?—I Wasn't—But I am Now

I am the Vice President of Human Resources for my company. I travel both domestically and internationally and have logged an average of over 220,000 air miles for each of the last fifteen years. In 2011, I attended the Health Benefits Conference in Clearwater, Florida and was captivated by Dr. Dee Edington's presentation wherein he talked about the value of a corporate wellness program. During that presentation, I was convinced that our company needed to develop and implement a wellness program for our employees.

Upon returning from the conference, I assembled a group of enthusiastic human resource professionals whose initial responsibility was to design a wellness program that included a mission and values statement, goals, activities and a budget for the following year. Our next task was to develop a plan on how to promote, educate and encourage employee participation in our wellness program. In the early part of 2012, I held employee meetings at our US locations to present the exciting details on our new wellness program. During those presentations, I also talked about the systemic US problem of obesity and the related problems and associated risks with diabetes, hypertension, and heart disease.

Our 2012 wellness initiative was a complete success. 93 percent of our employees completed all of the programs and activities that were a part of our first wellness program. I was honored with an invitation to speak at the 31st Annual Wellness in the Workplace Conference held in March of 2012 at the University of Michigan where I talked about how our Company developed and implemented its first Wellness Program. In 2013, I again took our new and improved wellness program on the road to our U.S. locations and met with all of the employees in our company. During my presentations, I again talked about health risks associated with obesity, high blood pressure, and elevated cholesterol and triglyceride levels. Our 2013 wellness program was again a complete success with a participate rate that far exceeded our goals and expectations. With these achievements, I truly considered myself to be a "wellness champion."

Much has been written about the vital role wellness champions play in determining the effectiveness and longevity of a wellness program. Wellness champions are an inspirational voice regarding employee health, well-being and work-life balance. Wellness champions must pursue innovative ways to increase employee participation and awareness in corporate wellness. Wellness champions must possess the ability to inspire and empower their co-workers to take responsibility for their own health. Wellness champion must also lead by example. In other words, a true wellness champion must "walk the talk."

When I introduced our company's 2012 and 2013 Wellness Initiative and when I spoke at the Wellness Conference at the University of Michigan, I was a whopping 80 pounds overweight. I had no sustainable exercise program, my eating habits were atrocious, and my blood pressure was through the roof. I was oblivious to my own precarious physical condition. I failed to heed or even hear the message I was delivering to my fellow employees.

However, I was brought back to reality during my August 2013 physical. My doctor told me that my blood tests revealed that I was pre-diabetic (impaired glucose tolerance). This diagnosis put me in a high-risk category for developing type II diabetic and cardiovascular disease with all their attendant life-shortening consequences. I was in total shock. I was now in a medical category that I was warning my co-workers against. I came to the quick realization that my co-workers to whom I talked about wellness programs must have thought: "how can this fat out-of-shape blob talk to me about obesity and the benefits of leading a healthy lifestyle." I no longer felt like a Wellness Champion.

My diagnosis of being a pre-diabetic was a life-changing event for me. I immediately decided to change my life. I attended diabetic classes at my local medical clinic where I learned proper nutrition and the importance establishing a regular exercise program. I completely changed to a healthy diet and began a rigorous daily exercise routine. I checked my blood sugar three times a day and watched with amazement the improvements that were made in my blood sugar readings.

In February of 2014, I announced to my co-workers the Company's 2014 Wellness Program. By that time, I had lost 60 pounds, I brought my blood sugar levels into normal levels, and my blood pressure was under control. During my presentations, I admitted to my co-workers that I had let them down—that I had no business preaching a healthy lifestyle when I could not lead one myself. I told them my story and emphasized that they did not have to wait for a life-changing event, like I did, before committing to a healthy lifestyle.

I have had many employees tell me that my 2014 Wellness presentation motivated them to change their lifestyle. And even though I felt that my 2012 and 2013 wellness presentations were inspirational and promoted the importance of leading a healthy lifestyle, I never received any such comments and commitments following those presentations. Time will tell whether our wellness endeavor will have a lasting impact. But I feel confident that it will. In 2014, our company selected a number of wellness champions based on their abilities to fill the criteria I set forth above, including their own achievement in leading a healthy lifestyle. I now felt a part of that group.

So I ask you: "Are you a wellness champion?" I wasn't—but I am now.

Randy Millard
Vice-President Human Resources
Elecmetal

11. Fortune Business Solutions

A Case Study in Participation of Health Risk Assessments Without Financial Incentives

Fortune Business Solutions, a human resource company in Tampa, Florida, began its efforts towards champion status after hearing Dr. Edington speak about *Zero Trends*. Senior management recognized the challenge of participation in Health Risk Assessments even when financial incentives were offered, and they wanted to create a culture of self-leadership.

They implemented a system designed by the Institute of Benefits and Wellness Professionals, which is highly inspired by Dee's teachings, reaches and case studies. We first made sure that management participated, supported, and understood the business case for wellness. This was absolutely essential. Without it, we would have walked away.

We then took steps to ensure to create an environment of trust. Our health risk assessment process was absolutely confidential, handled by a third party, and not tied to their health insurance carrier. No names, no social security numbers—100 percent confidential. Even though their health Insurance provider offered free resources in this area, the company felt the additional trust gained by using a third party was more important than a free resource. They have 46 full-time employees and 43 completed the surveys. So how did they achieve a 93.3 percent participation in completing the health risk assessments biometrics without any financial incentives?

We then held employee meetings to learn about the wellness strategy. The health risk assessment was provided at the end of the meeting at no charge to the employees, and was 100 percent paid for by the employer. It was offered voluntary, and to all employers (regardless if they were on the health plan or not). What was said at the meeting, and the powerpoint slides used, was absolutely crucial to our industry leading participation rate of over 90 percent. We create an experience—employees felt comfortable and empowered, not penalized or talked down to. We talked about what was in it for them, not what was in it for the company.

Clearly this company beat the normal participation level in health risk assessments, and they did it without financial incentives. This is so important as they now can build their wellness program knowing the risk factors facing employees and their readiness to change, and no longer have to build their wellness program in the dark. All of this will help them bend the cost of health care in the future by focusing on "wellness first" rather than feeding our "wait for sickness" medical system.

Kimberly Eckelbarger
Owner
Tropical Benefits and CBWA certified by IBWP

12. Haylor Freyer & Coon, Inc., Communicate & Connect

To consistently improve employee health, productivity, and morale, and control rising health plan costs employers must "Communicate & Connect" with employees... it all begins and ends there.

As a professional in the benefit management business for nearly 20 years I found most employers in the past controlling annual health insurance rate increases by shifting more of the cost to employees by raising copays and deductibles and/or having employees pay more towards the monthly premium. These strategies worked reasonably well for many years; especially back in the mid 90's when employers offered HMO plans with $5 dollar office visit copays and single plan premiums were less than $100/month.

Forward to 2015: Premiums have risen to $400/month for single coverage and family coverage is now more than $1000/month in most cases. At the same time as premiums have significantly risen, employers have increasingly moved towards high deductible health plans that expose employees to very high up-front deductibles. Between the rising cost of premiums and higher deductibles many employees have felt their income erode; because often the increase in the cost of health insurance and deductible exposure is higher than their annual pay increases.

Employers and employees are losing ground in the fight for insurance affordability. The 2014 Towers Watson/National Business Group on Health (NBGH) Employer Survey on Purchasing Value in Health Care reported that employees now pay over $100 more per month for health care than they did just three years ago. The average employer share of health insurance costs continues to climb at a greater rate than the Consumer Price Index (CPI) and wages—to $9,505 in 2014; nearly 28 percent more than employers paid just five years ago. During the same period employee costs have risen 32 percent.

The Affordable Care Act (ACA) is adding more financial pressures:

Employers: For employers to avoid significant "Play or Pay" fines (taxes) the Affordable Care Act (ACA) requires large group employers to offer minimum essential single plan health insurance coverage to full-time employees at a premium cost that is no more than 9.5 percent of the employee's annual W-2 income. This limits the amount of the annual increase in premiums the employer can continue shifting to employees. This "cap" on the premium shift has resulted in employers shifting the plan cost by offering plans with higher deductibles. In 2015 employers can offer ACA-compliant coverage to employees that has $6600 annual deductibles for single coverage and $13,200 annual deductibles for family coverage.

Employees: Most American citizens are now subject to the ACA's individual mandate. If an individual doesn't have minimum essential coverage, and they do not obtain an exemption, they will pay a "shared responsibility fee" for each month they are without minimum essential coverage. In 2016 the annual fee will be $695 per adult and $347.50 per child up to $2,085 per household OR 2.5 percent of their annual household income— whichever is higher.

What Can Be Done?

Fortunately there is a solution that will work in the long-term if employers and employees "communicate & connect" and truly become accountable to each other. The only solution to controlling the rising cost of health insurance is employees and their dependents not using the health insurance as much; because they're healthier.

The good news is that most of the cost in the healthcare system is driven by high claimants, it's the 80/20 rule. On average 80 percent of the insurance claims are spent each year by only 20 percent of the plan members, and the vast majority of those expenses are driven by very high "catastrophic" conditions. This is good news because so many high claims are associated with heart disease, strokes, and cancer. Why is this good news? Because almost all of those conditions are driven by our behavior—it's a choice! In fact, the Centers for Disease Control reported in 2009 that if Americans chose to do four things: 1) keep a healthy weight, 2) exercise regularly, 3) eat nutritious food and 4) didn't use tobacco <u>at least</u> 80 percent of all heart disease, heart attacks, strokes, and diabetes would be avoided; and 40 percent of all cancers.

A study done by Purdue University in 2010 reported that an astounding 87.5 percent of every dollar spent on healthcare can be tracked back to being created by a person's lifestyle. Poor lifestyle choices create health risks, and health risks eventually create conditions requiring medical attention.

Daniel J. Elliott
Haylor Freyer & Coon, Inc. VP
Group Benefits Department

13. HealthNEXT™

Over the last 5 years we have been studying benchmark culture of health efforts and developed a methodology to help other employers achieve similar results.[1] More recently we have deployed our methodology with a few alpha clients to test it. The case study below chronicles our work with an international manufacturing company with approximately 3000 employees in the United States. Our program focused on this domestic population.

Background

We were approached by the Head of Human Resources in the Americas in 2009 to assist them with their strategy to control a double-digit increase in their healthcare costs. Historically they had tried to stem these increases through benefit design as many others have done without success. After initial discussions it was clear that their human resource team were receptive to a new approach that would foster a culture of health and elevate the health status of their workforce.[2]

Assessment

Using a proprietary toolset including the Employer Health Opportunity Assessment™ (EHOA™) we visited worksites, reviewed all health related vendor reports, compared their benefit design with the best evidence-based approaches and interviewed all layers of the organization from the C-suite to union leadership. Our assessment tool scores companies based on 218 identified elements that contribute to a culture of health in 10 categories. Some of the categories are highlighted in this book including; data warehousing and analytics, corporate environment, leadership and management and vendor integration. This company was very early in its journey and scored only 255 points out of 1000 or putting it another way was only 35-40 percent of its way to a benchmark score of 700.

Early Recommendations

Our approach was to assist this employer three ways. Increase the accountability of the employee population, enhance the corporate approach to wellness and facilitate closer relationships with the popular primary care providers who care for the majority of the covered lives. To increase the accountability of employees we implemented our Individual Health opportunity Assessment™ (IHOA™) modeled after the benchmark program developed at Crown, Cork and Seal[3] by Dr. David Spratt and behaviorist Eddie Haaz.[4] To enhance the corporate approach to wellness we converted the gaps from benchmark identified in the EHOA™ into a three-year strategic plan. Lastly to facilitate a closer relationship with the popular primary care providers we worked with their health plan administrator to identify those practices and then deployed another proprietary tool the Community Provider Opportunity Assessment™ (CPOA™) to assess their care delivery and determine ways where their care could be improved.

Early Findings

As is often the case the initial assessment of health risks and conditions found the workforce to have a significant illness burden. There were clear connections between identified health risks such as hypertension and hypercholesterolemia and higher incidences of cardiac and stroke-related disease in their high-cost claims and disability reports. Making these connections were essential to obtain by in from leadership, management and ultimately the covered population. Little effort was being extended at the manufacturing sites to promote health. Many of the workers relied on vending machines for sustenance and there were little in the way of healthy options. Much of the workforce were on rotating work schedules interfering with sleep patterns and circadian rhythm. Perhaps most remarkable a sizeable portion of the workforce and their dependents were "medically homeless" having no relationship with a primary care practice.[5] Additionally many of the popular primary care practices were not performing anywhere near the levels promoted by the patient-centered medical home movement PCMH.[5]

Progress over the Following Four Years

This employer did a number of things to remedy their gaps from benchmark COH companies such as adjusting their benefit structure to be more consistent with evidence-based benefit design and building a data warehouse with the assistance of their health benefit consultant6. As a consequence their EHOA scores approached 550-600. They deployed the IHOA on an annual basis which included a proprietary Health Risk Assessment, biometric screening and a face to face review of the results by a physician to establish an individual action plan and a behaviorist to move the participant through the stages of behavior change.[7] Those identified with health risks of conditions were referred to health coaches and care managers. Aggregate results demonstrated that the participants' health improved over time and roughly 80 percent of the workforce and many spouses were impacted by this effort. Additionally the physician and behaviorist worked hard to identify participants who were "medically homeless" and refer them into the practices that were already connected to this employer by the CPOA™ activities. Through this process we were able to document, a reduction in the "medically homeless" and improved scores as the popular practices pursued care delivery improvements at our recommendation sponsored by this large employer. In one case, this employer subsidized the purchase of an electronic medical record system. This practice was taking care of a significant portion of the workforce in this rural area to justify the investment.

The Results

Over time this employer bent the healthcare cost curve. In fact, in the fourth year their healthcare costs decreased—truly "bending the curve." Additionally their "total weighted health risk" reduced year over year and there were remarkable population health achievements in blood pressure control and cholesterol management. The popular primary care providers improved their processes and one practice achieved Level 3 PCMH status. Remarkably over the time that we worked with this self-insured client their company stock doubled in value.

Conclusion

By working with an employer interested and motivated to improve the health status of their workforce it is possible to produce a culture of health and wellness over time. To accomplish this our research suggests the need to focus on the accountability of the individual participants, the corporate environment and the community providers directing care. The benefits of this effort are many. Individuals get healthier, providers deliver better care, and the employer obtains a competitive advantage in the marketplace.

Ray Fabius, MD
Chief Science Officer
HealthNEXT

References

1. www.healthnext.com
2. Nash, David, JoAnne Reifsnyder, and Valerie Pracilio. *Population Health: creating a culture of wellness*. Jones & Bartlett Learning, 2010.
3. www.crowncork.com/about/env_commitment.php
4. www.corporatehealthsolutions.com
5. Peikes, D., Zutshi, A., Genevro, J., Smith, K., Parchman, M., & Meyers, D. (2012, February). *Early evidence on the patient-centered medical home*. Final report (Prepared by Mathematica Policy

Research, AHRQ Publication No. 12-0020-EF). Rockville, MD: Agency for Healthcare Research and Quality.

6. Colwill, Jack M. "A Case Of 'Medical Homelessness.'" *Health Affairs* 29.5 (2010): 1067-1070.

7. *Employer Health Asset Management Roadmap—A Roadmap for Improving the Health of Your Employees*—published by the Change Agent Workgroup (CAWG) 2009.

8. Prochaska et al; *Systems of Psychotherapy: A Transtheoretical Analysis*; 7th edition, Belmont, CA; Brooks/Cole, Cengage Learning; 2009.

9. Fabius, Raymond, R. Dixon Thayer, Doris L. Konicki, Charles M. Yarborough, Kent W. Peterson, Fikry Isaac, Ronald R. Loeppke, Barry S. Eisenberg, and Marianne Dreger. "The link between workforce health and safety and the health of the bottom line: Tracking market performance of companies that nurture a 'culture of health.'" *Journal of Occupational and Environmental Medicine* 55, no. 9 (2013): 993-1000.

14. Henry Ford Health System

In July 2009, Henry Ford Health System (HFHS) CEO, Nancy Schlichting and Senior Vice President of Community Health, Equity & Wellness, Kimberlydawn Wisdom, MD, convened a Wellness steering committee comprising senior leaders to review the wellness practices of other major U.S. health systems, and discuss potential strategies for wellness and prevention initiatives at HFHS. As a result of the recommendations set forth by the steering committee, two reports were developed—one was a systematic review of the more than 80 wellness programs across HFHS and the other provided a platform for establishing wellness as a key strategic initiative.

In January 2011, the findings from these reports were shared with the CEO's Executive cabinet which commissioned that a Wellness Center of Excellence (Henry Ford LiveWell) be established. Later that same year, HFHS named Dr. Wisdom as Chief Wellness Officer and announced its new vision statement: "Transforming lives and communities through health and wellness—one person at a time."

In 2012, the core functions of Henry Ford LiveWell are coordination, collaboration and innovation across three areas of focus: engaged and empowered people (including HFHS patients, employees and community members), clinical preventive services and healthy environment. Underpinning all of the Henry Ford LiveWell strategic objectives is the goal of eliminating health disparities.

Kimberlydawn Wisdom, MD
Chief Wellness Officer, Senior Vice President of Community Health & Equity
Henry Ford Health System

15. Independent Group Home Living Program, Inc.

Independent Group Home Living Program, Inc. (IGHL) currently has 1,500 employees and serve 350 people located throughout Suffolk County on Long Island. IGHL is a non-profit organization headquartered in Manorville, New York. The company includes a diverse residential program comprised of fifty homes for people of all ages who have developmental and physical disabilities. IGHL strives to identify ways to meet employees' changing lifestyles by addressing financial, emotional, physical, social, and mental needs. In 2005 we launched a health improvement campaign, which is now known as *Health is Wealth*™. One of the fundamental principles in launching this initiative was a top-down leadership approach—we understood that we must lead by example.

In 2013, in an effort to promote family wellness, we expanded the program to include employees' spouses and dependent adult children. Health is Wealth™ not only requires employees to participate in the biometric screening and health assessment, but also requires their spouses and adult dependents to do the same.

Over the years we also found that for any successful wellness program, communication to employees is key. They need to be informed and made aware of the options they have available to them in order for them to stay engaged. IGHL sends a number of memos to communicate to employees what is being offered through the program. Every location has a Health is Wealth™ corkboard where all communications are posted for employees. Details on specific Health is Wealth™ classes are also recorded daily on a designated phone extension at the human resources department. In addition, in 2013 we launched a Health is Wealth™ website that allows employees to view all class offerings, schedule their own classes and track their progress throughout the year. ding parking lots and vehicles, went smoke-free. We have dieticians conducting cooking classes for our chefs to prepare healthy meals. We have our own garden on site and supply fresh vegetables to all of the group home houses.

The transformation of the overall health of our workforce has been incredible. Catastrophic events such as heart attacks have reduced from four to ten percent per year down to three in 2013, the lowest ever. While the national average of insurance costs over the last five to six years has gone up 41 percent, IGHL's costs have increased 10 percent mostly administration costs, not claims costs. IGHL has also seen a reduction in claims over a two-year time frame. We have saved money on training because employee retention improved by 4.3 percent.

Recruiting and training costs have gone down since retention increased and morale has improved overall.

Doris Geier
Sr. Director, Health is Wealth™ Program
Independent Group Home Living Program, Inc.

16. International Business Machines (IBM)

IBM is a multinational technology and innovation company with over 400,000 employees across approximately 100 countries. Addressing the health needs of such a dispersed, diverse population relies on a steadfast commitment from senior leadership and a strategic, integrated approach.

The specific goal of health promotion at IBM is to reduce health risk and build vitality among employees and their families, in order to enhance well-being, enable high performance, and mitigate avoidable health-related costs. IBM has embraced WHO's healthy workplace guidelines, to help refine company health priorities and objectives.

IBM's "Commit to Health" approach begins with long-standing corporate support with an integrated strategy which reflects a shared commitment and responsibility for health between both the company and employees. All IBMers are encouraged to commit to healthy living and vitality building, engagement with regular preventive care, and active involvement in healthcare decisions. In turn, IBM commits to helping employees succeed by making the healthiest choice the easiest choice, by putting the required resources directly in their hands. This is brought to life through IBM's online Commit to Health community, using its internal social connections and collaboration hub. Thousands of employees around the world visit and interact in the online community, sharing ideas and reviewing timely health education.

Employees are proactively and meaningfully involved during various steps of the program development process. Examples include:

- Focus groups to test new program concepts, such as a new children's health program to assist parents in addressing healthy behaviors at home.

- Beta testing of new tools to improve user experience, such as the testing of a new web-based tool designed to encourage mindfulness and resilience.

- Piloting of new programs before full implementation, such as training for HR professionals and managers on mental well-being support.

Recently, IBM has leveraged innovative social analytics technology to capture "mini pulse" feedback from employees as they interact with health programs. This real-time, practical input is invaluable when serving such a large, dispersed population such as IBM's.

In order to provide structure in program design and delivery, IBM established ten global priorities for health promotion which include: health assessment, active living, healthy eating, sleep and rest, mental and emotional well-being, preventing tobacco, alcohol, and drug abuse, injury and violence-free living, infection prevention, clinical prevention and engagement strategies. These priority areas are addressed through common global processes and systems, an integrated network of health professionals, and a combination of cross-border and local initiatives. Since the relative importance of each topic area varies around the world, particularly between major market and growth market countries, the model allows for additional flexibility and prioritization at the local level.

Specific targets across the framework are driven by IBM's formal Well-being Management System, which provides the means for integrated planning, alignment to corporate objectives, and effective monitoring of progress. Annual improvement plans, periodic reporting, and formal audits provide the processes to enable efficiency and progress. Creating a network of cross-border support and collaboration has helped to maximize internal subject matter expertise and program efficiencies around the world.

Several key global initiatives demonstrate IBM's continued innovation. A new global health risk assessment tool has been acculturated and adapted for use in 130 countries and is available to employees in twenty-six languages. In the United States, typically 60 percent of IBM employees complete the HRA, and initial launches in the United Kingdom and India have already reached twenty percent and ten percent respectively, through use of lotteries to win wellness-related products. IBM's global Virtual Health Fair event represents an exciting new approach to delivering health and safety education in a twenty-four-hour live online event featuring integrated health Services experts and IBMer interaction. The fair featured twelve webcasts on topics ranging from sleep to stress and travel health. Roughly 10,000 employees visited the first virtual health fair, with 13,000 webcast views and 19,000 resource downloads in eight different languages. IBM also embarked to create a new program model called, wellness advisor which aims to bring together EAP, medical support and wellness coaching services to improves access and support as well as create a less stigmatized entry point for EAP services.

specific targets are set related to integration across all four pillars of integrated health services (safety, medical, health benefits, and health promotion). Also, considerable cross-functional development has been done to integrate health promotion efforts into the health benefits design and delivery processes. Outside of the integrated health services department, projects are also underway to more deeply integrate with other HR functions, such as work/life and workforce analytics. All such cross-functional integrations not only increase the impact of Health Promotion efforts, but also support sustainability.

IBM was recently recognized as one of the three best workplaces supporting employee health in the world at the Global Healthy Workplace Award Summit in Shanghai April, 2014. IBM has also contributed to industry research on workplace health promotion, publishing various peer-reviewed manuscripts on the impact of programs on healthy behaviors and business costs.

Stewart Sill
Manager, Global Health & Vitality
IBM Integrated Health Services

Megan Benedict
Global Vitality Manager
IBM Integrated Health Services

17. Life Time[SM]

The Company was founded in 1992 with the mission to provide an entertaining, educational, friendly and inviting, functional, and innovative experience that meets the health and fitness needs of the entire family. With unwavering commitment on the member point of view, Life Time has since been credited with transforming the health and fitness industry. As the Healthy Way of Life Company, Life Time helps organizations, communities, and individuals to achieve total health objectives, athletic aspirations and fitness goals by engaging in their areas of interest—or discovering new passions—both inside and outside of Life Time's distinctive and large sports, professional fitness, family recreation, and spa destinations, most of which operate twenty-four hours a day, seven days a week. The company's holistic healthy way of life approach enables customers to achieve this by providing the best places, people, and programs of uncompromising quality and value.

Additionally, through Life Time's development of best-in-class nutrition products, proprietary metabolic assessments and testing, and heart rate training protocols, personal training and nutrition consultation, the award-winning healthy lifestyle magazine, Experience Life, nationally renowned athletic events, full-service spas and cafes, and comprehensive corporate health programs, it has become far more than the typical "health club" or "gym" chain, and continues to have a significant impact on the health and wellness of consumers.

Specific to the area of corporate wellness programs, we lend our deep expertise in physical assessments and exercise and nutrition, led by a best-in-class coaching approach designed to engage large employee populations. As a component of this, we have incorporated Edington Associates' Self Leadership Project. Today, we offer two methods for our corporate clients to set goals that support lasting behavior change.

The first option utilizes the self-leadership online learning modules as self-directed programs. Each module is easy to understand, engaging and actionable. Participants are able to easily learn the concepts and reinforce their personal development through various exercises that get them applying the concepts to their everyday life.

The second option combines Life Time's exercise and nutrition expertise with Edington's behavior change model. Recognizing that personal responsibility is at the core of taking charge of one's health, our coaches begin every client interaction with an assessment of that individual's self-leadership aptitude. This provide valuable insights regarding how their values, purpose and strengths dictate their lifestyle, how they deal with change and difficult decisions, and how resilient they are when distractions and temptations take them off a healthy way of life path.

Our coaches are able to collect and interpret this data via the individual's responses to our proprietary health risk assessment, which includes several life skill questions, along with motivational interviewing techniques designed to draw out strengths and weaknesses in each of the four areas of self-leadership. once the coach understands that individual's current aptitude, they begin developing a plan. For strong self-leaders, they are able to focus on setting bigger goals directly related to exercise, nutrition, stress and sleep. For others, coaches focus on small goals first, building the necessary skills needed to be successful with behavior change. Over time, the desired outcome is to ensure each individual becomes a strong self-leader able to establish and uphold new healthy habits that will help them sustain a healthier and happier way of life.

Andrea Puckett
Director myHealthCheck Operations
Life Time The Healthy Way of Life Company[SM]

18. Manatee County Government

Manatee County has a much different view of ROI than some in the industry. For us, the return on our investment is first knowing that we are doing everything we can to help our employees find what works for them and their family members to move to a higher level of well-being and health status, doing the right thing is important to us. Secondly, we see that our employee exit interviews give highest marks for the benefit and wellness programs and annually we hear of the employee who because of the plan design established with a physician and discovered that he had colon cancer and was able to obtain treatment that he wouldn't have otherwise or the woman with diabetes who for years has had a critically high HbA1c value and was not engaged in treatment, but after continual outreach, finally got engaged and for the first time in 8 years, has a manageable HbA1c value and reports she is a new person at home and work.

Measurably, we see that as a result of specific programming, our member's body mass indexes, blood pressures and stress levels are improving. We have a high compliance rate for medications and generic medication utilization is 85 percent and the completion of preventative care according to guidelines is close to 100 percent and the use of primary care is extremely high. In terms of our financial ROI, we recognize that change is a process and what we spend now, will not show return in a subsequent year, but our history has proven to us that the programs we have in place, have absolutely given us a return on our investment in that we have a negative 2.5 percent trend since 2009 on our self-funded health plan without shifting costs to our employees. We believe that our trend is a direct result of the plan design paired with the onsite clinical programs and supportive Advocates who work together with the member to help them achieve better health and a higher level of well-being. Our success has been fostered by our leadership's commitment to a culture of health and all of our members who have struggled to find what works for them, but have taken advantage of the services and have made longstanding changes for the better. All of this results in lower costs to the County, lower costs to our members and taxpayers and a higher level of service provided to our community.

This is our ROI:

- Negative trend with no cost shifting to employee

- 98 percent of exit interviews give highest marks for benefits and wellness program

- Reductions in biometrics and labs

- High usage of primary care

- 85 percent generic prescription usage

- 17 percent less than PBM book on PMPM Rx costs

- Employee feedback

Kim Stroud MA, LMHC
Benefits Manager
Manatee County Government

19. Marathon Health

Marathon Health, Inc. is a Vermont-based company founded in 2005. It was founded on the principles of patient empowerment and a holistic approach to health. Its primary focus is on creating trusting relationships between the clinicians and the patients they serve Marathon Health believes when people understand the choices that impact their health they gain a new perspective—one that isn't about being treated when sick, but rather about achieving their best possible health.

Zero Trends' business concept that excess costs follow excess risks encapsulates Marathon Health's population health risk management model. Population risk management looks at all the factors impacting an individual's health, including genetic predisposition to disease, environmental conditions such as the quality of the air and water, and, in particular, lifestyle risk such as tobacco use, alcohol and substance abuse, eating habits, and levels of physical activity. Population risk management also embodies whether people with chronic conditions such as diabetes and asthma are able to manage their condition and are at the standard of care, an important factor in preventing serious complications.

The key to population health management is working with patients of all risk levels, not just the medium and high-risk patients. Because, as the Edington data indicates, as workers move out of the medium- and high-risk categories, others are already moving in. Companies need programs that prevent the upward flow from low-risk to medium- and high-risk. "Not getting worse" is imperative in containing costs for employers.

Marathon Health has demonstrated how employers can and should begin looking at their healthcare costs as the end product of a system absolutely within their control. Healthcare should be thought of in the same way as production, distribution, and other business systems: a set of interdependent parts that can be measured, benchmarked, and improved. But improvement will not occur without managing a total population's health—from the fit and healthy to the obese—and providing a lasting health and wellness culture.

The key to helping the individual assume greater responsibility and accountability for their own health is the ability of the healthcare professional to function as a coach. Marathon Health makes all hiring decisions based on the belief that the core competencies and core behaviors of an ideal health coach include approachability, compassion, and listening skills, as well as being organized, action-oriented and driving for results.

Zero Trends talks about the five fundamental pillars for a successful health management strategy: senior leadership, operations leadership, self-leadership, reward positive actions, and quality assurance. Transformation will occur when all of these factors are aligned and health becomes an integral part of a company's culture.

Marathon Health has found that a successful worksite healthcare program is dependent upon a shared vision for health and a passion for influencing change on an organizational and individual level. The attributes and values that characterize the Marathon Health client base include:

- Management, operations, and culture are aligned around health as an important business driver
- Leadership actively demonstrates support of innovative health programs
- A demonstrated, long-term interest in the health and well-being of employees and their families
- A desire to become or maintain a status as an "employer of choice" in the community
- A fundamental belief that the current healthcare system is broken and that new, innovative solutions are needed

Change will occur when these criteria are met. Below are some case studies of clients who demonstrate all of these attributes, as well as the Five Fundamental Pillars.

City of Plantation, Fla.

Plantation is a city in Broward County, Fla. with a population of 85,000. The City's health center is open to 750 employees plus 690 spouses and dependents age 12 and over.

Services offered include primary care, health coaching, disease management, and medication dispensing.

Marathon Health began providing onsite total population health management to Plantation in April 2010. In the first year of operations, 52 percent of Plantation's employees visited the health center, and only 31 percent of that number were engaged in health coaching. In just four years, participation rose to 100 percent of employees visiting the health center and 93 percent engaged in health coaching. Hundred percent of employees and 100 percent of spouses have received full biometric screenings, which help to stratify the population to identify high health risks and chronic conditions. In the most recent year 475 employees (58 percent of total) were identified as have high health risks or chronic conditions. Ninety-eight percent of that target is engaged in health coaching.

Of all the at-risk patients, 66 percent made progress on blood pressure, 54 percent made progress on blood sugar, 47 percent made progress on total cholesterol, and 48 percent made progress on triglycerides. As a whole, 66 percent of at-risk patients made improvements. This translates to a cumulative savings of $7.8 million in Plantation's medical claims in the health center's first 48 months of operation—an ROI of 3.6:1.

Bendix Commercial Vehicle Systems

Bendix Commercial Vehicle Systems LLC, headquartered in Elyria, Ohio, develops and supplies leading-edge active safety technologies, air brake charging and control systems, and components under the Bendix brand name for medium –and heavy-duty trucks, tractors, trailers, buses, and other commercial vehicles throughout North America. Marathon Health provides total population health management to 415 employees and 480 spouses and dependents for the company's manufacturing campus in Huntington, IN. Services offered including primary care, health coaching, disease management, and medication dispensing.

Marathon Health began providing onsite total population health management to Bendix in 2013. In the last 18 months, 74 percent of employees patients were identified as having high health risks or chronic conditions. Marathon Health clinicians engaged 96 percent of the high-risk population, and 71 percent of the high-risk population made progress toward normal ranges.

Tracey Moran
Vice President of Marketing
Marathon Health | For Life.

21. Medical Mutual of Ohio (A HERO Interview)

Medical Mutual of Ohio is the oldest and largest health insurance company headquartered in the state of Ohio. The company employs approximately 2,300 people and is headquartered in Cleveland, Ohio with offices throughout the state. Despite being a healthcare company, Medical Mutual of Ohio faced employee health challenges that it wanted to improve. When the health plan first implemented its employee wellness program in 2003, the initial goals were to

- assess and impact the health risks of their unique employee population while empowering employees to be conscientious healthcare consumers,

- develop wellness strategies and interventions that were dynamic and targeted identified risks, and

- evaluate the impact of program interventions through data-driven metrics and analysis.

Medical Mutual of Ohio's program started with a few core programs and has evolved into a comprehensive and strategic program. Branded Wellness for Life, the program has been recognized with multiple industry awards, including the C. Everett Koop Health Award, the National Business Group on Health's "Best Employers for Healthy Lifestyle" award (multiple year winner), the American Heart Association, and various local awards.

Medical Mutual of Ohio offers a comprehensive health promotion program that includes a broad scope of activities ranging from health assessments, biometric screenings, educational opportunities, physical activity, company-wide challenges and environmental initiatives focused on building a healthy company culture. The Wellness for Life program is tied to the company's benefits structure, has strong leadership support, and takes a data-driven approach to program refinement.

To make sure it continues to evolve and improve, the company benchmarks its efforts against quality scorecards and conducts objective studies of its risk reduction programs. The program has demonstrated risk reduction for a cohort of employees, and cost analysis found that those who participate in programs at a higher level showed lower increases in healthcare costs and short-term disability.

The Wellness For Life program is comprehensive, so we're able to evaluate the program in many ways, which allows us to feed back into it and to keep improving it. We have a well-thought-out and strategic structure. We try to make it a good mix of what employees want and will participate in and what we know we need to offer in order to impact and improve our health risks.

We've found that the core foundation to a successful employee wellness program is that your program is employee centric, yet driven by data about your own workforce. If it's not employee centric in these ways, it won't work.

There are three key things that we've learned from which other employers could benefit:

- If you're so focused on the data and not on developing programs and modalities that employees really are willing to engage in and are interested in, your results won't be as strong. Recognize the need to establish a connection with employees to truly engage them; and recognize that employees bring a mixed bag of wellness needs to the workplace each day.

- You need to be equitable across all your work sites and employee audiences.

- Ensure you are providing employees with a variety of information and resources to help them reach their personal health and biometric goals, especially if you're moving toward an outcomes-based incentive strategy.

Constance Buetal
Director Wellness
Medical Mutual of Ohio
Adapted from a HERO Interview in 2013

22. NextEra Energy (Florida Power and Light)

The NextEra Health & Well-Being program was implemented 23 years ago at the direction of the CEO of then Florida Power and Light (FPL) as an employee wellness program for FPL employees and their families. The program was created primarily as a benefit for employees to help improve their overall health and well-being. A secondary motivation for investing in employee health was the belief that encouraging employees to take charge of their health could help the company control healthcare costs. The initial program included on-site fitness centers and exercise programming, health promotion programming, and an employee assistance program (EAP).

During the program's early years, a network of volunteer wellness coordinators supported the small staff at the corporate headquarters. Together, they worked to engage FPL employees by delivering wellness programs and services to the company's many sites throughout Florida.

Leadership has been fundamental to the program's success. Since its inception in 1991, the program has enjoyed strong support from senior leaders. In fact, leadership constitutes three of the five pillars that support NextEra Energy's corporate culture of health:

1. Senior leadership demonstrates its support by incorporating employee health into the company culture and including health as a potential core competency for senior management, operational leaders, and employees.

2. Operational leaders add further support by encouraging employee participation in wellness programs and being flexible with employees who want to participate in programs during work hours.

3. Management encourages employees to practice self-leadership in health matters by assuming responsibility for their own health and the health of their families.

4. The company reinforces employees' self-leadership and positive health behaviors through well-placed program incentives.

5.   Measurement across all aspects of the program—risk status changes, costs, engagement, participation, vendor performance, health claims data, and performance indicators – drives future program growth and direction.

With senior leadership support, NextEra Energy has ingrained wellness into all aspects of the work environment. The company has tobacco-free policies in all facilities, and cafeterias offer subsidized wellness meals. On-site exercise opportunities thrive even in moderate-sized work sites, and signage and coworker watchfulness reinforce safety policies.

Basic health and wellness programming is structured along five focus areas:

1.   Fitness centers offer exercise prescriptions, group classes, specialty classes, personal training, fitness assessments, team challenges, and independent exercise opportunities.

2.   Health promotion includes office and field ergonomic assessments, health screenings, flu shots, tobacco cessation options, massage therapy, and wellness challenges.

3.   Health centers include annual physicals, preventive screenings, primary care, disease management, body composition analysis, allergy shots, physical therapy, dietary counseling, and immunizations.

4.   Nutrition and weight management offers personal nutrition counseling, group nutrition presentations, dietary consultation for company cafeterias, catering services, and healthy options for on-site vending machines.

5.   EAP and mental health programming includes personal consultation, triage, and referral and group presentations and workshops on behavioral health issues.

The NextEra Health & Well-Being program consists of many programs and activities:

- Steps to Success is a personalized, long-term weight management program that pairs individuals who are obese or over-weight and have multiple risk factors with a health team, including a dietitian, fitness center staff member, and EAP counselor, who help them lose weight and sustain weight loss.

- Healthy Back/Healthy Neck is an exercise and lecture series designed to prevent musculoskeletal injury, and discomfort by strengthening the back, core, and neck and teaching proper body mechanics.

- Active Parenting Now is a video-based parent education program led by an EAP specialist who uses video vignettes to demonstrate parenting skills and lead a discussion on positive discipline and communication techniques.

- NextEra Health & Well-Being staff and safety group teamed up to create the Back Reinjury Prevention Program, which includes specialized materials on stretching, lifting, and body mechanics for employees who have experienced a loss-time back injury.

- A Personal Health Team delivers an integrated approach to health and well-being in the form of confidential, one-on-one support for employees and family members with multiple risk factors or maternity or chronic health needs. A team of twelve health professionals, staffed by the company's contracted health insurer , coach participants to achieve optimal health through education, intervention programs, and assistance working with the healthcare delivery system.

Short-term or seasonal programs complement the ongoing programs and keep the offerings fresh and employees engaged. The 20-20-20 Challenge, which motivates employees to exercise at least twenty minutes each day for a month, is an example of a seasonal program. Employees earn tokens for each workout and increase their chances to win a raffle with each additional token they earn. In another seasonal program, Spring Into Fitness!, fitness center members are encouraged to engage in physical activity and exercise routines with weekly challenges and prizes, including a prize for referring a new member to one of the fitness centers.

Company and program managers continuously measure the success of the NextEra Health & Well-Being program in terms of participant health maintenance and improvement. Although health for any large population is distributed along points of a continuum, the program's founder holds a core belief that success depends on some key items:

- Keeping risk low for healthy people
- Encouraging behavior change to reduce risk for marginally healthy people
- Providing effective programs for people with chronic conditions or catastrophic health events

The program's success starts with strong participation from employees and their family members:

- Eighty percent of employees participated in at least one on-site program in 2012, a six percent increase over 2010.

- Forty-five percent of employees reported they had participated in the program continuously for three years in 2012, an eight percent increase since 2010.

- In 2012, 78 percent of employees eligible to receive incentives had taken the annual health assessment, and 68 percent had participated in a health screening.

- Participation in the on-site health centers increased by 10 percent from 2010 to 2012, with a total of more than 20,000 visits in 2012. The average return on investment (ROI) for the company's three health centers was $2.36 for every dollar spent in 2012.

- Flu shots were administered to 41 percent of employees in 2012, an increase of 7 percent over the previous year.

- In the company cafeterias, 27 percent of employees chose the healthy food option in 2012, an increase of four percent since 2010. These healthy options represented 39 percent of the total cafeteria sales in 2012.

- With 66 fitness centers across the company, ample opportunity exists to use an on-site facility; 64 percent of eligible employees are enrolled in their on-site fitness center. In 2012, the total number of fitness center visits increased by 5 percent compared with 2010.

- The internal EAP staff counseled 1,845 employees and family members in 2012.

Strong employee participation is an important component of the company's multiyear health benefits strategy. In 2009, the program encouraged employees to participate in health assessments and screenings to "know their numbers" and to reduce their risks by participating in behavior change programs. The company reinforced these behavior changes by offering health incentives to employees who participated in the assessments and took action to reduce identified risk. In 2011, NextEra Energy began matching incentives with healthy outcomes. Employees who meet certain biometric indicators are eligible to receive a credit to their health reimbursement account. This approach was incorporated into the employee benefit plan for 2012.

Andrew Scibelli
Manager Health and Well-Being
NextEra Energy

23. Ottawa Kent

"Inspired by the research included in Zero Trends, and fuelled by our desire to deliver real solutions to our clients (not just insurance policies), we designed, built and implemented our own benefits risk management division at Ottawa Kent. The objective of this 'loss control for benefits' unit was to provide access to processes and programs—including giving employees access to their very own wellness coach—to consistently raise the wellness bar in order to deliver to employers an amazing 97.6 percent average employee participation in health risk assessments—*with no financial incentives.*

The process used by Ottawa Kent is nearly identical to the property/casualty risk management process. We start out by identifying our client's risk exposure. Then, we analyzed their loss data and develop strategies to control or eliminate those losses. It is only after completing these three steps that we even discuss insurance as a way to finance the costs of risk. The final, ongoing step is monitoring and measuring results."

Fasteners, Inc.

Fasteners, Inc., a retailer of tools and accessories for the commercial and residential building trades headquartered in Grand Rapids, Michigan with one hundred employees, has found great success with Ottawa Kent's approach. They've had the same wellness coach meet with their employees one-on-one, face-to-face since 2006. According to John Szlenkier, President of Fasteners, Inc., it just makes sense. "As a company, one of our services is maintaining and repairing tools for our customers," says John. "We see Ottawa Kent's process as a maintenance program for our most important asset—our employees. It's a no-brainer."

Tom Rickers, Fasteners, Inc.'s VP of Operations, agrees. "We've saved tens of thousands of dollars on health insurance costs and workers' compensation costs simply by implementing Ottawa Kent's risk management programs," says Tom. "In addition to savings, we've boosted both employee job satisfaction and long-term health and safety. This is important to Fasteners, Inc.—it's not just about the money. It's about making a positive impact on our employees' lives."

"It's imperative to motivate employees to become healthier," Says Dustin Boss, a Certified Risk Architect with Ottawa Kent. "Our program has a great track record. We provide an implementation process that 'turns employees on' to wellness right from the beginning and then reinforces this message through one-on-one wellness coaching meetings that help employees set SMART (Specific, Measurable, Attainable, Relevant, Time-bound) goals. By getting employees interested in their wellness from the beginning, we are able to avoid the lag between generating participation and delivering real improvement in health risk status. The fact that we get the results without incentives, and that employee participation averages over 97.6 percent, shows the power of one-on-one wellness coaching.

Randy Boss
Certified Risk Architect
Partner at Ottawa Kent

24. Premera Blue Cross

Program Impact Measure

Employers expect more than efficient claims administration from their health plans. Premera Blue Cross is asked to deliver health and productivity services to our employers and have the analytic horsepower to prospectively measure their opportunity to impact their future health and productivity costs. Based on that opportunity, employers want a roadmap for making it happen. Zero Trends provides a conceptual framework to do this. We translated the five pillars into an actionable and measurable roadmap that we could use to structure targeted services for our customers. We partnered with Dr. Edington to develop the Program Impact Measure (PIM) integrating qualitative information integrating the five pillars with claims, health risk, industry, demographic, and programmatic participation data into a unified qualitative and quantitative data set for analysis.

Purpose of the PIM

The PIM assesses the health engagement of an employee population and estimates the potential for future improvement of the health and productivity of that workforce. This is translated into a numerical score between 1 and 100 that is directionally indicative of future health and productivity costs. The algorithms and sub scores within the PIM provide scoring around the employers' relative opportunity (based on industry, demographics, and geography) for taking specific action. Think of this metaphorically as a type of automotive computer diagnostic. It doesn't do the repair, but identifies the critical issues and guidance for improvement.

Unlike many modeling tools, the PIM ties traditional healthcare data (claims, health risk, demographics, etc.), cultural data (policies, communication strategies, corporate support, etc.), and levels of participation for the services previously delivered. The PIM integrates both structured and unstructured data to assess all of these elements and provide the foundation for a strategy and a mechanism to measure ongoing progress toward achieving the strategy over time.

The PIM is a mixture of qualitative and quantitative data requiring a mixture of interviews and data input. The process includes

- a series of interviews with key stakeholders across the organization
- claims, demographic, and other health data entered into the PIM
- PIM algorithms, developed with Dr. Edington, generate the PIM score showing potential healthcare and productivity savings. The PIM also ranks where the greatest areas of opportunity for improvement reside

- Premera consults with the client to determine where to target interventions to raise the score.

- Premera delivers final set of recommendations for strategy.

Benefits of the PIM

- Demonstrates the impact a 'culture of health' strategy can have regarding the health of a workforce population based on the best employer health research.

- Provides the employer a strategic and tactical roadmap (programs, policies, communications, and incentives) for achieving the health and productivity improvement.

- Helps employers make informed purchasing decisions around health & productivity initiatives.

- Provides an ongoing objective mechanism for measuring progress and for fine tuning implementation.

Neal Sofian
Engagement Officer
Premera Health System

25. Schindler Elevator Corporation: A Call for "Going Stealth"

In 2013, Julie Shipley, Manager of General Training (now Senior Human Resources Business Partner) at Schindler Elevator Corporation, reached out to Motion Infusion (a well-being provider based in San Francisco) to inquire about the possibility of incorporating well-being into an upcoming leadership development program for the company's rising top managers. This initial conversation blossomed into what has now become a multi-year "Odyssey" series that has created a ripple effect of enhanced well-being throughout the organization. The success of the first "Leadership Odyssey" workshop (held in the spring of 2014) has sparked follow-up events including "Safety Odyssey," "HR Odyssey" and additional "Leadership Odyssey" workshops.

Like other wellness providers, I had felt continually frustrated by the lack of time and resources that are typically afforded wellness programs. "Going stealth," I have discovered, may be our best bet in getting around this chronic shortage. As outlined in my book *Workplace Wellness That Works*, a stealth strategy simply calls for embedding wellness and well-being concepts into non-wellness programs, such as leadership development, safety training, culture change initiatives and onboarding, and swapping out wellness language, such as health improvement and stress management, for "stealth" terms, such as energy and human performance improvement. The idea is to focus is on something other than health and well-being (such as improved leadership skills), and allow improved health and well-being to emerge as a byproduct. Sounds sneaky, but it's really just a smarter way to go where the money is and move toward what is deemed "essential" (especially in the eyes of senior leaders) in helping the organization to achieve its core objectives. Below are some best practices you can apply in building your own "stealth" initiatives:

Identify top organizational priorities: Every organization has its top core objectives, and as we all know, improved employee well-being is rarely one of them. After clarifying already existing top priorities and associated initiatives, look for ways to embed wellness and well-being concepts into these initiatives. For example, one of Schindler's core organizational objectives is "Building winning teams." In keeping with this objective, a key component to the Leadership Odyssey series is helping managers draw the vital connection between well-being (starting with their own) and high performing teams.

Form strategic, interdisciplinary partnerships: Having identified these core objectives, who are the people you need to connect with? In the case of Leadership Odyssey, the Organizational Development team at Schindler partnered with Motion Infusion, and in the case of the follow-up Safety Odyssey, Schindler's Organizational Development team partnered up with both Safety and Motion Infusion.

Rename: In taking a stealth approach, it's critical to rename wellness and well-being in non-wellness terms. The Organizational Development team at Schindler has successfully employed words like energy, sustainability, renewal, balance, and healthy culture to build its movement of well-being. In the Year 1 Leadership Odyssey workshop, managers were introduced to a "Sustainable Growth Model" that has provided a visual on the why behind investing in both well-being and building a culture of sustainability.

Use nudges and cues: Nudges, or environmental prompts, make the healthy choice the easy choice. Cues, or cultural prompts, make the healthy choice the "normal" choice. Nudges and cues are effective ways to shift the focus from the individual toward optimizing the environment and the culture. In follow up to Leadership Odyssey and Safety Odyssey, Schindler has now implemented ongoing nudges and cues. For example, Schindler now requests that the caterer provides healthy selections for all meetings. In addition, the Organizational Development team has taken the lead in positioning "high boy" tables in natural meeting spots (such as at the bottom of the escalators in the lobby) to nudge people into gathering more and standing more. Most importantly, participating managers are now "cueing" their team members into investing in their health and well-being on an ongoing basis. In addition, Schindler now incorporates well-being into everything they do, whether it's an informal walking meeting with a coworker or a training program or the choice of a restaurant for a group dinner. Schindler even includes a mandatory personal goal around well-being and culture in its employee merit program.

Rather than continuing to beat the drum on the value of wellness, we, as health and well-being providers, can get smarter. We can simply "go stealth," allowing receptivity to wellness to arise as an outcome. This changed mindset in leaders is exactly what we have continued to witness as a result of our stealth initiatives at Schindler.

As best told by one of the participating managers at the conclusion of the first Leadership Odyssey, "We desperately need this type of content to separate ourselves from the competition. If one aspect of our strategy and priority is to build winning teams, well-being is critical to driving the motivation that makes our good employees want to get up and come to work every day. It is also a valuable recruiting tool—and we need to get it right. This [well-being] is a critical element of differentiating ourselves from our competition in our ability to grow the business over time."

Laura Putnam
CEO, Motion Infusion, and Author, *Workplace Wellness That Works*

25. Simplicity Health

Many American working adults are living paycheck to paycheck, living longer and saving less. Most understand the need to save for their retirement and live within a budget, yet the hardest part of achieving personal financial security is to know where to find the money to save in the first place. While traditional financial education and wealth management planners are important, providing education and awareness to individuals about the health to wealth connection is the most important first step in the financial wellness equation.

Over the years we have seen the impact of health risk assessments that help individuals identify personal health risks so that the information can be used as an educational launching pad to promote behavior change to improve physical health. To support individuals in a similar way, the Health Index Calculator (HIC) is a tool designed to help people realize and visualize that they are spending too much on their health, potential savings within their control also based on the promotion of behavior change. Unlike the Health Assessment, the HIC allows individuals to forecast monetary gain based on their behavior changes related to their risk. The reveal of real dollars intrinsically motivates action.

"This kind of new innovation can radically impact the vast majority of Americans to change the way they think about physical and financial wellness. Behavior change is never easy, but this assessment tools supports positive, incremental steps to healthier habits that will prevent costly chronic disease and transform good health into wealth," said Simplicity Health Plans CEO Gregory James Hummer, MD.

Lisa M. Holland, RN, MBA,   Gregory J. Hummer, MD
CCWS President StayFit™   CEO Simplicity Health Plans

26. St. Jude Medical Center

After years of researching and evaluating best practice models, there appears to be no cookie-cutter approach to designing the perfect wellness program within the healthcare industry. The unique and dynamic healthcare environment challenges us to look for new and innovative approaches. At St. Jude Medical Center, rather than presenting a calendar of activities throughout the year, we have adopted a philosophy and commitment to intentionally integrate wellness into the fabric of our culture.

We have gone beyond traditional health risk assessments and biometric screenings, to offering a spectrum of well-being resources for applications at both home and work, from practical to just simply fun. This includes creating a "break away lounge" for employees to work out, play billiards, or just sit back and de-stress. We also provide an onsite farmers' market, chair massage by appointment, walking trails and clubs, kickball and softball leagues, one-minute mindfulness exercise during hand-washing, and financial wellness planning...to name a few.

In the coming years, the burden of stress and compassion fatigue will continue to weigh heavily on all hospital employees. We hope to continue inculcating the practices of Jon Kabat-Zinn's Mindfulness Based Stress Reduction methodologies into our leadership team and front-line staff. We are committed to creating a wellness framework in our environment where making healthy choices is made easy.

Jane Wang
Wellness Manager
St. Jude Medical Center

27. US Preventive Medicine

The workforce is the engine that drives the economy—and the health of the workforce is a performance driver that can impact both top line revenue as well as bottom line cost savings for employers—which leads to healthier communities with healthier economies.

Workplace health and wellness initiatives now reach millions of workers with prevention and health management services typically impacting employees many hours per month compared to the minutes spent in a primary care physician's office each year. By embracing a preventive medicine and health promotion strategy employers have the capability and expertise to meet the challenges of creating a more resilient, more engaged workforce.

The fundamental business value proposition of population health management is simple: good health is good business. Employers are realizing that excess health costs follow excess health risks.[1] Therefore, finding ways to manage financial risk by improving health status makes sound economic sense. To bring about real change to the corporate bottom line, employers must look beyond healthcare benefits as a cost to be managed toward the benefits of good health as investments to be leveraged.

US Preventive Medicine has created an innovative information technology solution for a personalized prevention solution, *The Preventive Plan*™. The Preventive Plan provides a suite of innovative tools and services that encompass an integrated primary prevention (wellness and health promotion), secondary prevention (biometric and lab screening as well as early detection/diagnosis), and tertiary prevention (early intervention and evidence-based chronic condition management).

The Preventive Plan leverages social cognitive concepts such as efficacy-building and self-regulatory mechanisms like goal setting and self-monitoring, which facilitate health behavior change. This web-based Prevention Plan allows individual users to complete a health risk appraisal, biometric reporting and lab testing to develop a customized Prevention Plan. The Plan provides users with knowledge of their health risks as well as suggestions to reduce those risks. In addition, each user is provided a suite of support tools, recommended risk-reduction activities and information that allows them to translate knowledge into action.

Users are able to complete a health risk appraisal, virtual coaching, live coaching, or social challenges to reduce their risks and are able to determine for themselves what level of engagement they prefer. All coaching programs are structured using risk-based educational modules. Live coaches can assist members to complete these modules telephonically, while virtual coaching allows completion of the same content, through self-directed online programs. Both coaching interventions utilize recommended action programs related to the risks identified from the risk appraisal, lab testing and biometric screening. They are focused on identification of barriers, goal setting and self-monitoring activities aimed at increasing self-efficacy. Live coaches utilize motivational interviewing as a method for engaging members in the coaching process, which is the only significant difference from the virtual coaching intervention.

In fact, published research studies in peer-reviewed journals have shown compelling health risk reductions of people participating in the Preventive Plan from US Preventive Medicine after one year and also after two years of participation.[2,3,4]

1. Edington D. *Zero Trends: Health as a Serious Economic Strategy.* Ann Arbor, MI: University of Michigan–Health Management Research Center; 2009.

2. Loeppke R, Edington D, Beg S. "Impact of The Preventive Plan on employee health risk reduction." *Population Health Management.* 2010; 13 (5):275-84.

3. Loeppke R, Edington D, et al. "Two Year Outcomes Show Effectiveness of the Prevention Program in Lowering Health Risks and Costs." Letter to the Editor. *Population Health Management.* 2011 14 (5): 265.

4. Loeppke R, Edington D, Bender J, Reynolds A. "The Association of Technology in a Workplace Wellness Program with Health Risk Factor Reduction." *Journal of Occupational and Environmental Medicine.* 2013 55 (3): 259-264.

The study published in the March, 2013 issue of the Journal of Occupational and Environmental Medicine (JOEM) evaluated the impact of The Preventive Plan on health risks in a cohort of 7,804 individuals across fifteen employers who were engaged in the Plan for 2 years.[4]

The net result of the health risk transitions of those 7,804 individuals, showed total population risk transition movement between baseline and two-year measurements as follows: the segment of the study population in the high-risk category was reduced from 11 percent to 6 percent; the segment in medium risk category was reduced from 29 percent to 23 percent and the segment in low-risk category was increased from 60 percent to 71 percent. Also, of those individuals that started in a high-risk category at baseline, 46 percent moved down to medium risk and 19 percent moved down to low risk category. Equally impressive is the number and percent of individuals remaining low risk (89 percent).

In analyzing the specific health risks of individuals at baseline and then after two years on their personalized prevention plan, it revealed reduction from high risk in all 15 of 15 health risk factors measured with a few of the notable findings as follows: 81 percent lowered blood pressure; 79 percent improved physical activity; 64 percent reduced stress; 61 percent reported fewer health-related sick days; 58 percent lowered cholesterol; 54 percent improved perception of their health; 43 percent improved fasting blood glucose and 35 percent quit smoking/tobacco use. A 12 percent decrease in high risk for body mass index was also seen in the population studied which correlates with other improvements in high risk.

We then performed a more detailed analysis of that study cohort to answer the following question: Is there a relationship between level of engagement and health risk reduction?[4]

To accomplish this, we grouped engagement types into stages based on how a user interacted with the Preventive Plan. Stage I engagement was informational in nature and included the completion of health risk assessment (HRA) and laboratory testing. Website access provides basic health-related information as well as a description of identified health risks and targeted messaging suggesting actions to reduce risks. Stage I engagement was further categorized into 3 subcategories defined by the number of times a user logged on to their personalized Prevention Plan website, Stage I(a) = 1 login, Stage I(b) = 2-4 logins, and Stage I(c) = 5 or more logins.

Stage II engagement was defined as virtual and/or social engagement and was comprised of completing one or more virtual coaching action programs and/or social challenges or both. Virtual coaching was accomplished through completion of self-directed activities, automated messaging and targeted reminders included as part of a risk-based action program. Social engagement was through the use of group challenges aimed at physical activity or healthy eating to track their progress and provide online comments of support to their teammates as well as observe their ranking compared to other teams.

Stage III engagement included live coaching interactions. We differentiated between live coaching alone and live coaching plus virtual and/or social engagement through the use of sub categories. Stage III(a) was live coaching without virtual and/or social engagements, while Stage III(b) included virtual and/or social engagement as well as live coaching interaction.

This analysis revealed that increased engagement resulted in greater health risk reductions statistically significant (p<.0001) level compared to natural flow for all Stages except Stage I(a).[4]

Even though Stage III engagement with live coaching yielded the greatest risk reduction, Stage I engagement demonstrated a dose response in improved risk reduction based on the number of times people logged in to their Prevention Plan and Stage II engagement with virtual coaching/ social engagement was also associated with dramatically significant (p < .0001) health risk transitions exceeding expected natural flow.

Therefore, these compelling results support the concept that leveraging technology with a web-based health management program with virtual coaching and social engagement are effective risk-reducing alternatives to live coaching interaction.[4]

Conclusion

Large-scale, population-based changes in health behaviors require a comprehensive and multipronged approach that sustains interest and promotes engagement. Participants in The Preventive Plan have shown excellent improvements in risk transitions toward a healthier status and reductions in absolute adverse health risks.

One of the key elements of successful population health management will continue to be the education and engagement of each individual. In fact, translating information into knowledge and knowledge into action to empower healthier behaviors at the individual level will yield better personal health management as well as population health improvement that will be a fundamental factor influencing the success of employer-based wellness programs, accountable care organizations and patient-centered medical home strategies.

These studies provides strong evidence that an innovative personalized preventive intervention with engaging technology and interactive Web-based tools as well as high-touch outreach by health coaches on an as needed basis, can reduce health risks by engaging individuals to be more proactive about their health. Furthermore, these studies yield more evidence for the business case that preventive medicine is an investment to be leveraged rather than a cost to be justified.

When an organization is at financial risk for the health and clinical risk of a population (e.g. self-insured employers, Taft Hartley trust funds, veterans administration, health plans, insurers, re-insurers, ACOs, PCMHs and others) they would benefit from an integrated population health management/comprehensive preventive solutions. The fundamental keys to success for comprehensive population health management initiatives are better health—and better health care—at lower costs.

The emerging body of evidence of the business value of health and the link between health improvement, productivity improvement and economic improvement is defining a new business case to invest in a more proactive, wellness-oriented, true "health system"—built on the pillars of preventive medicine to form the foundation of population health improvement. It is clear that this is not only a fiscal and clinical imperative—it is a moral imperative.

The bottom line is that good health is good business—as well as good medicine for individuals and our national economy.

Ron Loeppke, MD
Vice Chairman
US Preventive Medicine

Appendix C
Full Wellness and Well-Being Landscape Assessment

Indicate with an "X" or "✓" whether you offer each type of resource outlined in the table below.

Type Of Support	Employees	Dependents	Retirees
Manage Disease	❑	❑	❑
Asthma	❑	❑	❑
Low Back	❑	❑	❑
Pain	❑	❑	❑
Cardiac	❑	❑	❑
Diabetes	❑	❑	❑
COPD	❑	❑	❑
High Risk Obesity	❑	❑	❑
Depression	❑	❑	❑
Chronic Pain	❑	❑	❑
Irritable Bowel	❑	❑	❑
Hypertension	❑	❑	❑
Lipidemia	❑	❑	❑
Metabolism (Met Syndrome)	❑	❑	❑
Case Management	❑	❑	❑
On Site Biometric Screening	❑	❑	❑
On-Site Health Equipment For Self Help I.E., BP Kiosk Scale	❑	❑	❑
On-Site Medical Management	❑	❑	❑
Telemedicine On-Site	❑	❑	❑
Coaching On-Site	❑	❑	❑
Clinical Services	❑	❑	❑
Home Visit	❑	❑	❑
Visiting Doctor Programs	❑	❑	❑
Reduce Risk—Help Healthy People Stay Healthy Wellness Programs:	❑	❑	❑
Weight Management	❑	❑	❑
Stress Management	❑	❑	❑
Nutrition Balance	❑	❑	❑
Physical Activity	❑	❑	❑

Type Of Support	Employees	Dependents	Retirees
Work Life Balance	❏	❏	❏
Smoking Cessation	❏	❏	❏
Preventive Services	❏	❏	❏
Dental Exam	❏	❏	❏
Vision Test	❏	❏	❏
Diabetic Foot	❏	❏	❏
Exam Flu Shot	❏	❏	❏
Vaccination Other Than Flu	❏	❏	❏
General Physical	❏	❏	❏
Bone Density Exam	❏	❏	❏
Colon Cancer Screening	❏	❏	❏
Mammogram	❏	❏	❏
Pap Test	❏	❏	❏
Prostate Cancer Screening	❏	❏	❏
Help Employees Thrive - Development Opportunities For Self-Leaders (Examples):	❏	❏	❏
Self-leadership Principles	❏	❏	❏
Change	❏	❏	❏
Resilience	❏	❏	❏
Decision Making	❏	❏	❏
Mindfulness	❏	❏	❏
Emotional Intelligence	❏	❏	❏
Brain Health	❏	❏	❏
Work-Life Balance Efforts	❏	❏	❏
Mind, Body, Spirit	❏	❏	❏
Stress Management	❏	❏	❏
Yoga	❏	❏	❏
Meditation	❏	❏	❏
Other	❏	❏	❏
Development Opportunities For Leaders And Managers:	❏	❏	❏
Positive Executive Leaders	❏	❏	❏
Positive Operational Leaders	❏	❏	❏
Positive Managers And Supervisors	❏	❏	❏
Positive "Champions" Or Ambassadors	❏	❏	❏
EAP Programs	❏	❏	❏
Family, Elder and or Childcare	❏	❏	❏
Financial Support Counseling	❏	❏	❏
Legal Counseling	❏	❏	❏
Referral Resource Support	❏	❏	❏

Appendix D
Additional Resources

What follows is a compilation of some of the resources that we have found useful during the evolution of our thinking. It is by no means a comprehensive list.

INTRODUCTION

- Christensen, Clayton M., Jerome H. Grossman, and Jason Hwang. *The Innovator's Prescription:* A Disruptive Solution for Health Care. McGraw Hill, New York.
- Smith, Adam. *The Wealth of Nations.* Bantam Dell a Division of Random House. 2003.
- Smith, Hedrick. *Who Stole the American Dream.* Random House, New York. 2012

SECTION I: AWAKENING

Chapter 1: The Win-Win Imperative—Taking Wellness and Well-being to the Next Level

- N/A

Chapter 2: What is Health, Wellness, and Well-being?

Foundations of Wellness and Well-being

- Ardell, Donald B. *High Level Wellness, an Alternative to Doctors, Drugs, and Disease.* Bantam Books, 1979.
- Hettler, Bill. *"Six Dimensions of Wellness."* National Wellness Institute (www. nwi. org), and http://www.hettler.com/(1976).
- Rath, Tom, and James K. Harter. *Wellbeing: The Five Essential Elements.* Gallup Press, 2010.
- Seligman, Martin EP. "Positive health." *Applied Psychology* 57, no. s1 (2008): 3-18.
- Travis, John. *Wellness: Small Changes You Can Use to Make a Big Difference.* Ten Speed Press, 1991.

Chapter 3: Context Matters

- Allen, Robert Francis, and Charlotte Kraft. *The Organizational Unconscious: How to Create the Corporate Culture You Want and Need.* Prentice Hall, 1982.

- Allen, Robert F., and Judd Allen. "A sense of community, a shared vision and a positive culture: core enabling factors in successful culture based health promotion." *American Journal of Health Promotion* 1, no. 3 (1987): 40-47.

- Blanchard, Ken, Susan Fowler, and Laurence Hawkins. *Self Leadership and the One Minute Manager.* Morrow, 2005

- Brown, Tim. *Change By Design.* Harper-Collins, New York. 2009

- Brown, Tim. "Design thinking." *Harvard Business Review* 86, no. 6 (2008)

- D-school https://dschool.stanford.edu

- IDEO/Design Kit Field Guide to HCD http://www.designkit.org/resources/1

- Kolko, Jon. *Exposing the Magic of Design: A Practitioner's Guide to the Methods and Theory of Synthesis.* Oxford University Press, 2010.

- Kolko, Jon. *Wicked Problems: Problems Worth Solving: A Handbook and Call to Action.* 2012. Available at: https://www.wickedproblems.com/.

- Silverzweig, Stan, and Robert F. Allen. *"Changing the Corporate Culture."* Sloan Management Review 17, no. 3 (1976): 33.

- Edington, Dee W. *Zero Trends: Health as a Serious Economic Strategy.* UM-HMRC, 2009.

- Goleman, Daniel. "Emotional intelligence: Issues in paradigm building." *The Emotionally Intelligent Workplace* 13 (2001): 26.

- Meadows, Donella H., and Diana Wright. *Thinking in Systems: A Primer.* Chelsea Green Publishing, 2008.

- Pritchett, Price. *New Work Habits For A Radically Changing World.* Pritchett Rummler-Brache, Plano TX, 1999.

- Rith, Chanpory, and Hugh Dubberly. "Why Horst WJ Rittel matters." *Design Issues* 23, no. 1 (2007): 72-91.

- Scharmer, C. Otto. *Theory U: Learning from the Future as it Emerges.* Berrett-Koehler Publishers, 2009.

- Schein, Edgar H. *Organizational Culture and Leadership.* Vol. 2. John Wiley & Sons, 2010.

- Senge, Peter M., C. Otto Scharmer, Joseph Jaworski, and Betty Sue Flowers. *Presence: An Exploration of Profound Change in People, Organizations, and Society.* Crown Business, 2005.

- Senge, Peter M. *The Fifth Discipline: The Art and Practice of the Learning Organization.* Broadway Business, 2006.

- Senge, Peter M. *The Fifth Discipline Fieldbook: Strategies and Tools for Building a Learning Organization.* Crown Business, 2014.

- Senge, Peter M. *The dance of change: The Challenges to Sustaining Momentum in a Learning Organization.* Crown Business, 2014.

Chapter 4: An Executive Summary of the Win-Win Journey Process

- N/A

SECTION II: CREATING SHARED VALUES—SHARED RESULTS

Chapter 5: Engage and Motivate Leadership

- Blanchard, Ken, and Phil Hodges. *The Servant Leader: Transforming Your Heart, Head, Hands and Habits.* Nashville, TN: Thomas Nelson Press; 2003.
- Blanchard, Ken, and Mark Miller. *The Secret: What Great Leaders Know and dD.* San Francisco, CA: Berrett-Koehler Publishers; 2001.
- Blanchard Ken, and Susan Fowler Woodring. *Empowerment: Achieving Peak Performance Through Self-Leadership.* Successories Library; 1998.
- Blanchard, Ken. *Leading at a Higher Level.* Prentice Hall, New York. 2006.
- Cameron, Kim S. *Positive Leadership: Strategies for Extraordinary Performance.* Berrett-Koehler Publishers, 2012.
- Dutton, Jane E., and Gretchen M. Spreitzer (editors). *How to be a Positive Leader: Insights From Leading Thinkers on Positive Organizations.* Berrett-Koehler San Francisco. 2014.
- Cameron, Kim S., Robert E. Quinn, Jeff DeGraff, and Anjan V. Thakor. *Competing Values Leadership.* Edward Elgar Publishing, 2014.
- Goleman, Daniel, and Richard Boyatzis. "Social intelligence and the biology of leadership." *Harvard Business Review* 86, no. 9 (2008): 74-81.
- Hamel, Gary, and C. K. Prahalad. *Competing for the Future.* Harvard Business School Press. 1994.
- Hooker, Charles, and Mihaly Csikszentmihalyi. "Flow, Creativity, and Shared Leadership." *Shared Leadership: Reframing the Hows and Whys of Leadership* (2003): 217-34.
- Quinn, Robert E. *Deep Change: Discovering the Leader within.* Vol. 378. John Wiley & Sons, 2010.

Chapter 6: Prepare for the Journey

- Lencioni, Patrick. *The Five Dysfunctions of a Team.* Jossey-Bass San Francisco. 2002.
- Presencing Institute—https://www.presencing.com/
- Society for organizational learning—https://www.solonline.org/
- Senge, Peter M. *The Fifth Discipline: The Art and Practice of the Learning Organization.* Broadway Business, 2006.

- Senge, Peter M. *The Fifth Discipline Fieldbook: Strategies and Tools for Building a Learning Organization*. Crown Business, 2014.
- Senge, Peter M. *The Dance of Change: The Challenges to Sustaining Momentum in a Learning Organization*. Crown Business, 2014.
- Scharmer, C. Otto. *Theory U: Learning From the Future as it Emerges*. Berrett-Koehler Publishers, 2009.
- Senge, Peter M., C. Otto Scharmer, Joseph Jaworski, and Betty Sue Flowers. *Presence: An Exploration of Profound Change in People, Organizations, and Society*. Crown Business, 2005.
- Senge, Peter M., C. Otto Scharmer, Joseph Jaworski, and Betty Sue Flowers. *Presence: Human Purpose and the Field of the Future*. Broadway Business, 2008.

Chapter 7: Define What You Care About

- Frankel, Viktor. *Man's Search for Meaning*. Pocket Books a Simon & Schuster division of Gulf and Western. 1963.
- Gantner, Rose K. *Workplace Wellness: Performance with a Purpose*. Wellworks Publishing, LLC Moon Township PA 2012.

Chapter 8: Assess Where You Are Today

- Cooperrider, David, Diana D. Whitney, and Jacqueline M. Stavros. *The Appreciative Inquiry Handbook: For Leaders of Change*. Berrett-Koehler Publishers, 2008.
- Cooperrider, David, and Diana D. Whitney. *Appreciative Inquiry: A Positive Revolution In Change*. Berrett-Koehler Publishers, 2005.
- Health Environment Check (HEcheck). Contact Edington Associates for information. www.edingtonassociates.com
- HealthLead™ Accreditation. http://www.ushealthiest.org/
- HERO Employee Health Management (EHM) Best Practices Scorecard; http://hero-health.org/scorecard/
- CDC. http://www.cdc.gov/workplacehealthpromotion/assessment/assessment_interviews/environmental-assessment.html
- Living and Thriving Assessment. Contact Edington Associates for information. www.edingtonassociates.com
- For more resources and a bibliography of Appreciative Inquiry research see: https://appreciativeinquiry.case.edu
- http://www.centerforappreciativeinquiry.net/more-on-ai/the-generic-processes-of-appreciative-inquiry/

- For more resources and a bibliography of Appreciative Inquiry research see: https://appreciativeinquiry.case.edu
- http://www.centerforappreciativeinquiry.net/more-on-ai/the-generic-processes-of-appreciative-inquiry/

Chapter 9: Determine Where You Want to Go

- Blanchard, Ken, and Jesse Stoner. *Full Steam Ahead.* Berrett-Koehler Publishers, San Francisco, 2003.
- *Moneyball*, Columbia Pictures, Culver City CA, 2011.
- Bickman, Leonard. "The functions of program theory." *New Directions for Program Evaluation* 1987, no. 33 (1987): 5-18.
- Chen, Huey T. *Practical Program Evaluation: Theory-driven Evaluation and the Integrated Evaluation Perspective.* SAGE Publications, 2014.
- Chen, Huey T. *Theory-driven Evaluations.* Sage, 1990.
- Chen, Huey T., and Peter H. Rossi. "The theory-driven approach to validity." *Evaluation and Program Planning* 10, no. 1 (1987): 95-103.
- Chen, Huey-Tsyh, and Peter H. Rossi. "The multi-goal, theory-driven approach to evaluation: A model linking basic and applied social science." *Social Forces* 59, no. 1 (1980): 106-122.
- Chen, Huey T. "Theory-driven evaluation: Conceptual framework, application and advancement." In *Evaluation von Programmen und Projekten für eine Demokratische Kultur*, pp. 17-40. Springer Fachmedien Wiesbaden, 2012.
- Chen, Huey T. "The roots and growth of theory-driven evaluation." *Evaluation Roots: A Wider Perspective of Theorists' Views and Influences* (2012): 113.
- Funnell, Sue C., and Patricia J. Rogers. *Purposeful Program theory: Effective use of Theories of Change and Logic Models.* Vol. 31. John Wiley & Sons, 2011.
- Logic model and program planning resources available at: http://www.cdc.gov/eval/index.htm

SECTION III: EVOLVING POSITIVE ORGANIZATIONAL HEALTH

Chapter 10: Outline How You are Going to Get There

- Funnell, Sue C., and Patricia J. Rogers. *Purposeful Program Theory: Effective Use of Theories of Change and Logic Models.* John Wiley and Sons, 2011.

- Bickman L. "The Functions of Program Theory" In *Using Program Theory in Evaluation*, edited by L. Bickman. San Franciso: Jossey-Bass.

Chapter 11: Create a Positive Environment, Culture and Climate

- Allen, Robert, F., Shirley Linde. *Lifegain: The Exciting New Program that will Change Your Health and Your Life.* Appleton-Century-Croffs, New York. 1981.
- Allen, Judd. *Wellness Leadership: Creating Supportive Environments for Healthier and More Productive Employees.* Human Resources Institute, LLC. 2008.
- *Integrating Employee Health: A Model Program for NASA.* National Academies Press, Washing D. C. 2005
- Cameron, Kim S., and Gretchen M. Spreitzer, eds. *The Oxford Handbook of Positive Organizational Scholarship.* Oxford University Press, 2011.
- Cameron, Kim S., Jane E. Dutton, and Robert E. Quinn. *Positive Organizational Scholarship.* Berrett-Koehler San Francisco. 2003.
- Cameron, Kim S. "Paradox in positive organizational change." *The Journal of Applied Behavioral Science* 44, no. 1 (2008): 7-24.
- Ariely, Dan. *Predictably Irrational.* Revised and Expanded Edition: The Hidden Forces That Shape Our Decisions. Harper Collins, Inc. Kindle Edition. 2009.
- Ariely D. *The Upside of Irrationality: The Unexpected Benefits of Defying Logic at Work and at Home.* Harper Collins, Inc. Kindle Edition. 2010.
- Brafman, Ori, and Rom Brafman. *Sway: The Irresistible Pull of Irrational Behavior.* New York, NY. Double Day. 2008.
- Heath, Chip, and Dan Heath. *Switch: How to Change Things When Change Is Hard.* New York, NY: Broadway Books; 2010.
- Kahneman, Daniel. *Thinking: Fast and Slow.* New York, NY: Farrar, Straus and Giroux. 2012.
- Thaler, Richard H., and Cass R. Sunstein. *Nudge: Improving Decisions About Health, Wealth, and Happiness.* New Haven, CT: Yale University Pres.; 2008.
- Robbin Phillips, Greg Cordell, Geno Church, and Spike Jones. *Brains on Fire: Igniting Powerful, Sustainable, Word of Mouth Movements.* 2010. John Wiley & Sons, Hoboken, New Jersey.

Chapter 12: Support Self-leadership and Positive Individual Health

- Covey, Steven R. *The 7 Habits of Highly Effective People: Powerful Lessons in Personal Change.* New York, NY: Simon & Schuster; 1989.

- Jones, Laurie Beth. *The Path: Creating Your Mission Statement for Life and Work*. New York, NY: Hyperion e-books; 1996.

- Putnam, Laura. *Workplace Wellness that Works. Ten Steps to Infuse Well-Being and Vitality into Any Organization*. 2015. Wiley & Sons. Hoboken, New Jersy.

- Blanchard, Ken, Susan Fowler, and Laurence Hawkins. *Self Leadership and the One Minute Manager*. Morrow, 2005

- Blanchard, Ken, and Susan Fowler Woodring. *Empowerment: Achieving Peak Performance through Self-leadership*. Successories Library; 1998.

- Blanchard, Ken, D. W. Edington, and Marjorie Blanchard. *The One Minute Manager Balances Work and Life* (original published as *The One Minute Manager Gets Fit*). Quill William Morrow, 1986.

- Doidge, Norman. *The Brain That Changes Itself: Stories of Personal Triumph from the Frontiers of Brain Science*. New York, NY: Penguin Group; 2007.

- Hanson, Rick. *Buddha's Brain: The Practical Neuroscience of Happiness, Love, and Wisdom*. Oakland, CA: New Harbinger Publications; 2009.

- Hanson, Rick. *Just One Thing: Developing a Buddha Brain One Simple Practice at a Time*. Oakland, CA: New Harbinger Publications; 2007:33.

- Fredrickson, Barbara L. "The role of positive emotions in positive psychology: The broaden-and-build theory of positive emotions." *American Psychologist* 56, no. 3 (2001): 218.

- Fredrickson, Barbara. *Love 2.0: How Our Supreme Emotion Affects Everything We Think, Do, Feel, and Become*. Hudson Street Press, 2013.

- Fredrickson, Barbara. *Positivity*. Three Rivers Press (CA), 2009.

- Langer, Ellen J. *Mindfulness*. A Merloyd Lawrence Book of Addison Wesley, New York. 1989.

- Seligman, Martin EP, and Mihaly Csikszentmihalyi. Positive psychology: an introduction. *American Psychologist*. 2000;55(1):5-14.

- Seligman, Martin EP. *Flourish: A Visionary New Understanding of Happiness and Well-being*. Simon and Schuster, 2012.

- Peterson, Christopher, and Martin E.P. Seligman. *Character Strengths and Virtues: A Handbook and Classification*. Oxford University Press, 2004.

- Tay, Louis, and Ed Diener. "Needs and subjective well-being around the world." *Journal of Personality and Social Psychology* 101, no. 2 (2011): 354.

- Covey, Steven R. *The 7 Habits of Highly Effective People: Powerful Lessons in Personal Change*. New York, NY: Simon & Schuster; 1989.

- Seligman, Martin EP. *Learned Optimism: How to Change Your Mind and Your Life*. New York, NY: Simon & Schuster; 1998.

- Seligman, Martin EP. *Authentic Happiness: Using the New Positive Psychology to Realize Your Potential for Lasting Fulfillment.* New York, NY: Simon & Schuster; 2002.

- Reivich, Karen, and Andrew Shatte. *The Resilience Factor: Seven Essential Skills For Overcoming Life's Inevitable Obstacles.* Three Rivers Press; 2003.

- Peterson, Christopher, and Martin Seligman. *Character Strengths and Virtues: A Handbook and Classification.* New York: Oxford University Press/Washington, DC: American Psychological Association; 2004.

- Peterson Christopher. *A Primer in Positive Psychology.* Oxford University Press; 2006.

- Dweck, Carol. *Mindset: The New Psychology of Success; How We Can Learn to Reach Our Potential.* Ballantine Books; 2007.

- Langer, Ellen J. *Mindfulness.* Da Capo Press, 2014.

- Langer, Ellen J. *Counterclockwise: Mindful Health and the Power of Possibility.* Ballantine Books, 2009.

- Lyubomirsky, Sonja. *The How of Happiness: A New Approach to Getting the Life You Want,* New York, NY: Penguin Books; 2007.

- Seligman MEP. *Flourish: A Visionary New Understanding of Happiness and Wellbeing,* New York: Free Press; 2011.

- Kegan, Robert, and Lisa Laskow Lahey. *Immunity to Change: How to Overcome It and Unlock the Potential in Yourself and Your Organization* (Leadership for the common good) Harvard Business Review Press; 2009.

- Ganter, Rose. *Workplace Wellness: Performance with a Purpose.* Wellworks Publishing, LLC. Moon Township, PA, 2012.

- Wagnild, Gail. *True Resilience: Building a Life of Strength, Purpose, and Meaning.* Cape House Books, Allendale, NJ, 2014.

- Christakis, Nicholas A., and James H. Fowler. *Connected: The Surprising Power of Our Social Networks and How They Shape Our Lives.* Little Brown, 2009.

- Keltner, Dacher, Jason Marsh, and Jeremy Adam Smith (Editors). *The Compassionate Instinct: The Science of Human Goodness.* WW Norton & Company, 2010.

- For more information on the science of human goodness, see: http://greatergood.berkeley.edu/.

- For more information on positive psychology, see: https://www.authentichappiness.sas.upenn.edu/.

- Positive Psychology News Daily. Archives: http://archive.feedblitz.com/416792, Subscribe: http://www.feedblitz.com/f/f.fbz?Sub=416792

- Csikszentmihalyi, Mihaly. "Flow." In *Flow and the Foundations of Positive Psychology,* pp. 227-238. Springer. Netherlands, 2014.

- Csikszentmihalyi, Mihaly. *Finding Flow: The Psychology of Engagement with Everyday Life*. Basic Books, 1997.
- Csikszentmihalyi, Mihaly. *Flow: The Psychology of Optimal Experience*. Vol. 41. New York: HarperPerennial, 1991.
- Csikszentmihalyi, Mihaly. *Creativity, Flow and the Psychology of Discovery and Invention*. HarperCollins e-books. 2007.
- Csikszentmihalyi, Mihaly. "Happiness and creativity." *The Futurist* 31, no. 5 (1997): S8.
- Hooker, Charles, and Mihaly Csikszentmihalyi. "Flow, creativity, and shared leadership." *Shared Leadership: Reframing the Hows and Whys of Leadership* (2003): 217-34.
- Rosen, Robert H. *Just Enough Anxiety: The Hidden Driver of Business Success*. Penguin Group, New York, 2008

Chapter 13: Create Conditions for Positive Personal Motivation

- Ballard, Elise. *Epiphany: True Stories of Sudden Insight to Inspire, Encourage, and Transform*. Harmony Books, New York, 2011.
- Deci, Edward L., and Richard Flaste. *Why We Do What We Do*. Putnam Publishing Group, 1995.
- Ng, Johan YY, Nikos Ntoumanis, Cecilie Thøgersen-Ntoumani, Edward L. Deci, Richard M. Ryan, Joan L. Duda, and Geoffrey C. Williams. "Self-determination theory applied to health contexts a meta-analysis." *Perspectives on Psychological Science* 7, no. 4 (2012): 325-340.
- Pink, Daniel H. *Drive*. Riverhead Books of Penguin Group, New York. 2009.

SECTION IV: MEASURING AND COMMUNICATING WHAT MATTERS

Chapter 14: Measures That Matter

- http://www.grossnationalhappiness.com/9-domains/psychological-well-being/).
- Pawson, Ray, and Nick Tilley. *Realistic Evaluation*. Thousand Oaks, CA: Sage Publications. 1997.

Chapter 15: Evaluation Methods that Engage

- Hektner, Joel M., Jennifer A. Schmidt, and Mihaly Csikszentmihalyi. *Experience Sampling Method: Measuring the Quality of Everyday Life*. Sage, 2007.

Chapter 16: Methods that Enhance Perspective

- Aiken, Leona S., Stephen G. West, and Raymond R. Reno. *Multiple Regression: Testing and Interpreting Interactions.* Sage, 1991.
- Chen, Huey-Tsyh. *Practical Program Evaluation: Assessing and Improving Planning, Implementation, and Effectiveness.* Sage, 2005.
- Chen, Huey-Tsyh. *Theory-driven Evaluations.* Sage, 1990.
- Dalkin SM, Greenhalgh J, Jones D, Cunningham B, Lhussier M. "What's in a mechanism? Development of a key concept in realist evaluation." *Implementation Science.* 2015 Apr 16;10(1):49.

Chapter 17: Communication that Motivates

- Duarte, Nancy. *Slide:ology: The Art and Science of Creating Great Presentations.* Toronto, ON: O'Reilly Media, 2008.
- Duarte, Nancy. *Resonate: Present Visual Stories that Transform Audiences.* John Wiley & Sons, 2013.
- Tufte, Edward R., and P. R. Graves-Morris. *The Visual Display of Quantitative Information.* Vol. 2, no. 9. Cheshire, CT: Graphics press, 1983.
- Tufte, Edward R. "Envisioning information." *Optometry & Vision Science* 68, no. 4 (1991): 322-324.
- Tufte, Edward R. *"Beautiful Evidence."* New York (2006).
- Further information, including a moderated forum and a number of articles by and about Edward Tufte, are available on his website: http://www.edwardtufte.com.
- United Kingdon Measures of National Well-being: http://www.neighbourhood.statistics.gov.uk/HTMLDocs/dvc146/wrapper.html.

Appendix E
Measurement That Drives Values—Bhutan and the United Kingdom

In chapter 14, we described the development philosophy of the country of Bhutan and their approach to measuring Gross National Happiness (GNH) as a means to guide their "development path with values." They view GNH as their "National Conscience guiding us towards making wise decisions for a better future." Bhutan's approach to measuring GNH is a great example of a measuring and communicating what matters. Bhutan has adopted an alternative to the financial indicator of the success, and sees their measurement process as a means to drive improvement in the things the country and its citizen's value.

The GNH Index wishes to respect diversity and freedom of choice and to also acknowledge the limitations of quantitative measures. Hence it identifies as happy any person who has achieved sufficiency in six of the nine dimensions, or in 66 percent of the weighted indicators. This allows for diversity in different ways. First, not all indicators are relevant to all people—wildlife damage to crops is not relevant to urban populations. Second, every person may not need sufficiency in 100 percent of the indicators to be happy; they may focus on some areas, depending on their own values and skills. Third, if people have a core of achievements, they may be able to compensate internally for other deficits. A person without education or electricity can find other routes to GNH."[233]

An interesting aspect of Bhutan's GNH index is that it uses two types of thresholds: sufficiency thresholds, and one happiness threshold. The index looks not only at the percent of its population who are happy, but the percent of dimensions in which "not yet happy" people "enjoy sufficiency." Bhutan's 33 indicators and nine dimensions are outlined in table 21, along with individual weighting for each indicator.

We include this example of measuring what matters in Bhutan (see table 21) because we believe it is relevant to our organizations for a number of reasons. Bhutan's dimensions closely parallel those that any organization should find meaningful. The dimensions reflect a deep sense of caring for the well-being and happiness of its citizens as well as a profound sense of compassion for the ecology and culture of the region. We believe that organizations should not only care deeply about the health of the organization, but also about the health of their employees, the health of the larger ecology, economy, and communities that surround them. For more information on the story of Bhutan's GNH philosophy, please see: http://www.gnhbhutan.org/.

Table 21. Bhutan's Gross National Happiness domains and indicators

Relative Weights

Domain	Indicators	Weight	Domain	Indicators	Weight
Psychological well-being	Life satisfaction	33%	Time use	Work	50%
	Positive emotions	17%			
	Negative emotions	17%		Sleep	50%
	Spirituality	33%			
Health	Self-reported health	10%	Good Governance	Political participation	40%
	Healthy days	30%		Services	40%
	Disability	30%		Governmental Performance	10%
	Mental health	30%		Fundamental rights	10%
Education	Literacy	30%	Community Vitality	Donation (time & money)	30%
	Schooling	30%		Safety	30%
	Knowledge	20%		Community relationship	20%
	Value	20%		Family	20%
Cultural Diversity & Resilience	Zorig chusum skills (13 arts & crafts)	30%	Ecological diversity & Resilience	Wildlife damage	40%
	Cultural participation	30%		Urban issues	40%
	Speak native language	20%		Responsibility towards environment	10%
	Driglam Namzha (Etiquette)	20%		Ecological issues	10%
			Living Standard	Per capita income	33%
				Assets	33%
				Housing	33%

United Kingdom

If the measurement approach of a small country in the Eastern Himalayas does not resonate with you, other Western countries are beginning to adopt similar approaches. In 2010, the United Kingdom augmented its Gross Domestic Product measures to include a much broader set of dimensions that include the health and well-being of its citizens. Table 22 outlines the UK's full set of dimensions and measures. Annual progress on each indicators is available in a very engaging and interactive infographic at
http://www.neighbourhood.statistics.gov.uk/HTMLDocs/dvc146/wrapper.html.

Table 22. Dimensions and Measures for National Well-being United Kingdom

Proposed domain and measure

Personal Well-being
- Percentage with very high rating of satisfaction with their lives overall
- Percentage with very high rating of how worthwhile the things they do are
- Percentage who rated their happiness yesterday as medium or high
- Percentage who rated how anxious they were yesterday as low or very low

Our Relationships
- Average rating of satisfaction with family life on a scale from 0 to 10
- Average rating of satisfaction with social life on a scale from 0 to 10
- Percentage who said they had one or more people they could really count on in a crisis

Health
- Healthy life expectancy at birth
- Percentage who reported a long-term illness and a disability
- Percentage who were somewhat, mostly or completely satisfied with their health
- Percentage with some evidence indicating probable psychological disturbance or mental ill health

What we do
- Unemployment rate
- Percentage who were somewhat, mostly or completely satisfied with their job
- Percentage who were somewhat, mostly or completely satisfied with their amount of leisure time
- Percentage who were somewhat, mostly or completely satisfied with their leisure time
- Percentage who volunteered in the last 12 months

Where we live
- Crimes against the person (per 1,000 adults)
- Percentage who felt very or fairly safe and walking alone after dark
- Percentage who accessed green spaces at least once a week in England
- Percentage who agreed or agreed strongly that they felt they belonged to their neighbourhood

Personal finance
- Percentage of individuals living in households with less than 60 percent of median income after housing costs
- Mean wealth per household, including pension wealth
- Percentage who were somewhat, mostly or completely satisfied with their income of their household
- Percentage who report finding it quite or very difficult to get by financially

Education and skills
- Human capital – the value of individuals' skills, knowledge and competences in the labour market
- Percentage with 5 or more grades A*–C including English and Maths
- Percentage ok UK residents aged 16 to 64 with no qualifications

The economy
- Real household income per head
- Net National Income of the UK (£ million)
- UK Net National debt as a percentage of Gross Domestic Product
- Consumer Price Inflation index (2005=100)

References

1 Porter, Michael E., and Mark R. Kramer, "Creating Shared Value," *Harvard Business Review* 89, no. 1/2 (2011): 62–77.

2 Grad, Frank P. "The preamble of the constitution of the World Health Organization." *Bulletin of the World Health Organization* 80, no. 12 (2002): 981-981.

3 Travis, John W., and Regina Sara Ryan. *The Wellness Workbook*. Ten Speed Press, 1988.

4 Travis, John W., and Meryn G. Callander. *Wellness for Helping Professionals: Creating Compassionate Cultures*. Wellness Assoc, 1990.

5 Travis, John. *Wellness: Small Changes You Can Use to Make a Big Difference*. Ten Speed Press, 1991.

6 Ardell, Donald B. *High Level Wellness, an Alternative to Doctors, Drugs, and Disease*. Bantam Books, 1979.

7 Ardell, Donald B. "The nature and implications of high level wellness, or why 'normal health' is a rather sorry state of existence." *Health Values* 3, no. 1 (1979): 17-24.

8 Hermon, David A., and Richard J. Hazler. "Adherence to a Wellness Model and Perceptions of Psychological Well-Being." *Journal of Counseling & Development* 77, no. 3 (1999): 339-343.

9 Hettler, Bill. *"Six Dimensions of Wellness."* National Wellness Institute (www. nwi. org), and http://www. hettler.com/sixdimen. htm (1976).

10 Yen, Louis Tze-ching, Dee W. Edington, and Pam Witting. "Associations between health risk appraisal scores and employee medical claims costs in a manufacturing company." *American Journal of Health Promotion* 6, no. 1 (1991): 46-54.

11 Burton, Wayne N., Chin-Yu Chen, Alyssa B. Schultz, and Dee W. Edington. "The economic costs associated with body mass index in a workplace." *Journal of Occupational and Environmental Medicine* 40, no. 9 (1998): 786-792.

12 Yen, Louis Tze-ching, Dee W. Edington, and Pamela Witting. "Prediction of prospective medical claims and absenteeism costs for 1284 hourly workers from a manufacturing company." *Journal of Occupational and Environmental Medicine* 34, no. 4 (1992): 428-435.

[13] Edington, Dee W., Louis Tze-ching Yen, and Pamela Witting. "The financial impact of changes in personal health practices." *Journal of Occupational and Environmental Medicine* 39, no. 11 (1997): 1037-1046.

[14] Yen, Louis Tze-ching, D. W. Edington, and Pam Witting. "Associations between employee health-related measures and prospective medical insurance costs in a manufacturing company." *American Journal of Health Promotion* 6 (1991): 46-54.

[15] Broadhead, W. Eugene, Berton H. Kaplan, Sherman A. James, Edward H. Wagner, Victor J. Schoenbach, Roger Grimson, Siegfried Heyden, GŌSTA TIBBLIN, and Stephen H. Gehlbach. "The epidemiologic evidence for a relationship between social support and health." *American Journal of Epidemiology* 117, no. 5 (1983): 521-537.

[16] Uchino, Bert N., John T. Cacioppo, and Janice K. Kiecolt-Glaser. "The relationship between social support and physiological processes: a review with emphasis on underlying mechanisms and implications for health." *Psychological Bulletin* 119, no. 3 (1996): 488.

[17] Uchino, Bert N. "Social support and health: a review of physiological processes potentially underlying links to disease outcomes." *Journal of Behavioral Medicine* 29, no. 4 (2006): 377-387.

[18] Staniute, Margarita, Julija Brozaitiene, and Robertas Bunevicius. "Effects of social support and stressful life events on health-related quality of life in coronary artery disease patients." *Journal of Cardiovascular Nursing* 28, no. 1 (2013): 83-89.

[19] Seligman, Martin E.P., and Mihaly Csikszentmihalyi. "Positive Psychology: an Introduction." *American Psychologist.* 2000;55(1):5-14.

[20] Schulman, P. "Applying learned optimism to increase sales productivity." *The Journal of Personal Selling and Sales Management. 1999;* 19(1): 31-37.

[21] Kamen, L. P., and Martin E. P. Seligman. "Explanatory style predicts college grade point average." *Unpublished manuscript,* University of Pennsylvania, Philadelphia (1985).

[22] Nolen-Hoeksema S, JS Girgus, MEP Seligman. "Learned helplessness in children: A longitudinal study of depression, achievement, and explanatory style." *Journal of Personality and Social Psychology.* 1986;51: 435-442.

[23] Peterson, Christopher, LC Barrett. "Explanatory style and academic performance among university freshman." *Journal of Personality and Social Psychology.* 1987;53:603-606.

[24] Sharot, Tali. "The optimism bias." *Current Biology* 21, no. 23 (2011): R941-R945.

[25] Maruta, Toshihiko, Robert C. Colligan, Michael Malinchoc, and Kenneth P. Offord.

"Optimists vs pessimists: survival rate among medical patients over a 30-year period." In *Mayo Clinic Proceedings*, vol. 75, no. 2, pp. 140-143. Elsevier, 2000.

[26] Schou, I., Ø. Ekeberg, and C. M. Ruland. "The mediating role of appraisal and coping in the relationship between optimism-pessimism and quality of life."*PsychoOncology* 14, no. 9 (2005): 718-727.

[27] Nyce, Steven, Jessica Grossmeier, David R. Anderson, Paul E. Terry, and Bruce Kelley. "Association between changes in health risk status and changes in future health care costs: a multiemployer study." *Journal of Occupational and Environmental Medicine* 54, no. 11 (2012): 1364-1373.

[28] Burton, Wayne N., Chin-Yu Chen, Daniel J. Conti, Alyssa B. Schultz, and Dee W. Edington. "The association between health risk change and presenteeism change." *Journal of Occupational and Environmental Medicine* 48, no. 3 (2006): 252-263.

[29] Edington, Dee W., and Shirley Musich. "Associating changes in health risk levels with changes in medical and short-term disability costs." *Health Productivity Management* 3 (2004): 12-15.

[30] Sweetman, David, Fred Luthans, James B. Avey, and Brett C. Luthans. "Relationship between positive psychological capital and creative performance." *Canadian Journal of Administrative Sciences/Revue Canadienne des Sciences de l'Administration* 28, no. 1 (2011): 4-13.

[31] Shany, Hadar, and Oren Kaplan. "Are Happy Customer Service Representatives More Efficient? The Relationship Between Happiness and Work Performance Among Insurance Company Call Center Representatives." In *Toulon-Verona Conference "Excellence in Services."* 2014.

[32] Seligman, Martin EP. "Positive health." *Applied Psychology* 57, no. s1 (2008): 3-18.

[33] McIntosh, Daniel N., Michael J. Poulin, Roxane Cohen Silver, and E. Alison Holman. "The distinct roles of spirituality and religiosity in physical and mental health after collective trauma: a national longitudinal study of responses to the 9/11 attacks." *Journal of Behavioral Medicine* 34, no. 6 (2011): 497-507.

[34] Seybold, Kevin S., and Peter C. Hill. "The role of religion and spirituality in mental and physical health." *Current Directions in Psychological Science* 10, no. 1 (2001): 21-24.

[35] Baldwin, Christina. "Life's Companion: Journal Writing as a Spiritual Quest." Bantam, 1991.

[36] Hettler, Bill. "Six dimensions of wellness." National Wellness Institute (www. nwi. org), and http://www. hettler. com/sixdimen. htm (1976).

[37] Csikszentmihalyi, Mihaly. *Finding Flow: The Psychology of Engagement with Everyday Life*. Basic Books, 1997.

[38] Zhang, Xuanping, Susan L. Norris, Edward W. Gregg, and Gloria Beckles. "Social support and mortality among older persons with diabetes." *The Diabetes Educator* 33, no. 2 (2007): 273-281.

[39] Tomaka, Joe, Sharon Thompson, and Rebecca Palacios. "The relation of social isolation, loneliness, and social support to disease outcomes among the elderly." *Journal of Aging and Health* 18, no. 3 (2006): 359-384.

[40] Repetti, Rena L., Shelley E. Taylor, and Teresa E. Seeman. "Risky families: family social environments and the mental and physical health of offspring." *Psychological Bulletin* 128, no. 2 (2002): 330.

[41] Harter, James K., and M.S. Sangeeta Agrawal. *Causal Relationships Among Well-being Elements and Life, Work, and Health Outcomes*. Gallup, Washington, DC. 2012.

[42] Brown, Stephanie L., Randolph M. Nesse, Amiram D. Vinokur, and Dylan M. Smith. "Providing social support may be more beneficial than receiving it results from a prospective study of mortality." *Psychological Science* 14, no. 4 (2003): 320-327.

[43] Grant, Adam M. "Does intrinsic motivation fuel the prosocial fire? Motivational synergy in predicting persistence, performance, and productivity." *Journal of Applied Psychology* 93, no. 1 (2008): 48.

[44] Grant, Adam M., Elizabeth M. Campbell, Grace Chen, Keenan Cottone, David Lapedis, and Karen Lee. "Impact and the art of motivation maintenance: The effects of contact with beneficiaries on persistence behavior." *Organizational Behavior and Human Decision Processes* 103, no. 1 (2007): 53-67.

[45] Bright, David S., Kim S. Cameron, and Arran Caza. "The amplifying and buffering effects of virtuousness in downsized organizations." *Journal of Business Ethics* 64, no. 3 (2006): 249-269.

[46] Cameron, Kim S., and Marc Lavine. *Making the Impossible Possible: Leading Extraordinary Performance - The Rocky Flats Story.* Berrett-Koehler Publishers, 2006.

[47] Crocker, Jennifer, Noah Nuer, Marc-Andre Olivier, and Sam Cohen. "Egosystem and ecosystem: Two motivational orientations for the self." *Unpublished manuscript* (2006). Accessed on August 14, 2015. https://www.google.com/?gws_rd=ssl#q=Egosystem+and+ecosystem:+Two+motivational+orientations+for+the+self.

[48] Joel M. Podolny, Rakesh Khurana, and Marya Hill-Popper. "How to put meaning back into leading." *HBS Working Knowledge* (2005).

[49] *Burden of Stress in America Survey.* NPR/Robert Wood Johnson Foundation/Harvard School of Public Health. 2014.

[50] Braunstein, Alexandra, Yi Li, David Hirschland, Tim McDonald, and Dee W. Edington. "Internal associations among health-risk factors and risk prevalence." *American Journal of Health Behavior* 25, no. 4 (2001): 407-417.

[51] Lyubomirsky, Sonja. "Can Money Buy Happiness?" *Scientific American.* http://www.scientificamerican.com/article. cfm (2013).

[52] Li, Hongbin, Pak Wai Liu, Maoliang Ye, and Junsen Zhang. "Does money buy happiness? Evidence from twins in urban China." *Manuscript, Harvard University* (2011). Accessed on August 13, 2015. http://scholar.harvard.edu/files/maoliangye/files/ye_march6_2014_doesmoneybuyhappiness. pdf.

[53] Aknin, Lara Beth. (2012). "On Financial Generosity and Well-being: Where, When, and How Spending Money on Others Increases Happiness." (*Doctoral Dissertation*). Accessed on August 11, 2015. https://circle.ubc.ca/bitstream/handle/2429/42059/ubc_2012_spring_aknin_lara.pdf?sequenc e=1.

[54] Shin, Doh Chull. "How People Perceive and Appraise the Quality of Their Lives: Recent Advances in the Study of Happiness and Wellbeing." (2015). Accessed on May 21, 2015. http://escholarship.org/uc/item/0hq2v2wx.

55 Tay, Louis, and Ed Diener. "Needs and subjective well-being around the world." *Journal of Personality and Social Psychology* 101, no. 2 (2011): 354.

56 Maslow, Abraham, and A. Herzeberg. "Hierarchy of needs." *Motivation and Personality*. New York: Harper, 1954.

57 Deci, Edward L., and Richard M. Ryan. "The 'what' and 'why' of goal pursuits: Human needs and the self-determination of behavior." *Psychological Inquiry* 11, no. 4 (2000): 227-268.

58 Ryan, Richard M., and Edward L. Deci. "Self-determination theory and the facilitation of intrinsic motivation, social development, and well-being." *American Psychologist* 55, no. 1 (2000): 68.

59 Ryff, Carol D., and Corey Lee M. Keyes. "The structure of psychological well-being revisited." *Journal of Personality and Social Psychology* 69, no. 4 (1995): 719.

60 De Charms, Richard. *Personal Causation: The Internal Affective Determinants of Behavior*. Routledge, 2013.

61 Csikszentmihalyi, M. (1988). *Optimal Experience*. New York, NY: Cambridge University Press.

62 Rittel, Horst WJ, and Melvin M. Webber. "Dilemmas in a general theory of planning." *Policy Sciences* 4, no. 2 (1973): 155-169.

63 Blakely, John. "Coaching and systems thinking. Institute of Leadership and Management." Accessed October 5, 2015. https://www.i-l-m.com/Insight/Edge/2013/May/coaching-and-systems-thinking.

64 Quinn, Robert E. *Deep Change: Discovering the Leader Within*. Vol. 378. John Wiley & Sons, 2010.

65 Fera, Rae Ann. *Ken Robinson on the Principles of Creative Leadership*. Fast Company; Accessed October 5, 2015. http://www.fastcompany.com/1764044/ken-robinson-principles-creative-leadership.

66 Edington, Dee W. *Zero Trends: Health as a Serious Economic Strategy*. Health Management Research Center, University of Michigan. 2009.

67 Goetzel R, Roemer E. Chung, RC Liss-Levinson, DK Samoly. "Workplace Health Promotion: Policy recommendations that encourage employers to support health improvement programs for their workers." 2008. Partnership for Prevention.

68 ODonnell, Michael P., Carol Bishop, and Karen Kaplan. "Benchmarking best practices in

workplace health promotion." *American Journal of Health Promotion* 1 (1997): 1.

[69] Pronk, Nicolaas P. "Population Health Management at the Worksite." In *ACSM's Worksite Health Handbook: A guide to Building Healthy and Productive Companies* / American College of Sports Medicine; Nicolaas P. Pronk, editor. 2nd Edition. 2009.

[70] Hunnicutt, David, and B. Leffelman. "WELCOA's 7 Benchmarks of Success." *Absolute Advantage* 6 (2006): 3-29.

[71] Berry, Leonard, Ann M. Mirabito, and William B. Baun. "What's the hard return on employee wellness programs?" *Harvard Business Review*, December (2010): 2012-68.

[72] Pronk, Nicolaas. "Best practice design principles of worksite health and wellness programs." *ACSM's Health & Fitness Journal* 18, no. 1 (2014): 42-46.

[73] US Department of Health and Human Services. *Healthy People 2010*. US Department of Health and Human Services, 2000.

[74] Kegan, Robert, and Lisa Laskow Lahey. *Immunity to Change: How to Overcome it and Unlock Potential in Yourself and Your Organization*. Harvard Business Press, 2009.

[75] See more at: https://www.presencing.com/node/119#sthash.igpLcMsR.dpuf

[76] https://www.youtube.com/watch?v=HOPfVVMCwYg

[77] Brown, Tim. "Design thinking." *Harvard Business Review* 86, no. 6 (2008): 84.

[78] *10 Steps for Developing Core Values. Accessed on October 29, 2015.*
http://deliveringhappiness.com/work/10-steps-for-developing-core-values/#sthash.ywYw7D6K.dpuf

[89] Marzec, M., Tom Golaszewski, P. Powers, and Dee W. Edington. "Effects of environmental changes on employee health risks: A pilot study." *International Journal of Workplace Health Management* 4, no. 3 (2011): 200-203.

[80] Hoebbel, Cassandra, Thomas Golaszewski, Mya Swanson, and Joan Dorn. "Associations between the worksite environment and perceived health culture." *American Journal of Health Promotion* 26, no. 5 (2012): 301-304.

[81] Golaszewski, Thomas, and Brian Fisher. "Heart check: the development and evolution of an

organizational heart health assessment." *American Journal of Health Promotion* 17, no. 2 (2002): 132-153.

[82] Golaszewski, Thomas, Judd Allen, and Dee Edington. "Working together to create supportive environments in worksite health promotion." *American Journal of Health Promotion: AJHP* 22, no. 4 (2007): 1-10.

[83] Cooperrider, David L., Diana Kaplin Whitney, and Jacqueline M. Stavros. *Appreciative Inquiry Handbook*. Vol. 1. Berrett-Koehler Publishers, 2003.

[84] Cooperrider, David, and Diana D. Whitney. *Appreciative inquiry: A Positive Revolution in Change*. Berrett-Koehler Publishers, 2005.

[85] Ludema, James D., David L. Cooperrider, and Frank J. Barrett. "Appreciative inquiry: The power of the unconditional positive question." *Handbook of Action Research: The Concise Paperback Edition* (2006): 155-165.

[86] Kolko, Jon. *Exposing the Magic of Design: A Practitioner's Guide to the Methods and Theory of Synthesis*. Oxford University Press, 2010.

[87] Blanchard, Ken, and Jesse Stoner. "The vision thing: Without it you'll never be a world-class organization." *Leader to Leader* 2004, no. 31 (2004): 21-28.

[88] Blanchard, Ken, and Jesse Stoner. *Full Steam Ahead!: Unleash the Power of Vision in Your Work and Your Life*. Berrett-Koehler Publishers, 2011.

[89] "Ken Robinson on the principles of creative leadership." Accessed on October 29, 2015. http://www.fastcompany.com/1764044/ken-robinson-principles-creative-leadership.

[90] Prochaska, James O., and Wayne F. Velicer. "The transtheoretical model of health behavior change." *American Journal of Health Promotion* 12, no. 1 (1997): 38-48.

[91] Becker, Marshall H., and Lois A. Maiman. "Sociobehavioral determinants of compliance with health and medical care recommendations." *Medical care* 13, no. 1 (1975): 10-24.

[92] Bandura, Albert. "Social cognitive theory: An agentic perspective." *Annual Review of Psychology* 52, no. 1 (2001): 1-26.

[93] Miller, W. R., and S. Rollnick. *Motivational Interviewing: Preparing People to Change Addictive Behavior.* New York: Guilford Press, (1991).

[94] Funnell, Sue C., and Patricia J. Rogers. *Purposeful Program Theory: Effective Use of Theories of Change and Logic Models.* John Wiley and Sons, 2011.

[95] Bickman L. "The Functions of Program Theory" In *Using Program Theory in Evaluation,* edited by L. Bickman. San Franciso: Jossey-Bass.

[96] Wholey, Joseph S. "Evaluability assessment: Developing program theory." *New Directions for Program Evaluation* 1987, no. 33 (1987): 77-92.

[97] Chen, Huey-Tsyh, and Peter H. Rossi. "The multi-goal, theory-driven approach to evaluation: A model linking basic and applied social science." *Social Forces* 59, no. 1 (1980): 106-122.

[98] Phillips, Robbin, Greg Cordell, Geno Church, and Spike Jones. *Brains on Fire: Igniting Powerful, Sustainable, Word-of-mouth Movements.* John Wiley & Sons, Inc., Hoboken, NJ. 2010.

[99] "Time use on an average work day for employed persons ages 25 to 54 with children." Bureau of Labor Statistics, American Time Use Survey. http://www.bls.gov/tus/charts/. Accessed January 17, 2013.

[100] "Buck Survey. Working well: A Global Survey of Health Promotion and Workplace Wellness Strategies. Executive Summary." Available from: http://www.hreonline.com/pdfs/ 04012011Extra BuckSurvey.pdf Published 2011. Accessed May 27, 2014.

[101] Hoebbel, Cassandra, Thomas Golaszewski, Mya Swanson, and Joan Dorn. "Associations between the worksite environment and perceived health culture." *American Journal of Health Promotion* 26, no. 5 (2012): 301-304.

[102] Pronk, Nicolaas. P., and C. U. Allen. "A culture of health: creating and sustaining supportive organizational environments for health." *ACSM's Worksite Health Handbook, Second Edition. A Guide to Building Healthy and Productive Companies.* Human Kinetics, Champaign, IL. (2009).

[103] Golaszewski, Thomas, Judd Allen, and Dee Edington. "Working together to create supportive environments in worksite health promotion." *American Journal of Health Promotion:*

AJHP 22, no. 4 (2007): 1-10.

104 Rousseau, DM. in *Macro-Organizational Factors*, Hurrell Jr, JJ, Lennart L, Murphy, LR, Sauter SL, Editor, *Encyclopedia of Occupational Health and Safety*, Jeanne Mager Stellman, Editor-in-Chief. International Labor Organization, Geneva. 2011.

105 Cameron, Kim S., Jane E. Dutton, Robert E. Quinn. (Editors). *Positive Organizational Scholarship: Foundations of a New Discipline*. 2003. Berrett-Koehler, San Francisco.

106 Cameron, Kim S., Gretchen Spreitzer. (Editors). *The Oxford Handbook of Positive Organizational Scholarship*. Oxford University Press, New York, 2012.

107 Dutton, Jane, MA Glynn, Gretchen Spreitzer. "Positive organizational scholarship." In J. Greenhaus and G. Callahan, (Eds.) *Encyclopedia of Career Development*, 2006, Sage, Thousand Oaks

108 Cameron, Kim S., David Bright, and Arran Caza. "Exploring the relationships between organizational virtuousness and performance." *American Behavioral Scientist* 47, no. 6 (2004): 766-790.

109 Schein, Edgar. *Organizational Culture and Leadership*. Jossey-Bass. 1992.

110 Lok, Peter, and John Crawford. "The effect of organisational culture and leadership style on job satisfaction and organisational commitment: A cross-national comparison." *Journal of Management Development* 23, no. 4 (2004): 321-338.

111 Tims, Maria, Arnold B. Bakker, and Despoina Xanthopoulou. "Do transformational leaders enhance their followers' daily work engagement?." *The Leadership Quarterly* 22, no. 1 (2011): 121-131.

112 Goleman, Daniel, Richard Boyatzis, and Annie McKee. *Primal Leadership: Unleashing the Power of Emotional Intelligence*. Harvard Business Press, 2013.

113 Kuoppala, Jaana, Anne Lamminpää, Juha Liira, and Harri Vainio. "Leadership, job well-being, and health effects—a systematic review and a meta-analysis." *Journal of Occupational and Environmental Medicine* 50, no. 8 (2008): 904-915.

114 Gurt, Jochen, Christian Schwennen, and Gabriele Elke. "Health-specific leadership: Is there an association between leader consideration for the health of employees and their strain and well-being?" *Work & Stress* 25, no. 2 (2011): 108-127.

[115] Michie, Susan, and Sian Williams. "Reducing work related psychological ill health and sickness absence: a systematic literature review." *Occupational and Environmental Medicine* 60, no. 1 (2003): 3-9.

[116] Cameron, Kim S., Jane E. Dutton, Robert E. Quinn, and Amy Wrzesniewski. "Developing a discipline of positive organizational scholarship." *Positive Organizational Scholarship. Foundations of a New Discipline,* Berrett-Koehler Publishers, San Francisco (2003): 361-370.

[117] Seligman, Martin EP. "The president's address." *American Psychologist* 54, no. 8 (1999): 559-562.

[118] Srivastva, Suresh, and D. L. Cooperrider. "Appreciative Inquiry into Organizational Life." *Research in Organizational Change and Development* 1 (1987).

[119] Burns, J.M. *Leadership.* NY: Harper and Row, 1978.

[120] Bass, Bernard M. *Leadership and Performance.* NY: Free Press, 1985.

[121] Bass, Bernard M., and Ron E. Riggio. *Transformational Leadership.* New Jersey: Lawrence Erlbaum Associates, Inc., 2008

[122] Hatter, John J., and Bernard M. Bass. "Superiors' evaluations and subordinates' perceptions of transformational and transactional leadership." *Journal of Applied Psychology* 73, no. 4 (1988): 695.

[123] Koh, William L., Richard M. Steers, and James R. Terborg. "The effects of transformational leadership on teacher attitudes and student performance in Singapore." *Journal of Organizational Behavior* 16, no. 4 (1995): 319-333.

[124] Bycio, Peter, Rick D. Hackett, and Joyce S. Allen. "Further assessments of Bass's (1985) conceptualization of transactional and transformational leadership." *Journal of Applied Psychology* 80, no. 4 (1995): 468.

[125] Barling, Julian, Tom Weber, and E. Kevin Kelloway. "Effects of transformational leadership training on attitudinal and financial outcomes: A field experiment." *Journal of Applied Psychology* 81, no. 6 (1996): 827.

[126] Howell, Jane M., and Bruce J. Avolio. "Transformational leadership, transactional leadership, locus of control, and support for innovation: Key predictors of consolidated-business-unit performance." *Journal of Applied Psychology* 78, no. 6 (1993): 891.

[127] Aarons, Gregory A. "Transformational and transactional leadership: Association with attitudes toward evidence-based practice." *Psychiatric Services* 57, no. 8 (2006): 1162-1169.

[128] Cameron, Kim S. *Positive Leadership: Strategies for Extraordinary Performance.* Berrett-Koehler Publishers, 2012.

[129] Owens, B., W. Baker, and Kim Cameron. (2011). *Relational Energy at Work: Establishing Construct, Nomological, and Predictive Validity.* Presented at the Academy of Management Meetings, San Antonio, Texas.

[130] Baker, Wayne, Rob Cross, and Melissa Wooten. "Positive organizational network analysis and energizing relationships." *Positive Organizational Scholarship: Foundations of a New Discipline* (2003):328-342.

[131] Seligman, Martin EP. "Positive psychology, positive prevention, and positive therapy." *Handbook of Positive Psychology* 2 (2002): 3-12.

[132] Buckingham, Marcus, and Donald O. Clifton. *Now, Discover Your Strengths.* Simon and Schuster, 2001.

[133] Clifton, Donald O., and James K. Harter. "Investing in strengths." *Positive Organizational Scholarship: Foundations of a New Discipline* (2003): 111-121.

[134] Sawyer, Keith. *Group Genius: The Creative Power of Collaboration.* Basic Books, 2008.

[135] Castelli, W. P. "Epidemiology of coronary heart disease: the Framingham study." *The American Journal of Medicine* 76, no. 2 (1984): 4-12.

[136] Christakis, Nicholas A., and James H. Fowler. *Connected: The Surprising Power of Our Social Networks and How They Shape Our Lives.* Little, Brown, 2009.

[137] Christakis, Nicholas A., and James H. Fowler. "The spread of obesity in a large social network over 32 years." *New England Journal of Medicine* 357, no. 4 (2007): 370-379.

[138] Fowler, James H., and Nicholas A. Christakis. "Dynamic spread of happiness in a large social network: longitudinal analysis over 20 years in the Framingham Heart Study." *BMJ* 337 (2008): a2338.

[139] Christakis, Nicholas A., and James H. Fowler. "The collective dynamics of smoking in a large social network." *New England Journal of Medicine* 358, no. 21 (2008): 2249-2258.

[140] Brafman, Ori, and Rom Brafman. *Sway: The Irresistible Pull of Irrational Behavior.* Crown Business, 2008.

[141] Heath, Chip, and Dan Heath. *Switch.* Vintage Espanol, 2011.

[142] Thaler, Richard H., and Cass R. Sunstein. *Nudge: Improving Decisions About Health, Wealth and Happiness.* UK: Penguin, 2012.

[143] Kahneman, Daniel. *Thinking, Fast and Slow.* Macmillan, 2011.

[144] Sunstein, Cass R. "Storrs Lectures: Behavioral Economics and Paternalism" *Yale LJ* 122 (2012): 1826.

[145] Fitzgerald, CJ. "Evolution in the office: How evolutionary psychology can increase employee health happiness and productivity." *Evolutionary Psychology.* 2012;10(5):770-781.

[146] Leather, Phil, Mike Pyrgas, Di Beale, and Claire Lawrence. "Windows in the workplace sunlight, view, and occupational stress." *Environment and Behavior* 30, no. 6 (1998): 739-762.

[147] Wells, Meredith, and Rose Perrine. "Critters in the cube farm: Perceived psychological and organizational effects of pets in the workplace." *Journal of Occupational Health Psychology* 6, no. 1 (2001): 81.

[148] Wood, Lisa, Billie Giles-Corti, and Max Bulsara. "The pet connection: Pets as a conduit for social capital?" *Social Science & Medicine* 61, no. 6 (2005): 1159-1173.

[149] Kellert, Stephen R. *Building for Life: Designing and Understanding the Human-nature Connection.* Island Press, 2012.

[150] Bodin, Maria, and Terry Hartig "Does the outdoor environment matter for psychological restoration gained through running?" *Psychology of Sport and Exercise* 4, no. 2 (2003): 141-153.

[151] Berman, Marc G., John Jonides, and Stephen Kaplan. "The cognitive benefits of interacting with nature." *Psychological Science* 19, no. 12 (2008): 1207-1212.

[152] Weinstein, Netta, Andrew K. Przybylski, and Richard M. Ryan. "Can nature make us more caring? Effects of immersion in nature on intrinsic aspirations and generosity." *Personality and Social Psychology Bulletin* 35, no. 10 (2009): 1315-1329.

[153] Ford, Rochelle L., Joanna Jenkins, and Sheryl Oliver. "A Millennial Perspective on Diversity & Multiculturalism." *American Advertising Federation* (2011).

[154] Brack, Jessica. "Maximizing Millennials in the workplace." *UNC Executive Development* (2012): 1-14.

[155] Stewart, James B. "Looking for a Lesson in Google's Perks." The New York Times —Business Day. 15 March 2013. Web. 24 July 2014. <http://www.nytimes.com/2013/03/16/business/at-google-a-place-to-work-and-play.html?pagewanted=all&_r=0>

[156] Caldwell, David F., and Charles A. O'Reilly. "Measuring person-job fit with a profile-comparison process." *Journal of Applied Psychology* 75, no. 6 (1990): 648.

[157] Kristof-Brown, Amy L., Ryan D. Zimmerman, and Erin C. Johnson. "Consequences of individuals' fit at work: a meta-analysis of person–job, person–organization, person–group, and person–supervisor fit." *Personnel Psychology* 58, no. 2 (2005): 281-342.

[158] Robinson, Ken. *Finding Your Element: How to Discover Your Talents and Passions and Transform Your Life.* K: Penguin, 2013.

[159] Wrzesniewski, Amy, and Jane E. Dutton. "Crafting a job: Revisioning employees as active crafters of their work." *Academy of Management Review* 26, no. 2 (2001): 179-201.

[160] Pratt, MG, and BE Ashforth. "Fostering meaningfulness in working and in work." In K. S. Cameron, J. E. Dutton, and R. E. Quinn (Eds.), *Positive Organizational Scholarship: Foundations of a New Discipline* (pp. 309–327). San Francisco, CA: Berrett-Koehler, 2003.

[161] Fried, Yitzhak, Adam M. Grant, Ariel S. Levi, Michael Hadani, and Linda Haynes Slowik. "Job design in temporal context: A career dynamics perspective." *Journal of Organizational Behavior* 28, no. 7 (2007): 911-927.

[162] Berg, Justin M., Amy Wrzesniewski, and Jane E. Dutton. "Perceiving and responding to challenges in job crafting at different ranks: When proactivity requires adaptivity." *Journal of Organizational Behavior* 31, no. 2-3 (2010): 158-186.

[163] Berg, Justin M, Jane E. Dutton, Amy Wrzesniewski. "Job crafting and meaningful work." In B.J. Dik, Z. S. Byrne & M. F. Steger (Eds.), *Purpose and Meaning in the Workplace* (pp. 81-104). Washington, DC: *American Psychological Association*, 2013.

[164] Wrzesniewski, Amy, and Jane E. Dutton. "Crafting a job: Revisioning employees as active crafters of their work." *Academy of Management Review* 26, no. 2 (2001): 179-201.

[165] Job Crafting Exercise. Accessed on October 29, 2015. http://positiveorgs.bus.umich.edu/cpo-ools/job-crafting-exercise/.

[166] Allen, Judd. *Bringing Wellness Home: How to Create a Household Subculture that Supports Wellness Lifestyle Goals.* Human Resources Institute, LLC. 2010.

[167] Senge, Peter M. *The Fifth Discipline: The Art and Practice of the Learning Organization.* New York: Doubleday, 2006.

[168] Values in Action Institute on Character. Accessed on October 29, 2015. http://www.viacharacter.org/www/.

[169] Seligman, Martin E.P. *Helplessness: On Depression, Development, and Death. Second edition.* New York: W.H. Freeman, 1991.

[170] Lyubomirsky, Sonja, Laura King, and Ed Diener. "The benefits of frequent positive affect: does happiness lead to success?" *Psychological Bulletin* 131, no. 6 (2005): 803.

[171] Glenberg, Arthur M., David Havas, Raymond Becker, and Mike Rinck. "Grounding language in bodily states." *TeAm YYePG* (2005): 115.

[172] Carney, Dana R., Amy JC Cuddy, and Andy J. Yap. "Power posing brief nonverbal displays affect neuroendocrine levels and risk tolerance." *Psychological Science* 21, no. 10 (2010): 1363-1368.

[173] Doidge, Norman. *The Brain that Changes Itself: Stories of Personal Triumph from the Frontiers of Brain Science.* New York: Penguin, 2007.

[174] James, William. "Habit." *Popular Science Monthly.* February 1887.

[175] Hanson, Rick. *Buddha's brain: The Practical Neuroscience of Happiness, Love, and Wisdom.* New Harbinger Publications, 2009.

[176] Luders, Eileen, Arthur W. Toga, Natasha Lepore, and Christian Gaser. "The underlying anatomical correlates of long-term meditation: larger hippocampal and frontal volumes of gray matter." *Neuroimage* 45, no. 3 (2009): 672-678.

[177] Kurth, Florian, Eileen Luders, Brian Wu, and David S. Black. "Brain Gray Matter Changes Associated with Mindfulness Meditation in Older Adults: An Exploratory Pilot Study using Voxel-based Morphometry." *Neuro: Open Journal* 1, no. 1 (2014): 23.

[178] Kaliman, Perla, Maria Jesus Alvarez-Lopez, Marta Cosín-Tomás, Melissa A. Rosenkranz, Antoine Lutz, and Richard J. Davidson. "Rapid changes in histone deacetylases and inflammatory gene expression in expert meditators." *Psychoneuroendocrinology* 40 (2014): 96-107.

[179] Ramanchandran VJ. *The Neurons That Shaped Civilization.* Ted Talk. 2009. Available at: http://www.ted.com/talks/vs_ramachandran_the_neurons_that_shaped_civilization/ transcript ?language=en#t-362000. Accessed May 1, 2015.

[180] Kahneman, Daniel. *Thinking, Fast and Slow.* New York: Farrar, Straus and Giroux, 2011.

[181] Kahneman, Daniel. Comment made in a Ted Talk. February, 2010. Accessed Jan. 20, 2013. http://www.ted.com/talks/daniel_kahneman_the_riddle_of_experience_vs_memory.html.

[182] Csikszentmihalyi, Mihaly. *Flow: The Psychology of Optimal Experience.* New York: Harper and Row, 1990.

[183] Csikszentmihalyi, Mihaly. *Flow and the Psychology of Discovery and Invention.* New York: Harper Perennial, 1997.

[184] Seligman, Martin E.P. *Authentic Happiness: Using the New Positive Psychology to Realize Your Potential for Lasting Fulfillment.* New York: Atria (div. of Simon & Schuster), 2002.

[185] Peterson, Christopher, and Martin EP Seligman. *Character Strengths and Virtues: A Handbook and Classification.* Oxford University Press, 2004.

[186] Clifton D.O., Harter J.K. (2003) "Investing in Strengths." In K.S. Cameron, J.E. Dutton, & R.E. Quinn (Eds), *Positive Organizational Scholarship: Foundations of a New Discipline* (111-121).

San Francisco, Berrett-Koehler Publishers, Inc.

[187] Grossman, Paul, Ludger Niemann, Stefan Schmidt, and Harald Walach. "Mindfulness-based stress reduction and health benefits: A meta-analysis." *Journal of Psychosomatic Research* 57, no. 1 (2004): 35-43.

[188] Hofmann, Stefan G., Alice T. Sawyer, Ashley A. Witt, and Diana Oh. "The effect of mindfulness-based therapy on anxiety and depression: A meta-analytic review." *Journal of Consulting and Clinical Psychology* 78, no. 2 (2010): 169.

[189] Bohlmeijer, Ernst, Rilana Prenger, Erik Taal, and Pim Cuijpers. "The effects of mindfulness-based stress reduction therapy on mental health of adults with a chronic medical disease: A meta-analysis." *Journal of Psychosomatic Research* 68, no. 6 (2010): 539-544.

[190] Zernicke, Kristin A., Tavis S. Campbell, Philip K. Blustein, Tak S. Fung, Jillian A. Johnson, Simon L. Bacon, and Linda E. Carlson. "Mindfulness-based stress reduction for the treatment of irritable bowel syndrome symptoms: a randomized wait-list controlled trial." *International Journal of Behavioral Medicine* 20, no. 3 (2013): 385-396.

[191] Ott, Mary Jane, Rebecca L. Norris, and Susan M. Bauer-Wu. "Mindfulness meditation for oncology patients: a discussion and critical review." *Integrative Cancer Therapies* 5, no. 2 (2006): 98-108.

[192] Davidson, Richard J., Jon Kabat-Zinn, Jessica Schumacher, Melissa Rosenkranz, Daniel Muller, Saki F. Santorelli, Ferris Urbanowski, Anne Harrington, Katherine Bonus, and John F. Sheridan. "Alterations in brain and immune function produced by mindfulness meditation." *Psychosomatic Medicine* 65, no. 4 (2003): 564-570.

[193] Aikens, Kimberly A., John Astin, Kenneth R. Pelletier, Kristin Levanovich, Catherine M. Baase, Yeo Yung Park, and Catherine M. Bodnar. "Mindfulness goes to work: Impact of an online workplace intervention." *Journal of Occupational and Environmental Medicine* 56, no. 7 (2014):721-731.

[194] Shapiro, Shauna L., John A. Astin, Scott R. Bishop, and Matthew Cordova. "Mindfulness-based stress reduction for health care professionals: results from a randomized trial." *International Journal of Stress Management* 12, no. 2 (2005): 164.

[195] Pink, Daniel, H. *Drive: The Surprising Truth About What Motivates Us.* New York: Penguin Group, Inc 138 (2009): 240.

[196] Personal conversation with and presentation by Ed Deci at the Wellness Underground Conference. January 2015. Orlando Florida.

[197] Deci, Edward L., and Richard Flaste. *Why We Do What We Do.* Putnam Publishing Group, 1995.

[198] Deci, Edward L., Richard Koestner, and Richard M. Ryan. "A meta-analytic review of experiments examining the effects of extrinsic rewards on intrinsic motivation." *Psychological Bulletin* 125, no. 6 (1999): 627.

[199] Deci, Edward L., and Richard M. Ryan. *Handbook of Self-determination Research.* University of Rochester Press, 2002.

[200] de Charms, R. *Personal Causation.* New York (1968).

[201] Deci, Edward L., and Richard M. Ryan. *Intrinsic Motivation and Self-determination in Human Behavior.* Springer Science & Business Media, 1985.

[202] Deci, Edward L., James P. Connell, and Richard M. Ryan. "Self-determination in a work organization." *Journal of Applied Psychology* 74, no. 4 (1989): 580.

[203] Consensus Statement of the Health Enhancement Research Organization. "Guidance for a reasonably designed, employer-sponsored wellness program using outcomes-based incentives." *Journal of Occupational and Environmental Medicine* 54, no. 7 (2012): 889-896.

[204] Capps, Katherine and John B. Harkey. *Employee Health and Productivity Management Programs: The Use of Incentives, a Survey of Major US Employers.* Lyndhurst, New Jersey: IncentOne (2007).

[205] Mattke, S., Kandice Kapinos, John P. Caloyeras, Erin Audrey Taylor, Benjamin Batorsky, Hangsheng Liu, Kristin R. Van Busum, and Sydne Newberry, *RR-724-DOL,* 2014 (available at www.rand.org/t/RR724).

[206] Findings cited in "Best Practices: How Efficient Use of Health Incentive Dollars Increase ROI, Drive Wellness Program Engagement, and Encourage Long-Term Behavior Changes." Corporate Wellness Magazine. January 11, 2014.

[207] Stone, Dan N., Edward L. Deci, and Richard M. Ryan. "Beyond talk: Creating autonomous motivation through self-determination theory." *Journal of General Management* 34, no. 3 (2009):75.

[208] Gagné, Marylène, and Edward L. Deci. "Self-determination theory and work motivation." *Journal of Organizational Behavior* 26, no. 4 (2005): 331-362.

[209] Ryan, Richard M., and James P. Connell. "Perceived locus of causality and internalization: examining reasons for acting in two domains." *Journal of Personality and Social Psychology* 57, no. 5 (1989): 749.

[210] Deci, Edward L., Richard Koestner, and Richard M. Ryan. "Extrinsic rewards and intrinsic motivation in education: Reconsidered once again." *Review of Educational Research* 71, no. 1 (2001): 1-27.

[211] Ariely, Dan, U. Gneezy, G. Lowenstein, and N. Mazar. "Federal Reserver Bank of Boston Working Paper No. 05-11," July 2005: NY Times, 20 Nov. 2008.

[212] Baumeister, Roy F., Ellen Bratslavsky, Mark Muraven, and Dianne M. Tice. "Ego depletion: is the active self a limited resource?." *Journal of Personality and Social Psychology* 74, no. 5 (1998): 1252.

[213] Gailliot, Matthew T., and Roy F. Baumeister. "The physiology of willpower: Linking blood glucose to self-control." *Personality and Social Psychology Review* 11, no. 4 (2007): 303-327.

[214] McGonigal, Kelly. *"The willpower instinct: How self-control works, why it matters, and what you can do to get more of it."* Penguin, 2011.

[215] Ballard, Elise. *Epiphany: True Stories of Sudden Insight to Inspire, Encourage, and Transform.* Harmony Books, New York, 2011.

[216] Official website of Bhutan. Accessed on October 1, 2015. www.gnhbhutan.org.

[217] "9 domains of psychological wellbeing." Accessed on October 29, 2015. http://www.grossnationalhappiness.com/9-domains/psychological-well-being/).

[218] Maslow, Abraham Harold, Deborah Collins Stephens, Gary Heil, and Warren Bennis. *Maslow on Management.* New York: John Wiley, 1998.

[219] Hektner, Joel M., Jennifer A. Schmidt, and Mihaly Csikszentmihalyi. *Experience Sampling Method: Measuring the Quality of Everyday Life.* Sage, 2007.

[220] Merriam Webster. http://www.merriam-webster.com/dictionary/ethnography.

References

221 Babamoto, Kenneth S., Kwa A. Sey, Angela J. Camilleri, Vicki J. Karlan, Joana Catalasan, and Donald E. Morisky. "Improving diabetes care and health measures among hispanics using community health workers results from a randomized controlled trial." *Health Education & Behavior* 36, no. 1 (2009): 113-126.

222 Evans, Dale. April 2011. *The Internet of Things: How the Next Evolution of the Internet is Changing Everything.* Cisco Internet Business Solutions Group. Accessed on 5/28/15: https://www.cisco.com/web/about/ac79/docs/innov/IoT_IBSG_0411FINAL.pdf.

223 Baxter, Siyan, Kristy Sanderson, Alison J. Venn, C. Leigh Blizzard, and Andrew J. Palmer. "The relationship between return on investment and quality of study methodology in workplace health promotion programs." *American Journal of Health Promotion* 28, no. 6 (2014): 347-363.

224 Berwick, Donald M. "The science of improvement." *JAMA* 299, no. 10 (2008): 1182-1184.

225 World Health Organization. *Health Promotion Evaluation: Recommendations to Policy-makers: Report of the WHO European Working Group on Health Promotion Evaluation.* (1998).

226 Pawson Ray, and Nick Tilley. *Realistic Evaluation.* Thousand Oaks, CA: Sage Publications. 1997.

227 Dalkin SM, Greenhalgh J, Jones D, Cunningham B, Lhussier M. "What's in a mechanism? Development of a key concept in realist evaluation." *Implementation Science.* 2015 Apr 16;10(1):49.

228 Wilson, Sandra Jo, and Mark W. Lipsey. "School-based interventions for aggressive and disruptive behavior: Update of a meta-analysis." *American Journal of Preventive Medicine* 33, no. 2 (2007): S130-S143.

229 Landenberger, Nana A., and Mark W. Lipsey. "The positive effects of cognitive–behavioral programs for offenders: A meta-analysis of factors associated with effective treatment." *Journal of Experimental Criminology* 1, no. 4 (2005): 451-476.

230 Tanner-Smith, Emily E., Katarzyna T. Steinka-Fry, Emily A. Hennessy, Mark W. Lipsey, and Ken C. Winters. "Can brief alcohol interventions for youth also address concurrent illicit drug use? Results from a meta-analysis." *Journal of Youth and Adolescence* 44, no. 5 (2015): 1011-1023.

231 Lipsey, Mark W., and David B. Wilson. "The efficacy of psychological, educational, and behavioral treatment: confirmation from meta-analysis." *American Psychologist* 48, no. 12 (1993): 1181.

[232] Lipsey, Mark W., and David B. Wilson. Practical Meta-analysis (Applied Social Research Methods). Sage Publications. Thousand Oaks, California. 2000.

[233] Lipsey, Mark W. "The primary factors that characterize effective interventions with juvenile offenders: A meta-analytic overview." Victims and Offenders 4, no. 2 (2009): 124-147.

[234] "Gross national happiness index explained in detail." Accessed October 5, 2015. http://www.grossnationalhappiness.com/docs/GNH/PDFs/Sabina_Alkire_method.pdf.

INDEX

About Edington Associates

The promise of Edington Associates and the Institute for Positive Organizational Health is a meaningful learning experience to ensure that health and well-being is a primary consideration in decisions of individuals, employer organizations, communities, and society.

Conferences and on-site consultations:

- Presentations (one-hour, half-day, full-day): Presentations are tailored to the intended audience, to the culture of the organization, and to the population of key stakeholders.
- Interactive dialog: Co-creative and collaborative interactions that combine brain-storming, specific real-world and thoughtful activities, and meaningful take-aways for something to do on Monday.
- Workshops (half-day, full-day, multiple day): Workshops are designed to engage participants in specific objectives and conducted typically in work teams.
- Culture consultation (on-going over several months): Adjusting the culture of a work team or a department or even the total organization requires a dedicated Associate working with committed participants.
- Individual or group consultations (one time or ongoing): Consultations are typically focused on a single objective of interest to the individual or group.
- Intensive training (two- to five-day workshops, ongoing training and development over an extended period of time): Extensive training in the understanding and use of concepts, methods, and materials of the win-win philosophy.
- Measurement and evaluation: Help organizations evaluate and communicate about progress toward the vision and objectives that matter to employees and the organization.

Products and Tools:

- Self-Leadership Project (Web-based Modules): Change, Decision Making, Resilience, and Self-Leadership.
- Landscape Assessment: Helps organizations understand their current state regarding support for employee health and well-being. Includes both qualitative and quantitative inquiry tailored to organization.
- Culture Assessment (More in-depth than the Landscape Assessment): Includes appreciative inquiry, environmental audit, survey of the culture and climate, and other exploratory methods to fully understand the culture of the organization (e.g., interviews, organizational ethnography, etc.).
- Living and Thriving Assessment: Next generation health assessment that examines employee health and well-being, as well as the culture of the workplace, home, and community.
- Health Environment Check (HECheck): Conducted as part of the Culture Assessment or as a stand-alone comprehensive audit of the organization's health-supportive environment.
- Program Impact Measure.

About the Authors

Dee W. Edington, Ph.D.

Dr. Edington is an Emeritus Professor at the University of Michigan having served as Professor and Director in the School of Kinesiology and Founder and Director of the Health Management Research Center. He spun off Edington Associates LLC in 2010 to help, "Organizations ensure a thriving, high performing and sustainable workplace and workforce." He is the author or co-author of over 1000 articles, presentations, and several books, including *Championship Age-Group Swimming, Biological Awareness, Biology of Physical Activity, Capstone Knowledge in Kinesiology, The One Minute Manager Balances Work and Life; Zero Trends: Health as a Serious Economic Strategy;* and now *Shared Values—Shared Results: Positive Organizational Health as a Win-Win Philosophy.*

Dee received his BS and PhD degrees from Michigan State University and completed his M.S. at Florida State University. He held a post-doctoral position at the University of Toronto and was on the faculty at the University of Massachusetts and Chair of Exercise Science before coming to Michigan in 1976. He has received Career, Lifetime, or Prestigious Lecture Awards from the American College of Preventive Medicine, American College of Occupational and Environmental Medicine, Thomas Jefferson College of Population Health, US Navy Medical and Safety, Society of Prospective Medicine; Health Enhancement Research Organization; Michigan State University, National Business Group on Health, Top 10 Human Resource Executive Leaders for 2014; State of Michigan Governor's Lifetime Achievement Award.

Jennifer S. Pitts, PhD

Jennifer Pitts, PhD, received her doctorate in Social Psychology, a masters degree in Experimental Psychology, a bachelors degree in Behavioral Sciences, and held a two-year Agency for Healthcare Research and Quality (AHRQ) postdoctoral fellowship at UCLA's School of Medicine. Jennifer has been exploring the health-related influence of social support, engagement in treatment decisions, and meaning in life and work for the past 25 years. Most recently, she has focused on the impact of positive organizational cultures on the ability of employees to thrive in their work and lives.

Dr. Pitts previously held positions at UCLA's Division of General Internal Medicine and Health Services Research, Kaiser Permanente Organization Effectiveness Division, and at Casa Colina Medical Rehabilitation Hospital in Pomona, California. She spent 12 years with Pfizer Health Solutions Inc (PHS) as the Director of Outcomes and Analytics before co-founding Edington Associates in 2010. Jennifer is Co-Founder and Chief Strategy Officer at Edington Associates, LLC. She recently founded The Institute for Positive Organizational Health, a non-profit with the mission of improving the health and flourishing of individuals and transforming the context, culture, ecology, and economy surrounding health in organizations, communities, and society.

Made in the USA
San Bernardino, CA
08 February 2016